Pornography

Rutgers Depth of Field Series

Charles Affron, Mirella Jona Affron, Robert Lyons, Series Editors

———————

Edited and with an Introduction by
Peter Lehman

Pornography

Film and Culture

Rutgers
University
Press
New Brunswick,
New Jersey and
London

Library of Congress Cataloging-in-Publication Data

Pornography : film and culture / edited and with an introduction by Peter Lehman.
    p. cm. — (Rutgers depth of field series)
  Includes bibliographical references and index.
  ISBN-13: 978-0-8135-3870-9 (hardcover : alk. paper)
  ISBN-13: 978-0-8135-3871-6 (pbk. : alk. paper)
 1. Sex in motion pictures. 2. Sex in mass media. 3. Pornography—Social aspects.
I. Lehman, Peter. II. Series.
  PN1995.9.S45P665 2006
  791.43′6538—dc22   2005035513

A British Cataloging-in-Publication record for this book is available from the British Library

Manufactured in the United States of America

For Russell Merritt
Teacher, Mentor, Friend

Contents

Acknowledgments

Thanks to Elle Wolterbeek for her help in preparing the manuscript for publication. As always, thanks go to Melanie Magisos, this time for good-naturedly walking through rooms countless times with episodes of *Dirty Debutantes* on the screen and even more countless pages of the Voyeurweb on the computer screen. This book is dedicated to Russell Merritt, who showed me as a graduate student that academia could be an open, intellectually exciting place where all aspects of popular culture from rock and roll to pulp westerns could be fruitfully studied with the same rigor brought to the traditional humanities. I have never discussed pornography with Russell and to the best of my knowledge he has no interest in it. When I told him years ago about my research on the representation of the penis, he promptly replied, "Who needs it?" Now, as then, I hope the finished project answers the question, for when Russell asks such a question it is always with the rarest gift: he is truly open to listening to the answer. Russell and I agree about little except the value of our disagreements, which in an academic world where some narrowly define friendship and betrayal along methodological lines this is the highest value I can imagine.

The essays in the Historical Context section of this book originally appeared in the publications credited on the first page of each essay, and we wish to thank them for permission to reprint.

Pornography

Introduction: "A Dirty Little Secret"—Why Teach and Study Pornography?

Why teach and research pornography? It is unusual, to say the least, that an editor or author would begin an introduction to his or her volume by questioning the very purpose of studying the subject to which the book is devoted but, as we will see, pornography is always a special case—frequently to the point of hilarity. An anthology on Westerns, comedies, horror films, dramas, or the European art cinema would be unlikely to raise such a question. In his outstanding volume in this Depth of Field Series, for example, my good friend and colleague Robert Eberwein begins his introduction to *The War Film* by diving into a list of wars that the essays explore. He quite rightly presumes that he does not have to ask the reader why we should bother researching and teaching how war has been represented in film. War, unlike something as apparently trivial as sex, is something we should obviously study and care about. Eberwein groups the essays in his volume around four categories—genre, race, gender, and history—and once again he need hardly apologize for the relevance of studying those as aspects of the war film. It is unlikely that there will be public outcry in Rochester, Michigan, or that administrators and perhaps some faculty within Oakland University will raise eyebrows, or worse.

Eberwein begins his introduction as follows: "The essays in this anthology explore films about the Civil War, World Wars I and II, the Korean War, and the Persian Gulf War. The one significant war not represented is, in fact, the first one to ever to be photographed with the motion picture camera: the Spanish-American War of 1898" (1). Imagine for a moment my introduction beginning with the following: "The essays in this volume explore heterosexual intercourse, homosexual intercourse, threesomes and more, and interracial sex. The one significant sexual act not represented is bestiality, although it is one of the oldest known forms of human sexual behavior." And, Eberwein's four categories could just as easily apply to the porn film as to the war film: porn is a genre just as much as the war film is one; issues of race and gender lie at the very center of the porn genre, as does the manner in which porn represents its historical moment.

All facetiousness aside, I hope the above serves to delineate some special issues surrounding the academic study of porn in the current academic and cultural climate within the United States. To be sure, historically there was a time not so long ago when suspicion of popular genres such as Westerns and detective films was strong and when groundbreaking scholars such as John Cawelti had to demonstrate the value of the enterprise in the face of highly skeptical colleagues. Cawelti, a scholar whom I have long admired and whom I had the pleasure of getting to know and spend time with at an Ohio University film conference in the late 1970s, spoke recently with great candor about his colleagues at the University of Chicago during the late 1960s, when he first proposed in a campus lecture the then preposterous idea that Westerns could be studied in the same manner as canonical literature. Undoubtedly the academy is now adjusting—or not, as the case may be—to the equally preposterous hypothesis that pornography should be studied in exactly the same way that film has been productively studied. Is it any more outrageous in the early twenty-first century to throw the names of the Mitchell Brothers and Radley Metzger/Henry Paris around in the company of Federico Fellini and Ingmar Bergman than it was in the 1970s to throw the names of John Ford and Howard Hawks around in the company of Herman Melville and Nathaniel Hawthorne? Is it any more outrageous to suggest that the porn film has a history that in some ways parallels that of the mainstream film industry, evolving from early silent "smokers" to theatrical features in the early 1970s, and then to video and the home market in the 1980s? Isn't it just as preposterous to suggest that the theatrical porn feature structures its meanings and pleasures similarly to that of the Hollywood musical as it was thirty to forty years ago to suggest that a John Ford Western could attain the level of artistry, sophistication, structure, and complexity of a Shakespeare play?

The essays in this volume are divided into two sections: the first reprints important debates and moments in the history of film scholarship on porn and the second presents current developments in the field, many of which push into new territory. John Ellis's "On Pornography" and Paul Willemen's argumentative response, "Letter to John," both place Porn Studies within the political, ideological, and cultural climate in England in 1980 and also squarely within the influential Marxist, feminist, semiotic approach to Film Studies at the time in *Screen*, undoubtedly then the most influential and prestigious English-language academic film journal. The next piece, "Generic Pleasures: Number and Narrative," published nine years later by Linda Williams in her groundbreaking book, *Hard Core*, dramatically initiated a new era in Porn Studies, complexly redefining the oft-assumed hegemonic response of feminists to porn. After Williams, it became common to use the term *pro-porn feminists* (more on that in my conclusion) in opposition to such "anti-porn" feminists as Andrea Dworkin and those in the Take Back the Night movement. The chapter from *Hard Core* I have chosen to reprint is the highly influential one comparing porn's narrative structure to that of the musical, with sexual numbers being the equivalent of musical numbers. While acknowledging the extraordinary insight that Williams brings to the feature theatrical hard-core films of the 1970s, I argue in my response, "Revelations about Pornography," that much about the nature of porn exhibition, advertisement, and spectatorship at the time militated against the unified narrative reading Williams offers in favor of a more momentary, fragmented model of pleasure.

The last two essays in the first section represent important contributions from feminist film scholars who, like Williams, approach pornography as complex texts rather than simple evils. Constance Penley's "Crackers and Whackers: The White Trashing of Porn," adds the important dimension of class to the analysis of pornography. Laura Kipnis's "How to Look at Pornography," excerpted from her book *Bound and Gagged*, argues that pornography is full of ideas that get to the heart of our culture and our notions of self. In hindsight it is somewhat ironic to read the late 1980s essays so disturbed by the subject of pornography by two men, Ellis and Willemen, in juxtaposition with the affirming essays written by two women, Penley and Kipnis, in the late 1990s.

The second section of the book presents new essays published for the first time. Henry Jenkins, in "'He's in the Closet but He's Not Gay': Male-Male Desire in *Penthouse Letters*," makes clear that film pornography should not be studied in isolation from other current forms of pornography such as the letters published in *Penthouse* magazine and the videos made and named after that popular section of the magazine. Jenkins argues that the letters promote risky, infinite diversity as compared to the carefully contained videos. Chuck Kleinhans addresses the important shift in the 1980s from theatrical feature porn to home video porn, arguing that economic factors are much more important than most analysts, including Williams, recognize. Marjorie Heins surveys the complexly shifting legal definitions of pornography and obscenity in the United States, concluding with a compelling analysis of the conservative attack on sexuality in the media at the current moment.

Nina K. Martin in her essay, "Never Laugh at a Man with His Pants Down: The Affective Dynamics of Comedy and Porn," addresses the complicated relationship of comedy and laughter through her analysis of a wide variety of porn films. An often overlooked element of porn is the presence of humor. José B. Capino, in "Asian College Girls and Oriental Men with Bamboo Poles: Reading Asian Pornography," concludes that it is possible to read Asian porn in a manner that redeems it from the attacks of feminist and critical race theories. Daniel Bernardi's "Interracial Joysticks: Pornography's Web of Racist Attractions," on the other hand, argues that we need an ideological analysis of race and porn currently lacking in both antiporn and radical feminist scholarship. The concluding essay, "Pornography: What Men See When They Watch" by Marty Klein, is informed by Klein's experience as a licensed practicing sex therapist and sex educator. He rejects the common notion of pornography as exploitative, arguing instead that it is a fantasy of abundance in which the desire to be sexual is normal and attractive.

The remainder of this introductory essay is less a traditional editor's introduction to the selections in this volume than an essay about the value of teaching and researching porn. Isn't the argument about it basically "same old, same old"? The more things change the more they stay the same? In part, undoubtedly yes, but the differences are at least as telling as the similarities. Perhaps the simplest way to describe this is as follows: when movies (or "films" and "cinema," as they were termed in effort to come up with words that had serious connotations as opposed to the mere entertainment of "movies," or worse yet, "flicks") were first taken seriously within the academy, it led to debates about the validity of the high art/low art distinction. Porn on the other hand has led to a new polarization: art/no art. Or, the old opposition can be rephrased as high art/popular culture in which case we now have culture/porn. In other words, what is presumably some form of culture and value is opposed to unregenerate porn that lacks any redeeming value. Indeed, not only does it lack value, it threatens all values. So within the area of sexual representation we have yet another version of the dichotomy: erotica/porn. The former, presumably, has some redeeming values, pleasures, and meanings to which decent, normal human beings can respond while the latter only appeals to so-called prurient interests.

So we are back to our original question in a slightly elaborated version: why would anyone with a Ph.D. in an established discipline research and teach a valueless, meaningless form that appeals to the prurient interests of presumably abnormal people, or perverts as they are commonly called? In 1990, I was invited to participate in the American Association of University Professors Conference on Academic Freedom and Artistic Expression at Wolf Trap. In a break-out session, a small group of us, led by a lawyer, discussed which forms of sexual expression were protected under the First Amendment and which forms were not. I had trouble with the discussion for two reasons: I felt that all forms of sexual expression held some meaning and value for someone and that there was, therefore, no such thing as pornography or obscenity that had no "redeeming social value." Some people may not like the nature of that value or the group who values it, but that is an entirely different issue. In a related point, I said that similar efforts to draw clear-cut distinctions between art and pornography were also doomed to failure. The leader of the discussion could not fathom what I was saying and simply asserted that the law required that we draw such distinctions so that we could protect speech with socially redeeming value.

Let me give a simple example, drawing upon Linda Williams's groundbreaking book *Hard Core*. Williams traces the above-mentioned history of cinematic porn from its origins in 16mm silent films, pointing out that such films were usually shown in private, all-male "smokers" in such contexts as bachelor parties and the like. Within such a context, the men laughed and joked and talked among themselves while watching the sexually explicit films about women, who though absent from the audience were the likely butt of the jokes, laughter, and rude remarks. Let us for the moment presume that these films contained no "meanings" within themselves (a false assumption) and appealed only to prurient interests. Nevertheless, they would still all contain social value—within this context, male bonding and camaraderie. Now, some might strenuously object to drinking, cigar-smoking men laughing and talking rudely, all the while strengthening what many would see as their misogynist bonds. But even such people would have to grant a meaning, value, and function to the porn-viewing experience, though it might be one they deplore. Perhaps they could counter that such social values are not "redeeming" but that is obviously part of a slippery slope rather than clear-cut categorization of either having or not having redeeming social value. Presumably, many who might condemn the above-cited male bonding might applaud it in the military, for example. Others might question whether male bonding in the service of killing people is a higher social value than male bonding for the purpose of sexual exploration and pleasure, however crude and rude. In both cases, it would seem, however, that male bonding is a social value, as it sometimes is among hunters, fishermen, football players, and Boy Scouts. To argue whether we like or approve of meanings and values is quite different than arguing about whether such values are present.

A similar situation arises with regard to arguments about the distinction between art and pornography. Oft-quoted lines are frequently best left alone for a while but the famous line by Supreme Court Justice Potter Stewart, "I don't know what it [hardcore] is but I know it when I see it," is an exception. It sounds dangerously close to the way Inspector Clouseau thinks: "I suspect everyone and I suspect no one." How do you argue with statements like that? Even if Justice Stewart's line is true, what does it tell us? If he boldly declared, "I don't know what a Western is but, I know it when I see it," few would hail this as an insight into Westerns. If we pressed him further on Westerns he could probably come up with a list of characteristics, such as taking place in certain parts of the American West during a certain time period of the nineteenth century and involving such characteristic actions as gunfights and battles between whites and Indians. Now if we pressed Justice Stewart, he could just as easily come up with a similar laundry list about, for example, the pornographic theatrical feature film of the 1970s: it has a slight plotline often involving a sexual problem that motivates the men and women in the story to have frequent sexual encounters with one another involving a variety of sexual positions and number of partners and culminating with an orgy. I have purposefully stayed away from any scholarly definition here: these are off-the-cuff observations with which anyone who has seen any number of Westerns or theatrical porn features could come up with quickly.

In fact, it is so easy to define a genre in such a manner that one suspects that it was quite convenient for Justice Stewart simply to claim that he didn't know what pornography was because, had he defined it, he would have had to defend that definition and he might have found himself in hot water quickly. Surely we all know a Western when we see one, right? Good guys and bad guys as well as whites and Indians alike ride horses. Horses are a part of the Western genre and cars are not. Does that mean there can't be a Western with a car? What about a number of Sam Peckinpah's classic Westerns, including *The Wild Bunch*? Well, okay, maybe you can show an occasional car (forget for the moment how many cars can be shown or how often a single car can be shown). But when were cars invented? Didn't we just define the genre as taking place in the nineteenth century? Okay, well, there seems to be some leeway and sometimes Westerns takes place in the early twentieth century (once again, let's bypass the question of what years are constituted by the term *early*). Well, we've still got the part about the American West! Or do we? Some films that common sense tells most spectators are Westerns take place in such parts of the country as upstate New York or what we now call the Midwest. Well, okay, it's usually the West but sometimes it is in wilderness areas that we now think of as the East or the Midwest. The point is fairly simple: once you strictly define a genre there will be blurry areas and some films will combine elements of two or more genres, such as the noir sci-fi films (e.g., *Blade Runner* and *Dark City*).

Let us return for the moment to the dubious assumption that pornography and art are two distinctly separate categories. However we define those categories, we cannot escape the blurring that takes place at the border. Let me pick the single most agreed-upon characteristic of the hard-core porn film and that which distinguishes it both from soft-core porn and from art: actual sex and penetration are graphically represented as taking place, not merely actors pretending to have sex. The hard-core feature must include shots that clearly show the erect penis and various forms of penetration such as oral, anal, and vaginal. This is not in question by anyone familiar with hard-core porn films and this seems like one of the most clear-cut distinctions between art and pornography imaginable.

But what, then, do we make of films such as *In the Realm of the Senses* (1976) and *Romance* (1999) that appear to belong to the international art cinema but contain graphic shots of erect penises and various forms of penetration? Nagisa Oshima, who had already established a strong international reputation as Japan's foremost filmmaker of his generation, directed *In the Realm of the Senses*. *Romance* was directed by Catherine Breillat, who cites such filmmakers as Ingmar Bergman, Federico Fellini, Robert Bresson, and Nagisa Oshima as important influences on her work that, as one might expect from that list, shares many attributes of the international art cinema in common with the films of those she admires. Since both films contain explicit shots of erect, penetrating penises, are they therefore porn?

Censors of course might be quick to declare so and both of these films have histories of various censorship problems. *In the Realm of the Senses* was seized by U.S. Customs and there was such a public outcry against *Romance* in France at the time of its release that such well-known filmmakers as Jean Luc-Godard publicly came to the film's defense in an effort to prevent it from being censored. But let us put censors aside for the moment since the grounds upon which they act reveal more about the law at any specific place and time than about the alleged essential nature of the distinction between art and pornography. Marjorie Heins's essay in this volume gives a clear account of how the law in the United States has evolved and changed in regard to this issue. While the legal perspective is very important in the larger picture, it is of little help here since we get caught in a circular argument: showing the sexual act is pornographic, therefore *In the Realm of the Senses* and *Romance* are porn films. Indeed, the production history of *In the Realm of the Senses* is interesting from this perspective: the film was shot in Japan and the undeveloped film was sent to Paris, where it was developed and where postproduction took place. This was necessary since Japan forbids any photographic representation of the penis (a law that would later plague the foreign distributors of that well-known porn film, *The Crying Game*). Had Oshima attempted to send the developed film out of the country, it could have been seized by censors and have never seen the light of day.

But common sense about the hard-core porn genre tells knowledgeable spectators that *In the Realm of the Senses* and *Romance* are not porn films or, at least, that they differ in significant ways from most other porn films. The same was true within the United States of Andy Warhol's *Blue Movie* (1969), which was seized by police in New York City and tried for obscenity in New York State. Once again, the movie clearly depicts sexual intercourse and, once again, any knowledgeable spectator will immediately recognize that this film differs drastically from other films in the genre at the time. And much like those familiar with the international art cinema will recognize its presence in *In the Realm of the Senses* and *Romance*, anyone familiar with Andy Warhol's previous experimental, avantgarde films will recognize many elements of them in *Blue Movie*, including the presence of such Warhol "superstars" as Viva. Much like we saw that some Westerns might have cars and take place in the twentieth century and that some noir films are set in the future like science fiction, these films blur boundaries or mix elements from both art and porn. Most knowledgeable spectators would probably classify them as art films with some porn elements, though some might call them porn films dressed up with the trappings of art.

In this discussion I have purposefully avoided value judgments about these genre-blurring films. My point here is not that *In the Realm of the Senses* and *Romance* are better than pure porn films but, rather, that they are demonstrably different and blur the alleged line between art and porn and that, once we establish such categories as art and porn, the borderline between the categories will inevitably be blurred by some filmmakers. But there is another, more serious problem for those that believe in the simple clear-cut distinction between art and porn: some films, novels, and works of art have moved squarely from one category to the other over time! If there is some simple clear-cut distinction between them and we know porn when we see it, how can this be? Could Justice Stewart see a film on Tuesday and immediately know it is porn and then see the same film on Friday and clearly recognize a work of art with socially redeeming value? To be slightly less facetious, could Justice Stewart recognize porn when he sees it in one decade (even though he doesn't know what it is) and then recognize art (presumably he knows what that is) where he had previously seen porn in the next decade? And if this remarkable scenario is possible, what does it tell us about the art/porn dichotomy?

To answer these questions, I want to turn to the history of art and litera-ture as well as film. What better place to start than the Marquis DeSade, perhaps the most infamous name in the history of porn. If ever there was an obscene, blas-phemous pornographer, it was the Marquis DeSade and apparently all the right people in the right places in nineteenth-century France knew it the minute they saw it and, among other things, his work was censored and he was thrown in jail. Yet, in the 1990s and 2000s, the works of Sade were published by some of the most prestigious, scholarly, university presses in the world and these books were sold, among other places, in university bookstores. Not only did no one get thrown in jail, but the publication of these editions of Sade's works attracted no particular attention since by then it was widely accepted that Sade was a serious writer whose works should be taught and studied. Indeed, such leading French intellec-tuals as Roland Barthes wrote about the importance of Sade's work. So this par-ticular obscene pornographer went from being banned and jailed in the one century to being published in scholarly editions and taught in the university cur-riculum in the next century!

Someone seems to have made a bad mistake. Some Americans would quickly reply, "Yes, and it is the French who have also mistaken that idiot Jerry Lewis as a great artist." But such a response actually helps rather than hurts the point I am making. If someone that many Americans perceive as a crude buffoon can be simultaneously hailed as a great filmmaker in another country, it merely shows that all such judgments and categorizations are not clear-cut and chiseled in granite. Furthermore, the university presses in question are English-language presses and the university curriculum to which I refer is American.

Japanese erotic woodblock prints supply an interesting example from the world of art. For centuries the same masters that created the now-legendary wood-block prints of nature and other such subjects made highly graphic sexual wood-block prints that included voyeurism, erections, and anal, oral, and vaginal penetration, among other things. They executed these prints with the same care, detail, and aesthetic accomplishment that they brought to their nonsexual sub-jects. After contact with the West, however, the Japanese came to see these prints as pornographic and rather than being proud of them, they became ashamed of them. In this instance what was once seen as nonpornographic came to be seen as pornographic because of contact with another culture. Of equal interest, the same "serious" artists were also the "pornographers." Imagine in Hollywood, for exam-ple, a tradition where Martin Scorcese and Blake Edwards simultaneously pursued careers making high-visibility dramas, comedies, and hard-core porn films.

When I was writing my book, *Running Scared: Masculinity and the Rep-resentation of the Male Body*, I wanted to reproduce some erotic Japanese wood-block prints that had been donated to the Boston Museum of Art. When I contacted them for permission, I was told they had in turn donated the prints to the Kinsey Institute at Indiana University. Whatever the context of this decision, it can hardly be coincidental that since art museums around the world value and display Japanese woodblock prints, the Boston Museum of Art deemed the explicit erotic imagery inappropriate to a fine arts museum and more appropriate to a collection on sexuality which, incidentally, also includes photographic and cinematic pornography. And, if one accepts the art/porn distinction, the decision is entirely defensible given that the explicit representation of the erect penis and various forms of heterosexual and homosexual penetration in the Japanese erotic woodblock prints are similar to the representation of the body and sexual acts of Western pornography.

Like art and literature, film, in its comparatively short history, has also witnessed such bizarre shifting of categories between art and porn. Russ Meyer, pioneer of what was then commonly called the "nudie," was in some ways the father of American film porn. Famous for their display of a fetish for women with extremely large breasts, Meyer's films were low-budget affairs that he frequently wrote, shot, and edited by himself from 1950 to 2001. Yet, when one of his classics, *Faster Pussycat! Kill! Kill!* (1966), was rereleased in the 1990s, it played the art house circuit! Trust me, when as an undergraduate at the University of Wisconsin–Madison, at the time, I drove to a nearby small town to see a Meyer double-bill, including *Mud Honey* made only the year before, my destination was not an art house, nor would anyone have mistaken it for one! The Internet Movie Database includes the following two observations about Meyer: "His works were considered pornographic at the time of their release, but contain very little graphic sexual content by today's standards"; and "His films are often studied in film schools and shown on the film festival circuit." Both observations are accurate and both may help account for two of his nicknames, "The Fellini of the Sex Industry" and "King Leer."

Radley Metzger is a more recent example. He made a long string of both soft-core and hard-core porn films from the 1960s to the 1980s, the latter under the pseudonym Henry Paris. Metzger's late 1960s and early 1970s soft-core films not only helped reinvigorate that genre, but were also recognized for their artistic accomplishment by the prestigious Museum of Modern Art when they were added to the museum's permanent collection. How could that be? Did the Museum of Modern Art not know porn when it saw it? Could it be (gasp, gasp) that the films made under the name Henry Paris are as good or even better than those credited as Radley Metger? Could it even be that the Museum of Modern Art may one day be showing Paris's *Opening of Misty Beethoven* and *Barbara Broadcast*? Banish the thought! Or should we? Indeed, since drafting this paragraph some "legit" and "art house" theaters have been screening *Deep Throat*, following the "legitimacy" given that classic hard-core film by the documentary *Inside Deep Throat* (2005).

The above brief accounts of Sade's writings, Japanese erotic woodblock prints, the films of Meyer and Metzger, and *Deep Throat* all demonstrate that pornography is at best a historically and culturally defined category and as such it changes over time periods and within and between cultures. It is not a simple, fixed category with essentialist features that one can see and "know," at least not outside one's limited cultural moment, even if one is a Supreme Court justice. That fact, combined with the previous examples of how filmmakers like Breillat and Oshima blur the line between art and pornography by clearly including some of the defining elements of hard-core porn in their films (Briellat has on two occasions even cast Rocco Siffredi, one of the world's leading porn stars and producers), should give us pause before we simply accept the art/porn dichotomy as truthful or even helpful. If there is both a blurry distinction between the two categories and if works can and do move freely from one category to the other, it might simply be best to dispose of the entire schematic and consider porn one form of artistic expression among others, one genre of filmmaking among many other genres. We should also consider that this is not merely an academic issue but one with far-reaching cultural and social implications.

Indeed, the strict enforcement of the art/porn divide has turned into a variation of the Freudian category of the abject, with porn becoming the site where all disgusting sexual perversion resides full of misogyny, pedophilia, racism, and every other horrible sexual thing of which we can think. But such a notion of porn is simplistic and is false and ironically, frequently works to let "serious art" and "legitimate entertainment" off the hook. In fact, misogyny, racism, and the sexualization of children run rampant in art, mainstream cinema, television, and advertising and understanding them there (emphasis on understanding as opposed to censoring) is every bit as important as understanding them in porn. By no means, should porn be exempt from such critical discourse nor, however, should it simplistically be described as a monolithic cesspool of no use or value to any decent human being in any place or at any time.

But regardless of how we classify porn, the question still remains, why teach and research it? Regardless of whether we think of porn as a genre, which I, and others like Linda Williams and Constance Penley do, or whether we think of it a cesspool that would best be cleaned up and eliminated, there are many good reasons for studying and researching porn. The essays that follow, for all their diversity of opinion and disagreement, all give eloquent testimony to this fact. Nevertheless, I want to make a few general preliminary observations.

For years, the media has been fascinated with the simple fact that porn is big business. Various figures and dramatic statements abound about this multimillion-dollar business, which some say is larger than that of the legitimate film and entertainment business. It is clear to everyone that porn is big business: most "legitimate" hotels offer pay-for-view adult movies, many video stores have adult movie rental sections and some cater exclusively to porn, and Internet porn sites have proliferated and attracted much attention. Yet, oddly, if we listen to "respectable" people talk about this phenomenon, they all act puzzled, as if they can't imagine who would look at this stuff. Obviously, in many social and professional circles, people use porn but do not admit to it. How could it be such big business if only some "perverts" whom nobody knows but everyone imagines exist out there somewhere used it? Two reasons to study porn emerge from this. First, as big business, we should understand its economic impact, which like everything else is now global. Second, large numbers of people use porn and obviously most of them are neither perverts nor criminals. As with all forms of media and popular culture, we should understand how porn impacts the life of those users, whether positively, negatively, or neutrally.

Pornography also should be studied as a way of understanding what it tells us about human sexuality. One of the many simplistic myths about pornography is that porn is one thing. In reality, however, like any genre or form of expression, it is many different things both at any moment in time and historically over periods of time. Why certain kinds of explicit forms of sexual representation arise at any given point in time can tell us much about sexuality at that moment. As scholars such as Linda Williams have noted, for example, the 35mm theatrical porn feature emerged around the time of the women's movement and the stories such films as *Deep Throat* tell that deal with a central problem surrounding female pleasure may reflect an anxiety the male filmmakers and their targeted audience have about sexually experienced women who have new expectations given "the sexual revolution."

From my perspective as a scholar of masculinity and the male body in film, porn is of particular interest in that astonishingly it is one of the very few places in our culture to this day where the penis is commonly represented! Looking at how it is represented is therefore of particular importance. Whereas anyone who has watched any porn films or videos since the late 1960s quickly notes the centrality of the large penis, this "genre convention," if we think of it as such, also has complex meanings beyond mere film form. Some of these meanings interrelate with other cultural issues such as race. For example, in accordance with cultural stereotypes, black men with large penises are prominently featured in porn and, indeed, there is an entire genre of interracial porn that features sex between blacks and whites. Yet, one searches in vain for the Asian male performers in heterosexual U.S. movies and videos, let alone for a genre of Asian men having sex with white women. In keeping with the cultural stereotype that Asian men have small penises and are undersexed, they are a profoundly disturbing absence in heterosexual porn, implying they are incapable of satisfying white women and of supplying the necessary and allegedly dramatic spectacle of phallic sex. While video stores and Internet sites are full of "Oriental" and Asian sex tapes, these tapes feature Asian women with white men! The Asian women are valued for their "exotic" beauty and assumed submissiveness. Ironically, from my perspective, Brandon Lee, the much-celebrated first gay Asian male sex star, is known for his eight-inch penis, which makes him just like his white counterparts! He is the exception that proves the rule.

Porn also bears study in relation to developing new technologies. The relationship is complex and includes both how technologies help represent and even create new sexuality (e.g., telephone sex and Internet sex) and how sex helps build technologies into big business. Modern pornography as most of us think of it now originated with the invention of photography and the cheap and easy dissemination of sexually explicit pictures to the masses, including the lower classes. Gone were the days when sexually explicit and erotic material was made for the wealthy and literate upper classes. The class issue remains to this day an important aspect of porn. The middle and upper classes sometimes develop a class-based hysteria based upon fears of what porn will unleash in the hands of the lower classes, sometimes envisioned as containing criminal types who can't control their impulses.

Two simple examples of the intersection of porn and technology include video and the Internet. With the advent of home video, people didn't need to go out to see porn; they could watch it in the comfort of their own homes. Indeed, they could make it in the comfort of their own homes! Home video cameras in their infancy were prominently advertised in *Playboy* magazine. The implicit message was couples could video themselves having sex, making it possible for the first time in history for people to film themselves having sex easily. Similarly, the Polaroid camera had made it simple and private for the first time for ordinary people to take nude pictures of themselves and others, and many did. Indeed, currently one popular category on some amateur Internet porn sites is posting old, "vintage" Polaroid photographs.

The Internet has had a profound impact on porn. Initially, much like video recycled old 35mm feature films for home use, the Internet reposted celebrity nude photos and frame grabs from nude scenes in films. In these instances, video and the Internet merely becomes a new technology presenting old sexual content. But just like home video porn evolved new forms far removed from the narrative theatrical features, the Internet evolved new forms, one of the more interesting examples being "amateur sites" that, like "amateur videos," feature nonprofessionals. But again the differences are profound.

Indeed, the very categorization celebrity/amateur nudes raises interesting questions. What does it mean to have an "amateur" body or to have "amateur" sex? In the simplest sense, the answer is easy and unsatisfactory: the celebrities and the professionals are paid for their modeling and performing and are widely recognized in the media while the rest of us make our living by other means and are comparatively anonymous. But why does our culture have such a fascination with the beauty and/or sexual performance of celebrities? What is the difference between that and the girl or boy next door? Indeed, many sex magazines acknowledged the fascination surrounding this distinction by featuring a girl or boy next-door section in each issue. Video amateur porn picked up on that and the Internet pushed it into the stratosphere. Why and what are the consequences?

Digital technology now makes it easy both to take the pictures or videos and to self-distribute them instantly around the world. And, unlike Polaroid photographs, the quality is high. The implications of this are immense. Before the Internet ordinary people had no means to self-distribute images of themselves, even if they had the technology to create those images. Furthermore, the self-distribution is instantaneous and enables instantaneous response. The Internet also enables people who were once physically or psychologically isolated in their sexual tastes or practices to become part of a community of people who share those predilections. It is difficult to exaggerate the impact of this on sexually explicit imagery.

The Voyeurweb, founded by "Igor" in 1997, is an excellent example of the creative impact of the Internet on pornography. Indeed, Igor is an Internet auteur in much the same manner that Radley Metzger is a soft-core film auteur and, under his pseudonym Henry Paris, a hard-core auteur. The Voyeurweb has undergone many permutations and much growth since 1997 but the concept remains the same. Pictures are exhibited within categories such as "Private Shots," "Free Style Photos," "Exhibitionist Photos," "Amateurs with Sites," "Explicit Red-Clouds," and "HomeClips Videos." The site includes many free sections and a couple pay membership categories such as the hard-core photo section "Red-Clouds" and the video section "HomeClips." All sections are reliant upon people submitting their photos and videos. Viewers can rate all entries and each category awards monthly cash prizes based upon viewer response. Comment sections for all posts enable viewers to give feedback to the contributors. All sections also include bulletin boards for discussion about the posts and other topics.

What began as a fairly simple amateur site has grown into a complex, multi-faceted site worthy of a detailed analysis I hope to do in the future. For now, I simply want to draw a few conclusions about technology and sexuality. The Voyeurweb tilts the balance in favor of amateurs over professionals in several important ways. The above-listed categories are in a sense "edited" and involve professionals making choices about which submissions to post and when to post them as well as to providing accompanying remarks that help provide an interpretive frame for the viewer. Some categories such as the RedClouds "E-Contris" allow viewers to post with little delay since the category is updated frequently throughout the day and pictures are posted the day they are submitted, without editorial comment. The Voyeurweb has opened the sexual representation of male and female bodies to a much wider variety of age, race, body type, and range of features in regards to cultural norms of beauty than previous forms of porn, sexual representation, or even artistic representation of the body. It used to be that when we walked through an art museum, for example, we could make observations about the overwhelming preponderance of female nudes to male nudes or about the changing ideals of the female body in different eras such as Peter Paul Reubens's "voluptuous" nudes or the thin, fashionable nudes of the late 1960s and 1970s, but there was nothing most of us could do to change and effect such representations.

I want to draw my primary example from my ongoing work on masculinity and the male body. In my book *Running Scared: Masculinity and the Representation of the Male Body*, I examine the representation of the penis in a wide variety of discourses and arts, including the medical profession, jokes, fine arts, movies, and literature, among others. I show the representation of the penis is carefully regulated within these discourses: the desirable big dick in porn, the pathetic small penis as the butt of the joke in humor, the medically normative penis measured in inches, and the tasteful aesthetic penis of high art. All these discourses are outside the control of individuals: the medical profession, the pornographers, the artists, and the anonymous jokesters. The Internet, however, destroys all the careful regulations and enables men with a full range of penis sizes to represent themselves worldwide, regardless of whether they take the pictures themselves or have heterosexual or homosexual lovers take them or even just photographers. Interestingly, this leads at times to competing discourses about penis size at any given point in time on the RedClouds "Maleplicit" board where pictures of men are posted and discussed. It is not uncommon on any single day to find a thread devoted to big penises and one devoted to small penises, with images of both and comments from both men and women expressing desire for and appreciation of all of them. In such instances, for example, the small penis normally held up to ridicule (while seldom being shown) in penis size jokes so common in movies is here an object of pride and desire rather than the butt of the joke.

Threads devoted to penis size also appear on the regular RedClouds board and the issue comes up in many of the posts of men and women engaged in various forms of sexual activity. Indeed, male nudes are also posted regularly on that board. Looking at the comments is particularly revealing: many heterosexual males ridicule the small men more than the women posters and some of both express their desire for and appreciation of the small men. Clearly some men or their partners revel in knowing that their penises do not conform to various norms of representation. As such, their pleasure can come from a variety of sources, including masochistic humiliation at being mocked for not living up to expectations or, at the other extreme, being desired precisely for that reason. Not surprisingly, similar competing discourses appear on breasts. At the moment of this writing, there is a thread on the RedClouds Explicit Photo BB entitled "A Cups and Smaller." The thread is in praise of women with the smallest breasts imaginable. But on any given day, there is almost always also a thread devoted to women with large breasts.

The Internet thus enables people to seize control not just of the representation of their bodies but the distribution of the images and the opportunity to enter into discourse with others about it! This is no small thing (pun intended) and extends well beyond the simple point that tastes vary. Never before in the history of the sexual representation of the body have so many people been able to participate so directly in breaking norms, challenging stereotypes, and diversifying the range of represented body types. Casting directors, models, publishers, producers, distributors, exhibitors, and curators have little or nothing to say about it. As such, ordinary people are helping to represent and shape sexual discourse about the body in an unregulated manner.

Finally, we should study pornography so that we have a complete history of the movies. Porn has been part of film history since the silent era and there is, to say the least, no sign that it is about to disappear. Much like Victorian literature scholars, for example, have studied the erotic and pornographic novels of that era in order to get a complete picture rather than focus all attention only on the classics, we miss much of what cinema has been about if we arbitrarily exclude the study of porn. Jon Lewis has gone so far as to argue that there was a crucial point in the early 1970s where Hollywood and porn came very close together, with porn features on *Variety*'s top grossing film charts and with Hollywood even contemplating moving into porn production. Eventually, Hollywood took the opposite approach of differentiating itself from porn with a new crop of prestigious movies and directors. And, of course, actors and directors, among others, have moved freely from the porn industry into the Hollywood industry.

Given all these and other reasons, why would the media be shocked, shocked, shocked to discover that Film and Media Studies programs around the United States in major research institutions are teaching courses with units on pornography and even entire courses devoted to pornography? On August 20, 2001, the *Boston Globe* ran a story on the subject under the heading: "Porn Is Hot Course on Campus." In addition to me, Linda Williams at the University of California–Berkeley; Constance Penley at the University of California–Santa Barbara; Chris Straayer at New York University; and Henry Jenkins at the Massachusetts Institute of Technology were all interviewed. When the article appeared we were all disappointed that, among other things, the title sensationalized the subject. The article was reprinted on Sunday, August 26, 2001, in the *Arizona Republic* with the equally sensationalized title "Pornography Latest Hot Course on Campuses Across Nation."

All of the above pales in comparison to the headline in a follow-up story that appeared in *The East Valley Tribune*, a Phoenix metropolitan area paper. The *Boston Globe* article was professional in tone and respectful of those professors who teach porn in the classroom, even using the subtitle "Professors Seek Meaning Behind Flourishing Market." Starting with a huge graphic "This Course Rated X," the *Tribune* article went on with the title "Debbie Does ASU: Porn in Academia" and was nothing short of "yellow press" at its best or worst, trying to create a controversy under the guise of reporting one, starting with "To some, it's a dirty little secret" (A1). Whereas the *Globe* proclaimed that porn was the "hot course on campus," the *Tribune* declared that at ASU, it was a "dirty little secret," what Shakespeare might well call a "seeming paradox." How can something be a hot course and a dirty secret at the same time? The answer of course is that porn on campus is neither. None of us interviewed for these articles use pornography as a way to create a "hot," large enrollment class nor do we withhold advertising our courses to keep them a "dirty little secret." Rather, as with all good pedagogy, we determine what is appropriate to teach at what level (freshmen and sophomores;

or juniors and seniors; or seniors and graduate students) and to whom (majors or nonmajors or both).

I raise the issue of media coverage since I want to encourage faculty to proceed with eyes wide open: reporters with political agendas lurk in many places. And, of course, radio and even TV talk shows drool in anticipation. Within this context, I want to also raise the related issues of film screenings, syllabi warnings, and student consent forms.

I have always screened porn films with student projectionists the same as I screened all kinds of films in all my film classes. A faculty member once told me that I should be present at all screenings so that if a student became upset, I could stop the film, turn on the lights, and talk about it. Such a screening procedure would create the very form of hysteria that the course attempts to study, understand, and defuse. Imagine, in medical school if every time a student got upset during an autopsy the instructor stopped the class to talk about it. The head pathologist of a medical school told me that if students faint during an autopsy, they drag them outside, revive them, and send them back in. Alas, in the belief that movies and dead bodies are not equivalent, I'm willing to let students go home but, lo and behold, no such fainting has ever taken place during one of my screenings. No vomiting. No nervous breakdowns. Indeed, by treating the screenings like any screening for any class, students are prepared in the best way to watch the films and talk about them later. The hysteria is all in the minds of others; students taking the class are fully capable of dealing with the films and studying them just like other texts. But, let's just presume the worst catastrophic scenario possible for the moment: a student gets upset. Imagine what for some people in our society is becoming the unimaginable: an adult college student encountering something upsetting! Actually, I tell all my students that if they can get through college without encountering disturbing, upsetting ideas that challenge the belief system they bring into college, they should ask for their tuition money back.

Content warnings or signed student consent forms are, however, a serious pedagogical issue. The topic came up for discussion at two Society for Cinema and Media Studies workshops on teaching pornography in which I participated. In 1995, I explained why I included a warning in my class at the University of Arizona and both Linda Williams and Constance Penley spoke against the use of such cautions. Williams has since written on the issue in her book *Porn Studies*.

In a perfect world I agree fully with Penley and Williams that such warnings should not be part of the syllabus. Indeed, they sound like part of the very porn hysteria I have criticized above. This, however, is one of the few times that men are in a more vulnerable and perilous position than women. "The porn classroom," as Williams calls it, is rife for potential sexual harassment issues. Before addressing this issue, I want to review briefly Williams's position, then present my syllabus statement and argue for the value of the warning.

Williams offered a warning on the syllabus the first time she taught the class, but then she removed it. She notes: "It is common in some women's studies classes presenting images, though not teaching the genre, of pornography to ask students to sign a consent form saying that they are warned that they may be viewing some possibly horrendous materials, but then to provide for the possibility for students to excuse themselves from screenings or images that offend them too much" (14). Williams calls this counterproductive and concludes, "The consent approach tends to make the course all about finding that moment of most extreme offense, when the offensive text does what it is all along expected to do" (14).

I caution faculty, especially untenured, assistant professors, against simply accepting such a fixed position. The kind of institution in which the course is being offered and the city and state are all important factors. I taught the exact same course at the University of Arizona (U of A) in Tucson and at Arizona State University (ASU) in Tempe in consecutive years and had entirely different experiences in regard to these issues even though the two cities are only about seventy-five miles apart from each other in the same state. Indeed, when I arrived at ASU, I was shocked when a colleague suggested that I have students sign a consent form. At the U of A, I simply included the warning in the syllabus. It never occurred to me to have adult college students sign a consent form to take a sexuality class but, in retrospect, I am deeply indebted to that colleague. The statement in my syllabus and the form are as follows:

> Course Description: This course examines issues related to explicit sexual representations in pornography, the art cinema, Hollywood, and independent film and video. Topics covered include the representation of the male and female bodies, gay and lesbian sexuality, medical discourses on sexuality, and an extended unit on race and sexuality.
>
> This class includes sexually explicit materials and anyone offended or disturbed by viewing, reading, or discussing such materials should not enroll in the class. If any material should prove unexpectedly disturbing, students should simply leave the screening or lecture and meet with the instructor to determine an appropriate alternative assignment. Similarly, if any students are uncomfortable with a discussion topic with classmates outside class, during office hours, or at any other time, they should simply indicate they are uncomfortable and do not wish to discuss the topic further. This course presumes that students have a mature interest in exploring and discussing issues of sexuality and representation in an open and un-pressured environment. It is not a required course. Screenings are restricted to students enrolled in the class.
>
> I have read and understand the above and want to take the class.
>
>
> _____   _____
> Signature   Date

mediocre, even if some are great, and even the great ones have to be viewed with an active, critical mind. Obviously, porn is the same but too often in recent years, in the attempt to salvage porn from the hands of those who have been simplistically condemning it, there has not been enough ideological analysis of porn. (For the record, I wrote this prior to reading Daniel Bernardi's essay in this volume that arrives at the same conclusion.) Scholars and some sex educators and therapists have focused their attention on tearing down the destructive, negative myths about porn and its users. In the process of performing this valuable service, in some cases the scales have tipped away from any or at least enough criticism of the rescued "bad object."

If positions on pornography are staked out in this "pro" or "anti" fashion, I clearly come down on the side of pro-porn: I believe pornography can be complex, meaningful, and pleasurable and that it should be studied to enhance our understanding of sexuality and culture, not to fuel hysteria. The problem for me, however, lies in the very categorization of pro- and antiporn. The polarity is a false and even dangerous one. In all my classes, I urge my students to never abandon being active critical viewers, no matter how "progressive" they think any film may be and no matter how much they like it, even, and perhaps especially, if it is a classic like *Citizen Kane.* To be "pro"-John Ford or "pro"-*The Searchers* should not mean denying there are disturbing elements that should be criticized in Ford's oeuvre or in *The Searchers*, his commonly acknowledged masterpiece. Why should porn be different? How can anyone embrace porn and say, "I'm pro-porn"? Yet, sadly, that seems to be the implicit assumption in much porn scholarship today. In reading Linda Williams's massive anthology *Porn Studies*, I was struck by how little criticism or even concern her former students show for any consequences of how anything is represented in porn, or, for that matter, how they offer no criticism of her positions. In an effort to correct the fear and hysteria surrounding porn, some scholars have gone too far in the direction of simply embracing it as clearly not being the evil object so many writers and people in our culture imagine it to be, as if that means we should not be concerned about race, class, and gender depictions that we are so rightly concerned about in other genres. It is far more important to be complex than it is to be pro or con and I hope the essays in this volume all contribute to a climate of such critical and analytical awareness of porn.

WORKS CITED

Abel, David. "Pornography Hot Course on Campus: Professors Seek Meaning Behind Flourishing Market." www.BostonGlobe.com. Reprinted as "Pornography Latest Hot Course on Campuses across Nation." *The Arizona Republic*, August 26, 2001, A15.

Cawelti, John. Keynote address, presented at the annual conference of the Society of Film and History, Kansas City, Missouri, November 2002.

Eberwein, Robert. *The War Film*. New Brunswick, N.J.: Rutgers University Press, 2005.

Imdb.com. 2005.

Lehman, Peter. *Running Scared: Masculinity and the Representation of the Male Body*. Philadelphia: Temple University Press, 1993.

Lewis, Jon. *Hollywood V. Hard-Core: How the Struggle over Censorship Created the Modern Film Industry*. New York: New York University Press, 2002.

Stern, Ray. "This Class Rated X: Debbie Does ASU: Porn in Academia." *The East Valley Tribune*. September 7, 2001, A1 and A8.

Voyeurweb.com. 2005.

Williams, Linda. *Porn Studies*. Durham, N.C.: Duke University Press, 2004.

———. *Hard Core: Power, Pleasure, and the "Frenzy of the Visible."* 2nd ed. Berkeley: University of California Press, 1999 [1989].

Historical Context

John Ellis

On Pornography

Preface

"Pornography" seems to me to be one of the urgent and unanswered questions that our culture presents to itself. The sense of urgency is provided by the constant activity in this area: police seizure of material; attacks by feminists on representations and those who market them; and the pornography industry's own attempts to get increased public acceptance. Now, the Williams Committee[1] has produced a series of recommendations for replacing the existing unworkable legislation in this area. My sense that the question remains unanswered is perhaps more contentious: several definitions of pornography do exist that are perfectly adequate for their protagonists. Yet they are purely moral definitions, concerned with recruiting for particular ideas of "what should be done" about pornography. They all assume that "pornography" is an inherent attribute of certain representations. This is an untenable assumption: "pornography" is rather a designation given to a class of representations that is defined by particular ideological currents active in our society. These ideological currents are crystallized into particular political groupings that produce their own definitions of "pornography" and propagate them through various kinds of actions against particular representations. Different criteria are used, so that the definition of "pornography," its supposed effects, and methods of limiting them, are areas of struggle between differing positions.

The combination of vagueness and moralism in existing definitions of pornography has several effects. First, "pornography" as a label always threatens to engulf any sexual representation that achieves a certain level of explicitness. There is no way that any representation—especially if it involves photography—can insure itself against such labeling. Second, it produces a real blockage in the analysis and the production of representations alike. A reticence about the portrayal of sexuality hovers over much British independent film production. I have felt a similar reticence in writing this essay. Not only do definitions of pornography have an inhibiting moral force to them, but as a result of their blanket definitions, adequate means of writing and portrayal of sexuality have not been developed. Pornography is difficult to discuss because there is no discourse that is analytic yet nevertheless engages the subjectivity of the individual uttering that

First published in *Screen*, Summer 1980, vol. 21, no. 1, pp. 81–108. Reprinted by permission of the author and the editors of *Screen*.

discourse. We are caught between personal confessions and general theoretical systematizations—mutually exclusive modes, each inadequate to the problems addressed.

I have written this essay to break through some of the problems of "pornography" by displacing the category itself. This involves a double approach. There is a preliminary investigation of how "pornography" is defined for us now, how a particular area of signification is separated out across a wide range of media. Then, I have used a particular approach that seems to be able to differentiate between kinds of representations that are usually lumped together as "pornographic," and thus can offer a perspective for progressive work in this central and neglected area.

Pornographic Definitions

Sexuality is never left unspoken in our culture: it is massively present, but always subject to limitations. It is exhaustively defined across a series of specialist discourses (medicine, psychiatry, criminology, etc.) but its more public manifestation is through allusion rather than description. Forms of humor, representations of women, clothing, and other diverse practices all invoke sexuality. But they cannot be said to describe or to define sexual practices: they indicate obsessively, pointing toward sexuality, but they never differentiate, never show, never speak directly. Prohibitions exist not upon speaking about sexuality, but on explicit descriptions of sexual activities. Prohibitions exist upon representations that refer to sexual activity or display the human body in an overtly sexualized manner; on the public representation of sexual activity and the circulation of such representations. The conjunction of sexual activity and representation, where the representation specifies sexual activity rather than referring to it by inference or allusion, is the area of particular taboos and is the traditional area of pornography.

An industry has developed to produce and market such proscribed representations, ensuring their circulation outside the normal channels. This pornography industry is a reaction to the historically specific definitions of pornography; it is called into existence as a separate sector by campaigns and laws against pornography. Essentialist approaches to pornography as a particular kind of representation begin from the nature of the contemporary pornography industry and produce a definition of all that industry's products. Such an approach ignores the conditions of production of pornography as a proscribed area of signification. The various strong and specific definitions of pornography themselves produce this area, and it is with them that investigation of the constitution of "pornography" must begin if it is to be examined in its specific existence at a particular historical moment.

There will be no one unitary definition of "pornography" but rather a struggle for predominance between several definitions. These definitions will work within a context defined by several forces: the current form of the pornography industry and its particular attempts at legitimization; the particular form of the laws relating to obscenity and censorship; and the general mobilization of various moral and philosophical positions and themes that characterize a particular social moment. It is beyond the scope of this essay to examine the articulation of such general moral and philosophical currents with the specific question of pornography in the particular contemporary British attempts at definition of the area. More immediate is the complex question of the legal forms that are currently in use in Britain. These are by no means easy to describe (the Williams Report concludes that, here, in England and Wales at least, "The law, in short, is in a mess," 2.29), yet their effects across various media are quite marked. In addition, censorship is often undertaken by bodies of no formal legal standing like the British Board of Film Censors, which exists as a convenient delegate and centralizer of local authority film censorship powers. At every point, however, whether in precensorship as with cinema, or prosecution after publication as with printed material, both the law and its individual implementations rely on contemporary morality and definitions of what might constitute permissible representations of sexual activity. The mid-nineteenth-century test of whether a particular representation has a tendency to "deprave or corrupt" is used in most existing legislation. This requires jurors to have a definite image of what corruption and depravity might consist in their contemporaries—a definition that cannot but rely upon prevailing definitions of "pornography," its supposed effects, and its presumed social role.

Legal action against representations of a sexual nature depends upon the current prevailing definition of pornography. Legal action, or the possibility of it, in turn defines the nature of the pornography industry or institution. Representations become clandestine because they are threatened with prosecution; equally, they confine themselves to particular ghettos to avoid the "public concern" that can be produced by vocal interest groups espousing definitions of pornography that entail censorship. At every point "pornography" appears to be an area of representations whose limits and nature are the subject of a struggle between differing definitions. Definitions with such powers as these are the product of wider and institutionalized political positions. In contemporary Britain there seem to be three main positions that have emerged in relation to pornography: the right-wing "Nationwide Festival of Light"; the feminist concern with representation of women; and the liberal attitude exemplified by the Williams Report. Each has a distinctive power base. The Festival of Light relies on traditional Christian notions, which are conceived as in decline and under threat. It incorporates Mary White-house's highly successful campaign to deliberalize television output, as well as many other such pressure groups, and has powerful support in the right-wing sections of the police force, for example, the Chief Constable of Greater Manchester (see Williams, 4.23). The feminist campaigns against pornography have come particularly from those sections of the Women's movement that see society as constituted by an antagonism between the sexes. This position finds its power base in a series of concerted campaigns, demonstrations, pickets of retailers of "pornography," sloganizing of sexist advertising material, and so on. It is not primarily directed toward exploitation or change of existing legislation; it aims rather for a wholesale change in public attitudes by a redefinition of what constitutes an offensive representation. The final major position put forward in Britain is a liberal position, seeing society as pluralistic, containing many points of view in uneasy coexistence. This has recently been articulated by the Williams Committee, which was convened to produce a report proposing and justifying rationalization of English laws relating to obscenity. It regards the law as "holding the ring," ensuring public safety and well-being, rather than as an interventationist instrument enforcing particular points of view. Thus the Williams Committee represents a particular and successful tactic by a liberal lobby: commissioned by a Labour Home Secretary, it has been delivered to a Conservative one. The choice that now faces the Home Secretary is one of maintaining the existing legal confusion or implementing something approximating to the Williams Report's recommendations.

Each of these positions defines "pornography" as a different object. They produce definitions that class certain forms of representation as "pornographic"; they produce arguments about the social place, function, and influence of these representations; and they advocate different forms of action toward these representations by judiciary and public alike. All have a definite basis within particular organizations and institutions, and are therefore able to make political interventions of a public and influential nature. These interventions and the struggle for general public acceptability between these definitions together bring about the current form of the pornography industry.

Festival of Light

An exposition of the Nationwide Festival of Light's position can be found in the Longford Report.[2] This is a curious publication, taking the form of a report from a commission set up by Lord Longford to collect evidence about the pornography phenomenon. It was published as a mass-sale paperback amid a blaze of publicity, aiming to capture the definition of pornography for a semi-religious right-wing position. The report has the overall style of a government report, with a panel commissioning research and receiving submissions from anyone who cared to make them, yet it has none of the scrupulousness about its statements and their veracity that usually characterizes a government report. The Longford Report takes pornography as an object that exists incontrovertibly in the world beyond its writings: its main aim is to define its influences. Pornography, it argues, is a representation that isolates one physical activity—sex or violence—from the social context that would justify it as an activity or portray its consequences.

Dr. Claxton describes both "hard" and "soft" pornography as "a symptom of preoccupation with sex which is unrelated to its purpose"—which he sees, of course, not exclusively in terms of the physical orgasm, but as a relationship that transcends the merely physical (205).

Pornography has as its aim the excitation of the viewer rather than, as Lord Clark argues, one of provoking thought and contemplation:

> To my mind art exists in the realm of contemplation and is bound by some sort of imaginative transposition. The moment art becomes an incentive to action it loses its true character. This is my objection to painting with a communist programme, and it would also apply to pornography. (100)

Pornography, it is argued, "stimulates in the audience the kind of behaviour that may lead to violence" (45). Many of its representations cause "extreme offence to the great majority of people" (193). It is a type of representation that is at once a symptom of a general decline of societal values (the "permissive society") and a cause of particular undesirable activities: perversions, rape, masturbation, dissatisfaction within marriages, and so on. The metaphor of "health" hovers over the report: healthy sexuality is a sexuality that is functional within a relationship; a healthy attitude toward representations is one of contemplation and uplift; a healthy society is one that contains no disruption of its tranquillity. Health defines the presumably normal: the report appeals to this sense of the average in order to promote it as the only acceptable form of behavior. It then defines as pornography any representation that is capable of producing or suggesting behavior outside this norm.

Pornography for the Festival of Light is a class of representations that are concerned with sex or violence without their social or moral context. The representations aim to excite the viewer and have a concentration upon violence. They stimulate antisocial behavior where it might not have existed before, and are a symptom as well as a cause of a wholesale decline in social value. Pornography should be banned wherever possible, and should certainly be kept away from children. Rigorously enforced legislation is seen to be the means to achieve this aim.

One Feminist Approach

The most dominant feminist position finds itself confused with the Festival of Light's position at certain points, despite its different constituency and forms of campaigning. It produces a very similar definition of the object "pornography," but traces its roots back to very different causes. Such a feminist definition of pornography points to violence, lack of social context of sexuality, and the symptomatic social role of pornography in the same way as the Longford Report.

Pornography is seen as "violent and mysogynistic, and nothing to do with the free expression of 'healthy' sex, but rather the truly 'perverted' desire to trample on another human being."[3] Pornography is also described as a depiction of sexual activity deprived of its social significance and offered to excite the viewer:

> Pornography's principal and most humanly significant function is that of arousing sexual excitement. . . . It usually describes the sexual act not in explicit. . . but in purely inviting terms. The function of plot in a pornographic narrative is always the same. It exists to provide as many opportunities as possible for the sexual act to take place. . . . Characterisation is necessarily limited to the formal necessity for the actors to fuck as frequently and as ingeniously as possible.[4]

Pornography is even seen as the symptom of wider social trends, and as having a potential link with forms of violence perpetrated by men on women:

> There is no evidence that porn causes rape directly, and there may be no causal link. But they are linked in spirit. Both are manifestations of the same attitude towards women and sex—of a desire to avoid interaction with a woman as another human being.[5]

However, a feminist position would not base its view of pornography on any notion of a "healthy" society and its attitude to sex. Instead, many feminists perceive pornography as the product of a general antagonism between the sexes. Men are the subjects of pornography, it is produced for their gratification and pleasure; women are the objects of pornography, reduced to being sexual objects, degraded and humiliated. Sexuality and its representation in our society are both profoundly marked by the interpellation of men as aggressors, women as their victims. This argument is capable of designating a whole series of representations as "pornographic," representations that do not feature in more conventional or right-wing definitions. A feminist definition based on the notion of an antagonism between the sexes sets up a continuum of representations of women classified according to their sexuality. This continuum stretches from many forms of public advertisement displays to hard-core pornography in the usual sense. Each representation is designated pornographic because it defines women as sexual objects offered for male pleasure. The terms of this contention are not found entirely in written arguments: it appears equally and publicly in propagandist activities such as writing or putting stickers on posters, particularly in the Underground in London. One such sticker is "Keep My Body Off Your Ads," which condenses many of the problems with this position. It (polemically) confuses the real with representation, but in doing so it reduces the representation to being that of "a body," and the aim of the campaign to that of repression, the banning of representations of bodies. Interestingly, it also has a central confusion about address. "I" refers to the collectivity of women; "you" is either the collectivity of men who in an undifferentiated way "portray women," or (as is more probable given the address of most posters) the power elite of marketing personnel. In the first case, it is only to those who already have access to such feminist arguments that such a reading is possible: the sticker has no effect as propaganda toward those who do not. In the second case, the (male) viewer is left in the same relationship to the poster plus sticker as he was to the poster alone: he is the voyeur to women speaking to the advertisers as he was voyeur to the woman performing in the poster.[6]

Attacking posters for their assumptions is one example of the distinctive forms of campaigning adopted by many feminists against all the manifestations that they perceive "pornography" to have. This campaign is one to change public attitude, to render unacceptable many things that are currently taken for granted, like advertising, forms of sexual humor, "beauty queens," and so on. The campaign includes a variety of signifying practices in an overall definition of "pornography," and relies on "popular opinion" to ensure that such forms fall into disuse. It is a campaign to change attitudes to sexuality and to women:

> I believe we should not agitate for more laws against pornography, but should rather stand up and say what we feel about it, and what we feel about our own sexuality, and force men to re-examine their own attitudes to sex and women explicit in their consumption of porn. . . . We should make it clear that porn is a symptom of our sexist society, a reflection of its assumptions.[7]

As a polemical and urgent task of redefinition, this feminist notion of pornography cannot rely on legislation or on traditional moral ideas. Its characteristic modes of operation are those of polemical writing, and forms of direct action such as those against advertising or the "Reclaim the Night" marches through many cities in November 1977. This widespread position is the only conception of "pornography" that is aware of itself as an active intervention, shifting and producing definitions. Such a self-awareness means that this basic position can give rise to a sophisticated debate that escapes sterile arguments about whether specific representations "should be banned or not," and traces the complex links that exist between representations of sexuality and the practical attitudes of individuals to their sexuality. Within the dominant forms of representation in our society, women are posed as the objects of men's activity, and particularly as objects of men's sexual activity. Women's sexuality is produced in representations as a commodity for men's pleasure. Feminist definitions therefore intervene within representational practices to displace this exploitative definition of sexuality. It is a measure of the distinctiveness of this position that it is incompatible with most of the basic assumptions of the Williams Report; it is a measure of its effectiveness that the Williams Committee took special pains to gain evidence from the Women's movement (1.2).

The Williams Report

The Williams Report is a major achievement for the liberal lobby for reform of the current laws relating to obscenity and censorship. Costing £99,692 and two years' work, it is able to summarize such positions as that of the Festival of Light rather more elegantly than that lobby itself can, and then to refute both its internal logic and the empirical "proofs" that it calls upon. Its recommendations are for an overall rationalization and liberalization of laws in this area, artfully calculated to appeal to a wide range of legislative sensibilities. Liberalization entails "one step to the left" in each medium, within an overall context of removing material that could "cause offence to reasonable people" from public view.

The report classifies representations as pornographic according to their function and content:

> We take it that, as almost everyone understands the term, a pornographic representation is one that combines two features: it has a certain function or intention, to arouse its audience sexually, and also has a certain content, explicit representations of sexual material (organs, postures, activity, etc). A work has to have both this function and this content to be a piece of pornography. (8.2)

It reserves an aesthetic distance from the majority of such representations: "certainly most pornography is also trash: ugly, shallow and obvious" (7.2). It differs from both the feminist and the Festival of Light characterizations of pornography because it makes a rigid separation between the realms of the public and the private. Both feminist and right-wing characterizations are based on the assumption that the public and the private are inseparable: they see attitudes as existing in a continuum between the two realms. The Williams Report maintains that the two are different because they entail different conceptions of freedom and impose different duties upon the legislature. The private is seen as the area of the purely personal, the area of freedom of choice and individual predilection, into which others (whether individuals, groups, or state) should make the least possible intervention. There should be no imposed morality, no attempt to legislate a prescriptive conception of the normal. The public is seen as the area of the uneasy coexistence of these plural private preferences. It is where individuals encounter each other and have effects upon each other, where individual activities have to be curbed for the safety and continued well-being of others. So the report provides as its first principle that there should be as little limitation upon the individual as possible, and that such limitation should be for the protection of the generality of other individuals. Pornography, however objectionable it might appear, should therefore be available for individuals unless it can be proved that its presence within society affronts other individuals going about their daily business, or indeed produces forms of antisocial behavior such as aggression toward particular individuals. Therefore if it can be ensured that adult individuals can come across pornography only by their own conscious choice, and if no proof or strong evidence exists of a causal link between pornographic representations and particular, antisocial acts, then pornography should be given a legal existence in society. For this reason the report devotes much space to refuting the Festival of Light's empirical proofs of links between pornography and particular acts of violence. Once this direct evidence is demolished, then more general assertions of indirect harmful effects upon society as a whole can be refused by asserting pornography's relative insignificance compared to "the many other problems that face our society today" (6.80), and the difficulty of distinguishing whether a particular phenomenon is a cause or a symptom of a particular social change (6.76).

The law is then framed to prevent the exposure of "reasonable people" who might find certain material "offensive." The "offensive to reasonable people" test then becomes the criterion for deciding what forms of representation should be restricted to particular designated sales points. If harm to individuals can be proved or strongly supposed to be involved in the production or dissemination of a representation, then it can be banned completely. So printed pornographic material is exempt from censorship except where its production has involved cruelty to those posing for it or the exploitation of children. Written matter is exempt from any censorship. However, potentially "offensive" material is only to be made available in separate premises that carry a standard designation and no other form of advertising. Most of the magazines currently available in ordinary newsagents' shops would then be restricted to these premises. Live entertainment would be prevented from staging actual sex acts, as this "carried some dangers of public order problems" (11.9), which is why they are no longer permitted in Denmark. Videotapes and their proliferation receive no attention in the report, for which it has been criticized. Film remains the only medium to be subject to prior censorship, and the report envisages that certain films could still be banned altogether. The report's considered assessments tend to collapse here, under a belief in a realist aesthetic:

> Film, in our view, is a uniquely powerful instrument: the close-up, fast cutting, the sophistication of modern make-up and special effects techniques, the heightening effect of sound effects and music, all combine on the large screen to produce an impact which no other medium can create. . . . We are more impressed by the consideration that the extreme vividness and immediacy of film may make it harder rather than easier for some who are attracted to sadistic material to tell the difference between fantasy and reality. (12.10)

The argument is framed in terms of the possible consequences of violent material: it is conceived as possible that it could lead to violent acts in some way. Film censorship would be retained, able to ban certain films on the grounds of excessive cruelty, and allocating various certificates that would ban children under a series of specific ages from seeing particular films. An appeal against banning could be lodged on the grounds of the "artistic merit" of a particular film. The present self-financing and advisory British Board of Film Censors would be abolished and replaced by an official state body allocating mandatory certificates. A new category of restricted film would be set up in addition to the current "X" certificate banning children under eighteen. Such films could only be shown in halls licensed for the purpose by local authorities, who would thus retain their censorship powers only in so far as they could refuse to license any cinema in their area for the showing of restricted films. A cinema so designated would continue to be able to show "*Bambi* in the school holidays if it wishes to do so" (12.39).

> In practice [there will be] two sorts of designated cinemas. One will be a blue movie house, which rarely if ever shows anything else. The other will be, to some degree, an "art" house, which shows a variety of films with various certificates, usually of minority appeal. (12.39)

The overall effect of the Williams Committee recommendations, if they become law, will be to heighten the conflict over the term *pornography*. Its explicit effect is to make the legal definition of pornography one that is variable with shifts in public opinion. It does so by defining pornography as a private matter, as existing in an area where the law "holds the ring" rather than intervenes with particular definitions. The effect then is to shift arguments about the legal definition of pornography into the public arena where a struggle takes place to define the public consensus. But this shift can only take place within a liberal notion of pornography as a private matter, a definition that neither feminists nor the right wing would accept. It is perhaps the kind of fiction that only liberals can believe. The Williams Report therefore embodies a particular liberal definition of "pornography," distinct from other positions, whose power lies in its possible influence on legal definitions, enabling a wider range of material to become available in more restricted marketing channels.

The Institution of Pornography

The right wing, liberals, and feminists have three distinct definitions of pornography that conflict in attempting to define what pornography might be. The articulation of these three major positions with the present, confused, legal definitions of "obscenity" produces a particular industry, the institution of pornography. This is an agglomeration resulting from a series of ad hoc distinctions between classes of representation across a number of media, which are recognized to have a common existence. Specialized marketing and production methods have been evolved within this institution, which exists rather separately from the conventional business operations in particular media.

    The current general rules in Britain are that the following will be designated "pornographic": any representation of male or female genitals (not breasts); any form of enactment of sex whether simulated or actual that is of any duration and level of explicitness; and any sustained reference to "perversions," particularly a use of sexually charged violence. Even representations whose general purpose is other than the excitement of the viewer for sexual purposes is liable to inclusion in this category. The boundaries are fluid and shifting, but a large-scale change has taken place during the last decade [ca. 1980] through which the "pin-up" (the female body deprived of any genitals by artful posing or photographic processes) has become nonpornographic. It is now available daily in popular newspapers. Similarly, it can be argued that much advertising makes use of themes and poses derived from pornography, without receiving many objections other than from feminists. Within the boundaries, another distinction takes place between classes of representation, depending upon an assessment of the likelihood of judicial seizure, and their acceptability to the potential advertisers of a wide range of consumer products. This distinction is usually designated "hard-core"/ "soft-core," terms that originate in an American distinction as to whether real sex or simulated sex has been involved in the production of a representation, but it no longer has such a particular meaning. Soft-core pornography, available currently in public cinemas, in magazines on open sale in newsagents, attracts advertisements; hard-core pornography does not. Along with these advertisements comes a whole series of journalistic practices, from circulation audits to particular modes of address within written texts.

Pornography can designate itself by various simple mechanisms. An institution that is defined largely from outside by the suspicion of many vocal pressure groups is able to signify itself by exploiting the connotations associated with that suspicion. Thus "Swedish," "X," "Emmanuelle," "Sins" are precise generic indicators, as is a certain size of magazine with a near-naked female body portrayed on the cover, even before the list of contents develops the connotation. Similarly "Books and Magazines," "Adult," and "Private" indicate "hard-core" emporia. This activity of self-definition continues within the texts themselves, with the intrusive "we" ("aren't we daring?") of editorial matter; the recurrence of models; and the habit in films of using the institution of pornography itself (e.g., photo sessions) as circumstances for sex. This process means that areas of representation constructed from outside as "pornographic" never have to use that term to define themselves. The ground is never explicitly conceded.

Pornography in Britain occurs across a diversity of practices, each with its own means of marketing and dissemination, nevertheless unified by processes of self-designation into an institution of signification. Each practice has its own particular emphases and potentialities, both for marketing and for signification. Cinema is sharply divided into the kinds of soft-core films available in public cinemas, and the grades of sexually specific material to be found in "clubs" of various sorts. The British Board of Film Censors ensures that public films are extensively cut from the form they take in other countries, reducing them to a traditional kind of "teasing"; Tatler Cinema Clubs (associated with the Classic Cinema chain) show uncut American soft-core films; other clubs in city centers show films of actual sex acts of various kinds. Videotapes for home consumption are a fast developing industry, providing both material developed for the format (e.g., the video magazine *Electric Blue*, developed on an analogy with soft-core magazines), and full recordings of films sometimes banned or censor-cut for cinema. Magazines comprise a large and diversified market, with the half-dozen upmarket soft-core monthlies (e.g., *Mayfair, Club International*) having sales of between 150,000 and 250,000 each, and the downmarket publications (*Fiesta, Knave*) possibly around 150,000 each.[8] Readership of each copy is conventionally calculated at something like four times the number sold.

> Their editorial contents, both fictional and allegedly "factual," extensively describe varieties of sexual experience but their illustrations, majoring on high-definition female nudity, will not generally cover scenes of intercourse. The magazines. . . would treat auto-eroticism fully, touch on bondage, but shun more extreme perversions.[9]

Magazines obtainable only in specialized shops, for which no figures are available, provide what the generally circulated ones do not. Live performance in Britain takes advantage of the lack of censorship of theater to present revues of various kinds in both "legit" theaters and cabarets, which stop short of actual sex on stage. Writing and the fine arts are virtually freed from the emphasis that they used to have as major channels for pornography because they lack the immediacy of the "photograph effect." Prosecutions occur occasionally, however, but for some years have not involved pleas for the material made on the grounds of its "artistic merit."

The institution of pornography has been called into existence by the articulation of legal restraint and particular, conflicting, definitions of pornography. It produces no real justification of itself, no major articulation of "pornography" as a class of representation no better and no worse than any other. To this extent, it accepts its own status as the pariah of representational practices. Practitioners in the industry tend to prefer silence to developing any kind of public definition of their activities. When forced into pleading their case, their definitions tend to weave through the interstices of other definitions, speaking of "social function," "liberation," "sublimation," and other such gleanings from vulgar Freudianism or sociology. When a case is made for the ending of censorship on the grounds of intellectual freedom, it is not the pornography industry that makes it, but groups of liberal intellectuals who, like the Williams Committee, regard pornography as unappealing, but better permitted than banned.

The institution of pornography is a reaction to the designation of certain classes of representation as in some way objectionable. This designation is nowhere fixed, not even in law, but is the subject of a constant activity of redefinition as a result of struggles between definitions, particular initiatives on behalf of or against specific representations, and wider changes in moral attitudes.

Interface

The next step for this analysis is to find a way of characterizing the representations designated as "pornography" so that they can be seen as contradictory and open to change, even as undergoing change at the moment. This is the necessary other half of answering the inevitable (correct yet vexing) question: "What position should be taken up in relation to the struggle between definitions?" In doing this I have employed a metalinguistic approach like that used in the previous passage. This approach is necessary as an initial gesture that seeks to define a terrain in which further work (and not solely analytic work) can take place. As writing, it describes and delimits other forms of utterance, and is content to do so from a position of surveying those utterances from the outside. As an expression of an author-figure, it tends to evacuate the question of subjective response that pornography brings to the fore through its compelling implication of a sexed observer. Such a metalinguistic approach tends toward the impersonal, even the magisterial. It is not particularly able to produce accounts of textual activity, of the process of *enunciation*; it tends toward characterization of the facts of the *enounced*. A metalinguistic approach has to be used before it can be displaced by more complex and supple forms of analysis that can sense the openness of specific texts, or by forms of filmmaking that develop along the lines of contradiction that metalanguage can delineate.

The passage that follows therefore uses a typology of regimes of visual representations to examine one particular manifestation of representations called "pornography." This is the startling appearance of female genitals in easily available photographs and films, even in magazines sold in newsagents and films that are widely shown. This phenomenon does not account for everything that appears in pornography. I have chosen to concentrate on one public fact of pornography that has particularly caught my attention, because I think it can be made to reveal a particular shift within the area of representations that is designated "pornography." It is therefore a question that may be able to reveal "pornography" as a contradictory area of signification, rather than as a regime of signification with a strong internal coherence.

Female Pleasure

The closest that a general typology of visual representations has come to a perception of a particular regime of representation involving particular audience positioning that is open to change is probably Laura Mulvey's highly influential essay "Visual Pleasure and Narrative Cinema."[10] This has been central to the examination of the regimes of visual representation exploited in "mainstream cinema," and particularly the centrality of women to that cinema. Through an examination of the forms of looking and their pleasures (informed by psychoanalytic theory), Mulvey is able to give an adequate characterization of such diverse phenomena as the star system, striptease, and the narrative function of women in "dominant cinema." This characterization indicates directions for filmmaking practice that try to undermine these forms. However, it seems to be unable to account for and analyze the ways in which current visual pornography is obsessed with women's genitals: "The directness [of vaginal imagery] radically questions the psychoanalytically based analyses of images of women undertaken by Claire Johnston and Laura Mulvey and the notions of castration fear and the phallic woman."[11]

Mulvey's typology includes a notion of fetishism that is based on the letter of Freud's text,[12] taking fetishism as necessarily involving the disavowal of woman's lack of a penis. Hence current pornography would seem to contradict Mulvey's analysis, although in other areas it has proved to be crucial.

Mulvey describes cinema as an activity of looking[13] in which three looks are involved: that of the spectator to the screen; that of the camera to the event; and that of the actors within the event between each other. In classic cinema these are carefully arranged so that they never coincide: the camera never looks at the space that the audience "occupies" (the 180° rule); the actors never look down the axis of the camera. This regime allows the full exploitation of all the "pre-existing patterns of fascination already at work within the individual subject and the social formations that have molded him".[14] The first is the pleasure in looking itself, the scopophilic drive directed toward submitting others to a controlling and curious gaze. This drive is partly developed into a narcissistic form through which the viewer identifies himself or herself with figures perceived as existing outside the self of the viewer. These two structures of looking exist in tension with each other, and are crossed by a further pair of contradictory structures produced within the castration complex: voyeurism and fetishism. Voyeurism is an active, mobile form, associated with change and narrativization. It "demands a story, depends on making something happen, forcing a change in another person, a battle of will and strength, victory/defeat, all occurring in a linear time with a beginning and an end."[15]

Fetishism, according to Mulvey, is in contradiction with voyeurism: it involves a fixation that impedes narrative, centers on repetition of situations, the display of a star. Fetishism is a form of looking that disavows castration and hence sexual difference, whereas voyeurism involves an acknowledgment of sexual difference in its attempts to demystify or punish woman as object of the look. In both forms ultimately, the meaning of woman is sexual difference, the absence of a penis as visually ascertainable, the material evidence on which is based the castration complex essential for the organization of entrance into the symbolic order and the law of the father.[16]

Fetishism in Mulvey's account is a disavowal of woman's lack of a penis, and therefore should always involve avoiding the direct sight of the female genitals and finding a substitute penis in particular fetish objects, or in the whole figure of the woman-made-phallic. Current pornography would seem to refute this characterization. Yet in every other respect, current visual pornography maintains the kind of textual structure that Mulvey associates with fetishism. It presents the repetition of events rather than narrative development toward the resolution of an enigma; it relies upon a concentration on the figure of the woman that tends to oust any other considerations, and "the image [is] in direct erotic rapport with the spectator."[17]

The fetishistic representation attempts to abolish the distance between spectator and representation. Voyeurism installs a separation of seer and seen as the very principle of its operation, allowing the seer a secure position over and against a representation that permits the seen to change without threatening the position of the seer. This permits the development of editing, scene dissection, and narrative in the cinema. Fetishism constantly attempts to reduce or annul this distance and separation. Hence it is only capable of producing an attenuated narration, a constant repetition of scenarios of desire, where the repetition around certain neuralgic points outweighs any resolution of a narrative enigma, any discovery or reordering of facts. At its most extreme, fetishism involves a concentration upon performance, explicitly posed for the viewer (sometimes involving the performer looking directly "at" the audience), or even upon the frame-edge, or the two-dimensional reality of the realist photograph. A fetishist regime attempts to annul the separation of image and spectator, to reinstall an immediate relation that promises (in vain) to provide satisfaction to desire itself.

Thus Mulvey's use of the concepts of voyeurism and fetishism contains much that is vital to a metapsychological characterization of the various modes of cinematic and photographic representation. It cannot be discarded simply because it is unable in its current formulation to deal with the single (fairly ubiquitous) fact of direct depiction of female genitals. Rather, its Freudian basis should be reexamined.

Fetish: Penis or Phallus?

According to the text of Freud's essay "Fetishism," the construction of a fetish represents a disavowal of the *physical* fact of sexual difference, occasioned by an actual glimpse of female genitals. The structure that Freud describes is one in which the knowledge of the woman's lack of a penis is retained, but the infant is saved from acknowledgment of it by the substitution of what is seen in the moment before the sight of the genitals for that sight itself. The desire that the woman should after all have a penis is transferred to a particular part of the body, to an object (e.g., shoes, fur, stockings), or to other sensations. This substitute object maintains the belief that the woman has a penis while the knowledge of this physical lack is also maintained: in clinical fetishists "the two facts persist side by side throughout their lives without influencing each other."[18] The structure of disavowal is this: "I know (woman has no penis), nevertheless (she has, through this fetish)." In clinical fetishism the sight of the fetish is a necessary aid to sexual arousal, and Freud states that he has only encountered this state in males. Fetishism as a structure of (usually visual) perception, however, can also be found in women: it is a matter of the fascination resulting from hesitation of the knowledge of sexual difference by a structure of disavowal, "I know, but nevertheless."

For Freud's account of fetishism, then, the penis, its presence or absence on the human body, is central.

Yet the presence or absence of a penis on a human body is only important in so far as it signifies, in so far as it already has meaning within a particular cultural formation of sexual difference. The penis, or its lack, operates as the inadequate physical stand-in for that signifier that institutes the play of signification and difference: the phallus. In effect Freud's essay is aware of this distinction, only formulated clearly thirty years later. The child is already aware of sexual difference in Freud's account: what he seeks is confirmation that this suspicion might not be true after all. The desire that the woman should have a phallus in spite of everything is what gives the strength to the fetish, and allows the promotion of the moment before the physical confirmation as a substitute. Fetishism as a disavowal of sexual difference is thus a disavowal of the phallus by promoting in its place something else that the woman does possess. As a disavowal, it nevertheless maintains the phallus and thus the possibility of difference and language.[19] The structure is therefore one of "I know that woman does not have the phallus, nevertheless she does have the phallus in this fetish."

The fetish is a signifier that stands in for the phallus. Freud's example of the "shine on the nose" can demonstrate how this substitution of signifiers takes place through a process of metaphor or metonymy. His patient could become sexually aroused only through the sight (real or supposed) of a shine on the nose of his partner. Freud's analysis of this fetish has two components: a story and a sliding of signifiers. The "little story" is that of the child seeing female genitals, and looking up at the woman's face to gain a reassuring "nevertheless" from the nose. Hence the story that lies hidden in the fetish is one of a glance that traverses the woman's body. The notion of the "shine" comes from the condensation of this "glance" and its story into the German *Glanz* or "shine." Yet the condensation holds another possibility within itself, that the "shine" could stand for a realization of being looked at:[20] the "shine" is that of the gaze of the woman returned to the inquiring child. It then becomes the woman's *look* in which the fetish is located, rather than the "shine upon the nose" that Freud indicates did not necessarily have to exist to other observers. The woman's gaze is where her phallus is located. If this is so, then the story of the child's gaze may well itself be a substitute for this complex (nose/glance/*Glanz*) around the phallic gaze of the woman. It would then be a substitute that is provided in analysis in the form of a narrative, and narrative is always a suspicious or inadequate form for satisfactory analysis because of its insistence upon the serial nature of events (narrative can be said to lie behind the notorious "stages" interpretation of Freud's explanations), and its tendency to invite us into a literal scenario (narrative fiction's constant lure).

Such an interpretation of Freud's celebrated example questions the centrality of the child's active gaze to the account. The "little story" of the child's horror at the woman's lack of a penis can legitimately be seen as a substitute for the central and powerful gaze that constructs the fetish. The way is then open to examine fetishism as a particular kind of substitution of signifiers that does not necessarily depend upon a "primal look." Indeed, fetishism does not necessarily involve looking: a fetish can equally be something that is felt, heard, or smelled. Fetishism can be concerned with any or all of the invocatory drives and not just with a particular one: scopophilia.

What seems to be necessary for a particular object to become a fetish is that it should be constituted as a sexual signification by its articulation in a discourse of sexuality. The parts of the body, the objects, and the sensations that usually become fetishes are those that are already delimited and sexualized by a whole culture.[21] Hence those objects prone to fetishization are those that are already sexualized: underwear, visible parts of the body, the sound of clothes rustling, the smell of sweat.

This account of fetishism is able to avoid the problems that are inherent in Mulvey's account, and equally in Freud's, where he is forced by his insistence upon the woman's literal physical lack of a penis and the child's actual understanding sight of this lack to stress the horror that would be involved in such a realization: "probably no male human being is spared the fright of castration at the sight of a female genital."[22]

This horror cannot be involved in the massive dissemination of images of female genitals that characterizes particularly still photography in the pornographic sector. It is rather one result (and not the necessary result) of the quasi-identity that is produced between the phallus and the penis, between signifier and physical stand-in. It also produces the confusion between physical sexual difference and the distinction masculine/feminine that Freud took such pains to avoid.[23]

Fetish: The Woman's Sexual Pleasure

Mulvey's account of fetishistic modes of representation shows much that can be found in current pornography: cyclic narrative forms that reenact scenarios of desire; particular stress upon performances addressed to the spectator of the representation and having only tenuous relation to any notion of verisimilitude within the representation; the reduction of diegetic space to the two-dimensional surface of the screen; the woman posed as phallus rather than as lack. In addition, the usual voyeuristic distance of spectator to representation is compromised such that the image poses itself as pure presence (as fulfillment of desire) rather than as present absence (as something photographed in another place, at another time). Such structures of fetishism appear in current visual pornography, but other phenomena also occur that cannot be readily accounted for in Mulvey's terms as they stand.

Besides the massive diffusion of vaginal imagery already remarked upon (imagery often described as "explicit" or "aggressive"), there also appears a concentration on lesbian activities in both film and photography, and on female masturbation, particularly in still photography where it is often implied strongly by various poses. Feminist critics usually condemn the representation of masturbation as reinforcing the "solipsism" of pornography,[24] but are much more equivocal about the representation of lesbianism. These diverse shifts in pornographic representations have appeared, particularly in the fairly public pornography of magazines available in local newsagents' shops and in films available in public cinemas.

The fetish offered by these representations is no longer a fragment of clothing, or even the deceptively smooth body of the phallic woman; it is now the woman's sexual pleasure. The woman nevertheless has the phallus in sexual pleasure; the woman's lack of a phallus is disavowed in her orgasm. Hence physical sexual difference is no longer unmentionable within public representations of women that are designated "pornographic." Physical sexual difference can be promoted within these representations because the fetish has been shifted from compensating for the woman's lack of a penis to the finding of the woman's phallus in her sexual pleasure.

In orgasm woman no longer is the phallus, she has the phallus. Films currently produced within the pornographic sector gain their impulsion from the repetition of instances of female sexual pleasure, and male pleasure is perfunctory in most cases. The films (and photographs) are concerned with the mise-en-scène of the female orgasm; they constantly circle around it, trying to find it, to abolish the spectator's separation from it.

Female sexual pleasure has been promoted to the status of a fetish in order to provide representations of sexuality that are more "explicit" for an audience conceived of as male. The pornography industry has regarded the process as one of the legitimate expansion of the very restricted and clandestine "hard-core" representations into the more public arena of "softcore." Thus the progressive revelation of pubic hair in photographs and of (limp) penises in cinema has been regarded as the stealthy emergence of "pieces" of the body into the daylight of soft-core representations. Yet the industry's own characterization of the process, though to some extent a determinant of it, is very far from being the whole truth. Female sexual pleasure has become perhaps the dominant fetish within current public pornographic representation as a result of this "stealthy extension" of the industry, but the consequences are many and difficult to assess.

First, not every form of female sexual pleasure has an equal emphasis. Lesbian activity and female masturbation, when contained within a narrative, are always shown as subsidiary forms of pleasure, as surrogates for sex with a male, or as a form of experience that the heroine gains on her odyssey toward sexual satisfaction. Even within these passages, the emphasis on dildos and other substitute penises is quite marked: a male presence is maintained even within scenes of masturbation or lesbianism. Sexual pleasure for women, then, is posited as being dependent upon a male. This provides a certain security to the inquiry into female sexual pleasure: it is a fetish because it is in the orgasm that the woman's phallus is refound. Woman finds her phallus in the orgasm; woman is given that orgasm and hence that phallus by men. Both security and abolition of separation from the representation are provided for the spectator by this arrangement. The male's phallus is the condition for female sexual pleasure, the condition for the always-expected, never-found fulfillment of desire. The phallus for the woman in the representation is provided by the male in the audience: it is a "gift" from a man or men that provides woman's orgasm.

Angela Carter calls this process "a gap left in the text of just the right size for the reader to insert his prick into."[25] The representation of female pleasure is addressed to an audience constructed as masculine, as possessing a phallus (usually but not exclusively a biological male), because it erects the phallus of the individual in the audience as the condition of female pleasure. Female pleasure is the result, ultimately, of the gift of the phallus from members of the audience. Hence the current regime of pornographic representation retains its security for a (male) audience: it completes the fetishistic regime by providing the viewer with a direct relation to the representation through the gift of the phallus as the ultimate condition of female pleasure.

This regime is unquestionably an advance upon previous modes of representation of women in association with sexuality: the pin-up, the star system, much advertising rhetoric. It is equally an advance upon many forms of construction of "woman" within other regimes of representation. The question of female sexual pleasure has remained unasked within public discourses for many decades in our culture: in pornography it is now receiving attention on a massive scale. The availability of vaginal imagery can be said to have a directly educative effect for both men and women, as well as tending to dispel the aura of strangeness produced by the centuries of concealment of the vagina in Western representations.

It is therefore an important shift in the representation of the female, a shift that is still the subject of a series of hard-fought battles, whether in legislation or in the streets. For it is a profoundly equivocal shift: all is not sweetness and light in this field, the shift cannot be counted as a simple advance, let alone a victory for feminism. The educative effects, the effects of dispelling a particular and deep-rooted form of disgust at part of another's body, these are little more than side-effects, especially given the current and probable future institutional connotations given to the forms of circulation of these images. For the fetishistic regime is maintained by the reassertion of the phallus as the possession of the male, and the female as dependent upon the phallus as access to pleasure. The male spectator is sutured into the representation as the possessor of this prerequisite, and thus confirmed in a particular psychosocial construction of self.

However, this regime of representation is profoundly unstable. It has asked the question "what is female pleasure?"—a question that cannot find its answer in representations. The tawdry British sex comedies (such as those produced by the likes of George Harrison Marks) at least were based upon a question that could receive an answer: "What does a nude woman look like?" Current pornographic films have gone further and asked the question that lies behind that of nudity—the question of the nature of pleasure. But all that can be shown in a film or a photograph is the conditions of pleasure, its circumstances and outward manifestations. These are never enough: all that the viewer finds as the reply to the question are the outward displays, what is *expected*. What *happens*, "the fading of the subject," eludes the representation if the representation seeks to discover the elusive nature of the experience of sexual pleasure. The pornographic film text responds by multiplying instances of possible pleasure by multiplying its little stories of sexual incidents. Either that, or, in its more hard-core manifestations, it turns upon the object of the inquiry, the woman, and vents its (and the audience's) frustrations at the impossibility of gaining an answer to the question by degrading and humiliating woman, by attacking her for her obstinate refusal to yield this impossible secret. This aggression reaffirms the power of the phallus in response to a terror at the possibilities of the woman's escape from that power.

The formulation of this question in terms of a fetishistic regime has one further consequence: it leaves the question of male pleasure unasked. Attention is directed toward women and through them, to woman; male figures are attenuated in the sense that their sexuality is never really in question. The closest that questioning comes is in the often portrayed incidence of impotence or timidity, always cured. Male pleasure is assumed rather than investigated; this provides the security of the male viewer. Yet in the very perfunctory treatment that it receives, the question begins to haunt the representation: a disparity between the pressure of desire and the inadequacy of its satisfaction begins to open the complementary question, "what is male pleasure?" A question that, itself, has no real answer apart from the tautology of "I know because I know it."

All this points to an instability in the current regime of pornographic representation of sexuality, especially in the cinema. It is in cinema that the most hysterical responses to this instability occur. Two disparate manifestations of this hysteria: the extremes of brutality practiced upon women within representations, and the proposal from the Williams Committee that cinema should be the sole medium in which active censorship is retained. The particular instability in this medium results from the cinema's ability to narrativize a response to the question of female pleasure, however inadequate the response might be. For the process of narrativization produces significations, "moves" the spectator, and definitively introduces a voyeuristic form of viewing that threatens the whole security of the fetishist regime of representation. This perpetual displacement/replacement of signification and spectator is beyond the scope of conventional photographic layouts usually employed in magazines. Such layouts serve to enact the placement of the phallus as the condition of female pleasure, but do no more than that. In cinema, the fetishistic regime only operates on the condition that it is established across a variation of image, a perturbation of any stability. A form of voyeurism is always present. In cinematic representations there appears most acutely the instability of the current regime of pornographic representation oriented around the question of female pleasure, initially posed as a fetish. The possibility exists, then, for some film work to begin to displace this fetishistic regime by foregrounding and promoting as the organizing principle of the text those questions that begin to raise themselves behind the fetishistic posing of the question of female pleasure. It is possible to throw into question the nature of male pleasure by examining and frustrating what construction of the feminine it demands in particular circumstances. This to some extent is the effect of Nelly Kaplan's *Nea* (1976), which appeared briefly in Britain within the institution of soft-core pornography as *A Young Emmanuelle* (in early 1978).[26] It is possible also to use the questioning of pleasure, both male and female, to promote the notion of desire as the structuring principle of the text: desire that is constantly pursued but always elusive. Such is the enterprise of *Ai No Corrida* (*Empire of the Senses*) sufficiently threatening to be liable to Customs seizure, and sufficiently enlightening for the Williams Committee to mention it as a film unjustly treated under the current regulation of film censorship. Stephen Heath has traced the film's concern with the impossibility of seeing, its hesitation of narration.[27] What is important here is the way the film demonstrates the possibilities that pornography offers for representations of sexuality and of women (and men). The instability of the current fetishistic regime, based on the question of female pleasure that is only partially answerable by the "gift" of the phallus, provides opportunities for filmmaking practice. This would aim at a displacement of existing representations through foregrounding the aspects of the question that trouble the regime of representation that asks it. The institution of pornography would then begin to ask the questions about whose space it occupies without being aware of it: "What is sexuality? What is desire?"

Postface

This metapsychological approach has tried to characterize "pornography" as a shifting arena of representation in which particular kinds of aesthetic struggle may be possible. The boundaries of this arena are defined by the major positions over "pornography," the way that they articulate together, and the ways that they cross other definitions of morality, sexuality, representation, and so on. If, because of its conception of representation as a process, this metapsychological approach has managed to move away from such definitions, then it should also have a rather different notion of politics in relation to the pornography question. In particular, to regard pornography as an area of struggle within representations necessarily involves a different conception of the role of legislation.

The major definitions of pornography all look to the law as a crucial power that can be recruited to enforce one conception of representation, one permissible "pornography," or another. When the pornographic arena is regarded as the site of a particular struggle over representations, the law can be regarded only as providing or securing certain conditions for that struggle. This by no means coincides with the recommendations of the Williams Report. In some ways this report does not tackle the real problems faced by those attempting to change representations, their uses and their potential in our society; in other ways it actively blocks certain directions of work. The law as it stands provides certain obstacles for those trying to intervene actively (through stickers or graffiti for instance) in the area of public advertising. Recent cases have resulted in punitive fines for feminists undertaking such activity.[28] The Williams Report is unable to formulate any recommendations in this area, though recognizing that "many people, as is clear from submissions to us, dislike [sexualized advertisements]" (9.9). Currently advertisements are regarded legally as private property (hence fines for defacing them), rather than as being in the public domain, on the grounds that their entire function is one of addressing all and sundry whether they choose to be so addressed or not. The implications of such an argument for legal reform are not considered by the Williams Report, and so in this sense it can be seen as not having tackled the problems for those attempting to change and challenge existing representations.

Other recommendations of the report may provide new obstacles. Its recommendations are based on a public disavowal of a representational activity that is designated "pornography" by general opinion. This will mean that the production of such representations will be confirmed as a separate industry, difficult to move into, closely linked with organized crime. The construction of pornography as "I know it exists, nevertheless I choose to ignore it" will deprive many practitioners of the flexibility to move in and out of particular forms of signification that is implied by the notion of "struggle within representations." Some work will be public, some will be in plain wrappers, behind discreet doors. Such designations will provide institutional determinants of the meanings that are being produced that will create severe problems. It may suit the industry to exchange relaxation of controls on representations for tighter controls on their dissemination, but this is bound to create further problems for disruptive representational work in the area of pornography.

The area of cinema is the only medium in which the Williams Report advocates specific censorship mechanisms. It allows that the defense of "artistic merit" may be applied to films against the activities of the censor. If there is to be censorship of films by a government body, then this should be a *public* process, similar to that used in Weimar Germany. The censorship body would have to publish arguments for specific alterations to films or bans upon films, which would then be argued out with the producers and distributors in public, if challenged. The potential would then be provided for censorship itself to become an area of struggle, rather than a secretive and unargued process as it is now.

It is too simple to support the Williams recommendations as they stand merely because they offer a possible liberalization. Similarly, it is too simple to reject direct attacks upon public representations because the form of the attack is often open to accusations of puritanism. A politics in relation to pornography must develop from a conception of "pornography" as a particular arena of representation in which certain displacements, refigurations, are or can be possible.

NOTES

An earlier version of this essay was given as a paper at the Communist University of London in July 1979. My thanks to all those present for the suggestions that have been incorporated here, as well as to Maria Black, Ben Brewster, and Film Studies graduate students at the University of Kent.

1. *Report of the Committee on Obscenity and Film Censorship* [Williams Report], November 1979, HMSO Cmnd 7772. References are to the numbered sections of the report. The report does not consider Scottish law.

2. *Pornography* [The Longford Report] (London: Coronet, 1972).

3. Ruth Wallsgrove, "Pornography: Between the Devil and the True Blue Whitehouse," *Spare Rib* 65 (December 1977).

4. Angela Carter, *The Sadeian Woman* (London: Virago, 1979), 12–13.

5. Wallsgrove, "Pornography."

6. In this respect, the sticker "Who does this poster think you are?" would be a more effective way of confronting the attitude that advertising promotes.

7. Wallsgrove, "Pornography."

8. Michael Brown, appendix 6 to Williams Report.

9. Ibid., 250.

10. Laura Mulvey, "Visual Pleasure and Narrative Cinema," *Screen* 16, no. 3 (Autumn 1975): 6–18.

11. Griselda Pollock, "What's Wrong with 'Images of Women'?" *Screen Education* no. 24 (Autumn 1977): 25–33.

12. Sigmund Freud, "Fetishism," in *The Standard Edition of the Complete Psychological Works*, trans. and ed. James Strachey (London: Hogarth, 1951–1973), vol. XXI.

13. Although addressed to cinema, much of Mulvey's analysis is relevant to still images.

14. Mulvey, "Visual Pleasure and Narrative Cinema," 6.

15. Ibid., 13.

16. Ibid.

17. Ibid., 14.

18. Sigmund Freud, "Outline of Psychoanalysis," in *Standard Edition*, vol. XXIII, 203. "Fetishism" is in vol. XXI.

19. Freud presents his clinical fetishists as in no real way discommoded: "usually they are quite satisfied with it, or even praise the way in which it eases their erotic life" (*Standard Edition*, vol. XXI, 152).

20. A bright point of light concentrated on the eyes of an actor is a standard indicator of an intense gaze in a film.

21. For an examination of this process, see Rosalind Coward, "Sexual Liberation and the Family," *m/f* no. 1 (1978), especially 14–17.

22. Freud, "Fetishism," in *Standard Edition*, vol. XXI, 155.

23. For a similar discussion of fetishism, see Metz's "The Imaginary Signifier," *Screen* 16, no. 2 (Summer 1975), especially 67–75. Metz, however, is only concerned with the fetishism of the cinematic apparatus.

24. A humanist notion dependent on conceiving sexuality as permissible *only* when involving more than one person.

25. Carter, *Sadeian Woman*, 16.

26. See *Monthly Film Bulletin*, December 1977, 263.

27. Stephen Heath, "The Question Oshima," in *Ophuls*, ed. Paul Willemen (London: British Film Institute, 1978).

28. Fines of £100 and over have been exacted for "creative" writing on London Underground posters.

Paul Willemen

Letter to John

Dear John,

While reading your article "On Pornography" in the last issue of *Screen* my initial admiration for the clarity and accuracy of your analysis gradually turned to a sort of irritation. This disturbance of the equilibrium in my libidinal economy sparked off an intense process of inner speech urging me to clarify my disagreements and to put my own reflections on the subject into a semblance of order.

I found our positions to be very similar—and in some cases where that was not so, your arguments convinced me that they should be—but that there were also passages that I thought skidded off the track. In the end, you arrived at a perfectly respectable destination although it is also a dead end. What does it mean to require porn to address the questions: "What is sexuality? What is desire?" Either it is the case that porn has solved those questions in its daily and durable practice because it trades on the exploitation of their answer, or these are questions only psychoanalysis can deal with at all adequately. To ask porn to deal with them strikes me as an evasion of the very issues you raised. By bracketing questions of specific social-historical signifying regimes defined as porn and by redirecting attention to philosophical and psychoanalytical issues posed in such a general and abstract manner, the specific institution of porn, that is, the terms on which it functions and changes, has been lost from sight. Of course I agree that we must try to go beyond the currently available positions and your essay provides some of the signposts for such a trajectory. All I hope to do in this letter is to pick up on those signposts and perhaps add a few more.

The focus of my irritation with the essay centered on your note number [20, reprinted in this volume] where you assert that "a bright point of light concentrated on the eyes of an actor is a standard indicator of an intense gaze in a film." That is a mistake. Such a bright light, whether a point or a beam of light on the eyes of an actor/character, if shown in close-up (a necessary extra specification), does not indicate an intense gaze in a film. True enough, it is the indicator of a look, that is to say, it functions as the signifier of a gaze, but not necessarily of a gaze *in* the film nor necessarily of an intense gaze anywhere. It may indicate that the actor/character is gazing intently at something or somebody, or that she or he is being gazed at intently, but it also may mean—and quite often does, as I pointed out in an analysis of *Pursued*[1]—that something is going on behind the eyes

First published in *Screen*, Summer 1980, vol. 21, no. 2, pp. 53–65. Reprinted by permission of the author and the editors of *Screen*.

of the character, in which case it functions as the signifier in a metonymic process substituting the container for the content. This metonymy is particularly common in noir films where a horizontal band of light across the eyes, leaving the rest of the image in relative obscurity but still plainly visible, tells us that the character is a psycho or has been traumatized. As often as not, such an image can have the character gazing at nothing in particular, signifying madness or blindness, or initiating a memory sequence. In other words, what is being shown as going on behind the eyes is not at all what is being gazed at. The look inscribed into such an image is by no means always a gaze contained within the diegesis between characters or from a character to an object.

On the contrary, I would argue that the primary function of such an image is to mark the look *at* the image, that is, the look of the viewer as distinct from that of the camera, two looks that in most films are mapped onto each other. While the look of the camera constitutes the frame, the beam of light on the eyes pinpoints a look which, although from the same position as the camera, is not coextensive with it, introducing negativity into the image, a mark of difference. A different look is being interpellated. If we can say that in classic cinema the frame is absented (it functions as a masking of a continuous, homogeneous plenitude: the diegetic world in which the characters continue to exist even when they are out of frame) and that the image as seen by the camera is thus naturalized, the beam or the point of light inscribes a different look that denaturalizes the image by presenting it in its "to-be-looked-at-ness."

Of course, that presentation can be and often is reintegrated into the diegesis by articulating it to a diegetically motivated look or assigning it to a diegetic light source, suturing the momentary fissure and binding the viewer's position back into the network of looks that sustains the narrative movement of the text. But such a recovery maneuver does not eradicate the moment of oscillation, the moment of risk. To put it somewhat crudely, and therefore perhaps misleadingly, the type of image you specify signifies (as opposed to "implies") that it is one pole of an axis, the other end of which is the viewer's eye. The look of the viewer is the signifier of that axis, including its three constituent terms: viewer, image, and the specular relation between the two. In that sense, its explicit inscription into the image functions as a mark of what in literature would be described as direct address. The mischaracterization of that type of image in the context of your discussion of fetishism (which is where the note occurs) is as significant as your selection of that particular example is revealing.

I think a comparison between the light-on-the-eyes image and other images that stress their perspectival or compositional features will clarify my point. Both looks are present in both types of image (the look of the camera at the profilmic event and the look of the viewer at the image), but whereas the "eyes-image" distinguishes the two, the others don't and thus correspond much more directly to the structure of fetishism and its regime of split belief: the emphatically composed image both indicates and denies simultaneously its "to-be-looked-at-ness," while the eyes-image designates the difference and thus goes against the grain of the fetishistic position, dislocating its regime of split belief to some extent. And I added that qualification only because there are more effective ways of designating the image as there "for my look," as Buñuel showed with a razor blade. It is interesting to note that the more fetishized image, the one that both draws attention to its to-be-looked-at-ness and effaces, naturalized if by covering it with the camera's look, is usually regarded as the more aesthetically satisfying one. Freud's textbook example of fetishism (the glance at the nose), which you quote, is also an example of two looks being mapped onto each other: the look at the vagina and the look at the nose, the latter cancelling out the anxiety generated by the former. In that sense, it is the frame that constitutes the cinematic equivalent of the "shine on the nose" and not the "light on the eyes" type of image that works in the opposite direction by dissociating the two looks. The two processes are radically different.

I want to return to the "to-be-looked-at-ness" of the image that goes together with the inscription of the look of the viewer, with the donation of the image to the looking eye/I. As I suggested earlier, the kinds of image that foreground compositional features such as strong perspectival arrangements or a double *mise-en-cadre* by having frames within frames, tend to play around, timidly, with the mapping of the camera's look onto that of the viewer and achieve an increased aesthetic effect. Such effects have come to be regarded as evidence of a strong authorial presence, as marks of the process of enunciation. But the fact that the eye-images you mention are in close-up separates them from the conventional forms of arty composition. Whereas images in classic narrative cinema (e.g., Budd Boetticher or Capra) use the frame as a mask, arty compositions (using that phrase as a slightly pejorative shorthand, although I am by no means prepared to dismiss all such images at all times) emphasize the frame and, in so doing, also stress that the look of the viewer is coextensive with that of the camera, that the two looks are one. In that way, they achieve an increase in their to-be-looked-at-ness in terms of an increase in aesthetic effectiveness while at the same time retaining the naturalization of frame as mask for a continuous and homogeneous diegetic world.

Such images, directly analogous to fetishes, stress the presence of an organizing "I" which uses—directs—the camera's look to circumscribe and organize the viewer's field of vision, thus denying the autonomy while acknowledging the presence of the viewer's look, making it present yet absent at the same time. However, the type of close-up you refer to puts no such stress on the addresser of the enunciation: it opens up a space for the emergence of the addressee's position. Obviously, when one of these two protagonists emerges, the other one tags along in its shadow. But what I am arguing is that the two different types of image, one extremely common and liable to fill an entire film, the other more of a punctuation image, both stress a different side of the process of enunciation.

It is interesting that you should have evoked the light-in-the-eyes image because, although it cannot do what you ask of it, it nevertheless provides a useful way of engaging with the process of enunciation characteristic of pornographic imagery, that is, direct address: "This is for you to look at." What is at stake here is the fourth look:[2] that is to say, any articulation of images and looks that brings into play the position and activity of the viewer as a distinctly separate factor also destabilizes that position and puts it at risk. All drives have active and passive facets and the scopic drive is no exception. When the scopic drive is brought into focus, the viewer also runs the risk of becoming the object of the look, of being overlooked in the act of looking. The fourth look is the possibility of that over-looking-look and is always present in the wings, so to speak. The fourth look is not of the same order as the other three (intradiegetic looks, the camera's look at the profilmic event and the viewer's look at the image), but a look imagined by me in the field of the other that surprises me in the act of voyeurism and causes a feeling of shame, as Jacques Lacan put it.[3]

When the look of the viewer is separated off from the look of the camera, the fourth look emerges particularly strongly when the viewer's scopic drive is being gratified in relation to an object or scene that heightens the sense of censorship inherent in any form of gratification. In simpler terms: the fourth look gains in force when the viewer is looking at something she or he is not supposed to look at, either according to an internalized censorship (superego) or an external, legal one (as in clandestine viewings) or, as in most cases, according to both censorships combined. In this way, that fourth look problematizes the social dimension, the field of the other of the system of looking at work in the cinematic institution as well as in the photographic and televisual ones.

Direct address imagery is offered explicitly "for me to look at," stressing the addressee's look as opposed to the addresser's intervention, and is particularly liable to bring that fourth look into play in full force. When you suggest that the "shine on the nose" image of Freud's example is produced as an avoidance of the woman's gaze back at the child, you correctly but perhaps inadvertently stress the presence of the fourth look in Freud's scenario. The child avoids the eyes of the woman whose nose allows him to disavow what he has (not) seen lower down, because to encounter that look would threaten the pleasurable and reassuring structure of fetishism he has just managed to install to avoid that very threat. Whether the woman was or was not actually looking back at the child is beside the point in this context.

Much has been written about the political importance of the activation of the viewer in relation to an imaged discourse and people such as Stephen Heath have commented on the importance of the look in that process.[4] But what has rarely been addressed (it has often been affirmed or denied but rarely addressed) is the question: how exactly, through which hybrid processes and in which mechanisms, can the interweaving, the articulation of the textual and the social, be traced in relation to the viewer? To my knowledge, only two credible processes partaking simultaneously of the textual and of the social situation within which it arises (as production or as reading) present themselves: inner speech and the fourth look. Inner speech is a complex problem I approached a couple of years ago.[5] The fourth look and its direct implication in both the social and the psychic aspects of censorship, of the law, introduces the social into the very act of looking while remaining an integral part of the textual relations.

The look at, say, a Wim Wenders film or an Altman film does not pose many problems. First, because the viewer's look is caught in the fetishistic process of disavowal through the play on framing and composition that simultaneously highlights and denies the incision effected by the frame. The looks of the camera and of the viewer are both inscribed, but as a unity, thus dimming the focus on the viewer's position and illuminating the marks of enunciation to be credited to the absent organizer of the discourse, that is to say, to the author who thus signals his or her desire to be recognized as artist.

Second, because the mapping of these looks binds the viewer into the spectacle, the fourth look is diverted and left dormant. Third, the problems inherent in the exercise of one's voyeurism having been contained (indeed, having been covered by the mantle of art), the decrease in the overtness of the look's sexual grounding facilitates displacement, sublimation, and a reversal of affect: instead of the risk of being caught looking, a positive valuation has now been bestowed upon the voyeur's activity. Some would even go so far as to want to be seen looking at an Altman film. This process of reversal forms the basis of the arguments around so-called artistic merit as distinct from the "free speech" arguments that are made in defense of a genre such as porn cinema.

The weakness of the artistic merit argument has to do with the need to identify marks of enunciation so that they can then be credited to or projected upon a mythic "source" of the discourse: the artist. No matter that discourses such as porn cinema are riddled with emphases on the marks of enunciation, the argument is displaced from the text on to the "quality," which invariably means the journalistic reputation of that mythic source, the artist.

The circularity of that trajectory is evident: if the text bears the hallmarks of an expressive subjectivity, it must have been done by an artist, and if it emanates from an artist, it must be art, and art can be distinguished by its emphatic marks of enunciation, and so on. This is the circle the liberal position on porn tries to break by extending the right of free speech to (some) nonartists.

Your reference to the "eyes-image" occurs when you are constructing a transition within a passage which is itself a transition. The example signals the shift from an account of Laura Mulvey's discussion of visual pleasure[6] to the proposition that female pleasure itself has become a fetish in porn representations. This passage is itself embedded in the shift from a partial but pertinent consideration of the institution of porn on the basis of the Williams Report[7] to an attempt "to find a way of characterizing the representations designated as porn so that they can be seen as contradictory and open to change," in the words of the essay.

This is perhaps not the place to argue that representations do not have to be contradictory to be open to change: no representation is so univocal and homogeneous that it must remain outside history. Being caught up in contradictions is not quite the same as being contradictory. However, this second transition eventually allows you to arrive at the conclusion that the questions at stake in porn are: What is sexuality? What is desire?

Interesting and important as these questions are, I would suggest that more relevant, less all-encompassing questions might be: What are the terms of the social circulation of representations of sex? What are the terms of their economic exploitation? Perhaps my two questions can be subsumed in the formulation you propose, again in a note: Who do porn representations think you are?

I have no answers to these questions, but the issues they raise allow the discussion initiated in your essay to be put into a more productive framework. The mode of address of porn imagery is characterized by a strange anonymity, a kind of emphatic anonymity. Porn films and photographs mostly are unsigned or signed with pseudonyms. This is not really to avoid prosecution since publishers, exhibitors, and retailers tend to carry the risk anyway. Besides, even where porn is legal, pseudonyms are still the rule.

At the same time, when compared to the smoothly flowing regime of mainstream cinema, porn is heavily marked by the process of enunciation. But there is no author to whom these marks could be credited and to whom can thus be delegated the responsibility for the fantasy articulated in and by the discourse. Moreover, the traditional strategies deployed by mainstream cinema to achieve an impersonal mode of narration, which nevertheless binds the viewer into the diegesis, are not open to the porn film.

The specificity of the genre requires a maximum number of sexually explicit images, which necessarily fragment the narrative, produce constant repetitions, and render suspense or an elementary sense of verisimilitude virtually impossible. The images must bear the marks of realist verisimilitude, the narrative cannot.

Strategies to elicit identification with a character are necessarily rudimentary because there is virtually no time and no context within which to construct such a figure. Hence the massive use of stereotypes and stock situations. Narrative is reduced to a minimum and becomes a barely (*sic*) motivated procedure for the juxtaposition of fantasy scenes whose combinatory logic is more that of the catalogue than that of narration.

In addition, the very arrangement of the figures in the image reinforces their status as specifically designed for "my" look. Their to-be-looked-at-ness is stressed by the absence of the taboo on the look into the lens, by the disposition of the body or bodies in the diegesis so as to grant direct access to the genital areas even if this means that the protagonists have to engage in most uncomfortable contortions, by the relentless use of punctuating close-ups of genitalia and their interactions, and so on. In porn there is no way the viewer can fade into the diegesis or, alternatively, shove responsibility for the discourse on to the author. The viewer is left squarely facing the image without even the semblance of an excuse justifying her or his presence at the other end of the look. Porn imagery may well be the most blatant and uncompromising form of direct address short of physical contact.

Besides, the substitution of the look for physical contact is precisely the essential precondition for porn and the specific difference that distinguishes it from other scopophilic regimes such as looking at family snapshots or at Hollywood movies. Porn involves a direct form of address in which the look substitutes for physical (sexual) contact in a structure determined by conditions of production along with the emphatic presence of the fourth look. It is via that look, imagined by me in the field of the Other, that porn imagery affects and is affected by the competing discourses and institutions that assign it its changing place within the register of signifying practices.

Crudely speaking, when mention is made of changes in the public presence and acceptability of porn, it is the institutionalization of the fourth look within a social formation we are talking about. Within that structure, there are different modes of looking. The dominant one is no doubt the fetishistic look because images themselves, as objects, sustain the belief in a presence in the face of our knowledge of absence. This founding fetishism can be overlaid, doubled by a second order and more specific fetishism when the depicted figure relaunches the need for some further disavowal. Obviously, the depiction of genitalia is a prime candidate for such a second-order disavowal. Hence the fact that in many, perhaps even in most, porn images the bodies depicted are shown as somehow contained, sheathed in paraphernalia such as boots, stockings, garter belts, or leather gear, making these bodies into representatives of the phallus according to the mechanisms lucidly described by Laura Mulvey in her essay on the work of Allen Jones.[8] The disavowal operates by making the body into a phallus or by inscribing elsewhere in the image, often in multiplied form, what is looked for and seen to be missing.

However, porn also often plays on a second, more reassuring type of looking that can quite easily coexist with the fetishistic look, although it is in some sense its inverse. It is less a disavowal of "her" castration than a confirmation of the viewer's phallic power. This specular relation is dependent on the emphatic direct address interpellating the viewer as possessor and donor of the phallus, the one who is required to complete the picture, as it were.

The representation of women experiencing pleasure is one variant on this theme. In most porn, women are the space onto (into) which male pleasure and phallic power is inscribed. This can take different forms: through the disposition of the body so as to grant maximum access to the look; through the imprinting on women of the traces of male pleasure (the come shot or money shot, as it's called in the trade, usually disperses its seminal signifiers onto the body of the woman, while her orgasm either precedes it, is triggered by it, or is left out of the picture altogether). Even when a woman is shown to be deriving pleasure from masturbation, her body is always arranged in "display" poses maximizing access of the look to her genital area, suggesting that the pleasure depicted is a narcissistic mirror for the viewer. Rare are the occasions when in such a scene the distinction between the look of the viewer and that of the camera is brought into play. The price the viewer pays for this guarantee of her or his phallic power is the price of porn itself: the radical separation from the object of desire required for the look to be able to function at all (as signifier of desire). The viewer's security depends on that separation: it is separation that guarantees (mostly) him phallic power. If it is true, as you suggest, that there is a proliferation of vaginal imagery and of women-in-pleasure images, then this is the very opposite of "an advance upon previous modes of representation of women," as you write. On the contrary, such a development constitutes an emphatic insistence on the centrality of phallic, male pleasure and suggests that the male population in Western societies now requires to be reassured more often, more directly, and more publicly than before. The increase in public visibility and availability of such imagery does address women: it tells them to stop threatening that centrality. The terms on which representations of sexuality appear to circulate at present seem to point to a severe crisis of male self-confidence. It would even be possible to confirm this by way of analyses of analogous developments in mainstream cinema: the proliferation of disaster movies about burning and collapsing skyscrapers, crashing planes, suffocating and exploding ships, toppled presidents, and so on.

This address of women through the public display of porn operates indirectly through the fourth look: public visibility here means that the look imagined by me in the field of the Other is that of a woman who sees the images that guarantee that female pleasure depends on a phallus. The more women object to this, the more effective the operation of the images is for men. Of course, to actually be caught looking, to be found out as needing reassurance, is quite a different matter. Nevertheless, that the proliferation of such images coincides with the growth of the Women's movement as well as with vocal demands for censorship is not a coincidence.

I would also like to make a few points about the social inscription of porn images in relation to fantasy. Fantasy images, framed image-objects, and what we see around us are three different things existing in different spaces. Each involves different relations between subject and look. The actualization of fantasy scenarios into framed image-objects (still or moving) necessarily passes through "the defiles of the signifier," as Lacan would say, as well as through the distortion processes unconscious signifiers are subjected to when passing into consciousness.

In relation to the imaged discourse, secondary elaboration and considerations of representability are extremely important. Figurative images, which is what porn images needs must be, require a social setting and an individuation that fantasy can do without. On the one hand, the surfeit of specific details due to the need for a frame to be filled produces an excess of signification. But this excess is also a loss: the lack of fit between the represented scenario and the fantasy transmuted into concrete images.

In porn, this inevitable mismatch plays a particularly important role because it is more acutely experienced. When a Western such as *Pursued* evokes the primal scene as a structuring fantasy, it does so in oblique and distorted ways.

Porn imagery directly addresses the viewer with the fantasy itself. The fantasy no longer needs to be reconstructed. But now it is the very incarnation of the fantasy that cannot but produce a mismatch: the actors' bodies (pimples and all), the lighting, the sets, the noises on the sound track, everything is excessively concrete and never quite coincides with the selective vagueness of a fantasy image. A sexual fantasy can proceed very satisfactorily without having to specify the pattern on the wallpaper. A filmic fantasy cannot. In porn, and perhaps in all films, it is the loss generated by the friction between the fantasy looked for and the fantasy displayed that sustains the desire for ever-promised and never-found gratification.

Porn, as an institution, thrives on this repetition of loss, of the double separation between viewer and representation and between the fantasy looked for and the one on offer. It is in the tension between approximation and separation in relation to the representation of sex that perhaps the explanation can be found for the compensatory activity associated with porn: masturbation. And that pleasure in return relaunches the desire for the tensions provoked by porn in the first place. The close connection between porn and masturbation tends to generate defensiveness . . . and further compensatory action. It is difficult to talk about porn without becoming too aggressive, too puritanical, too jokey, too excessive in one way or another. (Hence also the slightly excessive and scandalous aspects of a direct address in the form of a letter intended to be overlooked by *Screen*'s readers.)

The most common defensive strategy in relation to porn is the mobilization of double entendres, sustained double meanings, witticisms, jokes, and so on. The verbal language that accompanies porn stresses this jokey aspect, insisting that it is not to be taken seriously. However, it is more than just a distancing device. Neither is the joke aspect of porn just a self-reflexive comment on the endlessly stereotyped and repetitive nature of the porn discourse itself. The way porn actualizes unconscious significations is analogous to the way jokes do.

Allowing for the differences between Freud's verbal jokes and cinematic porn, there is at least one striking similarity between their discursive mechanisms. It is a similarity relating not so much to the place of the fourth look in the process but to its function as a space. Perhaps even the only space, as far as the viewer is concerned, where the social and the textual mesh. Tzvetan Todorov, in his book *Théories du symbole*,[9] schematizes the process of enunciation involved in rude jokes: A (the man) addresses B (the woman) seeking to satisfy his sexual desire; the intervention of C (the rival) makes the satisfaction of desire impossible.

Hence, a second situation develops: frustrated in his desire, A addresses aggressive remarks to B and appeals to C as an ally. A new transformation occurs, provoked by the absence of the woman or by the need to observe a social code: instead of addressing B, A addresses C by telling him a rude joke; B may well be absent, but instead of being the addressee she has become (implicitly) the object of what is said: C derives pleasure from A's joke.

The only modification I would want to make to this scenario is that C, the rival addressed by the joke and the one who becomes the subject of its pleasure, does not have to be another person. Any censorship mechanism, whether internal or external to A, is equally effective in setting in motion the series of substitutions and displacements described.

Taking into account that the mode of address in visualized discourse operates through the organization of a network of looks, the structure of address underpinning the joke process is very similar to that in play in porn: a man ends up showing a rude image of a woman (usually) to another man who becomes the subject of its pleasure. The male addressee arrives in that place because the woman has been expelled from it. But as Poe demonstrated in his story of the purloined letter, messages always reach their destination. The initial demand of the man addressed to the woman was a demand for his gratification, that is to say, it was a demand for self-gratification through the detour of the woman. The rival is in fact this narcissistic double whose gratification is at stake. It is the addresser in another place of the discursive process. His pleasure stands in for mine. In that process, the woman has been eliminated and relegated to the field of the Other, whence she, the repressed, returns as the subject of the fourth look. This allows the men to function as subjects and objects at the same time: one is the object of a look, the other is the subject of an enunciation. The representation of sexuality men circulate substitutes for an address of a woman who is thus relegated to a space below the barrier of repression, whence her look returns as the one that overlooks the male in his reassuringly defensive games of substitution.

This mechanism offers a way of understanding how a feminist politics can have effects within porn as a signifying practice. The historically changing content of porn imagery provides figurations of the contours, the imprint of women's struggles on the representations of male desire and its objects. The distance between the woman imagined as the subject of the fourth look and the woman (not) addressed in the first place measures the extent to which feminisms have impinged on male sexuality.

The porn industry addresses itself to women by representing back to them those changes—the crisis provoked in male sexuality—but it does so obliquely: the images are not for women to look at, they are for women to overlook. To get annoyed by that mirror may be understandable, but it is a little beside the point. Which is not to say that one shouldn't oppose aspects of the porn industry: that business institutionalizes and exploits both the crisis in male sexuality and the real women who are required to model for the images and the films. On the other hand, to oppose the representation of (sexual) fantasy merely modifies the regime of representation, not the fantasy.

Postscript

Talking about changing the representation, not the fantasy, in Fleming's anemic version of *Dr. Jekyll and Mr. Hyde* (1941), there is a strange sequence that appears to have been caused by such censorship. But it is the way the fantasy circumvented the censorship that is rather interesting in the context of a discussion about pornography. The passage occurs when Spencer Tracy/Hyde comes to visit Ingrid Bergman/Ivy in the secret apartment where Hyde keeps her to gratify his beastly desires. She is seen in a fairly distressed state when he enters. He starts by teasing her: "What shall I ask you to do tonight, dear?" (or words to that effect). He then proceeds to build up the tension, suggesting a series of innocent-sounding activities that are immediately rejected. He gets more and more excited as he gets closer to enouncing the awful, beastly thing he will require from her. Gradually, the full horror of what he is about to ask her to do dawns on her and she starts to whimper and moan in helpless despair: "No, no . . . not *that!*" Tracy replies: "Yes . . . Yes, my dear . . . you shall . . . *Sing* to me." And then we are treated at length to the anguished, tearful face of Bergman as she is forced to submit to this filthy perversion.

I think there are few scenes in the cinema that avoid showing sex in so blatant and graphic a manner. (Perhaps in *Susan Slept Here*, the middle-aged Dick Powell/Mr. Christopher and the seventeen-year-old Debbie Reynolds/Susan dancing throughout their wedding night, with dialogue lines about being able to keep it up all night, qualifies as another such sex scene.) This substitution of singing (and dancing) for sex may give a clue to the popularity of musicals.

Musicals do have a marked structural similarity with porn films. In both cases the importance of the generically obligatory sequences makes for a weak narrative as the story is simply there to link the graphic sex/musical numbers with fairly predictably coded transitions from the narrative to its interruptions, with the interruptions functioning as self-contained pieces. Moreover, the need to include such relatively autonomous segments arranged as spectacles "arresting" the look and thus, at least to a significant extent, suspending the narrative flow, makes for films that proceed with a halting rhythm. Also in both genres, such a structure makes it easier to add or to cut scenes without substantially altering the plot development. Finally, in both genres the interrupting segments consist of bodies displaying their physicality either in isolation or in rhythmical unison.

All this makes the precise point where the narrative tends to give way to a musical number rather interesting. It cannot be a mere coincidence that moments of "discovery" (when the lovers discover they are in love) or of "union" tend to be the obvious points where the rhythmical interactions are be inserted. Other key moments are when one of the lead characters displays her or his body for seduction, for the look of the Other: there too the narrative tends to swell into a musical number. Perhaps there is material here for a comparative study between Egyptian, Hindi, and U.S. musicals? One pertinent difference might be that in Hollywood the display of the male body is at least as significant as that of the female body, perhaps even more so (e.g., Astaire, Kelly).

NOTES

1. Paul Willemen, "Pursued—The Fugitive Subject," in *Raoul Walsh*, ed. Phil Hardy (Edinburgh: Edinburgh Film Festival, 1974).

2. Paul Willemen, "Voyeurism, the Look and Dwoskin," *Afterimage* 6 (1976).

3. Jacques Lacan, *Le Séminaire*, XI (Paris: Editions du Seuil, 1973).

4. Stephen Heath, "Anata mo," *Screen* 17, no. 4 (Winter 1976–1977): 49–66.

5. Paul Willemen, "Cinematic Discourse: The Problem of Inner Speech," in *Cinema and Language*, ed. T. de Lauretis and S. Heath (Bethesda, Md.: University Publications of America, 1981).

6. Laura Mulvey, "Visual Pleasure and Narrative Cinema," *Screen* 16, no. 3 (Autumn 1975): 6–18.

7. *Report of the Committee on Obscenity and Film in Censorship* [The Williams Report], HMSO Cmnd 7772, November 1979.

8. Laura Mulvey, "You Don't Know What You're Doing, Do You Mr. Jones?" *Spare Rib* 8 (1973).

9. Tzvetan Todorov, *Théories du symbole* (Paris: Editions du Seuil, 1978).

Linda Williams

Generic Pleasures: Number and Narrative

In becoming legal, feature-length, and narrative, hard-core film joined the entertainment mainstream. No matter how much it might still be regarded as a pariah, the new "porno" was now more a genre among other genres than it was a special case. As if to insist on this fact, hard-core narratives went about imitating other Hollywood genres with a vengeance, inflecting well-known titles and genres with an X-rated difference. Films with titles such as *Sexorcist Devil* (1974), *Beach Blanket Bango* (1975), *Flesh Gordon* (1978), *Dracula Sucks* (1979), *Downstairs Upstairs* (1980), and *Urban Cowgirls* (1981) were now exhibited in movie theaters that looked—almost—like other movie theaters. Stories, too, were almost like other film stories. Audiences, though still disproportionately male, were becoming more like other film audiences. By the early 1980s, this normalization of hardcore would be further dramatized in the many videocassette rental outlets that offered X-rated adult videos on the same shelves as or adjacent to the latest horror film or teen comedy.

This chapter examines this "genre-among-genres" quality of feature-length hardcore. The goal here is not to celebrate a hard-core coming of age or the achievements of the genre's emerging auteurs; rather, it is to explore the significance of hardcore's now-mainstream popularity. This new popularity with and appeal to more general audiences, it seems clear, represents an unprecedented mass commercialization of sex as visual pleasure and spectator sport. But the particular form that this commercialization has taken has not been adequately appreciated, owing to the embattled nature of the pornography debates. We must begin, then, with a basic question: of what, apart from the essential ingredient of the money shot, and its placement within some kind of narrative, does the genre consist?

On its face, the answer is easy: hardcore consists of sexual action in, and as, narrative. This action is now rendered in color and sound in films and, increasingly, videotapes that run at least sixty minutes. Since hard-core action cannot be filmed or taped without the performance of sexual acts, it might be tempting to say that hardcore is synonymous with sex itself, for we now see the sex act as event more than we see the sexual show of the stag film. But if we have learned anything about the money shot, it is that although the physical act of sex obviously must take place in order to be filmed, the visual spectacle of external penile ejaculation is a tacit acknowledgment that such real-live sex acts can be communicated to viewers only through certain visual and aural conventions of representation. What, besides the money shot, are these conventions, and how do they function? Most of this chapter will be taken up with exploring the iconography of the various sexual numbers and their relation to narrative. Before turning to this subject, however, we need to examine the conventions arising from the genre's most striking new source of realist effect: its belated integration of sound technology.

The Sounds of Pleasure

The hard-core quest for an involuntary, self-evident "frenzy of the visible" has revealed that what passes for a confessional frenzy is really just another way of speaking about and constructing the apparent "truths" of sex. The metaphor of speech—of discourses of sexuality as ways of talking about sex—has been crucial to this construction. And yet real speech has been remarkably absent thanks to the genre's unusually prolonged silence. Thirty years after the rest of cinema had been wired for sound, the stag film still relied on the power of its images alone, persisting in the "exquisite embarrassment" of silence.

It is worth asking, then, just what difference sound made when it did become a necessary ingredient in the genre. To a certain extent, sound functions in hardcore the way it does in mainstream narrative cinema: to situate and give realistic effect to the more important image. Rick Altman (1980, 69) has noted that the single most important difference between silent film and sound film is the latter's increased proportion of scenes of people talking to one another. In showing the source of sound, then, narrative cinema employs sound as an anchor to the image.

All sound, whether music, sound effects, or speech, thus functions to bolster the diegetic illusion of an imaginary space-time and of the human body's place within it. Extradiegetic music brought in from outside the depicted scene may enhance the mood and establish rhythms that complement the movements of bodies and smooth over the temporal-spatial gaps created by editing. Sound effects give solidity and spatial dimension to the depiction of the diegetic world. And synchronous speech ties the body to the voice.

Theorists of cinema sound such as Pascal Bonitzer (1976), Rick Altman (1980), Alan Williams (1980), Mary Ann Doane (1980), and Kaja Silverman (1988a) have emphasized the way these uses of sound create the illusion of the viewing subject's unity.[1] Silverman in *The Acoustic Mirror*, for example, stresses the different organization of male and female voice in mainstream cinema and the importance of nonsynchronization of female body and voice in avant-garde practices that deconstruct the dominance of the image, especially the patriarchal, fetishized image of women.

In hard-core film and video, however, the relation of sound to image differs from that in dominant cinema, though without having the function of avant-garde deconstruction. In these films, when characters talk their lips often fail to match the sounds spoken, and in the sexual numbers a dubbed-over "disembodied" female voice (saying "oooh" and "aaah") may stand as the most prominent signifier of female pleasure in the absence of other, more visual assurances. Sounds of pleasure, in this latter instance, seem almost to flout the realist function of anchoring body to image, halfway becoming aural fetishes of the female pleasures we cannot see.[2]

The articulate and inarticulate sounds of pleasure that dominate in aural hardcore are primarily the cries of women. Though male moans and cries are heard as well, they are never as loud or dramatic. Other sounds of pleasure include the smack of a kiss or a slap, the slurp of fellatio and cunnilingus, the whoosh of penetration-engulfment, not to mention the sounds of bedsprings; they can also be actual words spoken by the performers during sex, from the clichés of "fuck me harder" and "I'm going to come" to less usual communiqués such as "I love you" or phrases like "ripe mango take two" (which only make sense in the particular narrative context—see below).

As in mainstream cinema, these sounds of pleasure augment the realist effect of what in cinema is the hierarchically more important visual register, lending an extra level of sensory perception to the pleasures depicted. But because of increasingly common postdubbing, these sounds are not invoked with the same realism as sound in the mainstream feature. Many sexual numbers, especially of early hard-core sound features, were and still are—like the musical numbers of musicals—shot "*mit* out sound." Sound is recorded elsewhere and added later in the "mix." (Ziplow [1977, 76], for example, tells his frugal would-be pornographer to order silence on the set to record some "room tone," and then to have his "sound man pick up some extra moaning and groaning" in "extra-curricular vocal work" from the performers.) In all cases, however, the effect of nonsynchronous sound is to detract from the spatial realism of synchronous sound. Prerecorded (or postrecorded) sound is achieved, unlike sound recording done on the set, by placing microphones close to the body. As Alan Williams (1981, 150–151) notes of sound in movie musicals, the purpose of this closeness, of this extrasonic presence of the body, is greater clarity in the music and sung lyrics—and for this reason, movie musicals do not record sound live.

In this respect hard-core films are more like musicals than like other kinds of narrative. While hard-core sound does not seek clarity of music and lyrics, it does seek an effect of closeness and intimacy, rather than of spatial reality. In hearing the sounds of pleasure with greater clarity and from closer up, auditors of hard-core sacrifice the ability to gauge the distances between bodies and their situation in space for a sense of connectedness with the sounds they hear. Williams (151) refers to this effect as one of spacelessness: "To imagine this effect outside of the musical, the reader has only to think of any badly dubbed foreign film. . . . The voices seem 'too close' and whatever implied spatial environment they do possess does not change."

This, indeed, is often the (surreal) effect of a great many postdubbed sex scenes, as well as of the dialogue sequences of the more cheaply made hard-core features. When the lip movements of the performer do not match the sounds that come from those lips, the hard-won illusions of suture are rendered null and void. It is worth asking, then, why this convention has been so popular in a genre apparently engaged in an interminable quest for realism. Certainly various practical reasons can be cited: it is both easier and cheaper to shoot sexual numbers without sound; camera operators can move close in without worrying about the sound they make; and since music, like voice and sound effects, is typically added later anyway, "live" sound hardly seems worth the added effort. But because many relatively big-budget hard-core films, which in their nonperforming, dialogue sequences do use synchronous sound, revert to nonsynchronous sound in the "numbers," this technique would seem to be an important *formal* feature of the genre's representation of sex. It is also a feature that places the hard-core film in close aural connection to the movie musical. To a great extent, in fact, the hard-core feature film *is* a kind of musical, with sexual number taking the place of musical number. The generic implications of this analogy will be explored below; for the moment, however, it is worth noting the similar rhythmic and melodic features of the sounds of pleasure on the one hand and the "sounds of music" on the other.

One observation to be drawn from this analogy is that visual and aural closeness are not commensurate. Although the movie musical and the hard-core porno prefer sounds to be "taken" from close up, there is no such thing as a close-up of sound, as there is of image. Alan Williams (1980, 53) has argued, in fact, that there is no such thing as sound in itself, and that sound recording is in no way parallel to image recording. In one sense, we could say that the close-up sound of pleasure attempts to offer the "spectacular" aural equivalent of the close-ups of "meat" and "money." Nevertheless, the aural "ejaculation" of pleasure, especially in postsynchronized sound, gives none of the same guarantee of truth that the visual ejaculation does.

A 1981 feature by Alan Vydra entitled *The Sounds of Love* illustrates this point well. In a narrative that is as (ineptly) based on the false analogy of audio overhearing to visual voyeurism as Brian de Palma's *Blow Out* is to Antonioni's *Blow Up*, a musician is determined to record and replay for his own apocalyptic pleasure the most perfect and expressive sound of female orgasm. He hires a young stud-detective to tap the phones and wire the bedrooms of numerous women in his quest for the most powerful, natural, and spontaneous of orgasms. Echoing *Deep Throat*'s fetishization of the invisible place of female pleasure, he says: "I must be able to hear the approaching orgasm from her throat." The film, however, does not quite trust this fetishization of sound-over image; all it offers (in Dolby to home viewers with the appropriate stereo equipment) are some very loud and often deep growly sounds emanating from women's throats.

The film is of interest for its failure to acknowledge the difference between the sounds and the images of pleasure. It proceeds as if the musician's quest was for a discrete single sound—a single note almost—that could do for the audiophile what the meat or money shot is presumed to do for the image fetishist. In the end the musician hears this sound in a live sequence of eavesdropping in which his own wife is brought to orgasm by the stud-detective. The musician's response is to blow them all—himself included—to kingdom come, whether out of jealousy or *jouissance* we do not know. But the film's feeble apocalyptic climax (in which sounds of an explosion accompany images of the same) merely underscores the fact that visual and aural voyeurism are very different things. The attempt to "foreground" the sounds of pleasure fails. As Mary Ann Doane points out in "The Voice in the Cinema" (1980, 39), sound cannot be "framed" as the image can, for sound is all over the theater; it "*envelops* the spectator." It is this nondiscrete, enveloping quality that, when added to the close-miked, nonsynchronous sounds of pleasure, seems particularly important in the hard-core auditor-viewer's pleasure in sound.

Although aspects of sound are measurable—in decibels, in pitch, in tone— diffuse, enveloping sound differs importantly from the discrete and framable image of the body. The allure of the sounds of pleasure resides at least partly in the fact that they come from inside the body and are often not articulate signs (meaningful combinations of sound and sense) but, rather, inarticulate sounds that speak, almost preverbally, of primitive pleasures. Although they seem to arise spontaneously, they are not involuntary as the "frenzy of the visible" of male orgasm is.

This apparent spontaneity is particularly important in the pornographic quest to represent the female desires and pleasures that come from "deep inside." *Deep Throat* is but one of many films and tapes to pose this problem, in which "depth" becomes a metaphor for getting underneath deceptive appearances. Thus depth of sound does not lend itself to the same illusion of involuntary frenzy as that offered by the visible. Nevertheless, although there can be no such thing as hard-core sound, there remains the potential for performers to converse with one another, in articulate or inarticulate vocables, about their pleasure.

Sexual Numbers

Let us return to the more central, visible iconography of the new hard-core feature. As we have seen, the money shot is crucial: "If you don't have the come shots you don't have a porno picture." But this shot cannot exist in isolation; it must be worked into a variety of narratives and a variety of sexual numbers. Perhaps the second most important feature of the genre, then, is that a little something is offered to satisfy a diverse, but not all-inclusive, range of sexual tastes. Stephen Ziplow, in his *Film Maker's Guide to Pornography* (1977), provides a checklist of the various sexual acts that should be included in a porno, along with the best way to film them. This extremely functional guide to the would-be pornographer is useful because it also goes to the heart of the genre's conventionality. The list includes

1. "Masturbation": with or without paraphernalia, but always including well-lit close-ups of genitalia. Although Ziplow does not specify the sex of the masturbator, it is clear from his description that he assumes the act will be performed by a female ("It's always a lot of fun to watch a pretty lady getting off on her own body," 31). Compared to the stag film, in fact, hard-core feature-length pornography has very few scenes of male masturbation.
2. "Straight sex": defined as male-female, penis-to-vagina penetration in a variety of positions, which Ziplow enumerates as man on top, woman on top, side to side, and "doggie" (31).
3. "Lesbianism": here Ziplow is terse; all he says is that it is "a major turn-on to a larger portion of your heterosexual audience" (31).
4. "Oral sex": defined as both cunnilingus and fellatio. Ziplow notes that "cunnilingus presents technical difficulties" of visibility, since the man's head obscures the "action," whereas "blowjobs," which present no such difficulty and have the further advantage of facilitating the money shot, are "always a hit with the porno crowd." His advice in both cases is to block out the action well in advance (31).
5. "Ménage à trois": a threesome with male or female as the third party (32). (It seems to go without saying that while two female members of such a configuration may involve themselves with each other, it is taboo for two men to do so in heterosexual hardcore.)
6. "Orgies": "a lot of people making it together." Ziplow warns that these can be expensive (32).
7. "Anal sex." Ziplow presumes the person receiving anal sex to be female (32).

These are the sexual acts that Ziplow deems essential to a hard-core feature circa 1977. But even a cursory look at a random sample of films from 1972 on suggests that to this list could be added at least one more "optional component," which I shall also define, in the jargon of the industry, as

8. "Sadie-max": a scene depicting sadomasochistic relations such as whipping, spanking, or bondage, performed with or without paraphernalia.

This list of sexual numbers, although quite varied—and many porno-graphic features do their best systematically to work in as many of these numbers as possible—is still far from inclusive. In heterosexual porno, for example, no male-to-male relations of any kind occur, nor is there any bestiality or "kiddie porn."

Iconography

The visual content of the acts listed above, including the way they are lit and pho-tographed, constitutes the conventional iconography of the genre. Iconography is simply the pattern of visual imagery one expects to see in a given genre. Just as we expect to see monsters in horror films, guns, suits, and hats in gangster films, and horses and cowboys in Westerns, so in porno do we expect to see naked bod-ies engaging in sexual numbers. Yet as Stephen Neale (1980, 13) notes in a useful pamphlet on film genres, lists of visual content are only the first step to under-standing genre; though helpful as descriptions of the elements of generic struc-ture, such lists do not begin to address the dynamics of structuration. Thus, although iconography attempts to define the visual specificity of a genre—that which makes it distinct from other genres—it cannot explain *why* such visuals are employed, except as reflections of reality.

In the case of the Western, for example, it is not sufficient to say that the genre simply reflects the historical reality of the American West; such a notion is tantamount to saying that the very aesthetic form of the genre itself is determined by the events of America's agrarian past (Neale 1980, 15). We have only to apply this reflective formula to pornography to see its limitation: does feature-length hard-core pornography simply reflect the sexual activities performed in American bedrooms in the wake of the sexual revolution? Is the money shot a realistic reflec-tion of these activities?

A more fruitful approach sees genre to be less a reflection of some deter-minant reality than a form of modern mythmaking—a way of doing something to the world, of acting symbolically upon it. Here iconography and narrative work together to intensify oppositions and contradictions that exist within a culture, in order to seek imaginary forms of resolution. To critics Leo Braudy and Thomas Schatz, for example, a film genre's success—its ability to continue to offer some-thing to audiences—depends on the significance of the conflicts it addresses and its flexibility in adjusting to audience and filmmakers' changing attitudes toward these conflicts (Braudy 1977, 109, 179; Schatz 1981, 38).

A particularly sophisticated example of the way genres address social problems is offered by Fredric Jameson in *The Political Unconscious* (1981). Jame-son (118–119) argues that originally the genre of medieval romance was devised to solve the problem, not important in earlier epic narratives, of how an enemy from one's own class could be thought of as an evil "other" who must be destroyed. The narrative form that, typically, tells the story of an unknown and hostile knight who will not say his name or show his face stages a struggle between same-class enemies in which the hostile knight is perceived as the malevolent other, much as in earlier epic forms pagans were. Once defeated, however, this knight asks for mercy, lifts his visor, and tells his name, at which point he is reinserted into the unity of the social class to which he belongs; he loses his sinister otherness. Jameson argues that this new genre—the story of the unknown knight who first seems evil and alien, then later seems similar—offers a formal, narrative solution to the problem of an evil that can no longer be permanently assigned to whole categories of "Other."

Jameson's analysis is useful because it does not see generic form as simply reflecting important aspects of history. The battles of medieval romance do not mirror knightly combat as it actually occurred any more than the stylized gunfights of Westerns reflect how cowboys really fought. Both scenes represent crucial moments in narratives that have reworked the reality of combat in ways that permit the resolution of deeper problems, not necessarily manifest on the texts' surface. Both medieval romance and Westerns rework some aspect of the past into a form for the present. Each is "talking to itself," as Colin McArthur (1972) puts it in regard to the gangster genre, about problems that have urgency and currency in the present moment. The repetitive forms of each seem to insist on the possibility of solutions, as long as the problems persist. These solutions themselves then become part of the social fabric and, in turn, important in the formation of new sociohistorical realities (Neale 1980, 16).

We can therefore ask of the current hard-core genre, What problems does it seek to solve? What is it "talking to itself" about? Obviously it is talking to itself about sex—specifically, about masturbatory, straight, "lesbian," oral, ménage à trois, anal, orgiastic, and sadomasochistic sex. By the same token, it is *not* talking to itself, except as a structuring absence, about male homosexual sex. We can also ask, What problems does the deployment of this iconography seek to solve? To answer this question, we need to understand more about how sexual iconography works with narrative.

Narrative and Number

Any of the sexual practices in the above list could be found somewhere in a stag film, as could some that are not listed. What is different about the hard-core feature, however, is the assumption, implicit in Ziplow's guide, that as many of these practices as possible will be worked into, or called forth by, the newly expanded narrative. Ziplow himself offers no description of narrative in the genre, but he is clear that it should exist; specifically, it should occupy approximately 40 percent of the screen time and should serve as a vehicle to the sexual numbers represented in the remaining 60 percent.

Although Ziplow does not explain why, narrative is assumed to be necessary to number. Now it is a commonplace for critics and viewers to ridicule narrative genres that seem to be only flimsy excuses for something else—musicals and pornography in particular are often singled out as being *really* about song and dance or sex. But as much recent work on the movie musical has demonstrated, the episodic narratives typical of the genre are not simply frivolous pretexts for the display of song and dance;[3] rather, narrative often permits the staging of song and dance spectacles as events themselves within the larger structure afforded by the story line. Narrative informs number, and number, in turn, informs narrative. Part of the pleasure of the movie musical resides in the tension between these different discursive registers, each seeking to establish its own equilibrium.

Steve Neale (1980), for example, notes the seemingly obvious but nevertheless important fact that all mainstream narrative cinema moves from relative equilibrium to disequilibrium and back. Certain genres achieve this equilibratory disruption and restoration in specific ways. In the Western, the gangster, and the detective film, for example, disequilibrium is figured as physical violence: through violence, equilibrium is reestablished (20–21). Violence exists in other genres, too, such as the horror film. But here the specificity of the genre lies not so much *in* violence as in the conjunction of violence with images and definitions of the monstrous. In this genre, order and disorder are articulated across categories (and images) of "the human" versus "the monstrous" (22). In the case of the musical and the melodrama, however—generic structures that bring us somewhat closer to feature-length pornography—narrative is set in motion neither by violence nor by the monstrous, but by the "eruption of (hetero)sexual desire into an already established social order" (22). In these genres, disequilibrium is specified as the process of desire itself and the various blockages to its fulfillment.

The advantage of Neale's formulation over more traditional descriptions of iconography and narrative form is its location of elements of generic specificity that may exist in different combinations in other genres. For instance, whereas heterosexual desire is found in a great many genres, the role it plays in the musical and melodrama is quite specific and central. What is unique in the musical is the specific inscription of music itself, especially of song and dance, into the narrative movement from equilibrium through disequilibrium and back; performance numbers woven into narrative thus become the key to particularly intense statements, and sometimes resolutions, of narrative conflicts. In the justly famous "Dancing in the Dark" number from the movie musical *The Band Wagon* (Vincente Minnelli, 1953), for example, Fred Astaire and Cyd Charisse's "spontaneous" discovery of their ability to dance together off stage in a park resolves their inability to dance on stage in a show, and so ultimately assures the success of that show. The number also resolves their earlier hostility toward each other and

Astaire's loneliness. Although not all musical numbers are so integrated into their narratives, all musicals do have numbers that either restate or resolve the problems posed by the narrative in other numbers (Mueller 1984, 33–35).

One can also examine how some numbers relate to other numbers in a narrative. In *Easter Parade* (Charles Walters, 1948), the story concerns Fred Astaire's attempt to prove to the former dancing partner who has jilted him that he can take any woman and make her into a star simply by dancing with her. The fact that the former partner is Ann Miller, known primarily for her dancing, and the new partner Judy Garland, known primarily for her singing, complicates the nature of the numbers that will allow Astaire to succeed. Nor does he succeed until he significantly revises his original sense of what it means to dance—that is, to perform a number—with a woman.

The resolution of these problems comes about not through the narrative, or through any one number, but through the relation of number to narrative and number to number. Astaire at first tries to fit Garland into the sophisticated ballroom-dancer mold of Miller. The result is a comic fiasco of sabotaged elegance as the feathers on Garland's overplumed gown fly and she dances wildly out of control, foiling all of Astaire's valiant attempts to recover their equilibrium. But if Garland can't dance like Miller, she can sing like no one else. And it is when she *sings* what had been Astaire and Miller's dancing theme song, "It Only Happens When I Dance with You," that Astaire finally falls for her and learns to appreciate her unique qualities. Professional success follows as they learn to sing and dance together in a more comic vein. The climax of this success occurs with the famous "Couple of Swells" number, in which each portrays a male tramp singing and dancing in a comic imitation of elegance.

But professional success does not automatically solve the problem of the mutually shared song-dance performance that expresses romantic love. And so, even in their triumph—and even though the *narrative* asserts that Astaire and Garland love each other—when Astaire is manipulated into performing one more time with Miller, a jealous Garland walks out. The real solution must be sought on the level of the number; the film must find the Garland-Astaire love song-and-dance that will better the Miller-Astaire performance. That number is the title song inflected by role reversal: Garland sends Astaire an Easter bonnet, and she takes *him* to the Fifth Avenue Easter Parade, where the number's grand finale is performed. Astaire may have succeeded in transforming her into a star, but in so doing he has had to adapt his own performance to the talents and desires of this particular woman.

These examples of the function of musical numbers in a movie musical can help us to understand the similar function of sexual numbers in the pornographic feature. To begin with, there is the obvious sense of the musical number, especially the romantic song-dance duet, as a sublimated expression of heterosexual desire and satisfaction. Beyond that there is the fact that the hard-core feature—unlike the silent stag—is quite literally a musical: original music and even

songs with lyrics (as, for example, the execrable *Deep Throat* theme song) frequently accompany numbers, especially the "big production" numbers. Finally,
there is the obvious sense in which the sexual acts listed above constitute a virtual
typology of numbers in the pornographic feature. Masturbation, for example, can
be seen as a solo song or dance of self-love and enjoyment—à la the "Singin' in the
Rain" number in the musical of that name; straight sex is like a classic heterosexual duet—as in "You Were Meant for Me," also from *Singin' in the Rain*—with oral
sex as a variation of this same theme; "lesbian" sex is like the narcissistic "I Feel
Pretty" number from *West Side Story*; ménage à trois is a trio—"Good Mornin'"
from *Singin'* or the beginning of the "Hungry Eyes" number from *Dirty Dancing*;[4]
"sadie-max" is a particularly violent and fetishistic dramatization of dominance
and submission—à la the Cyd Charisse–Gene Kelly number in the "Broadway
Melody" section of *Singin' in the Rain*; and orgies are like choral love songs celebrating the sexual union of an entire community—"Broadway Rhythm" in *Singin'* or the "everybody-out-on-the-dance-floor" number of communal integration
that ends *Dirty Dancing* ("The Time of My Life").

A major difference between the genres, however, is the fact that many
more of the numbers in hardcore are, in a sense, "love" songs expressing the desire
for or act of union. Although movie musicals certainly emphasize the love song
or dance, many solos, duets, trios, and so forth have nothing to do with desire or
longing. Nevertheless, feature-length hard-core films still closely resemble musicals structurally in their tendency to give one particular number the conflict-
resolving function or expression of ultimate satisfaction of the musical's love song
(like "Dancing in the Dark," "You Are My Lucky Star," or "The Time of My Life").
In *Deep Throat*, for example, oral sex—specifically fellatio—has this status. The
problem that the fellatio number eventually solves is introduced in another number: the uninspiring "straight sex" that Linda Lovelace engages in at the beginning
of the film.

In this last respect, however, the hard-core genre is not entirely parallel to
the musical. For in the musical, the always-sublimated expression of desire in the
love song or dance is a priori pleasurable, whereas in feature-length pornography
unsublimated sex, especially that occurring early in the film, is often not pleasurable at all to at least one of its participants. In *The Resurrection of Eve* (Mitchell
Bros., 1973), *Angel on Fire* (Roberta Findlay, 1979), and *Taboo* (Kirdy Stevens,
1980), for instance, the initial numbers range from simply listless to overtly distasteful to one or more of the characters involved. A most peculiar quality of this
narrative form of the genre, then, would seem to be this paradox: although built
on the premise that the pleasure of sex is self-evident, the underlying and motivating anxiety is that sometimes it is not. Out of this contradiction comes the
need for a combined solution of narrative and number.

In hard-core narrative we might say that sex numbers can function in the
following ways: (1) as regular moments of pleasure that may be gratifying either
to viewers or to the characters performing the acts; (2) as statements of sexual con-

flicts that are manifest in the number (in *Taboo*, for example, the film begins with a fellatio number between a husband and wife; the husband insists on leaving the light on; the wife resists and does not enjoy their encounter; the performance continues to the point of his orgasm, but her dissatisfaction is apparent); (3) as statements, or restatements, of conflicts that are manifest in the narrative; or (4) as resolutions of conflicts stated either in the narrative or in the other numbers. In other words, as in the movie musical, the episodic structure of the hard-core narrative is something more than a flimsy excuse for sexual numbers: it is part and parcel of the way the genre goes about resolving the often contradictory desires of its characters.

Male and Female Centers of Power

In his impressive book *The American Film Musical*, Rick Altman (1987, 16–27) writes that the distinctive episodic structure of the genre is basic to the way it goes about resolving the contradictory desires and needs of its characters. Noting that number does not simply interrupt narrative but rather that the two function in carefully orchestrated parallel scenes involving both the male and the female protagonist, Altman suggests that the dynamic principle motivating narrative in the musical must be the fundamental difference between male and female.

To express this most basic opposition, the narrative structure of the musical diverges from the classical Hollywood norm of chronological, linear progression and causal sequence. The MGM operetta *New Moon*, for example, proceeds via parallels in narrative and number between the male and female protagonists, played by (none other than) Nelson Eddy and Jeanette MacDonald. MacDonald plays a wealthy French aristocrat onboard a ship carrying her to New Orleans in 1789. She is asked to sing for the other nobles on the deck. Her song is drowned out by another song that comes from below deck—a group of poor Frenchmen about to be sold into slavery sing to forget their troubles. They are led by a young nobleman in disguise, Nelson Eddy (17–19).

Altman argues that the sequence is less a causal relation between two events than a setting forth of paired oppositions: "*She* sings on deck, *he* sings in the hold; *she* sings to entertain a bevy of society women, *he* sings to relieve the misery of a group of penniless men" (17). The film thus develops two centers of opposed power (male and female), each provided with a set of secondary characteristics that are also opposed: "*the female*—rich, cultured, beautiful, easily offended; *the male*—poor, practical, energetic, tenacious. Yet they share one essential attribute: they both sing" (19).

This dual focus of the musical, constructed on parallel stars of opposite sex and divergent values, is a defining feature of the genre and can help us to pin down Neale's general observation about the centrality of heterosexual desire in some genres. If male and female are the primary oppositions of the musical genre, their basic resolution occurs through the mediation of secondary oppositions. In *New Moon*, for example, both narrative and number operate to resolve the secondary oppositions (rich/poor) as each protagonist adopts characteristics of the other: Eddy learns some of MacDonald's restraint, and MacDonald takes on some of Eddy's energy (19–20).

Altman's point is that although most movie musicals divide the world into male and female in order to bring the two sexes together in some sort of implicitly monogamous happily-ever-after, in the end it is the *secondary* oppositions that this union actually mediates. From *The Gold Diggers* to *Gentlemen Prefer Blondes* to *Gigi*, the most common opposition has been that between female beauty (the most prevalent female "center of power") and male riches (the most prevalent form of male power). (Here Altman [25] quotes Marilyn Monroe's famous line from *Gentlemen Prefer Blondes*: "Don't you know that a man being rich is like a girl being pretty?" Recent musicals often reverse these terms—with rich *girl* and pretty *man*.) Sexual union performs the merger of the primary gender oppositions, but only with the help of secondary oppositions.

We can begin to see how this mediation occurs in hard-core film by looking at *The Opening of Misty Beethoven* ("Henry Paris," a.k.a. Radley Metzger, 1975). Since this movie is itself a loose reworking of George Bernard Shaw's *Pygmalion*, familiar to many in its musical incarnation as *My Fair Lady*, some of the parallels to musical-genre structure will be a little too neat. But since these parallels are only more consistent in this film than in others I will use them to get to the heart of the structures that to some degree are found in most hard-core narrative.

Like a classic musical, *Misty Beethoven* is about heterosexual desire. To use Altman's terminology, it is narratively structured on a fundamental male/ female opposition accompanied by opposed secondary characteristics. *He* is Dr. Seymour Love (Jamie Gillis), a wealthy, sophisticated sexologist. *She* is Misty Beethoven (Constance Money), a poor, unsophisticated whore who makes her living giving "hand jobs" to old men in a porno theater in Pigalle and working in an adjacent brothel.

They meet in the theater, where Seymour is doing research and where Misty has left her chewing gum on a seat back. (Earlier we saw Misty give a hand job to an old man named Napoleon who ejaculates—in a typical money shot—in unison with the screen performer. The title of the film they watch is *Le sexe qui parle*.) Seymour hires Misty to study her. They go to a private room where a vulgarly made up, gum-chewing Misty, wearing a T-shirt with AMERICAN EXPRESS and MASTER CARD emblazoned on the front, recites her repertoire: "I do a straight fuck, I don't take it in the mouth, I don't take it in the ass," and even "I don't take it in the bed"—presumably she prefers the movie theater. But Seymour, the cold scientist, is only interested in interviewing her: he finds her vulgarity fascinating; she is the "perfect specimen" of a "sexual civil service worker."

Seymour arrogantly boasts that he could transform even this unlikely material into the most desired sexual performer of the international jet set: the "Golden Rod Girl." What Henry Higgins did with Eliza Doolittle and vowels, what Fred Astaire did with Judy Garland and a few dance steps, Seymour proposes to do with Misty and sexual technique. As in these musicals, too, the fundamental issue underlying linguistic, musical, or sexual performance is power—for what all these men have in common are those most typical characteristics of the male center of power: money, class, and knowledge (the last typically being, in hardcore, knowledge of sex). And what Eliza, Judy, and Misty have in common is the raw material of the most typical characteristics of female power: beauty and talent. In a Foucauldian sense, then, the knowledge of sexual technique that Misty stands to gain is offered by Seymour as a potential form of power. But in typical male-chauvinist style, he sees this power as the gift that only he, sophisticated author and sexologist, has the knowledge to give.

In his New York mansion-cum-training school—where the constant sexual activity in the background creates an atmosphere similar to the rehearsals of a Busby Berkeley backstage musical or the workouts in a boxing film—Misty begins training. Dressed in a jogging suit, she practices manual and oral sexual techniques on plaster cast penises and ubiquitous live male "models" who double as servants. With Seymour's coaching, Misty is supposedly learning to convert a "mundane routine, a daily act, into something stimulating."

But there is something in the rote repetition of the training itself—and especially its mechanical use of fellatio—that belies this goal. In fact, the initial emphasis on fellatio tends to posit this particular sexual act much as "straight sex" is posited in *Deep Throat*—as ordinary, run-of-the-mill sexual performance, against which more inspired and interesting performances will eventually shine. At first, however, Seymour's emphasis on high-class techniques for sucking and licking a penis stands in direct opposition to Misty's crude pleasure-giving method: the no-frills hand job that we saw her give the old man.

Like Nelson Eddy and Jeanette MacDonald, Seymour and Misty not only possess opposing secondary characteristics, but these characteristics are also restated, mediated, and ultimately resolved in the sexual numbers. Misty's no-frills approach to both life and sex is contrasted to Seymour's connoisseurship. At first the contrast is posed as a simple professional difference over which technique does the job best. But soon it is linked to a more fundamental and familiar opposition expressed as the antagonism between the sexes. Misty and Seymour state this antagonism succinctly early in the film: "I think men stink," she says in response to Seymour's arrogant coaching. "They think you stink," he replies; "it's one of the most perfectly balanced equations in nature."

Actually, the "equation" is not perfectly balanced at all, either "in nature" or in Misty's relation to the men she must learn to please. Her unequal position as sexual trainee in the one-sided giving of pleasure to men is quite typical of women's position within a phallogocentric symbolic system. It forces her to accommodate her sexuality and her desire to that of the male. Not all hard-core narrative states this opposition so baldly, but as in the movie musical, some form of this classic, and unequal, battle between the sexes seems to animate the conflicts that both genres seek in their own ways to resolve. (In *Deep Throat*, for example, the opposition is posed as pure anatomical difference, with the resolution coming through the right number with the "right" man, though in fact the fellatio "solution" really works *for the male*. In the 1987 *Careful, He May Be Watching* [Henry Pachinko] the solution is more complex: a married woman [Seka] is, unbeknownst to her airline pilot husband, a porno star. He loves his wife but wants to spice up their relationship, introducing another woman into their bed. The wife is reluctant. Resolution occurs when, in her double life as porno star, the wife tries a "lesbian" girl-girl number and likes it. When her husband brings home an airline stewardess, she is ready for further experimentation. The finale of the film is a ménage à trois that is satisfying to all and "solves" the minor skirmish between husband and wife. Resolution occurs, but again, its terms are ultimately the man's.)

Like the female protagonists of musicals, Misty knows that the larger power structure in which she operates constructs the woman in the image of male desire. The only power she stands to gain will come from following the advice of her Pygmalion and giving the man what he wants. A reluctant Galatea, she does her maker's bidding and achieves her first triumph seducing an Italian nobleman in the toilet of the Rome Opera. The seduction scene itself is intercut with Seymour's verbal representation of what, in his careful orchestration of the event, should be happening at each moment. As he narrates and we see the events happening according to his plan, we also see Seymour being simultaneously and mechanically "serviced" by one of the many female servant-trainers who inhabit his sexological empire.

Misty's second challenge is more difficult: she must seduce an art dealer in Geneva whom Seymour initially describes as "impotent" but whose appearance is visually coded as gay. The training for this seduction-performance involves more elaborate rehearsals, leading, for the first time in the film, to a number that exhibits something more than mere professional technique. Seymour has enlisted two experienced women friends, Geraldine and Tania, to aid in his training of Misty. Through elaborate cross-gender role-playing—with Tania playing Misty and Geraldine playing the role of the man Misty will seduce—he has them rehearse Misty's next seduction before a movie camera. He also has Tania talk through each stage so that Misty later can listen in to the record of this rehearsal (through an earphone) and let the audio cues trigger visual memories. Misty watches this rehearsal on the set as Seymour, all the while being fellated by another one of his anonymous female trainers, directs the "action."

This elaborate cinematic rehearsal for Misty's next seduction offers an image of sexual relations as complicated sexual role-playing aimed at, and directed by, a male voyeur-viewer who "gets off" at the performance. Although the scene employs two female participants in what looks like a standard "lesbian" scene, the fact that one of these woman is acting the part of the male seducee calls attention to a quality inherent in many of the seemingly "obligatory lesbian" scenes of 1970s narrative hardcore: the women in them are not enacting their own desires but are going through motions aimed more at pleasing male viewers than one another. Seymour's presence as aroused director-viewer calling the shots and telling the women what to do while having one of them "play" the male herself is a remarkably self-reflexive commentary on the male control exercised in such scenes.

Yet the role of seducer that Misty is learning to play will eventually emphasize her "masculine" control of the scene. (The number will end, for example, with Misty on top.) Seymour tells Tania, who is playing Misty's seducer's role, to say to Geraldine, who is playing the gay male seducee: "I'm going to lick your cock like it's the inside of a ripe mango." A mango's "inside" is not a particularly apt simile for an erect penis, in spite of the presence at its center of what in Spanish, at least, is called the "bone." But it is precisely this sexual ambivalence—between hard bone and soft flesh whose "inside" is licked—that this entire rehearsal seems designed to express. It could be that this particular director simply takes a special delight in confounding sexual role-playing (as other films by Radley Metzger seem to confirm). But it could also be that scenes like this, as well as the much simpler "lesbian" girl-girl numbers of most hard-core films, show how readily cross-gender identification takes place.

This question of cross-gender identification raises the further question of whether the "lesbian" number is a sexual event in its own right. In many stag films and hard-core pornos the "lesbian" number is presented, as it is here, as a warm-up or rehearsal for a "better," more satisfying, number that will follow. (The "lesbian" scene above, for example, is followed immediately by Seymour's getting into the act himself.) It would indeed be strange for heterosexual hard-core films aimed primarily at male audiences to posit the "lesbian" number as the "big production" key to satisfaction. Yet as this complex number in *Misty Beethoven* suggests, to dismiss the girl-girl number would be to define hardcore as consisting totally of the action of the phallus and to explain the so-called obligatory "lesbian" number only as a setup for girl-boy numbers.

If a "lesbian" number is constructed so that one woman gives pleasure to the other, then the woman giving the pleasure typically shows, and often also speaks, her knowledge of what pleases the other. Putting aside for the moment the question of how women might identify with and take pleasure in such action, it certainly seems possible that male viewers can identify with the active woman, with her superior knowledge of how the more passive woman feels. But perhaps we should not rule out less active forms of identification—that is, identification with the passive woman who is given pleasure and abandons herself to the control of the other. Spectatorial pleasure in such scenes may very well involve the ability to identify both ways.

In *Misty Beethoven* the cross-gender identifications are written into the film in defiance of the participants' genders: Geraldine, a woman, plays the role of the passive male who will be seduced by Misty; after this "lesbian" rehearsal, Tania, the seducer playing Misty, asks to do the "sequel" right away, this time with Seymour as the seducee. The "big production" number that follows thus shows an apparently aroused and envious Misty (wearing a perhaps symbolic green dress) watching her own stand-in perform a sexual number with Seymour. This number contrasts strongly with all the film's previous numbers. Considerably longer, it develops in several major sections, each with a distinct mood, and creates a sense of spontaneous and sustained passion—like a sexual jam session where some members of the combo put down their instruments to watch and listen as the others perform. Although this number's sexual content consists only of a highly conventional progression from oral sex to straight sex to money shot, much of the number is in a straight sex dorsal-ventral position that is most favorable to visibility of the full frontal female body while simultaneously showing the insertion of penis in vagina.

In this section of the number, Tania, the more active seducer, proceeds from fellatio to sitting on Seymour's penis as he lies nearly supine and she leans back. Thus both sexual position and the elaborate movements of an overhead, circling camera privilege this number as more special, and more spectacular, than anything previously shown. The number takes on significance in relation not only to the narrative—as a contrast to the businesslike professionalism espoused by Misty and Seymour—but also to other numbers. For example, its length, relative spontaneity, and passion are contrasted positively and in ascending order to Misty's crude hand job, to the many previous, overrehearsed fellatio training sessions, and to the "lesbian" rehearsal. Even its "end" offers something more: Seymour and Tania continue to embrace and laugh together after the money shot, exhilarated and delighted by their own performance.

Misty, however, in her new position as audience to a rehearsal that, like so many of those magical rehearsals of backstage movie musicals, is already a showstopper, doubts her ability to emulate such a spectacular performance. The question of her own sexual desire in all this is worth pondering, given her marked presence as on-scene spectator to both the "lesbian" and the heterosexual rehearsals for her own upcoming performance. What does Misty want? And with whom might she identify in these two numbers? Does she identify with the passive enjoyment of the man (first played by a woman) who is seduced, or with her own female stand-in? Or with both? Her momentary displacement from performer to spectator poses, but does not answer, these questions. Moreover, these are precisely the questions that need to be asked of the female spectator of pornography in general. *Misty Beethoven*'s way of posing the question seems to suggest that a purely passive identification with the woman performer is not the whole story.

Significantly, Misty at this moment begins to question the entire enterprise. She tries to back out of the seduction, saying that she won't be able to fool anyone, that she would be crazy to "try to sell phony merchandise. . . . On the street it's simpler; everybody does their own number, but nobody fools anybody." Misty's "number," we must remember, is the no-frills hand job. To attempt a more elaborate number—ultimately, one that would pretend not even to be a number—is, in her mind, simply "phony." Seymour's counter to this challenge is contradictory. On the one hand, he tells her that she isn't a phony, since her talent has aroused his own interest—here he holds out to her a vague promise of getting to know her better when the project is over. On the other hand, he provides her with the listening device that feeds her the verbal directions from the rehearsal number. Not only does the device cue her on what to say and do in the actual seduction scene, which takes place on the floor of an art gallery, but it also allows her memory to see what the film audience sees: black-and-white images of the rehearsal film. In other words, Seymour's goal of passing off his Galatea as the most desired woman of sophisticated sexual circles is thoroughly saturated with the calculated values of engineering in opposition to real spontaneity. The work of the film, however, will be to resolve this contradiction by foiling his too perfect sexual creation.

Seymour's apparent goal is to transform Misty from an "honest whore" who gets direct payment for services into a pleasure-giving automaton whose indirect payment is access to a higher social class. In the process, however, he forces Misty to rely increasingly on complex technological aids, which in turn become fetishized as necessary to the pleasure. In the seduction scene, for example, Misty parrots the "mango" line from the rehearsal film, to which she is simultaneously listening, and then unwittingly repeats Tania's ad lib indicating her desire to continue the rehearsal: "ripe mango take two." Taking the line as part of Misty's own kinky fantasy, the seducee replies, "Roll it," and leans back to enjoy Misty's performance on his sexual organ.

But even though Misty's performance is a "success"—measured in the art dealer's ejaculation in a money shot—and even though she gains proficiency in ever more complicated numbers, each of these numbers stands in contrast to the spontaneity and emotion of Tania and Seymour's prolonged duet. Her final triumph, for example, is the seduction of Larry Layman, a vain Hugh Hefner–style editor of a famous men's magazine and the unofficial power behind the election of the "Golden Rod Girl." In this number Misty takes charge, even improvising on Seymour's plan of attack as she takes on not only Layman but his woman friend Barbara as well. In a ménage à trois with paraphernalia—which climaxes (for Layman at least) in a daisy chain that has Layman penetrating Barbara frontally while being penetrated from the rear by Misty, who wears a dildo—complexity defeats both spontaneity and involvement.

In this number Misty's control is absolute. Like Seymour during the rehearsal, she wields the phallus *and* she calls the shots. But although she functions successfully as the unmistakable catalyst to Layman and Barbara's pleasure, she is just as unmistakably an accessory to it. It is Layman and Barbara who connect.

Misty enhances that connection, but, as the dildo demonstrates, she is not quite connected herself. As in her final training session, where Misty makes three male models ejaculate simultaneously—the equivalent of the "By George, She's Got It!" number in *My Fair Lady*—her proficiency is a tour de force of mere technique. She herself is no more involved than when she jerked off Napoleon while watching the money shot in the porno film.

After her "triumph" with Layman, Misty encounters Seymour at the same party. He is casually engaged in his own two-woman ménage à trois while dressed (or half-undressed) as Julius Caesar and telling misogynistic stories about how to handle women. Disappointed and angry because she had taken his earlier promise of a date seriously, Misty turns to leave. Seymour arrogantly orders her to stay with the inducement, "You can have Caesar." "Why? I already have Napoleon," she says.

With Misty gone, the cocky Seymour deflates. He looks for her back in the porno theater in Pigalle, endures the humiliation of gossip that suggests that his Galatea has gone to live with Layman, mopes about his mansion watching the old training films of Misty as he is listlessly fellated by one female servant after another. While he is engaged in this activity, Misty returns and takes over fellatio during a change of shifts that Seymour doesn't even notice because he is so absorbed in watching Misty on screen.

Soon, though, he becomes aware of her touch. Delighted but pretending not to be, he complains of the screen Misty that "she never did get it right. She was too stupid, unexciting—a sexual civil service worker." In answer, the real Misty bites his penis. A verbal argument ensues. Seymour talks fast. Misty gives him back one of his own lines: "People have sexual problems because they talk too damn much." In answer, he kisses her. The straight sex number that ensues is the film's duet finale—the equivalent of MacDonald and Eddy's reprise of "Lover Come Back to Me" in *New Moon*, Astaire and Rogers's "Cheek to Cheek" number in *Top Hat*, the "Easter Parade" number in *Easter Parade*, and "The Time of My Life" in *Dirty Dancing*. Significantly, this number contains no fellatio, no anal penetration, no sexual paraphernalia, and only the briefest of money shots.

Misty and Seymour make love all over the room in a variety of positions and moods, but the emphasis throughout is on romantic and spontaneous involvement rather than complex gymnastics. At the end, a close-up of penis and vagina, apart but still drawn to each other, confirms the impression of this number as the fulfilled expression of romantic heterosexual desire enacted primarily through male and female genitals. In a coda, we find Seymour's sexual training school flourishes, but now with Misty as head instructor and with Seymour as a docile student in dog collar and chain.

To return to our musical analogy, we can see that Altman's notion of the musical as structured by the dynamic opposition between male and female centers of power operates forcefully in *Misty Beethoven*. "Men stink/women stink" seems to be its plainest expression. Also as in the musical, secondary oppositions function to resolve the contradictory desires and needs of the primary opposition between male and female characters. As male and female, Misty and Seymour constitute opposing (and, we should never forget, unequal) centers of power. But these primary oppositions are then mediated through the merger of secondary oppositions—his sophisticated connoisseurship and technique, her directness and honesty.

As we have seen, this mediation occurs not in any one moment of the narrative or in any one sexual number but through meanings created by the structured oppositions of both narrative and numbers. Misty's honesty is asserted in the narrative in her speech about what numbers she does and does not do and in her sustained criticism of phoniness; Seymour's connoisseurship is asserted in his constant exploitation of cinematic and sexual technique and encouragement of complex, even kinky, sexual expressions. Over the course of the film, Misty becomes more sophisticated and kinky, while Seymour becomes attached (literally, in the dog collar at the end) to Misty alone.

Thus the original source of their differences lies both in sex itself—their obvious and original male and female sexual differences—and in their different attitudes toward the performance of sex. And it is in these *secondary* oppositions concerning sexual performance that mediation occurs. The numbers are structured initially to contrast Misty's no-frills hand job with Seymour's insistence that she cultivate technique and learn to "take it in the mouth." As rehearsals and performance proceed in alternation, Seymour's method of complexity and sophistication gains; Misty's no-frills directness wanes. But the real mediation leading to the final duet in which Misty fulfills all of her initial conditions ("I do a straight fuck, I don't take it in the mouth, I don't take it in the ass . . . I don't take it in the bed") yet merges them with Seymour's greater connoisseurship comes from the film's discovery of something more, something that has been lacking all along in both their approaches.

This lack is spontaneity: an involvement in the number that transcends its performative aspect, turning it into something more than a number, more than a performance of sex—into a utopia of desire and fulfillment. These spontaneous, unstaged, and unrehearsed events occur as if of their own accord out of the merged desires of the sexual performers. The first introduction of spontaneity, of course, occurs midway through the film in the impromptu "sequel" to the overchoreographed rehearsal. In this number Tania and Seymour "jam" together while Misty watches. This freewheeling quality—expressed in neither Misty's nor Seymour's original sexual credo—emerges to undermine and transform the original opposition between "plain" and "fancy" sex into a merger of both through spontaneous involvement.

The final number between Misty and Seymour effects this merger. It is "fancy" compared to Misty's original no-frills approach, but it is "plain" compared to the highly choreographed rehearsals or to the final performance with Layman, in which Misty is a smooth-functioning accessory to Layman's pleasure. In short, this final number—like the "Dancing in the Dark" number in *The Band Wagon*—

takes on significance through the dramatized opposition between it and the increasingly complex, but alienated, rehearsal and performance numbers. In both cases the successful performance—of sex or of song and dance—depends on the number's seeming not to *be* a performance but to arise naturally and spontaneously from the sexual desires of the performing couple.

In her fine book *The Hollywood Musical*, film critic Jane Feuer has shown that the musical as a genre is founded on a contradiction between highly engineered, choreographed, and rehearsed numbers (which all filmed song-and-dance numbers necessarily are) and the desire to make these numbers seem unrehearsed, as if they arose naturally and spontaneously out of the rhythms and harmonies of song and dance itself. This contradiction, Feuer (1982, 1–23) argues, animates the musical's extreme valuation of certain myths—of spontaneity, of performers' communion with audience, of community integration through song and dance—myths that in turn work to overcome the "original sin" of cinema itself: the fact that, as a mass art of canned performance, cinema can never really bring audience and performer together; that it must always be elaborately rehearsed and choreographed for camera and lighting to be right and for lips to synchronize to prerecorded sound. In an age of mechanical reproduction, postmodern simulacra, and heightened voyeurism, the rhetoric of the genre must work overtime, so to speak, to compensate for what has been lost. Even the most elaborate production numbers, which historically have been the most highly engineered and rehearsed of all the Hollywood product, rhetorically attempt to "cancel" or "erase" this engineering through the appearance of what Feuer (3–4), borrowing from Lévi-Strauss, calls "bricolage": making it up as you go along out of whatever materials are at hand.

Thus the most complexly engineered of the famous songs and dances by the great movie performers have been the numbers that most gave the illusion of being created spontaneously out of the materials at hand: an umbrella, a puddle, a lamppost. This erasure of rehearsal and professional performance by a supposedly natural, unstudied bricolage operates both within numbers—as in "Singin' in the Rain"—and between numbers—as in the contrast between Kelly's "natural" song-and-dance ability and the engineered phoniness of this film's nonsinging, nondancing villainess.

As we have seen, similar contradictions seem to animate the myths of the pornographic feature as well, at least in the (vast majority of) films that work toward what I have been calling the solution to the problem of sex through the performance of sex. In such films, sex as a spontaneous *event* enacted for its own sake stands in perpetual opposition to sex as an elaborately engineered and choreographed *show* enacted by professional performers for a camera. And just as the filmed musical number must rhetorically do everything in its power to deny its engineered, choreographed professionalism, so the hard-core sexual number must as well. Indeed, it must do even more, for it is in this most directly sexual context that the sense of the word *number* rejoins that of the prostitute's performed and choreographed "trick" and thus mirrors the entire problematic of hard core's utopian project of offering visual proof of authentic and involuntary spasms of pleasure.

From this perspective we can see that in *The Opening of Misty Beethoven* the isolation of, and solution to, the problem of "phoniness"—of insincere sexual performance—is absolutely central to what the feature-length hard-core genre is all about. Just as *Deep Throat* posed and then "resolved" the problem of the authenticity of Linda Lovelace's pleasure, so in a more complex way—a way that might be said to constitute both a classical statement and a more meditative self-reflexive formulation of what the pornographic feature-length narrative is "talking to itself" about—*Misty Beethoven* poses and then solves the problem of sexual performance as "trick" or show played for the camera versus spontaneously pleasurable real event.

The comparison between the two movies is instructive. Both feature male sexologists, who occupy the position once held in literary pornography by the traditional figure of the libertine. The sexologist's professional-scientific interest in sex can thus be viewed as a thin disguise for traditional libertine pleasures. But it is also something more. Whether presented as the comic professor who invents an aphrodisiac (as in *Blondes Have More Fun* [John Seeman, 1975]), a serious psychiatrist who tries to effect a cure (as in the takeoff on *10*, *11* [Harry Lewis, 1981], in which an apparently unarousable male client undergoes therapy to learn to fantasize the woman of his dreams), or the disembodied voice of therapeutic authority (as in *Carnal Haven* [Sharon Thorpe, 1976], in which the unhappy sex lives of four married couples and their stay in a sex-therapy clinic are commented on), these figures are not simply pleasure seekers. Their expert discourse also functions to define the very terms of the quest for the knowledge of pleasure. And it is this scientific knowledge of the pleasure of sexuality (often, but not always, posed as male knowledge of female pleasure) that leads in many of these films to the great variety of sexual numbers that characterizes the form.

In *Deep Throat* this quest for scientific knowledge culminates in a gimmick that "solves" the problem by locating pleasure fancifully in deep-throat fellatio. As if in self-conscious response to this well-known hard-core solution, *Misty Beethoven* poses fellatio as one of the more "mundane" of its panoply of sexual numbers, building instead a complex set of oppositions between professional gimmicks and tricks and the spontaneous, mutual pleasure located in rigorously heterosexual, but not unimaginative, straight sex. In both movies, however, sexual performance poses a problem, and the exploration of a range of different sexual acts ultimately leads to the "solution."

Even without the presence of the sexologist-hero we can see how this quest for the knowledge of sexual pleasure operates within the parameters of a "diff'rent strokes for diff'rent folks" sexological framework. In the first installment of the popular *Taboo* series of hard-core family melodrama, the woman who was described above as objecting to having the light on while engaged in fellatio with her husband is left by him for his young secretary. On her own now, the woman tries the world of swinging singles but is embarrassed by the public orgies in which she is invited to participate. At home later, she masturbates in the dark to the visual fantasy of sexual coupling with a not quite discernible mate. Disturbed by a noise, she wanders into the bedroom of her college-aged son who is having a bad dream. Spontaneously aroused by this son, she begins to make love in the dark room to his still-sleeping body; meanwhile, the fleeting images of her masturbatory fantasy are staying on the screen longer, eventually to merge with the present number. The son awakens to find his mother fellating him; with an amazed "Jesus Christ" he joins in, moving to a straight sex position with the mother on top reaching her orgasm and saying "I'm coming" as the son continues to thrust. The money shot occurs later as he places his penis between her breasts and comes onto her face.

Taboo offers a particularly interesting—and popular[5]—opposition between spontaneous, exciting (good) sex and unexciting, unspontaneous, phony, or contrived (bad) sex. In this film, spontaneity is located in the taboo incestuous coupling of mother and son in a dim room hidden from the rest of the world. This dark, secret sex functions in opposition to the brightly lit sex of the opening and to the communal, public scene of the orgy, neither of which turns the mother on. Remarkably few repercussions attend the breaking of what is often taken to be the most fundamental of sexual taboos. The mother offers only weak resistance to subsequent encounters. (In a sequel, *Taboo IV*, the mother will undergo therapy to rid herself of this nagging desire.) In this first film, when the mother confesses her problem to a female friend, instead of shock or disapproval the friend's only reaction is to masturbate in vicarious excitement. In the end the mother establishes a relationship with an employer who proposes marriage; although she refuses marriage, she does agree to keep him as her lover. The implication is that he will offer a good cover to her ongoing secret relationship with her son.

"Good" sex, in other words, might be located almost anywhere—in fellatio (as in *Deep Throat*), in anal sex (as in *Loose Ends* [Bruce Seven, 1984]), in straight sex (as in *Misty Beethoven*), or even in incest (as in *Taboo*). "Diff'rent strokes for diff'rent folks" is, after all, the guiding ethic. Yet despite the apparent inclusiveness, some "strokes" remain genuinely taboo within the heterosexual limits of the genre: father-son incest, for example, is unthinkable. What counts is not so much the intrinsic content of the sexual numbers, but how they are played (that is, performed, lit, shot, edited) and how the film constructs the knowledge of the "truth" of that sex. Here we depart from our model of the musical. In the musical, one type of number, the romantic duet, is generally privileged over all others in the reconciliation of opposites that is the means to heterosexual union. In feature-length pornography, however, any one of the possible numbers listed by Ziplow could perform the reconciliation of opposites if set up properly with respect to narrative and other numbers. In the musical, the romantic dance duet and love song are the most appropriate vehicles for communicating heterosexual desire; in the hard-core feature, while all the numbers potentially communicate sexual desire and pleasure, some numbers do so more than others.

Fellatio is the most common number used to express maximum spontaneous pleasure in the films of the 1970s. Displacement of female genital pleasure onto oral satisfaction offers only a provisional, and ultimately unstable, solution to the problem of fixing visual pleasure. It is a solution that is already gently parodied in *Misty Beethoven*. Seymour, for example, tries to teach Misty to look with pride on an erection achieved through fellatio, to say to herself, "I made that." But as we have seen, the film as a whole views fellatio as the overused gimmick that by the late 1970s it had indeed become, and thus as the antithesis to spontaneous sex. To a certain extent the money shot's original value as a solution to the problem of sex depended on a novelty that by the 1980s had begun to wear thin. Of course, in the context of an older literary pornographic tradition the representation of fellatio is really not very novel at all. There was novelty, though, in its cinematic reproduction in a nonliterary, mass-entertainment form consumed by both men and women. For this more general audience fellatio, and its less familiar, less visible counterpart, cunnilingus, stood momentarily for the very idea of sexual exploration exposed by the then-expanding "sexual revolution." Precisely because oral sex had once seemed an exotic, even forbidden, practice, one not mentioned in the traditional prerevolutionary "marriage manuals," it could function as the sexual act most apt to generate spontaneous desires. That it could just as easily become the rote number that *Misty Beethoven* parodies in 1975 attests to the importance in this genre of always seeking the "new" and spontaneous sexual solution to the problem of sex.

In other films the solution could be an orgy, as in *Behind the Green Door* (1972) and *The Resurrection of Eve* (1973) by the Mitchell Brothers; a ménage à trois, as in *Insatiable II* (Godfrey Daniels, 1984) and *Careful, He May Be Watching* (Richard Pachinko, 1987); a dramatically privileged form of straight sex, as in *Throat—Twelve Years After* (Gerard Damiano, 1984); or sadie-max, as in *New Wave Hookers* (Dark Bros., 1975) and *Insatiable* (Godfrey Daniels, 1980). And in many films a voyeuristic twist is added to the above acts to provide a mediatory solution to the problem of sex. In the bizarre *Café Flesh* (F. X. Pope, 1982), for example, we find the pure voyeurism of postapocalyptic "sex negatives" who can only watch the sexual performances of "sex positives." In the more conventional *I Like to Watch* (Paul G. Vatelli, 1983), voyeurism is the device that gets everyone to join in. And in *Talk Dirty to Me One More Time* (Anthony Spinelli, 1985), it is a voyeuristic husband's view of his wife that finally cures him of impotence.

In all, however, at least until the early 1980s, one rarely sees the dramatic climax of pleasure figured without the ubiquitous money shot. Nor do practices like cunnilingus—especially "lesbian" cunnilingus, in which a penis performs no important role—although frequently depicted, receive the same climactic emphasis as mediator of opposites that the above numbers do. This situation will, however, begin to change when more women take on the task of directing hard-core films in the mid-1980s.

Conclusion

One conclusion to be drawn from this chapter's comparison of feature-length pornography and Hollywood musicals is that in hardcore a wider variety of numbers can be used to mediate the oppositions that structure the narrative, though certain numbers do remain genuinely taboo, most significantly male-to-male sex. A corollary, and more important, difference between hardcore and the movie musical is that narrative equilibrium does not necessarily lie in the permanent union of the couple. Although *Misty Beethoven* does imitate the musical model by celebrating, with its straight sex emphasis, a heterosexual union, the other examples we have considered suggest that within the genre as a whole numerous sexual pleasures with diverse partners can, if properly placed in the narrative and in relation to other numbers, succeed in solving problems in the realm of sex. The formation of a couple, Susan Sontag (1969, 66) has noted, is not primarily what pornography is about.

As we have seen, what this new cinematic form of pornography is about is not only the multiplication of depictions of graphic sexual acts but also the conventionalized deployment of these acts within narratives that aim, as Foucault (1978, 63) puts it, not just at "confessing" sex, but at "reconstructing, in and around the act . . . the images, desires, modulations, and quality of the pleasure that animated it."

In this intensification of pleasure in the very *knowledge* of pleasure, the hard-core narrative film resembles more "legitimate" recent deployments of sexuality, whether medical, sexological, or psychiatric. As in these other discourses, sexuality is constructed as a problem that a greater knowledge of sexuality will "solve." Also, as in these other discourses, the problem of differences between the sexes, or of the different pleasures derived from various sexual practices, becomes increasingly paramount. Of these discourses, pornography and sexology are the most alike, in both purpose and narrative form.

That the "solutions" to the problems of sex are most often constructed from the dominant power knowledge of male subjectivity should come as no surprise. Classic movie musicals, as we have seen, do much the same thing. What may surprise, however, especially in contrast to the earlier stag film, is the extent to which sexual difference itself, together with its corollary of (unequal) male and female centers of power and pleasure, has moved to the foreground of hard-core generic expectation. In place of the musical's utopian solution of a couple united through the harmony and rhythm of song and dance, hard-core narrative offers a materialism of different varieties, quantities, and qualities of sexual pleasure as the utopian solution to all sexual ills, including that most fundamental ill: the lack of sexual accommodation between men and women.

NOTES

1. Sound has been much slower to be analyzed by film theorists, partly because sound arrived late to film, long after the cinematic image had been firmly ensconced as the central element of cinematic signification, and partly because sound has traditionally played only a supportive role as anchor to the image. Other theorists who have written about sound include Stephen Heath (1981) and Michel Chion (1982).

2. Stephen Heath (1981, 189) writes that a "whole gamut of pants and cries" functions to "deal with the immense and catastrophic problem . . . of the visibility or not of pleasure, to provide *vocal image* to guarantee the accomplishment of pleasure."

3. It is remarkable how much fine work on the movie musical film scholarship has been produced in the last five years, work that has considerably aided me in my effort to understand the functions of number and narrative in the hard-core feature. A precursor of much of this work is the anthology of essays edited by Rick Altman, *Genre: The Musical* (1981), followed by Jane Feuer's *The Hollywood Musical* (1982), and then by Altman's own *The American Film Musical* (1987). Gerald Mast's *Can't Help Singin'* (1987) has added to the riches.

4. There is, of course, a hard-core "version" of this musical entitled *Very Dirty Dancing*.

5. No fewer than two popular cycles of films are based on variations of incest themes: *Taboo* (I–IV) and *Taboo American Style,* Parts 1–4. The latter film series is a continuing soap opera-style family melodrama, complete with a millionaire matriarch played by Gloria Leonard, that advertised itself as "Beyond Dallas." The first installment, *Taboo American Style, Part 1: The Ruthless Beginning*, was chosen by the X-Rated Critics Organization as Most Erotic Film of 1985 (Rimmer 1986, 427).

WORKS CITED

Altman, Rick. "Moving Lips: Cinema as Ventriloquism." *Cinema/Sound* (special issue). *Yale French Studies* 60 (1980): 67–79.

———. *Genre: The Musical—A Reader.* Bloomington: Indiana University Press, 1981.

———. *The American Film Musical* Bloomington: Indiana University Press, 1987.

Bonitzer, Pascal. *Le regard et la voix.* Paris: Union Generale d'Editions, 1976.

Braudy, Leo. *The World in a Frame: What We See in Films.* Garden City, N.Y.: Anchor, 1977.

Chion, Michel. *La voix au cinema.* Paris: Editions e l'Etoile, 1982.

Doane, Mary Ann. "The Voice in Cinema: The Articulation of Body and Space." *Cinema/Sound* (special issue). *Yale French Studies* 60 (1980): 67–79.

Feuer, Jane. *The Hollywood Musical.* Bloomington: Indiana University Press, 1982.

Heath, Stephen. *Questions of Cinema.* Bloomington: Indiana University Press, 1981.

Jameson, Fredric. *The Political Unconscious: Narrative as Socially Symbolic Act.* Ithaca, N.Y.: Cornell University Press, 1981.

McArthur, Colin. *Underworld USA.* New York: Viking, 1972.

Mast, Gerald. *Can't Help Singin': The American Musical on Stage and Screen.* Woodstock, N.Y.: Overlook, 1987.

Mueller, John. "Fred Astaire and the Integrated Musical." *Cinema Journal* 24 (Fall): 28–40.

Neale, Stephen. *Genre.* London: British Film Institute, 1980.

Rimmer, Robert. *The X-rated Videotape Guide.* New York: Harmony, 1986.

Schatz, Thomas. *Hollywood Genres: Formulas, Filmmaking, and the Studio System.* New York: Random House, 1981.

Silverman, Kaja. *The Acoustic Mirror: The Female Voice in Psychoanalysis and Cinema*. Bloomington: Indiana University Press, 1988.

Williams, Alan. "Is Sound Recording Like a Language?" *Cinema/Sound* (special Issue). *Yale French Studies* 60 (1980): 67–79.

———. "The Musical Film and Recorded Popular Music" In *Genre: The Musical—A Reader*, ed. Rick Altman, 147–158. London: Routledge & Kegan Paul, 1981.

Ziplow, Stephen. *The Film Maker's Guide to Pornography*. New York: Drake, 1977.

Peter Lehman

Revelations about Pornography

The title of the 1984 film *On Golden Blonde* puns in a manner characteristic of porn on the 1981 Hollywood film *On Golden Pond* starring Jane Fonda.[1] Linda Williams does not discuss this or any other type of porn humor in *Hard Core: Power, Pleasure, and the "Frenzy of the Visible,"* her brilliant 1989 book-length study of pornographic cinema. No book, let alone the first one on a topic, can be expected to cover every possible aspect of its subject. Nevertheless, the importance of fleeting moments of humor in porn relates to other aspects of porn Williams overlooks, overemphasizes, or underemphasizes. In this essay, I want to outline those areas. My reason for granting Williams centrality is quite simple: precisely because her book is so good and because it is the first one of its kind, it is central to the growing study of pornography in general and feminism and pornography in particular. The following critique is a tribute to the profoundly thought-provoking insights Williams has brought to the area.

When discussing the hard-core feature that she dates from 1972, Williams, in my estimation, overemphasizes the importance of narrative structure. In the process of doing so, she falls into a somewhat conventional form/content split. Williams pays virtually no attention to the specific manner in which the erotic content she analyzes is represented in any of the films. Erotic response, as any other kind of response, is shaped by form, and we should pay careful attention to the manner in which any single film or video scene or even moment within a scene is represented in regards to lighting, camera position, cutting patterns, and so forth.[2]

Although Williams does identify several crucial stylistic features of the genre such as the "meat shot" and the "money shot" (to which I return later), she never deals with a more specific level of formal analysis. As such, her study bears comparison with Carol Clover's insightful analysis of the horror film, *Men, Women, and Chain Saws* (1992). Clover devotes her attention almost exclusively to narrative patterns. She identifies a major stylistic feature which she terms the "I-camera," the use of a Steadicam to represent the killer's point-of-view. As such, the "I-camera" is comparable to the "meat shot" and the "money shot"; they are pervasive, recurring features of their genres. While such stylistic observations are extremely important, we need to extend the analysis of style in such genres as horror and pornography to a more localized level or we will miss much of what is horrific or erotic in these films. I want to return here, however, to other consequences

First published in *Film Criticism*, vol. 20, nos. 1–2 (Fall/Winter 1995–96), pp. 3–16. Reprinted by permission of the author and the editors of *Film Criticism*.

of the manner in which Williams overemphasizes the function of narrative in the hard-core feature.

In the 1970s and early 1980s, for example, when many of the films she analyzes were being made in 35mm and exhibited exclusively in theaters, most spectators randomly entered the theaters without the usual regard for the starting time of the feature and frequently left without waiting for it to end or to see what they had missed at the beginning. This reverses the norm of "legitimate" cinema and also changes the significance of narrative patterns. It also helps explain how it is possible that a sex scene on a pool table in *Insatiable* (1980) could be repeated in its entirety in *Insatiable II* (1984). Although Williams analyzes the pool table scene in *Insatiable* in some detail, she does not even note that it is repeated in the later film, although she also discusses it. The mere fact that such a repetition is possible suggests that much of the appeal and meaning of the sexual number lies outside its narrative contextualization.

The resolution of any narrative problem a film may pose (e.g., will a character find sexual pleasure?) is less significant for a spectator who has not been present when the problem was posed or may not be present when it is solved. Indeed, the comings and goings of porn audiences were so standard that I remember being shocked in the 1970s when, after Leonard Bernstein among others had conferred social chic on *Deep Throat*, I passed a theater in mid-town Manhattan on a Saturday afternoon and found a line of people, shopping bags in hand, waiting for the next show to begin. What were they doing there? I wondered. Why didn't they go in? Rather than being symptomatic of a defining moment in the development of hardcore, I suspect it was a bizarre aberration that quickly passed, leaving spectators to once again furtively duck in and out of theaters at will.

Remember that most porn movie schedules at the time were not even published in the newspaper, so that even if people would have wanted to see the film through from beginning to end, it would have meant showing up in an area like mid-town Manhattan and standing in line or hanging out for an indefinite period of time to do so. With the sole exception of the *Deep Throat* phenomenon, I do not ever recall seeing any lines outside porn theaters. Given that start times still are not even published, it is reasonable to assume that for the vast majority of spectators narrative patterning is at best a disrupted aspect of theatrical porn watching.

Needless to say, with the advent of home video, the precarious status of narrative in porn is intensified. The video format invites spectators to fast-forward through scenes, replay other scenes, and even slow-motion and freeze-frame favorite moments within scenes. Such a context reeks havoc with narrative structure since it is quite literally possible for the spectator to elide it totally (e.g., fast-forwarding through all the narrative parts and just watching the sex scenes) or to restructure it temporally. Indeed, porn made for the video market acknowledges this reality since it deemphasizes narrative structure in comparison to the theatrical hard-core feature. Concomitantly with her overemphasis on narrative, Williams underestimates the function of the porn star system. This is particularly ironic since if there ever was a genre built upon the star system it is porn. Much like in the 1950s, for example, many fans would go to any John Wayne Western or in recent decades any Clint Eastwood Western or cop film, porn watchers may see everything with, for example, Marilyn Chambers. Indeed, this aspect of the porn star system is so strong that some stars like Chambers even have their name in the titles of some of their films. I have argued elsewhere that porn does not maintain the classical distinction between the actor and the fictional role (1993). Some porn actors like John Holmes virtually become synonymous with and even referred to with a name of a fictional character like Johnny Wadd and others like Chambers play themselves in such films as her Private Fantasies series.

Since porn does not invest much in the believability of its fictional world, it acknowledges that spectators are really watching actors perform sexually, not characters. Even fans who believe that actors like Wayne and Eastwood "play themselves" in their films have some investment in the various characters or repeated characters (e.g., Harry Callahan) that those actors play. Porn fans, I would argue, have little or no such investment, displacing their star fascination entirely upon the actor and his or her body. As the oft-noted masturbatory function of porn indicates, rather then lose themselves in identification with the fictional bodies on the screen, porn spectators direct their attention to their own bodies. It is hard for someone to masturbate without knowing what she or he is doing.

For a spectator watching a Marilyn Chambers film, her presence may be a more significant portion of the pleasure of the form than the narrative structure in which she appears. Thus, although Williams perceptively classifies several Chambers films in quite different narrative categories (e.g., *Behind the Green Door* [1972] as a "separated utopia" like the backstage movie musical and *The Resurrection of Eve* [1976] as an "integrated utopia"), the continuity of her star presence may, for many spectators, be more important than the narrative dissimilarity between the films. With the shift of porn exhibition to the video market in the 1980s, both the tenuous nature of porn narration and the emphasis on star presence even further qualify Williams's reading since spectators may deemphasize narrative form and overemphasize the star body in a fetishist's dream of near total control over the temporal flow, watching it as many times as he or she wants, or in slow-motion and freeze-framing it.

Both the theatrical and the home video viewing contexts of porn, then, suggest a less unified structure for pleasure than Williams grants and the importance of stars points to a central area of pleasure that not only further threatens the primary importance of narrative structure but also points to a crucial feature of the form: fleeting moments of pleasure. Much as individual porn watchers may derive erotic pleasure from the physical appearance of a star they find attractive, they may also derive pleasure from brief, fragmentary visual and aural moments such as a passing facial expression or a particular moan. Indeed, porn stars have different styles of fucking in terms of how they use their bodies, faces, and voices, and these repeat across films.[3] Though Williams is correct in emphasizing such standard industry practices as the "money shot" and the "meat shot," she overlooks the wealth of nonstandardized, idiosyncratic details that permeate porn sex scenes. In a conventional sense, these mean nothing and go noplace, but if we grant erotic pleasure a meaningful place within porn, these unclassifiable moments may be central to viewer response if not narrative patterning.

It is precisely within this highly unusual context of heterogeneous, fleeting, and fragmentary pleasures that I believe we can understand porn humor. The porn industry's humorous titling of many of its films basically consists of isolated, single jokes. Neither the joke nor the laughter it may generate, in other words, is integrated into the film that follows. In this regard, Hollywood has to take its titling more seriously than porn. People expect the title to bear some relevance to the film they are about to see and would be understandably upset if the tone and nature of the following film completely departed from the title. Hollywood cannot afford to title a social seriousness drama about AIDS, *The Naked Gun 33-1/3*, just for a moment of humorous pleasure. Yet, that is precisely what *On Golden Blonde* does since the film's narrative does not even remotely relate to *On Golden Pond*. If we go to a Hollywood film entitled *Malcolm X* (1992), we expect a drama about a historically important figure; if we rent a porn film entitled *Malcolm XXX* (in production in 1992), we may be amused at the clever manner in which the title simultaneously puns on a recent Hollywood film and the X-rating, but we still expect a typical hard-core film that at most will have a few trappings surrounding the subject of its biographical title.

Advertising in porn video functions somewhat similarly to the frequent use of title humor. Images used on the boxes often do not appear in the films. The box of *Wild and Wicked* (1991), for example, shows a woman on both the front and back playing seductively with a large chain. On the back cover, she pulls it between her legs. In the video itself, however, not only do these images not appear, but there is no chain in any scene. An initial response might be to consider the promise of this undelivered image false advertising—a deplorable trick to get the consumer to buy or rent the video. Upon reflection, however, this is not a satisfactory explanation. What would motivate the industry to disappoint or anger its clientele regularly? If customers are sometimes disappointed, it must not be a major disappointment or they would be up in arms complaining to video store managers or the companies that sell the tapes. Clearly, porn watchers do not expect all advertising images to appear in the films any more than they expect the titles to be accurate. Indeed, the images on the boxes resemble photographic poses like those in porn magazines rather than narrative images that have been frozen and pulled out of context. Rather than being a false promise, they are yet another unintegrated pleasure, something that can be enjoyed in addition to the video images. Hollywood sometimes advertises films with formally constructed images that do not appear as if they have been pulled from a narrative flow, but there is a major difference. If we see a film advertised with an image of Clint Eastwood holding a rifle, he had better hold a rifle in the movie or, if we see John Wayne throwing a punch, he had better be involved in a fist fight in the movie. These are not images to be enjoyed on their own but, rather, what John Ellis has called narrative images that are directly related to the film they advertise. Although porn advertising images usually bear some relation to the video they advertise (the actors shown on the boxes, for example, usually appear in the tape, or a disclaimer is printed on the box), the relationship is less integrated than that typical of Hollywood films.

Williams's model for studying the history of porn bears an uncanny resemblance to that of such film historians as David Bordwell, Janet Staiger, and Kristin Thompson, who have analyzed the classical style of filmmaking. What Williams terms the stag film is equivalent to what many film historians now term the primitive cinema, and what she terms the hard-core feature is equivalent to what historians term the classical style, which also involved an expansion to feature-length narration. Indeed, her analysis of the centrality of such devices as the "meat shot" and the "money shot" bears comparison with the manner in which historians have identified central stylistic devices such as shot-reverse-shot editing in the classical cinema. From this perspective, which seems to me valid, the history of pornography recapitulates the history of cinema in general, moving from a primitive mode in one exhibition context to a classical mode within a changing exhibition context. The stag smoker, for example, would compare with the nickelodeon and the theatrical hard-core feature with the classical feature exhibited in legitimate theaters. The analogy may, however, only work so far.

Once the classical style was established it maintained a remarkable dominance, especially in regard to such aspects of narration as feature-length and the dominance within the style of narrative. But something much different may be happening in pornography. The hard-core theatrical feature may have been more of an aberration than a major stylistic development, and while the reasons for this are complex and varied and involve exhibition, economics, and technology, the fate of the hard-core feature bears on the argument I have been developing about Williams's lack of attention to certain aspects of those features and her over-attention to cohesive narrative patterns.

The development in the 1980s of porn made on video and aimed directly at the home market obviously was shaped by technology and economics. Using video equipment, these tapes are produced much more cheaply and quickly than their 35mm theatrical precedents. If one measures them against the hard-core feature, they show a loss of both production values (such as lighting) and narrative development—that is, even by the limited standards of narrative development in the theatrical features, many of the videos are even less developed. Rather than reify a golden age of theatrical 35mm porn as, incidentally, many of the 1970s porn auteurs did by abandoning the form altogether and attempting to move into legitimate filmmaking, perhaps we need to consider the less developed video forms as moving porn back into a format that is more closely aligned with many of its heterogeneous and fleeting moments of pleasure. From this perspective, the fact that certain early

Femme Productions as well as some gay and lesbian videos have moved toward collections of short, unrelated segments may be significant. Whereas economics may seem to explain these developments fully, I suggest that there are other issues related to porn's pleasures that may account for the willingness to move away from the near total reliance on narrative features that for so long completely characterized heterosexual commercial porn. Though even from this perspective it is interesting to ponder something that Williams completely overlooks—the popularity of many types of compilation videos that, for example, will simply present sex scenes taken from a variety of films featuring a particular star and edit them together outside any narrative context. The popularity of such tapes (some of which are organized around types of sex scenes such as anal or oral) suggest an uneasy and perhaps forced relationship between the scenes themselves and the original narrative context in which they appeared. One does not, for example, find popular videos that present nothing but a collection of John Wayne Western shootout scenes. These porn compilation tapes almost announce that they are nothing but "getting down to business" by dispensing with the usual preliminaries. As such they may have an honesty to them that reflects back on the form from which they come.

Within Hollywood, once the feature was established, culturally denigrated forms were relegated to the status of shorts. The Three Stooges, with their crude vaudeville form of slapstick humor, are a good example of this tendency. By chance, my exposure to pornography offering alternatives to mainstream, heterosexual hardcore has come in the form of short compilations: *Clips* (1988), a lesbian tape, consists of three ten-minute unrelated segments, and a gay Asian porn tape entitled *Up My Bunzai* (various copyright dates) also consists of three short segments. Similarly, such early Femme Productions (porn made by women for women and the couples market) as *Urban Heat* (1984) and *Femme* (1984) are comprised of short, unrelated segments with little narrative.

Williams does note the reliance on vignettes in early Femme Productions, but she attributes it to a need to return to the origins of porn in order to discover alternative forms of representation. While this may be true, as it was for Andy Warhol, the segments in both *Clips* and *Up My Bunzai* also have little or no narrative and characterization. As such I suspect that all three tapes betray an affinity with what I have characterized as the heterogeneous, brief, and fleeting nature of many of porn's pleasures. Porn may never have been suited fully to the feature format. Porn features developed out of an exhibition context that appealed to viewers by promising them the features that they expected when they went to the movies. The porn industry, like the early film industry (and perhaps like many porn patrons), may also have desired a respectability that features with characters might help confer upon the films. From this perspective the narrative might be a little like the oft-joked-about articles and interviews in *Playboy*. While those writings undoubtedly constitute a *Playboy* "philosophy," the jokesters quite rightly knew what the relationship between the pictorials and that philosophy was. Iron-ically, an article that appeared in a recent issue of *Playboy*, "How Dirty Pictures Changed My Life," by Lisa Palac, is revealing about how porn films function erot-ically. Palac, a former antiporn crusader, chronicles her encounters with porn and her changing perceptions of the form. Of her first porn viewing experience, she remarks, "The plot was forgettable. I vaguely remember a contrived sex scene on a pool table" (81). Of her first masturbatory experience with porn, she refers to "replaying certain close-ups over and over" (88). Indeed, her general recollection is that "I spent more time fingering the fast-forward button than anything else . . . I scanned for cute guys with long hair, punk, butchy women, plots with lots of psy-chological tension, come shots where he doesn't pull out and, most of all, genuine female orgasms" (145). For Palac, plot is unimportant with, at most, individual, iso-lated scenes retaining importance; parts are fast-forwarded and others are repeated. Significantly, the tapes are even "scanned" for interesting plots with psychologi-cal "tension." It may seem at the very least paradoxical to fast-forward looking for plot elements since plot and character development are precisely what we nor-mally think of as requiring careful attention to the entire film. But even this within porn can function in a more isolated manner (and one that Williams totally over-looks). One can, as Palac does, isolate individual scenes within porn wherein the character situations and interactions have special erotic appeal for the viewer. In this regard, Palac's desire for "psychological tension" has less to do with the psy-chological development of rounded characters typical of the classical narrative and is, in fact, on a par with her desire for images of "cute guys with long hair."

Revelations, a 1992 Femme Production written and directed by Candida Royalle, is an atypical film within the context of porn narrative that sheds light on these issues. On the one hand, the film is an unusually serious and highly nar-rativized porn film about a futuristic society that carefully regulates sexual con-duct for the good of the state. All sexually explicit materials are outlawed. At the beginning of the film, the central female character comes across a man being dragged out of his apartment by the police. She surreptitiously enters the apart-ment and discovers a back room with sexually explicit photographs and video tapes. She watches a tape and returns twice to watch others. At the end, the police burst in on her, catch her in the act of watching the forbidden tapes, and arrest her.

In addition to this strong narrative structure, *Revelations* develops an explicit theme about the evils of censorship. The film envisions a nightmare future and at its conclusion a written message urges viewers to fight the growing cen-sorship climate in the United States that will lead to such a dystopia. The scenes showing the woman having state-approved sexual intercourse with her husband are frightening representations of fascistic procreation devoid of any sense of eroti-cism or sexual pleasure; they have sex to produce "little soldiers" for the state. The film derives its title from the revelations the heroine has from watching the banned videos. She learns that sex can be erotic, beautiful, and pleasurable and, most significantly, watching the tapes culminates in her masturbating while watching. We see the tapes the woman watches almost in their entirety; Royalle only cuts away briefly to shots of the watching woman.

What makes *Revelations* so extraordinary is the nature of the sexually explicit tapes that supply the revelations of the title: they are almost totally non-narrativized. There is *no* plot, *no* character development, *no* thematic development in the films within the film. Although a brief title appears at the beginning of each tape (the first two identify the beginning and later stages in a couple's relationship and the third, which shows lesbians, is introduced as forbidden sex), no further reference or development occurs. The titles simply label and identify what follows. The woman, for example, sees what love was like for new lovers and between two women in a society that allowed such forms of sexual expression, even if it disapproved of some of them. The erotic value of these revelations, however, lies entirely outside narrative. Royalle emphasizes this by having the woman remember isolated images from the tapes that are intercut as we see her having sex with her husband and bathing. Her revelations about eroticism and the way sex could be as opposed to the way it is and has been for her are based upon non-contextualized images that hold a particular fascination and erotic impact for her. She recalls intensely charged images outside even the context in which they occurred rather than narratives, characters, or themes.

From this perspective, *Revelations* is bizarrely contradictory; it is a highly narrativized and thematized porn film about the extraordinary erotic value of totally non-narrativized, nonthematized porn. As such, the film is an explicit embodiment of the contradictory tensions that lie at the center of hard-core narrative features. These tensions are further highlighted by the manner in which Royalle treats both the narrative and the films within the film. The narrative is invested with much more thematic significance and stylistic sophistication than is typical for the hard-core feature. Some images such as the poetic, highly manipulated ones at the beginning and conclusion and the extreme close-ups of parts of the woman's face as she narrates her story stylistically resemble the European art cinema and the avant-garde. In addition to the anticensorship message, Royalle boldly explores the potential role of female vision and sexual pleasure in a context presumed by many to be the sole domain of males. It is no coincidence that it is a man's apartment that the woman enters. Royalle's anticensorship message and her suggestion that women use porn for their own sexual pleasure are not simple pretexts for hard-core scenes—these are urgent matters.

On the other hand, in the typical hard-core feature, the sexual numbers at least involve the main characters, however flimsy their characterization may be. In *Revelations*, however, the films within the film are simply put in a VCR and shown. In the first two, we see two lovers about whom we know virtually nothing, and who are not characters in the film, making passionate love. The point could obviously be made thematically by simply letting us glimpse those tapes rather than watching them fully. For Royalle, showing us the non-narrativized erotic tapes is as important as her highly thematic, futuristic narrative.

Revelations, then, is at one and the same time both more narrativized than the typical hard-core feature with sexual numbers that are less integrated into that narrative. As such, the film embodies the profoundly unstable nature of the hard-core feature while reminding us that there are differences between instabilities and essences. I am not, in other words, arguing that Williams misses the "essence" of pornography; pornography has no "essence." I do think, however, that her work on the hard-core feature misses the instabilities that result from the contradictory tensions that arise from wanting to narrate and thematize while simultaneously arouse with images and sounds that lie at the furthest extremes from narration; many of the erotic pleasures of hard-core porn lie outside narration, characterization, and thematization.

In 1984, I argued strongly against what had become the dominant manner in film studies of pitting the political and ideological significance of the avant-garde against the narrative feature. The former, I felt, was hailed beyond all reason for its powerful, positive effects, while the latter was condemned as little more than the embodiment of the deplorable, dominant ideology. I do not want to suggest ten years [ca. 1995/1996] later we should create a porn opposition between narrative and non-narrative reminiscent of that which lay at the center of the avant-garde/commercial feature opposition in the 1970s and early 1980s. As *Revelations* itself demonstrates, there are profoundly important porn feature-length films. Porn has also been used in safe-sex films. It can, in other words, be used across a complete spectrum ranging from totally non-narrative, brief segments to hard-core features to safe-sex films. These should not be pitted against each other in a manner where, for example, the non-narrative short is seen as the true or liberating embodiment of porn's pleasures and the hard-core feature is reduced to a sham that simply obscures what porn is all about. The relationship between the various forms of pornography is much more complex.

Williams has very perceptively analyzed the narrative patterns of hard-core features and their significance. Ironically, however, far from characterizing what is most significant about most of those films, she may have emphasized aspects of them that are less central to many of porn's pleasures and perhaps even counter to them. That some porn today has willingly cast off the degree of narrative and characterization typical of the theatrical feature and embraced short, unrelated segments may have less to do with economic necessity and technology (stories can be told cheaply on video) and more to do with a sense of liberation from the constraints of a narrative respectability that did not sit well with much of the pornographic impulse. If the narrative feature itself tended to legitimize hardcore, Williams has somewhat similarly legitimized the study of it. In the process, however, she may have inadvertently given her subject too much respectability (i.e., meaningful narrative patterns) while she overlooked the heterogeneous, brief, and fleeting nature of porn's less reputable pleasures. Those pleasures may in fact have held an uneasy relationship with the admittedly fascinating narrative structures in which they were encased. Williams's analysis is in part a reaction to a cliché that the narrative in porn is merely a pretext for the sex scenes. On the contrary, she argues, those narratives are structured into meaningful patterns as in other Hollywood genres, particularly the musical. While that is the case, Williams has lost sight of the fact that there also is validity to the equally clichéd disclaimer so frequently muttered by porn watchers that the narrative is indeed a pretext. How does a narrative about a woman seeking sexual pleasure for herself relate to a film in which a male spectator may derive his most intense moment of pleasure from watching a fleeting expression cross her face while listening to her utter an inarticulate sexual moan? For better or worse (and I think for better), pornography really is dirtier than Williams acknowledges. Tom Gunning has distinguished between the cinema of attractions and the development of narrative in early film history. Something of the unusual nature of the hard-core feature emerges if we consider it from this perspective. The cinema of attractions was one of display rather than storytelling. Attractions acknowledge the spectator in a manner that makes cinema more exhibitionistic than voyeuristic and offer visual curiosity rather than interest in narrative enigmas. Attractions also have a different sense of time than narratives do since they do not build temporal patterns so much as display and remove what has been seen: "Rather than a development which links the past with the present in such a way as to define a specific anticipation of the future (as an unfolding narrative does), the attraction seems limited to a sudden burst of presence" (6). As such, attractions are characteristically brief and do not develop expectations based upon patterning. The suspense of the attraction is not how but when it will occur: "The act of display on which the cinema of attractions is founded presents itself as a temporal irruption rather than a temporal development" (7).

At first glance, it might seem that porn is just another form of the cinema of attractions; it is highly exhibitionist in its display of the body and shamelessly acknowledges in spirit, if not always in technique, what the spectator is there for. From theater advertising to video boxes to reviews, the makers, exhibitors, and critics of porn all openly acknowledge its sexually arousing and even masturbatory function. It is all perhaps summarized by the manner in which magazines replace the usual ratings categories such as one to four stars and thumbs up or down with such things as penises ranging from limp to fully erect or a range of one to four erect penises. The institution of porn openly revels in what it is about.

In the hard-core feature, however, sexual display is anything but brief, and it is strongly linked to patterns based upon expectation. Indeed, perhaps nothing in cinema is more ritualistically patterned and less full of surprises than the hard-core number with its predictable "meat shots" (close-ups of the penis thrusting in and out of the vagina) and "money shots" (visible ejaculation, frequently on the body of the woman). This type of patterning, however, is not like the patterning that Gunning attributes to the narrative. Although the lengthy sexual numbers typical of the hard-core feature include arousal, various types of sexual activity (e.g., anal and oral), and various positions (e.g., woman on top, rear entry), all of which culminate in the money shot, the patterning has little or nothing to do with narrative or character. Time is connected into a past, present, and future, but it is not the enigmatic time of narrative. What lies at the center of the hard-core feature is a hybrid whereby the attraction that is still based upon the exhibitionist display of the body and taboo subjects is both extended and patterned, but within a pattern of curiosity, arousal, display, and satisfaction rather than one within a diegetic framework. The hard-core feature's diegesis has little or nothing to do with its display of sexual attractions. To put it another way, Gunning notes that the distinction between the cinema of attractions and the narrative cinema is not total; the former includes narrative elements, and the latter found a place for attractions within it. The place of the attraction within the hard-core feature, however, is distinctly different than its place within the classical narrative.

The hard-core theatrical feature upon which Williams concentrates is intensely and perhaps even paradoxically contradictory in its nature. It is torn apart at its very center by conflicting impulses that shatter even its strongest illusions of meaningful cohesiveness. As we expand our study of pornography, it is important that we do not lose sight of the fleeting moments of heterogeneous pleasure that are at one and the same time so central to porn and so repugnant to our culture. In the name of genre and narrative, Williams has redeemed too much. Using her own terminology, I would argue that all forms of porn have more "separated" pleasures than she acknowledges.

NOTES

An earlier version of this essay was presented at the 1993 Console-ing Passions Conference in Tucson. I am deeply indebted to Connie Penley and Diane Waldman for the comments they made at the conference and to Robert Eberwein for his later comments. I would also like to thank Melanie Magisos for her help with revisions.

1. For an analysis of the function of porn in humor, see Lehman, 1996, 45–54.

2. For a more detailed formal analysis of porn, see Johnson (1993).

3. For a fascinating semiological analysis of the fleeting and often uncontrollable facial expressions that characterize porn, see MacCannell (1989). MacCannell's discussion of verbal patterns and inarticulate vocal communications during intercourse is also relevant.

WORKS CITED

Bordwell, David, Janet Staiger, and Kristin Thompson. *The Classical Hollywood Cinema: Film Style and Mode of Production to 1960.* New York: Columbia University Press, 1985.

Clover, Carol J. *Men, Women, and Chain Saws: Gender in the Modern Horror Film.* Princeton: Princeton University Press, 1992.

Ellis, John. *Visible Fictions: Cinema, Television, Video.* Boston: Routledge, 1982.

Gunning, Tom. "'Now You See It, Now You Don't': The Temporality of the Cinema of Attractions." *The Velvet Light Trap* 32 (Fall 1993): 3–12.

Johnson, Eithne. "Excess and Ecstasy: Constructing Female Pleasure in Porn Movies." *The Velvet Light Trap* 32 (Fall 1993): 30–49.

Lehman, Peter. "*Twin Cheeks, Twin Peeks,* and *Twin Freaks*: Porn's Transgressive Remake Humor." In *Authority and Transgression in Literature and Film*, ed. Bonnie Braendlin and Hans Braendlin, 45–54. Gainesville: University Press of Florida, 1996.

———. *Running Scared: Masculinity and the Representation of the Male Body*. Philadelphia: Temple University Press, 1993.

———. "The Avant-Garde: Power, Change, and the Power to Change." In *Cinema Histories, Cinema Practices*, ed. Patricia Mellencamp and Philip Rosen. Los Angeles: American Film Institute, 1984.

MacCannell, Dean. "Faking It: Comment on Face-Work in Pornography." *American Journal of Semiotics* 6, no. 4 (1989): 153–174.

Palac, Lisa. "How Dirty Pictures Changed My Life." *Playboy* 41, no. 5 (May 1994): 80–82, 145–146.

Williams, Linda. *Hard Core: Power, Pleasure, and the "Frenzy of the Visible."* 2nd ed. Berkeley: University of California Press, 1989.

Constance Penley

Crackers and Whackers:
The White Trashing of Porn

White Trash Theory

Before getting into my topic—porn's predilection for white trash looks and tastes—I want to say something about the benefits to one's theoretical formation that can accrue from growing up white trash. This brief comment is not a digression from my topic, because it was precisely my white trash upbringing that gave me the conceptual tools to recognize that predilection and the language to describe and explain it. I cannot imagine any better preparation for grasping the intricacies of contemporary theory and cultural studies than negotiating a Florida cracker childhood and adolescence. I understood the gist of structuralist binaries, semiosis, the linguistic nature of the unconscious, the disciplinary microorganization of power, and the distinguishing operations of taste and culture long before I left the groves of central Florida for the groves of academe. At the University of Florida in Gainesville, the University of California at Berkeley, and the Ecole des Hautes Etudes en Sciences Sociales in Paris, I encountered the ideas of Saussure, Lévi-Strauss, Barthes, Althusser, Lacan, Foucault, and, somewhat later, Certeau and Bourdieu. In those ideas I immediately recognized the home truths of white trash or, as Barthes would say, white trashnicity.

How does such theoretical precociousness emerge in cracker culture? Consider, for example, the intense conceptual work involved in figuring out the differential meanings of white trash—what it is because of what it is not, a regular down-home version of honey and ashes, the raw and the cooked. A Southern white child is required to learn that white trash folks are the lowest of the low because socially and economically they have sunk so far that they might as well be black. As such, they are seen to have lost all self-respect. So it is particularly unseemly when they appear to flaunt shamelessly their trashiness, which, after all, is nothing but an aggressively in-your-face reminder of stark class differences, a fierce fuck-you to anyone trying to maintain a belief in an America whose only class demarcations are the seemingly obvious ones of race.

From *White Trash: Race and Class in America*, edited by Matt Wray and Annalee Newitz. New York: Routledge, 1997: 89–112. Reprinted by permission of the author and Taylor & Francis Group, LLC.

If you *are* white trash, then you must engage in the never-ending labor of distinguishing yourself, of codifying your behavior so as to clearly signify a difference from blackness that will, in spite of everything, express some minuscule, if pathetic, measure of your culture's superiority, at least to those above you who use the epithet *white trash* to emphasize just how beyond the pale you are. This is hard going because the differences between the everyday lives of poor blacks and poor whites in the rural South are few and ephemeral. I am not denying the difference of race—and how that difference is lived—but trying to point to the crushing weight, on all those lives, of enduring poverty and the daily humiliations that come with it.

Even someone with as impeccable white trash credentials as my own can recall only one "distinction": white people don't eat gopher but blacks do (gopher is crackerese for a variety of land turtle). Perhaps I remember the socioanthropological distinction "gopher/not gopher" because it intersected with so many other distinctions marked by race, gender, and economic class that would, as I came to realize, both help and hinder me as I grew up and out into the world.

I made money as a kid by catching the slow-moving gophers in the white-owned groves and selling them for a quarter each to my teenage cousin Ricky, already a reprobate but a shrewd entrepreneur. Ricky would turn around and sell the gophers for fifty cents in East Town, the black neighborhood where I, as a white girl, was not allowed to go. I progressed from being grateful to my cousin for giving me the odd quarters to chafing at the restrictions on my mobility and my own budding entrepreneurship. This was especially so after Ricky had rounded up a crew of gopher-catchers from whose labor he was able to extract for himself at least as much as the minimum wage Disney pays its workers now toiling on our old hunting grounds.

But crackers are not always content merely to learn the complex stratagems of maintaining the tenuous distinctions of white trash culture; they sometimes go beyond that understanding to devise the critical method of using white trash against white trash. The epithet *white trash* can be deployed in a similar way to the original usage of "politically correct" within left circles, where a group would adopt the phrase to police its own excesses. My brother and I had a favorite game, which was to try to figure out which side of the family was the trashiest, our mother's Tennessee hillbilly clan or our father's Florida cracker kin. The point of the game wasn't to come to a definitive conclusion (we agreed it was pretty much a toss-up) but to try to selectively detrash ourselves, to figure out just how trashy we were so as to monitor and modify our thinking and behavior as much as possible. We vied to amass the most self-humiliating family statistics by claiming for Mom's or Dad's side the greatest number of cousins married to one another, uncles sent up the river for stealing TV sets, junked cars on blocks in the front yard, converts to Jehovah's Witnesses, or grandparents who uttered racist remarks with the most vehemence and flagrancy. Why my brother and I came to want to engage in this funny but painful detrashing project is a long story that must wait for another day, but the fact that we created this game demonstrates that white-trashness does not just involve the effort to make distinctions in response to a label coercively imposed from above ("Hey, at least we don't eat gopher!") but can also be a prime source for developing the kinds of skills needed to grasp the social and political dynamics of everyday life.

Growing up white trash, then, can give one the conceptual framework for understanding the work of distinction and the methods of criticism. But the real advantage lies in the way that upbringing helps a nascent theorist grasp the idea of agency and resistance in an utterly disdained social group whose very definition presumes it to have no "culture" at all.[1] The work of distinction in white trash can be deployed downward and across, but also up, to challenge the assumed social and moral superiority of the middle and professional classes.

White Trashing Practice

Considering the ways that white trash can be deployed up as a form of populist cultural criticism brings me to pornography. We already have several good discussions of the class nature and class politics of pornography, although the research on earlier periods is more extensive than that on the products of today's commercial industry. The contributors to Lynn Hunt's *The Invention of Pornography: Obscenity and the Origins of Modernity, 1500–1800* give a wealth of examples of the way pornography was used during that period to challenge absolutist political authority and church doctrine, variously linked as it was to free-thinking, heresy, science, and natural philosophy.[2] In *The Literary Underground of the Old Regime* Robert Darnton describes the workings of the eighteenth-century literary underground, a counterculture that produced smutty, muckraking, libelous literature and images that mocked and eroded the authority of the Old Regime.[3] In *The Secret Museum: Pornography in Modern Culture* Walter Kendrick argues that nineteenth-century pornography had no typical content of its own but consisted solely of dangerous and seditious images and ideas that the ruling classes wanted to keep out of the hands of the presumably more susceptible lower orders.[4] Defense attorney Edward de Grazia's *Girls Lean Back Everywhere: The Law on Obscenity and the Assault on Genius* tells story after story of early and mid-twentieth-century attempts to defend books such as *Ulysses, Tropic of Cancer, An American Tragedy, The Well of Loneliness, Howl,* and *Naked Lunch* against the efforts of the state, the police, and religion to ban this material from public and popular consumption.[5]

But where are the defenders of contemporary works like *Tanya Hardon, The Sperminator,* or *John Wayne Bobbitt: Uncut?* The more mass-cultural the genre becomes, and, it seems, the more militantly "tasteless," the more difficult it is to see pornography's historical continuity with avant-garde revolutionary art, populist struggles, or any kind of countercultural impulses. Add the feminist antiporn polemic and this low-rent genre appears unredeemable artistically, socially, or otherwise. Exceptions do get made, of course, for quality politically oriented gay male videos, such as Jerry Douglas's *Honorable Discharge,* about gays in the military; Candida Royalle's "couples erotica"; Fatale's lesbian-made videos for lesbians; and educational porn, which includes Gay Men's Health Crisis's safer sex videos or porn star and feminist Nina Hartley's guides to better fellatio and cunnilingus. But within mass-commercial videos, the great majority of the titles are seen to merit little critical, much less feminist, interest.

Two writers have suggested why this might be the case. In the "Popularity of Pornography" chapter of Andrew Ross's *No Respect: Intellectuals and Popular Culture,* Ross argues that the feminist disdain for pornography is a Victorian holdover, a conditioned middle-class female revulsion for anything associated with the lower orders, a revulsion that leads directly to, as Judith Walkowitz has shown in the case of nineteenth-century feminism, the political strategy of legislating an outright ban (the temperance movement) or engaging in moral reform and public hygiene efforts (getting prostitutes off the street and into "proper" jobs as maids and factory workers).[6]

Laura Kipnis builds on Ross's argument about feminism and the class politics of porn in "(Male) Desire, (Female) Disgust: Reading *Hustler.*"[7] She tells us how she made herself overcome her revulsion for the magazine to be able to sit down one day and actually look at it. Kipnis discovered that this most reviled instance of mass circulation porn is at the same time one of the most explicitly class-antagonistic mass periodicals of any genre. *Hustler,* she found, was militantly gross in its pictorials, its cartoons, its editorials and political humor, with bodies and body parts straight out of Rabelais, all put to service in stinging attacks on petit-bourgeoisiehood, every kind of social and intellectual pretension, the social power of the professional classes, the power of the government, and the hypocrisy of organized religion. Although Kipnis remains grossed out by *Hustler,* her reading of the magazine gives herself and us an invaluable insight into the class-based reasons for that revulsion and the social and political uses of grossness. She is careful to point out, however, as Darnton does in his study of the eighteenth-century French literary underground, that the libertarian politics here are not always or necessarily progressive but still serve an important role in questioning repressive and pretentious assumptions of morality and authority. You can be sure that if Newt Gingrich is *Hustler*'s "Asshole of the Month," Oprah Winfrey will have the honors next time (and they did, in consecutive months, in 1995).

What Kipnis calls *Hustler*'s grossness could also be characterized as an ingenious deployment of white trash sensibilities. Don't look to this magazine for the kind of witty and bitter barbs that issue forth from the mouths of Brecht's working-class antiheroes. When *Hustler* maneuvers into class position, it stations itself firmly on the bottom of the sociocultural chain of being. Its deliberately stupid humor, its savaging of middle-class and professional codes of decorum, its raunchiness and sluttiness all scream white trash. But this kind of lumpen bawdiness is not unique to *Hustler*. It pervades contemporary mass-commercial porn as well as the entire history of U.S. porn production, far more so than does the "classier" tone of *Playboy* and *Penthouse*.

To me and to the students in a course I teach on pornography as a popular American film genre, the most striking feature of the films we survey, beginning in 1896, is the ubiquitous use of humor, and not just any kind of humor, but bawdiness, humorously lewd and obscene language and situations.[8] From the 1910s to the late 1960s the predominant form of pornographic film was the short, usually black-and-white, anonymously produced film known variously as the stag film, blue movie, or "smoker," so-called because of the smoke-filled rooms where men would gather for clandestine screenings organized by itinerant projectionists. In a recent sympathetic evaluation of Linda Williams's *Hard Core: Power, Pleasure, and the "Frenzy of the Visible,"*[9] the (yes, I'll say it) *seminal* book on pornographic film, Peter Lehman worries that she misses some crucial aspects of porn by overestimating the importance of narrative structure and neglecting the role of "fleeting moments of humor in porn."[10] His argument about the relatively greater importance of "fragmentary pleasures" over narrative resolution is persuasive but his assessment that there are only "fleeting" moments of humor in porn falls short. Stag films are full of humor, and the narrative, which, as Lehman notes, is often more vignette than fully developed story, is itself structured like a joke. And here we are talking about really bad jokes, ranging from terrible puns to every form of dirty joke—farmer's daughter, traveling salesman, and Aggie jokes. Of course not all of the sexually explicit films of this period exhibited the bawdy, farcical character of the stags. The short peep show loops consisted of earnestly direct views of sexual action with little set-up and no story. But the majority of the few hundred American stag films made for collective male viewing depended on this popular brand of humor. This is especially the case with the pre–World War II films that were made on the edges of the entertainment world and thus shared the qualities of both burlesque and silent film comedy.[11]

Given the enormous success of the feminist antiporn movement—and their strange bedfellows, the religious right—in shaping the current prevailing idea of porn as nothing but the degradation of women and the prurient documentation of the most horrific forms of violence waged against women, it may be difficult to recognize that the tone of pornography—when one actually looks at it—is closer to *Hee Haw* than Nazi death camp fantasies. Also difficult to recognize because it so goes against the contemporary typification of porn as something *done* to women, is that the joke is usually on the man. And if the man is the butt of the joke, this also contradicts Freud's description of the mechanism of the smut joke, in which any woman present at the telling of the joke is inevitably its butt.

On the Beach (a.k.a. *Getting His Goat*) is a classic stag film from 1923 that illustrates both the kind of humor and the level of commentary on masculinity found in the typical stag film of the era. The narrative is that of a practical joke, played on a hapless man. The man (Creighton Hale, better known as the professor in D. W. Griffith's *Way Down East*) is daydreaming while leaning on a fence at the beach. "Idylwild Beach," the intertitle tells us, "Where the men are idle and the women are wild." He spies three playful, laughing women who disrobe to go for a swim, and steals their clothes. The women agree to have sex with him to get their garments back, but only if he forks over money and has sex with them through a hole in the fence. The punning alternate title of the film tells you what's coming next: what the man believes is "the best girl I've ever had" is a goat the women back up to the hole in the fence. The women take all his money, which he happily gives, and prance away down the beach. At some unspecified time later, the three women reappear. On spotting the erstwhile daydreamer, one tucks a pillow under her dress to simulate pregnancy, and the women again extract money from the bewildered man, once more "getting his goat." The women in the film are not portrayed as motivated by some intrinsic female evil but rather a kind of charming mischievousness, and the man is shown deserving what he gets because of his sexual and social ignorance. "Watch your step. There's one born every minute," says the final intertitle in a cautionary address to the male audience not to be fools to their own desires.

The low-level humor of many stag films can be traced back to the bawdy songs and dirty jokes that inspired them. If Linda Williams's breakthrough was to get us to think of pornographic film as *film*, that is, as a genre that can be compared to other popular genres like the Western, the science-fiction film, the gangster film, or the musical (porn's closest kin, she says), and studied with the same analytical tools we take to the study of other films, the next logical step, it seems, would be to consider pornographic film as popular culture. We would then be able to ask what traits pornographic film shares with the production and consumption of a whole range of popular forms.

Reading through Ed Cray's *The Erotic Muse: American Bawdy Songs*, it is striking to see, for example, the similarity between the lyrics of the dirty song tradition and the plots of stag films. Anticlericalism is big, of course, in both bawdy songs and porn films, as it is in the endlessly recyclable joke, "Did you hear the one about the priest and the rabbi . . ." Cray tells us that songs about licentious ecclesiasticals were so popular that English obscenity law evolved from court actions to suppress them.[12] In the several versions of the bawdy song "The Monk of Great Renown," the monk engages in rape, anal intercourse, and necrophilia. The somewhat tamer stag films that I have seen prefer to attack the hypocrisy of the clerical class by having the priests and the nuns get it on in all sorts of combinations. Most of the anticlerical films were imports from France or other heavily Catholic countries, except for the classic *The Nun's Story* (1949–1952). The American stag films preferred to mock the mores of the professional classes, which were depicted as exploiting professional power for sexual purposes, in films such as *The Casting Couch* (1924), *The Dentist* (1947–1948), *Doctor Penis* (1948–1952), and *Divorce Attorney* (1966–1967).

Surprisingly (although why should it be?), stag films also share with bawdy songs an emphasis on female agency, with the woman both initiating sex and setting the terms for the sexual encounter. In "The Tinker" and related bawdy songs, the housewife cajoles the workingman into having sex with her and then all the other women in the house, but turns on the tinker when he decides to screw the butler too. In one stag film from the late 1910s or early 1920s (that looks like a French import) two women undress, drink wine, and fondle each other. One says to the other, "I brought Jacques," and straps on a dildo. A few moments later an intertitle tells us that the hairdresser is at the door. One woman fellates the hairdresser while he works on the other woman's hair and then they pull him into a three-way. In another film of the same period two women are out mushroom-hunting in the woods and come across a penis poking through the underbrush. They examine the penis with a magnifying glass before deciding that they've discovered a new species of mushroom. An intertitle tells us that "the mushroom was enjoyed in all kinds of sauces" and we then see the two women, and the naked man revealed to be attached to the penis, in various combinations. In *Goodyear*, from the 1940s, a man and a woman are sitting on a couch and the woman pulls a condom out of her bag and demonstrates its use to the man. After a blow job, intercourse, and another blow job, the woman flips the man's limp penis from side to side, shaking her head with disappointment. In *The Wet Dream*, from the Horny Film Corporation (1935–1945), the woman in the man's dream won't let him get on top after she's been on top of him. He finally does manage to get on top but only after she has put a French tickler on him, presumably for her pleasure. This film also ends with the woman's disappointment with the man's now completely limp penis. In one of the best known stag films of all time, *Smart Aleck* (1951) with Candy Barr, she refuses to go down on the man, especially when he starts to force her. She gets up in disgust and calls a female friend who does want to have oral sex with the man. While that's going on, Candy gets back into the scene to get the man to go down on her. Here, like the lady in "The Tinker," it is the woman who orchestrates the sexual activity.

Another important trait shared by the bawdy song and the stag film is the theme of the penis run amok. Such penises appear, for example, in meldings of the bawdy ballad and the sea shanty, where you get descriptions like "With his long fol-the-riddle-do right down to his knee" (Cray 1992, 35) or "Hanging down, swinging free. . . . With a yard and a half of foreskin hanging down below his knee" (36). The Tinker rides to the lady's house "With his balls slung o'er his shoulder and his penis by his side" (31) but gets in trouble by fucking the butler when he is supposed to be fucking all the ladies and, in another variant, fucks the Devil. Wayward and wandering giant organs abound in everything from fraternity songs, such as "Do Your Balls Hang Low?" to cowboy and Vietnam-era lyrics about efforts to exert some control over the penis, such as "Gonna Tie My Pecker to My Leg" (192–193, 336–337).

Animated films of the stag era, unconstrained by physical reality, were able to depict the run-amok penis better than live action films. *Buried Treasure* (ca. 1928–1933) features Everyready Hardon. Poor Everyready's penis runs off on its own, gets bent and has to be pounded back into shape, goes after a woman but accidentally fucks a man, and runs into the business end of a cactus, among other, often painful, mishaps. In *The Further Adventures of Super Screw* (also ca. 1928–1933) the hero's penis is so big that he must drag it along on the ground, where it gets bitten by a dog and then run over by a bus. While his gargantuan penis is in a sling at the hospital a nurse decides to cut it down to size. After they have ribald sex, he goes into the lab and starts screwing a chimp who impales him on its own giant penis. After returning to the operating room to get his penis restored to its original dimension, he finds an ape to screw. Since the producers and consumers of these films were unquestionably male, the ubiquity of this theme of male humiliation demands to be accounted for in some way.

Laura Kipnis points out that in *Hustler*, as we have seen in the films, jokes, and songs noted above, sex is an arena of humiliation for men, not domination and power over women: "The fantasy life here is animated by cultural disempowerment in relation to a sexual caste system and a social class system" (Kipnis 1992, 383). Rather than offering the compensatory fantasy found in the more upscale *Penthouse* and *Playboy*, where the purchase of pricey consumer goods will ensure willing women and studly men, *Hustler* puts into question a male fantasy that represents power, money, and prestige as essential to sexual success, which "the magazine works to disparage and counter identification with these sorts of class attributes on every front" (383). *Hustler* puts the male body at risk, Kipnis says, which helps to account for its focus on castration humor and ads that are addressed to male anxieties and inadequacies, such as ads for products promising to extend and enlarge penises. *Hustler* and other deliberately trashy magazines (my favorite is *Outlaw Biker*)[13] are the print progeny of the stag films and related forms of smutty folklore.

Ed Cray underestimates the centrality of bawdy humor to the porn film when he contrasts what he sees as the lack of prurience in folk balladry to the dearth of humor in pornography. Although he recognizes that folk balladry can easily veer toward the pornographic and does so often, he is not as ready to acknowledge that pornographic titillation can incorporate bawdiness; "pornography is rarely humorous" (Cray 1992, xxviii), he says. But ribald humor is equally important to the two forms and, moreover, bawdy songs are often much wilder sexually than porn films. Only the animated films can play with the kind of hyperbolically exaggerated body parts and wildly impossible sexual positions that are a staple of the bawdy song. It would be more accurate to say that both popular forms are fundamentally based in a kind of humor that features attacks on religion (and, later, the professional classes), middle-class ideas about sexuality, trickster women with a hearty appetite for sex, and foolish men with their penises all in a twist, when those penises work at all.

It is illuminating to see which forms or figures from popular culture are cited in the stag films to reinforce these themes. The sound track added on to *The Casting Couch* is a recording of Mae West's riff on the importance of education, where she gives a man a lesson in mathematics: "Addition is when you take one thing and put it with another to get two. Two and two is four and five will get you ten if you know how to work it." Subtraction is when "a man has a hundred dollars and you leave him two." Another film of the same era, *The Bachelor Dream*, ends with a shot of *Mad Magazine*'s mascot, Alfred E. Neuman.

While it is true that stag films borrowed heavily from the oral culture of joketelling, it is also important to note that the films were themselves oral culture in the way they were consumed by male audiences. The American Legionnaires, Shriners, Elks, Dekes, and Kappa Sigs counted on the films' humor to help them manage a relation to the sex on screen and to each other, a kind of "comic relief" regulating the guilt and discomfort of the viewing. No film exists without its audience, but the stag film especially so because the backtalk and verbal display sparked by the film is an integral part of the film experience. Thomas Waugh's history of gay male photography and film briefly suggests that such humor may have appealed to gay men in the audiences as well, even though it has long been recognized that the linguistic antics surrounding the films traditionally functioned to shore up the homosocial heterosexuality of the audiences against any hint that a bunch of men looking at penises together were gay.[14] Waugh thinks it would be a stretch to claim that stag film humor reflects a gay camp sensibility but he does believe that "the stag film's coy mixing of levels of cultural affectation with sexual innuendo and vulgarity would not have fallen on deaf gay ears" (Waugh 1996, 320). If Waugh found few gay male films among the stag films he researched, he still thinks it is possible that gay pleasures were nonetheless to be found in both the straight stag films and the oral culture in which they were embedded.

Although porn is usually conceptualized and debated as a stigmatized "other," completely beyond the moral and cultural pale, its desires, concerns, and uses are not that different from those found in other popular forms throughout U.S. history. Here, I took the example of bawdy songs but those other forms include the dirty jokes told everywhere, every day in offices, on playgrounds, and now in faxes and on the Internet. Folklorists like Alan Dundes and Gershon Legman tell us that smutty joketelling is the warp and woof of American working life, a kind of humor that is a major form of symbolic communication that expresses and forms our changing ideas and anxieties about a number of issues but especially sexuality and the relations between the sexes.[15] Other closely related popular forms are *America's Funniest Home Videos, Mad Magazine*, and World Wrestling Federation wrestling, which, like porn, is a physical contact sport requiring a similar suspension of disbelief.

When my course on pornographic film was protested by the local antiporn group (based in local churches) and Pat Robertson in a *700 Club* special on godlessness in public schools, it became clear that my critics' biggest fear was that studying pornography as film or popular culture would normalize it. That's why Pat Robertson called my course "a new low in humanist excess" right after making the wonderfully curious statement that "a feminist teaching pornography is like Scopes teaching evolution."[16] And if the antiporn people have been following the culture wars, they would also know that another danger lurked for them beyond the threat of normalization: the risk that scholars who take popular culture seriously might start asking of porn what they ask of all other forms of popular culture. These questions would include "What is the nature of the widespread appeal?" "To what pleasures and ideas do these films speak?" "What desires and anxieties do the films express about identity, sexuality, and community, about what kind of world we want to live in?" "What kind of moral, social, and political counterculture is constituted by the producers and consumers of porn?"[17] If the study of porn as film and popular culture reframes it as a relatively normal and socially significant instance of culture, this goes a long way toward disarming those who depend on its typification as sexual violence to crack down on moral and political dissidence. But enough of cracking down, let's get back to the issue of cracking up.

The bawdy humor, at the expense of the man, tends to drop out of porn films only during the so-called golden age of 1970s big-budget, theatrically released, feature-length narrative films like *Behind the Green Door, Inside Misty Beethoven, The Resurrection of Eve*, and *The Story of Joanna*. In an era in which the makers of adult films were trying to respond at once to the sexual revolution, Women's Lib, and the possibility of expanding their demographics beyond the raincoat brigade and fraternal lodge members, the narratives began to center, albeit very anxiously, around the woman and her sexual odyssey. While there are some eruptions of egregious punning and willfully vulgar humor in these "quality" films meant for the heterosexual dating crowd (for example, Linda's friend in *Deep Throat* who asks the man performing cunnilingus on her while she leans back and puffs away on a cigarette, "Do you mind if I smoke while you eat?"), they are far more "tasteful," even pseudo-aristocratic, in their demeanor and depicted milieu than the great majority of films of the earlier stag era. But the stag films, which Linda Williams characterizes as lacking in narrative and more misogynistic in their "primitive" display of genitals and sexual activities than the golden age pornos, may not be as misogynistic as Williams says if they can be recognized more as strong popular joke structures than weak film narratives.

What I have observed is that as porn films "progressed" as film, technically and narratively, and began to focus on the woman and her subjectivity, they became more socially conservative as they lost the bawdy populist humor whose subject matter was so often the follies and foibles of masculinity. And while it is true that stag films usually just peter out, so to speak, without any narrative closure, such closure may not be so desirable. Most of the golden age pornos have closure, all right: like Hollywood films they end in marriage or some other semi-sanctioned kind of coupling, while the stag films are content to celebrate sex itself without channeling it into the only socially acceptable form of sexual expression, heterosexual monogamous marriage. It may also be that insofar as the golden age films focus on women's sexuality and subjectivity, the pat solution of the marriage ending may have been an attempt to resolve anxieties those films inadvertently raised in the course of a narrative about women's new sexual and social freedoms.

Fortunately, in the 1980s and 1990s, porn films got trashy again as producers threw off the "quality" trappings of the golden era to start manufacturing product for the rapidly expanding VCR market. Suddenly, many more people, women included, could consume porn and many more people could produce it, even those who lacked money, technical training, or a sense of cinema aesthetics. Sure, there are always going to be pretentious auteurs in porn as everywhere else, such as Andrew Blake and Zalman King, but during this period amateur filmmaking ruled. So popular were amateur films that the professional adult film companies started making fake amateur films, "pro-am," in which recognizable professionals, even stars, would play ordinary folks clowning around the house with their camcorder, or were paired with amateur "video virgins." As porn became deliciously trashy again, it coincided with a new female media deployment of white trash sensibilities against the class and sexual status quo not seen since the goddesses of burlesque reigned. Roseanne, Madonna, Courtney Love, Brett Butler, and Tonya Harding would certainly be on the list but it should be extended to include some significant male talent.

Howard Stern and Mike Judge (the creator of *Beavis and Butthead*) would have to be ranked among the most ingenious of such deployers, with *Saturday Night Live*'s Wayne and Garth in the running, but not really, because their raffishness is shot through with too much redeeming sweetness. All of these white trash theorists and practitioners understand the politically strategic value of making a spectacle of masculinity. Jeff ("You're a Redneck If . . .") Foxworthy, offers, by comparison, just a soft celebration of hick manhood.

When James Garner called Howard Stern "the epitome of trailer trash," Stern responded, in his typically scatological fashion, "I can't believe this guy wants a war with me. He should be busy worrying if he's gonna have a solid bowel movement." We know, of course, from Stern's now two best-selling memoirs that neither his parents nor his own Long Island suburban family live in a trailer. His nontrash origin goes to show that you do not have to be white trash to use white trash sensibilities as a weapon of cultural war, although the fact that white trash's rocket scientist, Roseanne, grew up so solidly trashy, reinforces the argument that early training counts. In a real shocker, feminist artist and critic Barbara Kruger came out as a Howard Stern fan and defender, on the cover of *Esquire* no less, claiming that his

sharp, extemporaneous brand of performance art, his unrelenting penchant for "truth"-telling, serves as a kind of leveler: a listening experience that cuts through the crap, through the deluded pretensions of fame, through the inflated rhetoric of prominence. . . . Zigzagging between self-degradation and megalomania, political clarity and dangerous stereotyping, temper tantrums and ridiculously humble ingratiation, he is both painfully unsettling and crazily funny.[18]

One feminist friend who is a longtime admirer of both Kruger's art and her critical writing expressed dismay and disappointment that Kruger could defend such a sexist, racist, homophobe. Is this postfeminism ad absurdum, she wondered? A couple of weeks after the shock of seeing Kruger's *Esquire* article, my friend called to tell me that she had been up late the night before and channel-zapped into something called "The Lesbian Dating Game." As she was marveling at the funniest, most nonjudgmental representation of lesbians she had ever seen on television or in the movies, she was chastened to realize that she was watching—and loving—the Howard Stern show.

Laura Kipnis argues that *Hustler* publisher Larry Flynt's obscenity trials did more to ensure First Amendment protection for American artists than any of the trials prosecuting much more culturally legitimate works of art and literature. In the same vein, Howard Stern's trashiness does more to counter the angry white men of America's airwaves (and elsewhere) than any liberal commentator because his target is precisely that masculinity that perceives itself to be under attack from all sides, a masculinity no longer sure of its godgiven privilege and sense of entitlement that was for so long the taken-for-grantedness of law, government, and religion. Stern puts his body on display, phobic, farting, flailing, a male body lashing out at all the feared others—women with beauty, smarts, and power; strong, sexually confident blacks; those men with the kinds of superior qualities that attract women but who willfully choose to be gay. He also makes it clear that he wants more than anything to be those others and to *be with* them. Feeding his hysteria, then, is his not having a clue how to pull that off. Who, after all, wants a skinny, neurotic (if not psychotic) white guy "hung like a pimple"? *This* angry white man gives us a brilliant daily demonstration of what that anger is all about. Rush Limbaugh and his ilk dress up their anger in the trappings of a (male) rationality and knowledge. Howard Stern needs all the trailer trashiness he can muster to cut through the false decorum of that unexamined fury.

Beavis and Butthead, too, have never lived in a trailer but they did burn down a trailer park. And the shabby den in which they watch TV makes Roseanne's house look like an Ethan Allan showroom. All of the pundits and parents who worry about kids mimicking these two delinquents have either never watched the show or have no idea of the way kids watch TV. Instead of simply modeling themselves after Beavis and Butthead, kids use these cartoon lumpen to teach themselves a very important social fact: that the only people who get to be that stupid and live are white guys, and they just barely do. A sure sign that *Beavis and Butthead* detractors do not know the show itself is that they never mention the role of Daria (called "Diarrhea," of course, by Beavis and Butthead). Daria is the smart, hardworking little girl who knows that she can't afford to be stupid and is more often than not the audience for the boys when they are variously humiliated by their out-of-control bodies or their sudden recognition of the limits of their stupidity.

Although the use of gross, dumb humor has been heavily censored in the television version of *Beavis and Butthead*, the two boys' trashiness still thrives in the album and comic book format. In *The Beavis and Butthead Experience* they get to play air guitar with Nirvana, sing along with Cher, and party on the Anthrax tour bus. The point of their greatest abjection comes when a member of Anthrax shows Beavis and Butthead some girly photos and Beavis runs off to the bathroom with them, where it becomes apparent to Butthead and the band members that Beavis does not know the difference between shitting and coming. The more you get to know of Beavis and Butthead, by the way, the more you realize that Butthead has a tad more IQ points than Beavis, of both the intellectual and emotional kind. The relatively (only relatively) greater awareness of Butthead means that he is often able to offer a critical perspective on their polymorphously perverse antics, to a lesser extent than Daria, of course, because he is, after all, a full participant in them.

For example, in the second issue of the Beavis and Butthead comic book the two young chicken-chokers decide that it would be cool (that is, not suck—see Lévi-Strauss, Bourdieu) to sneak into the morgue of a funeral home. The following dialogue ensues:

BUTTHEAD: Whoa! Huh-Huh-Huh Look at all th' stiffs? They're . . .

BEAVIS: . . . NAKED! Heh-Heh-Heh Yeah . . . there's one stiff on that slab . . . and one in my pants. Heh-Heh

BUTTHEAD: Uhhh . . . I'm afraid I've got some bad news for you,

BEAVIS: . . . Huh-Huh These are all naked GUYS!

BEAVIS: Oh . . . Heh-Heh Yeah, I forgot! Heh-Heh

Beavis's sexual orientation is only one of many things he can't quite keep track of and Butthead is always there, not to straighten him out, but to remind him of the price to pay if he fails to achieve standard issue masculinity, as if Butthead has a chance himself. If Howard Stern takes on the psychopathology of angry white men, Mike Judge addresses the panicky arrogance of these horny pale adolescents as they try to figure out what they are entitled to, as white guys, even though they know (or Mike Judge and we know) that they have zip going for them other than what used to be the automatically privileged white guy status. Where Beavis and Butthead fail is that they don't even know how to work the one advantage they sort of have. They also are not capable of noticing when Judge throws in their path a way out, a possible ally, but Beavis and Butthead fans do.

The first story, "Dental Hygiene Dilemma (Fart 1)" (March 1994), of the first *Beavis and Butthead* comic starts off with an extended homage to feminist performance artist and NEA Four member Karen Finley. The two boys pull up their bikes to a small store called Finley's Maxi-Mart that seems to sell only yams, recalling the yams that the artist stuffed up her vagina in one of her many performances on the powerful desires of women and the social and psychical wounds inflicted on their bodies. Beavis and Butthead cheat an elderly man, a customer at Finley's Maxi-Mart, out of his money and his yams. "Diarrhea" walks by (perfect timing) and chides the boys for their cruelty while explaining the idea of karma to them, trying to get them to understand that their stupid actions will have consequences for them later.

Mike Judge would have been even more appreciative of Finley's strategies for attacking the sexual and social status quo if he had known then the details of the second censorship scandal she would be involved in. In early 1996 Crown Publishers canceled its contract to publish Finley's decidedly Beavis and Butthead–like parody of domestic tastemaker Martha Stewart's *Living Well* when they found it just too gross with its tips on coffin building, rude phone calls, and cuisine that mixes Oreos, Ring Dings, and beer. For Valentine's Day, Martha Stewart recommends choosing chocolate with care, since taste varies considerably: "Choose Valbrona chocolate from France or Callebaut from Belgium." Finley, of course, is almost as well known for smearing chocolate on her nude body as for the yam insertion trick. Crown, also Martha Stewart's publisher, decided that graciousness and grossness do not mix.[19]

Jesse Helms is more right than he knows when he calls Karen Finley's work "pornographic," because so much of the sensibility of her performances and writing, like that of Howard Stern and Mike Judge, arose from the porn world's now decades-long use of such trashy, militantly stupid, class-iconoclastic, below-the-belt humor. But my interest here isn't to demonstrate porn's trickle-up influence on art and media even if it is illustrative to chart just how large that influence is.[20] Rather, I want to show that the male popular culture that is pornography is a vital source of countercultural ideas about sexuality and sexual roles, whether those ideas are picked up by the more legitimized areas of culture or not.

One of contemporary porn's most brilliant organic intellectuals has to be Buttman, John Stagliano, the white trash Woody Allen, who has made a score of films documenting Buttman's travels and travails as he goes around the world (and Southern California) seeking the perfect shot of a woman's perfect ass. Buttman, played by Stagliano himself, gets mugged, evicted, bankrupted, rejected, and ridiculed, all in his single-minded quest for perfection. Licking ass, caressing ass, ogling ass, and only occasionally fucking ass, if the woman insists, Buttman does for anal fetishism what Woody Allen does for neurosis, and it's not always a pretty picture. In thrall to his obsession, things get even worse when he doesn't stay true to his own fetishistic commitments. In *Buttman's Revenge* (1992), the erstwhile ass worshiper falls on hard times after foolishly trying to branch out by making a disastrous "tit film." No longer a star, his business associates and friends reject him and he ends up living on the street, although they later relent and help him with his comeback by surprising him with Nina Hartley, celebrated for having the most beautiful ass in the business. As in so many of the stag films, the man, this time Buttman, is the butt of the joke.

In *The Hearts of Men* Barbara Ehrenreich constructs a history of male rebellion against the status quo from the Cold War era through the 1970s, and men's production and consumption of porn deserves a place in that history.[21] The gray flannel rebels, the Playboys, the beats, the hippies, all tried to conceive of less restrictive versions of masculinity, ones not subject to the alienation of the corporate world, alimony-hungry wives, dependent children, monogamy, or mortgages. Ehrenreich appreciates the impulse fueling much of this masculine refusal but faults all of the various strategies for either disregarding or blaming the woman. When we put porn into this history we find a male popular culture that, by contrast, neither disregards nor blames the woman in its attempt to renegotiate the sexual and social status quo, a male popular culture that devotes itself—to a surprising degree—to examining the hearts of men. What's in the hearts of men according to porn? A utopian desire for a world where women aren't socially required to say and believe that they don't like sex as much as men do. A utopian desire whose necessary critical edge, sharpened by trash tastes and ideas, is more often than not turned against the man rather than the woman.

How else to explain that *John Wayne Bobbitt: Uncut* is practically a feminist chef d'oeuvre? The year 1995 was a glorious one for the white trashing of porn, to which much credit must first be given to Tonya Harding. The porn industry couldn't resist re-creating Tonya's story again and again, including circulating the wedding night videos that her ex-husband put up for sale to the highest bidder. Of the several porn takeoffs of the scandal on ice, the best has to be *Tanya Hardon*, which revels in "Tanya à la Cardigan"'s trashiness over and against "Nancy Cardigan"'s pseudo upperclassness. Tanya and her husband Jeff shove empty beer cans off the kitchen counter to fuck while planning how to wreck Nancy's skating career with a blow to the knee. Although one could point out how reminiscent this scene is of Roman Polanski's brilliant rendering of the eroticism of the Macbeths' roll in the marital bed as they plot the killing of the king, that wouldn't be the point now, would it? *Tanya Hardon* celebrates Harding's white trash verve over Kerrigan's refined pathos ("Why *me*, why *me*?") but also the whole genre's love of white trash sensibilities to deflate upper-class pretensions and male vainglory. In the best scene in the film, which has fairly high production values for an adult film—there are even insert shots of a skating rink—Tanya has stolen Nancy's boyfriend and is sharing him with another skater in the rink's dressing room, when Nancy walks in on the threesome. Aghast yet riveted, she blurts out, "Why *not* me, why *not* me?" but Tanya is so mean that she won't let Nancy join in. Jeff, of course, is dead meat by this time, having hooked up with the Beavis and Butthead of henchmen to carry out the knee-whacking operation.

Former porn star Ron Jeremy's direction of *John Wayne Bobbitt: Uncut* is the epitome of how white trash can be deployed to criticize male attitudes and behavior. Given the chance to tell "his own story," the on-camera Bobbitt doesn't realize that the film is telling a story about his story, and it's not flattering. The deeply dim ex-Marine, called Forrest Stump by *Esquire*, narrates and reenacts the night his wife, Lorena, cut off his penis and doctors labored for nine and a half hours to reattach it. The ever-so-slightly fictionalized aftermath of the surgery shows women everywhere, from Bobbitt's hospital nurses to the porn stars he meets because of his new celebrityhood, avidly pursuing sex with him to find out if "it really works." It sort of does.

Early on in the video we see Bobbitt and his buddies at a nude dance club, drinking beers and ogling the performers. When he arrives home, late and drunk, and falls into bed, Lorena (played by Veronica Brazil) is already asleep after a hard day's work at the nail parlor. He climbs on top of his sleepy wife who rouses only to complain about the late hour and his drunkenness and to tell him clearly that she doesn't want to have sex with him. He pays no attention to her refusal, screws her for a few seconds, and then, just as Lorena is starting to wake up and get into it, falls off and passes out. The unhappy and sexually frustrated Lorena muses to herself for a while before leaving the bed to get a knife. Standing over her unconscious husband, she tries repeatedly to wake him, to get him to respond to her needs, before she resorts to cutting off his penis in despair at his insensitivity and inattentiveness. (Because contemporary porn won't show even a hint of violence, we get no special effects of the penis being cut off but only, hilariously, a shot of her hand clutching the severed penis and the steering wheel as she flees the house in her car.)

Although the film offers a sometimes disparaging portrait of Lorena—for example, showing her stealing money from her boss at the nail parlor—the film's sympathies are with the wife whose husband thinks marital rape is how a man has sex with his wife. The more we see of John on screen, the more we hear his attacks on Lorena and his rationalizing of the faults in their marriage, the deeper a hole he digs for himself. Julie Brown's 1995 HBO spoof of "Lenora Babbitt" was, by contrast, much less sympathetic to a Lorena it portrayed as entirely unreasonable in her demands for mutual sexual satisfaction. So, too, Brown's companion spoof of "Tonya Hardly" exhibited little of the affection for the skater's trashiness found in *Tanya Hardon*. In both HBO stories it's the women who get their comeuppance, not the men. Also to be noted is that Julie Brown's version, the supposedly more progressive, even avant-garde rendering of these characters and events, offers a racial stereotyping of Lorena—Carmen Miranda with a blade—much more blatant than anything found in the porn version.

Radical sex writer Susie Bright says she can't believe John Wayne Bobbitt lets this video be shown because it demonstrates for all the world to see that "this man does not know how to give head to save his life," and indeed he doesn't.[22] Nor is he good at much else. In one unscripted scene in the film where two women are laboring mightily to get John hard, without much success, and he seems to be tentatively trying out cunnilingus, Ron Jeremy walks into the scene and begins expertly giving head to two other women that he has brought onto the set. Lore has it that Bobbitt did not know that the director was going to put himself into the movie; he certainly didn't know Jeremy's plans for shamelessly upstaging him, the supposed hero of this video. Next, and in pointed contrast to Bobbitt's scarce tumescence (his two fluffers are clearly flagging at this point) Jeremy whips out his own much larger and fully functioning penis, which he applies immediately, and again expertly, to the female talent. Jeremy may have lost his porn star looks, staying behind the camera these days for good reason, but here he reappears on screen to make a pedagogical point, to remind us that porn's expertise, what it promises to teach viewers, is good sexual technique.

What's the moral of *John Wayne Bobbitt: Uncut* for men? If you don't learn better sexual technique and start being more sensitive to your partner's needs, you're going to get yours cut off too, and, what's more, you'd deserve it! Who would have thought that the porn industry would give us the 1990s version of Valerie Solanas's *SCUM Manifesto*, brilliantly disseminated in the form of a tacky, low-budget (by Hollywood standards) video sold and rented to millions of men?

That tackiness also takes aim at Hollywood. The center of commercial adult film production is North Hollywood and Northridge, making those two shabby cities the tinny side of Tinseltown. The adult industry so loves producing knockoffs of Hollywood films that it is impossible to keep track of all of them. The knockoffs can't be intended simply to ride the coattails of popular Hollywood films because most consumers know that the porn version seldom has much to do with the themes, characters, and events found in the original film. What is more likely, as Cindy Patton says of films such as *Beverly Hills Cocks, Edward Penishands*, and both gay and heterosexual versions of *Top Gun (Big Guns)* is that they are meant as "an erotic and humorous critique of the mass media's role in invoking but never delivering sex."[23] I would add the gay male film *The Sperminator* to her list because of the way it rewrites *The Terminator* to expose the closeted homoeroticism of so much Hollywood film (Kyle Reese and John Conner get together to "sperminate" the Sperminator). In the new videos, Patton says, types of sex are rarely presented as taboo in themselves, only as representationally taboo—what Hollywood or television is unwilling to show. With Hollywood under attack by the family values crowd and liberals and conservatives alike clamoring to V-chip to death television's creativity (the industry having immediately caved in), porn and its white trash kin seem our best allies in a cultural wars insurgency that makes camp in that territory beyond the pale.

NOTES

1. In *Roll, Jordan, Roll: The World the Slaves Made* (New York: Vintage, 1972), Eugene D. Genovese argues that white trash folks have no culture of their own because it is entirely borrowed from poor blacks. He, too, as I did, claims that the everyday lives of poor blacks and poor whites are very similar, and were so even during the period of slavery. But he credits those similarities to a massive poor white appropriation of black culture, seeing in white trash culture a

degraded version of black food, religion, and language. He even says that white trash folks lacked the desire for literacy and education that was so strong in black culture. Genovese would not, then, buy my argument, admittedly a slightly tongue-in-cheek one, that growing up white trash offers one of the best possible preparations for a theoretical and political engagement with the world. To do so he would first have to acknowledge the productively creative hybridity of white trash culture in its exchange with black culture, and the corresponding capacity for white trash social agency, both of which he disavows in his book. Genovese does, however, have a fascinating and persuasive account of the origins of "white trash" as an epithet. He believes black slaves derived the term, but their hostility toward poor whites was fostered by wealthy landowners wanting to prevent any interracial unity that might be turned against a system that oppressed both blacks and whites. Like the epithet "fag hag," then, it is meant to drive a wedge between natural allies.

2. Lynn Hunt, ed., *The Invention of Pornography: Obscenity and the Origins of Modernity, 1500–1800* (New York: Zone, 1993).

3. Robert Darnton, *The Literary Underground of the Old Regime* (Cambridge, Mass.: Harvard University Press, 1982).

4. Walter Kendrick, *The Secret Museum: Pornography in Modern Culture* (New York: Viking, 1987).

5. Edward de Grazia, *Girls Lean Back Everywhere: The Law on Obscenity and the Assault on Genius* (New York: Random House, 1992).

6. Andrew Ross, *No Respect: Intellectuals and Popular Culture* (New York: Routledge, 1989). Judith Walkowitz, *Prostitution and Victorian Society: Women, Class, and the State* (New York: Cambridge University Press, 1980).

7. Laura Kipnis, "(Male) Desire and (Female) Disgust: Reading *Hustler*," in *Cultural Studies*, ed. Lawrence Grossberg, Cary Nelson, and Paula Treichler (New York: Routledge, 1992), 373–391.

8. I teach the course on pornographic film in the Film Studies Program at the University of California, Santa Barbara. I would not have been able to put together a historical survey of the genre without the help of the Institute for the Advanced Study of Human Sexuality in San Francisco, which provided many of the films and much needed historical information on producers, venues, and collateral industries such as magazine publishing and sex toy manufacturing.

9. Linda Williams, *Hard Core: Power, Pleasure, and the "Frenzy of the Visible,"* 2nd ed. (Berkeley and Los Angeles: University of California Press, 1989). Thanks very much to Linda Williams and the students in her fall 1995 "Pornographies On/Scene" class at UC–Irvine, where I first tried out the arguments in this essay that I had been developing with my students at UC–Santa Barbara.

10. Peter Lehman, "Revelations about Pornography," *Film Criticism* (1995): 3.

11. The figures on the number of stag films are understandably not as reliable as one would want. At this point I am relying on the fact that the few researchers on the stag film are all using approximately the same figures, which are based on Ado Kyrou's "D'un certain cinéma clandestin," *Positif* nos. 61–63 (June–August 1964): 205–223; and Al Di Lauro and Gerald Rabkin's *Dirty Movies: An Illustrated History of the Stag Film, 1915–1970* (New York: Chelsea, 1976). Di Lauro and Rabkin base their figures on their own viewings in Europe and America; Kyrou, on the Kinsey collection, Scandinavian catalogues from the 1960s and early 1970s, and the catalogue listings of a private collector who did not want his identity revealed. Thomas Waugh says these figures match what he has found thus far: "The corpus of the stag film seems to include about two thousand films made prior to the hardcore theatrical explosion of 1970, of which three quarters were made after 1960. Of the group made prior to World War II, which is the present focus, I have found documentation for only about 180, about 100 American, 50 French, plus a sprinkling of Latin American, Spanish, and Austrian works." *Hard to Imagine: Gay Male Eroticism in Film and Photography from Their Beginnings to Stonewall* (New York: Columbia University Press, 1996), 309.

12. Ed Cray, *The Erotic Muse: American Bawdy Songs*, 2nd ed. (Urbana: University of Illinois Press, 1992), 40. Cray does not neglect women's talent for bawdiness. He collects, for example, the songs known among sorority women as the "rasty nasty," with lyrics that celebrate the women's nastiness and sluttiness, such as "We Are the Dirty Bitches" (351–352). For further evi-

dence of this talent he refers the reader to Rayna Green's "Magnolias Grow in Dirt, The Bawdy Lore of Southern Women," *Southern Exposures* 4, no. 4 (1977).

13. Thanks to Deborah Stucker for her analytical insights on *Outlaw Biker* and its role in the creation of a lumpen or working-class sexual and social counterdiscourse for women and men.

14. Waugh, *Hard to Imagine*, 319–320.

15. Alan Dundes and Carl R. Pagter, *Urban Folklore from the Paperwork Empire* (Austin: American Folklore Society, 1975) and *When You're Up to Your Ass in Alligators: More Urban Folklore from the Paperwork Empire* (Detroit: Wayne State University Press, 1987). Gershon Legman, *Rationale of the Dirty Joke: An Analysis of Sexual Humor, First Series* (New York: Grove, 1968) and *No Laughing Matter: Rationale of the Dirty Joke—An Analysis of Sexual Humor, Second Series* (New York: Breaking Point, 1975). Carl Hill's *The Soul of Wit: Joke Theory from Grimm to Freud* (Lincoln: University of Nebraska Press, 1993) has a good discussion of class bias in joke theory in chapter 7, "At Witz End," where he shows Freud's (failed) attempt to separate the high-minded Witz from the lowly Komik.

16. The special on godlessness in public schools was broadcast during April 1993.

17. For a discussion of pornography as a moral counterculture, see Paul R. Abramson and Steven D. Pinkerton, *With Pleasure: Thoughts on the Nature of Human Sexuality* (New York: Oxford University Press, 1995), especially chapter 7, "Porn: Tempest on a Soapbox."

18. Barbara Kruger, "Prick Up Your Ears," *Esquire*, May 1992, 95. A slightly different version of the article appears in Kruger's collection of essays, *Remote Control: Power, Cultures, and the World of Appearances* (Cambridge, Mass.: MIT Press, 1994), 25–30.

19. "What Is a Book Publisher to Do When a Parody Hits Home?" *New York Times*, February 12, 1996, C1, C4.

20. For porn's influence on contemporary art, see Carla Frecerro, "Unruly Bodies: Popular Culture Challenges to the Regime of Body Backlash," *Visual Anthropology Review* (Fall 1993): 74–81 (on Madonna and 2 Live Crew); Elizabeth Brown, "Overview of Contemporary Artists Interacting with Pornography," lecture for the Sex Angles Conference, University of California, Santa Barbara, March 8, 1996; and Linda Williams, "A Provoking Agent: The Pornography and Performance Art of Annie Sprinkle," in *Dirty Looks: Women, Pornography, Power*, ed. Pamela Church Gibson and Roma Gibson (London: British Film Institute, 1993), 176–191.

21. Barbara Ehrenreich, *The Hearts of Men: American Dreams and the Flight from Commitment* (New York: Doubleday, 1983).

22. Susie Bright made this comment in "Deep Inside Dirty Pictures: The Changing of the Guard in the Pornographic Film Industry and American Erotic Spectatorship," a lecture she gave at a conference on "Censorship and Silencing: The Case of Pornography," at the University of California, Santa Barbara, November 5, 1994.

23. Cindy Patton, *Fatal Advice: How Safe Sex Education Went Wrong* (Durham, N.C.: Duke University Press, 1996).

WORKS CITED

Cray, Ed. *The Erotic Muse: American Bawdy Songs*. 2nd ed. Urbana: University of Illinois Press, 1992.

Kipnis, Laura. "(Male) Desire and (Female) Disgust: Reading *Hustler*." In *Cultural Studies*, ed. Lawrence Grossberg, Cary Nelson, and Paula Treichler, 373–391. New York: Routledge, 1992.

Waugh, Thomas. *Hard to Imagine: Gay Male Eroticism in Film and Photography from Their Beginnings to Stonewall*. New York: Columbia University Press, 1996.

Laura Kipnis

How to Look at Pornography

Pornography grabs us and doesn't let go. Whether you're revolted or enticed, shocked or titillated, these are flip sides of the same response: an intense, visceral engagement with what pornography has to say. And pornography has quite a lot to say. Pornography should interest us, because it's intensely and relentlessly *about* us. It involves the roots of our culture and the deepest corners of the self. It's not just friction and naked bodies: pornography has eloquence. It has meaning, it has ideas. It even has redeeming ideas. So what's everyone so wrought up about?

Maybe it's that buried under all the nervous stereotypes of pimply teenagers, furtive perverts in raincoats, and asocial compulsively masturbating misfits, beneath all these disdainful images of the lone pornography consumer, is a certain sneaking recognition that pornography isn't just an individual predilection: pornography is central to our culture. I'm not simply referring to its immense popularity (although estimates put its sales at over $11 billion a year). I mean that pornography is revealing, and what it reveals isn't just a lot of naked people sweating on each other. It exposes the culture to itself. Pornography is the royal road to the cultural psyche (as for Freud, dreams were the route to the unconscious). So the question is, if you put it on the couch and let it free-associate, what is it really saying? What are the inner tensions and unconscious conflicts that propel its narratives?

Popularity doesn't tell you everything, but it can tell you a lot. Like the Hollywood blockbuster or other cultural spectacles, what transforms a collection of isolated strangers with different lives, interests, and idiosyncrasies into a mass audience is that elusive "thing" that taps into the culture's attention, often before it's even aware that that's where its preoccupations and anxieties are located. Audiences constitute themselves around things that matter to them, and stay away in droves when no nerve is struck. Behind mass cultural spectacles from *Jurassic Park* to Ross Perot to the O. J. Simpson trial or any other spectator attraction, what commands our attention, our bucks, our votes are the things that get under our skin, that condense and articulate what matters to us. I want to suggest however, perhaps somewhat perversely, that the endless attention pornography commands, whether from its consumers *or* its protesters (who are, if anything, even more obsessed by pornography than those who use it), has less to do with its obvious content (sex) than with what might be called its political philosophy.

From *Bound and Gagged: Pornography and the Politics of Fantasy in America*. Durham: Duke University Press, 1999: 161–178. Reprinted by permission of the author.

When writing about the pornography of the past, whether visual or literary, scholars and art historians routinely uncover allegorical meanings within it, even political significance. The question of how its content relates to its social moment and historical context supersedes questions about whether it should or shouldn't have existed, or how best to protect the public from offense to their sensibilities. Historians have made the case that modern pornography (up until around the nineteenth century) operated against political and religious authority as a form of social criticism, a vehicle for attacking officialdom, which responded, predictably, by attempting to suppress it. Pornography was defined less by its content than by the efforts of those in power to eliminate it and whatever social agendas it transported.[1]

Even knowing this, it seems quite impossible to begin to think about contemporary pornography as a form of culture, or as a mode of politics. There's zero discussion of pornography as an expressive medium in the positive sense—the only expressing it's presumed to do is of misogyny or social decay. That it might have more complicated social agendas, or that future historians of the genre might generate interesting insights about pornography's relation to this particular historical and social moment—these are radically unthought thoughts. One reason for this lacuna is a certain intellectual prejudice against taking porn seriously at all. Those who take pornography seriously are its opponents, who have little interesting to say on the subject: not only don't they seem to have spent much time actually looking at it, but even worse, they seem universally overcome by a leaden, stultifying literalness, apparently never having heard of metaphor, irony, symbolism—even fantasy seems too challenging a concept.

I've proposed that pornography is both a legitimate form of culture and a fictional, fantastical, even allegorical realm; it neither simply reflects the real world nor is it some hypnotizing call to action. The world of pornography is mythological and hyperbolic, peopled by characters. It doesn't and never will exist, but it does—and this is part of its politics—insist on a sanctioned space for fantasy. This is its most serious demand and the basis of much of the controversy it engenders, because pornography has a talent for making its particular fantasies look like dangerous and socially destabilizing incendiary devices.

Sweating naked bodies and improbable sexual acrobatics are only one side of the story. The other is the way pornography holds us in the thrall of its theatrics of transgression, its dedication to crossing boundaries and violating social strictures. Like any other popular-culture genre (sci-fi, romance, mystery, true crime), pornography obeys certain rules, and its primary rule is transgression. Like your boorish cousin, its greatest pleasure is to locate each and every one of society's taboos, prohibitions, and proprieties and systematically transgress them, one by one.

As the avant-garde knew, transgression is no simple thing: it's a precisely calculated intellectual endeavor. It means knowing the culture inside out, discerning its secret shames and grubby secrets, and knowing how to best humiliate it, knock it off its prim perch. (To commit sacrilege, you have to have studied the religion.) A culture's pornography becomes, in effect, a very precise map of that culture's borders: pornography begins at the edge of the culture's decorum. Carefully tracing that edge, like an anthropologist mapping a culture's system of taboos and myths, gives you a detailed blueprint of the culture's anxieties, investments, contradictions. And a culture's borders, whether geographical or psychological, are inevitably political questions—as mapmakers and geographers are increasingly aware.

Pornography is also a form of political theater. Within the incipient, transgressive space opened by its festival of social infractions is a medium for confronting its audiences with exactly those contents that are exiled from sanctioned speech, from mainstream culture and political discourse. And that encompasses more than sex. Our legacy of Puritanism makes sex a vehicle for almost anything subject to repression and shame: sex becomes a natural home for all forms of rebellion, utopianism, flaunting, or experimentation. Like adolescents who "use" sex to express their rebellion, anything banished from social sanction can hitch its wagon to sex and use pornography as a backdoor form of cultural entrée. (Of course, that any kind of social rebellion is instantly dismissed as adolescent is indicative of how shaming and silencing tactics are employed to banish a vast range of meanings. Which is precisely why pornography becomes such a useful vehicle for hurtling those meanings back into view.) Pornography has many uses beyond the classic one-handed one.

Like the avant-garde's, pornography's transgressions are first of all aesthetic. It confronts us with bodies that repulse us—like fat ones—or defies us with genders we find noxious. It induces us to look at what's conventionally banished from view. Pornography is chock full of these sorts of aesthetic shocks and surprises. Here's another one: in a culture that so ferociously equates sexuality with youth, where else but within pornography will you find enthusiasm for sagging, aging bodies, *or* for their sexualization? There is indeed a subgenre of porn—both gay and straight—devoted to the geriatric. The degree of one's aesthetic distress when thumbing through magazines with titles like *40+*, with its wrinkly models and not-so-perky breasts, or *Over 50*, with its naked pictorials of sagging white-haired grandmothers (or the white-haired grandfathers of *Classics*, with their big bellies and vanishing hairlines, and, turning the page, the two lumbering CEOs in bifocals and boxer shorts fondling each other), indicates the degree to which a socially prescribed set of aesthetic conventions is embedded in the very core of our beings. And our sexualities.

It also indicates the degree to which pornography exists precisely to pester and thwart the dominant. The vistas of antediluvian flesh in *Over 50*, or its features like "Promiscuous Granny," counter all of the mainstream culture's stipulations regarding sex and sexual aesthetics. One may want to argue that these subgenres of pornography simply cater to "individual preferences" or to dismiss them as "perversions," depending on how far you carry your normativity. But for the individual viewer, it's not just a case of different strokes for different folks. Pornography provides a realm of transgression that is, in effect, a counter-aesthetics to dominant norms for bodies, sexualities, and desire itself. And to the extent that portraying the aging body as sexual might be dissed as a perversion (along with other "perversions" like preferring fat sex partners), it reveals to what extent "perversion" is a shifting and capricious social category, rather than a form of knowledge or science: a couple of hundred years ago, fat bodies were widely admired.

Why a specific individual has this or that sexual preference isn't my concern here, in the same way that why Mr. Jones is or isn't a sci-fi fan isn't the concern of a popular-culture critic. What the cultural critic wants to account for is the "why" behind forms of fandom, and behind the existence of particular genres of popular culture, and to distill from them the knowledge they impart about the social: she might say, for example, that sci-fi is a genre in which anxieties about human possibilities in the context of expanding science and out-of-control technologies can be narratively articulated. We know, or learn, certain things about ourselves because we find them registered in our cultural forms. So, too, with the existence of these variegations within pornography. What shapes these subgenres—their content, their raw materials—are precisely the items blackballed from the rest of culture. This watchfully dialectical relation pornography maintains to mainstream culture makes it nothing less than a form of cultural critique. It refuses to let us so easily off the hook for our hypocrisies. Or our unconsciouses.

The edges of culture are exquisitely threatening places. Straddling them gives you a very different vantage point on things. Maybe it makes us a little nervous. (And what makes us nervous makes us conservative and self-protective.) Crossing that edge is an intense border experience of pleasure and danger, arousal and outrage—because these edges aren't only cultural: they're the limits that define us as individuals. We don't *choose* the social codes we live by, they choose us. Pornography's very specific, very calculated violations of these strict codes (which have been pounded into all of us from the crib) make it the exciting and the nerve-wracking thing it is. These are the limits we yearn to defy and transcend—some of us more than others, apparently. (And of course taboos function to stimulate the desire for the tabooed thing *and* for its prohibition simultaneously.)

The danger and thrill of social transgression can be profoundly gratifying or profoundly distasteful, but one way or another, pornography, by definition, leaves no social being unaffected. Why? Because pornography's very preoccupation with the instabilities and permeability of cultural borders is inextricable from the fragility and tenuousness of our own psychic borders, composed as they are of this same flimsy system of refusals and repressions. Pornography's allegories of transgression reveal, in the most visceral ways, not only our culture's edges, but how intricately our own identities are bound up in all of these quite unspoken, but quite relentless, cultural dictates. And what the furor over pornography also reveals is just how deeply attached to the most pervasive feelings of shame and desire all these unspoken dictates are. Pornography's ultimate desire is exactly to engage our deepest embarrassments, to mock us for the anxious psychic balancing acts we daily perform, straddling between the anarchy of sexual desires and the straitjacket of social responsibilities.

Pornography, then, is profoundly and paradoxically social, but even more than that, it's acutely historical. It's an archive of data about both our history as a culture and our own individual histories—our formations as selves. Pornography's favorite terrain is the tender spots where the individual psyche collides with the historical process of molding social subjects.

This may have something to do with the great desire so many pornography commentators have to so vastly *undercomplicate* the issue, to ignore studiously the meanings that frame and underlie all the humping and moaning. It's as if they're so distracted by naked flesh that anything beyond the superficial becomes unreadable, like watching a movie and only noticing the celluloid, or going to the revolution and only noticing the costumes. It is not *just* sex, *just* violence, *just* a question of First Amendment protection. It's exactly because the experience of pornography is so intensely complicated and fraught with all the complications of personhood, in addition to all the complications of gendered personhood, that pornography is so aggravating. It threatens and titillates because it bothers those fragile places. It tickles our sensitive spots. Tickling is in fact one of the categories of pornography that's particularly interesting in this regard. Why is there a variety of pornography devoted to the experience of tickling, being tickled, and, especially, being tickled against one's will?

Of course, neither the culture nor the individual have had their particular borders for very long. These aren't timeless universals. The line between childhood and adulthood, standards of privacy, bodily aesthetics, and proprieties, our ideas about whom we should have sex with, and how to do it—all the motifs that obsess pornography—shift from culture to culture and throughout history.

The precondition for pornography is a civilizing process whose instruments are shame and repression. One of pornography's large themes is that we're adults who were once children, in whom the social has been instilled at great and often tragic cost. (And by definition incompletely, if you follow the Freudian understanding of the unconscious as a warehouse for everything that's repressed in the process of becoming a social being—for example, wanting to fuck your parents.) Of course, one major thing our society doesn't want to contemplate in any way, shape, or form is childhood sexuality. If you regard pornography in these somewhat more complicated terms (that is, if you start out from the presupposition that it *has* cultural complexity), then many of its more exotic subgenres may start to seem a little less peculiar, particularly since so many of them—from your standard bondage and dominance to the slightly more kinky terrain of spanking and punishment, to the outer frontiers of diapers and infantilism—seem such evident, belated, poignant memorials to the erotics of childhood.

In *Strictly Spanking*, an array of fairly ordinary-looking men and women get what's coming to them, and good. The spanker is always a woman. (Mother-dominated child-rearing *is* the norm in our society.) A frilly yellow dress is hiked up to reveal the red flush of recently spanked buttocks; a scary Joan Crawford–ish suburban matriarch is poised to do some serious damage to your posterior with the business end of a hairbrush; you're forced to bend over a pillow and get a good thrashing for whatever naughty thing you did. The standard poses include naked and facing the corner, garments around the ankles, or bent over the disciplinarian's knee. Hairbrushes, paddles, and switches are the preferred disciplinary apparatuses. You've been bad and need to be punished. You can almost hear the running commentary under the sound track of rhythmic thwacking: "This hurts me more than it hurts you," "When will you ever learn?" "Clean up your goddamn room!" There's no particular mystery about the origin of the erotics of humiliation.[2]

I mentioned tickling. In "A Plume for the Pledge," the lead feature in the premiere issue of *Tickling*, we're introduced to Tess and Helen: "Tess waits patiently—though a bit on the nervous side. Helen, a junior, knows that a feather can hurt more than a paddle. . . . It's initiation time on campus. The pledges are going through Hell Week. Paddles have been outlawed, but the university authorities forgot that tickling can be the most excruciating form of punishment." Let's think about the tone of this for a minute—after all, it's not exactly high realism. There's a certain knowingness about the enterprise: the creation of a fantasy scenario with stock elements. Two interchangeable twentyish ponytailed blondes in white underwear inhabit the living room of Sorority House, USA. Helen holds the pledge's hands behind her back, tickling the bottoms of her feet mercilessly with feathers. Soon the underwear comes off, and the tickling continues. Twenty black-and-white pictures of the same two girls, the same scene, the same feather, with minor variations. A few closeups on feet. A rope is produced; now Tess is tied down—she doesn't seem to mind, though, she's laughing away. A few photos catch Helen looking a little pensive, maybe a bit melancholy, but she quickly returns to her usual fun-loving self and it's just another gigglefest at Delta Gamma.

What sort of homage is this? As psychoanalyst Adam Phillips points out, "A child will never be able to tickle himself. It is the pleasure he can't reproduce in the absence of the other. The exact spots of ticklishness require—are—the enacted recognition of the other. To tickle is above all to seduce, often by amusement."[3] For Phillips, this would seem to be something of a memorial to childhood seduction, but seduction in the sense that we all crave it: as a form of attention and recognition. And perhaps, in the case of tickling, one charged with erotics as well. It's this erotic component of childhood that's routinely censored and goes widely undiscussed. Phillips points out that psychoanalysis too is essentially a theory of censorship—a catalogue of materials that are repressed and not allowed into consciousness. Pornography, which as we see covers quite a similar terrain (which is what makes psychoanalytic theory such a useful explanatory device for it), is similarly subject to the wrath of censors—both internal and state—border police both. Tickling is one of those permeable borders: between play and sex, between sadism and fun, certainly between adult and childhood sexuality.

This border between childhood and adulthood is both the most porous and the most zealously patrolled, which may be why a magazine like *Diapers* is so consternating—even though it's just a series of pictorials of a winsome young man, maybe late twenties, but dressed throughout in extra-large Pampers, rubber pants, and a succession of pretty bonnets and frocks. Speaking of censorship, it's interesting to note that when Freud's notorious quote, "Anatomy is destiny," is cited, it's invariably employed to refer to the differences between male and female sex organs, and to taunt Freud for his always-lurking misogyny. But Freud actually used this quote (a paraphrase from Napoleon) twice, and the other reference is to the psychological consequences of nature's weird decision to put the sex organs and elimination functions into the same "neighborhood," as Freud so charmingly puts it.[4] His point is that this proximity has a series of affective consequences: from the disgust that so often seeps over into sex to the child's sexual arousal during parental hygiene ministrations. There are certain things we just don't want to know about ourselves, and about our formations as selves. These seem to be precisely what pornography keeps shoving right back at us.

Well, if you want to go around in diapers, why not just do it in the privacy of your own home, or under your rock? Why do these people have to parade their squalid little obsessions in front of the rest of us? One reason is that pornography would be nowhere without its most flagrant border transgression, this complete disregard for the public/private divide. Flaunting its contempt for all the proprieties, it's this transgression in particular that triggers so much handwringing about the deleterious effects on society of naked private parts in public view. These deeply held standards of privacy of ours are, of course, relatively recent, historically speaking. They're a modern invention, tied to the rise of the middle class, the invention of the modern autonomous individual, and the consequent transformations of daily life into an elaborately complicated set of negotiations between body, psyche, and the social. Equally modern, and perhaps even more relevant, are the corresponding inventions of sexual and bodily functions as sites of shame and disgust, which arise simultaneously, around the early Renaissance, further fueling the necessity of privacy.[5]

But this public/private boundary is ever shifting. In fact, it's flip-flopping so fast these days it's hard to keep up, and it's precisely these shifts that form the subtext of so much else that's disturbing the cultural equilibrium: for example, the recent focus on the pervasiveness of incest and domestic violence, privacy rackets both. This question of privacy is by no means a simple one. Pornography is often cited, by antiporn feminists, as a causal factor in many bad things that happen to women. But the fact is, these domestic abuses depend completely on the protections of privacy (which is clearly not the Arcadia pornography's critics would have us believe), whereas pornography's impulse is in the reverse direction: toward exposure, toward making the private public and the hidden explicit. Given the kinds of power abuses that privacy so usefully shields, and the social changes that exposure can, at times, engender, the privacy/publicity opposition doesn't have any clear heroes.

What's often referred to as the tabloidization of American culture also reflects shifting standards of public and private. When lower-middle America takes to the airwaves to brandish the intimate details of their lives—their secret affairs, their marital skirmishes, their familial contretemps—and talk show guests duke it out on air, high-minded critics invariably respond with contemptuous little think pieces snorting about what bad taste this all is. But taste is a complicated issue, and the history of the concept is entirely bound up with issues of social class and class distinctions.[6] "Keeping things to yourself," the stiff upper lip, the suppression of emotions, maintenance of propriety and proper behavior, and the very concept of "bad taste" are all associated historically with the ascendancy of the bourgeoisie and their invention of behaviors that would separate themselves from the noisy lower orders. All of our impulses (and snobbery) about what should be private or what shouldn't be public are enormously complex, historically laden cultural machinery. Given that all these public/private dilemmas are intricately connected to governing affects of deep and overwhelming shame and embarrassment, our immediate impulses and our "taste" aren't always the most reliable indicators of anything but obedience to a shifting set of conventions, whose purposes we're constitutionally disinclined to question, as *Hustler* makes so clear.

This recent dedication to exposure and propriety violations, this "tabloid sensibility" that seems to now dominate American cultural life, may not be unrelated to the economic decline that has forced downward mobility down the throats of a once economically optimistic Middle America. If a lifetime of hard work is no longer any guarantee of financial security—of a home, or continued employment, or a pension—and if upward aspirations now look like so much nostalgia for earlier times, why adopt the deportment or the sensibility of the classes you can't afford to join? Class, after all, isn't simply a matter of income, or neighborhood. It's also embedded in a complex web of attitudes and proprieties, particularly around the body. (This is something "Roseanne" viewers know all about.)

Pornography, of course, dedicates itself to offending all the bodily and sexual proprieties intrinsic to upholding class distinctions: good manners, privacy, the absence of vulgarity, the suppression of bodily instincts into polite behavior. It's not only porn's theatrics of transgression that ensure its connotation of lowness, it's also pornography's relentless downward focus. This is one explanation for why pornography doesn't appear ripe for serious critical interpretation. Imagine culture as a class system, with the "top" of culture comprised of rarefied, pricey, big-ticket cultural forms like opera, serious theater, gallery art, the classics, the symphony, modernist literature. Moving down a bit you get your art house and European films; down a bit more, public television, Andrew Lloyd Webber, and other middlebrow diversions. If you keep moving on down through the tiers of popular culture—down through teen-pics, soap operas, theme parks, tabloid TV, the *National Enquirer*, Elvis paintings on velvet—then right down at the very bottom rung of the ladder is pornography. It's the lowest of the cultural low, on perpetual standby to represent the nadir of culture, whenever some commentator needs a visible cultural sign to index society's moral turpitude.

But let's be honest about this cultural hierarchy. If pornography is at the bottom of a cultural class system whose apex comprises the forms of culture we usually think of as consumed by social elites with deep pockets—after all, take a look at the price of an opera ticket, or at the clothes at the opening night of the symphony—then questions of social class seem to lurk somewhere quite near all this distress over pornography. If culture is grouped along a hierarchy from high to low, and the rest of our social world is grouped along a hierarchy from high to low, then this puts pornography into analogy with the bottom tiers of the social structure. This isn't to suggest that the "lower classes" are pornography's consumers, but that insofar as porn is relegated to a low thing culturally, it takes on all the *associations* of a low-class thing.

Take the dual associations antipornography feminists make between pornography and violent male behavior. It hardly needs saying that the propensity to violence is a characteristic with strong class connotations—you might even say stereotypical connotations. A propensity to violence is in opposition to traits like rationality, contemplation, and intelligence, which tend to have higher-class connotations: the attributes associated with the audiences of higher cultural forms like theater or opera. The argument that pornography causes violent behavior in male consumers relies on a theory of the porn consumer as devoid of rationality, contemplation, or intelligence, prone instead to witless brainwashing, to monkey-see/monkey-do reenactments of the pornographic scene. This would be a porn spectator who inherently *has* a propensity to become violent (not presumably the members of the Meese Commission, who spent years viewing pornography without violent consequences). Maybe it becomes clearer how fantastical this argument is when you consider how eagerly we accept the premise that pornography causes violence—and are so keen to regulate it—compared to the massive social disinclination to accept that *handguns* cause violence (and it's certainly far more provable that they do): guns, without the same connotation of lowness, don't seem to invite the same regulatory zeal, despite a completely demonstrable causal relation to violence.[7]

The fantasy pornography consumer is a walking projection of upper-class fears about lower-class men: brutish, animal-like, sexually voracious. And this fantasy is projected back onto pornography. In fact, arguments about the "effects" of culture seem to be applied exclusively to lower cultural forms, that is, to pornography, or cartoons, or subcultural forms like gangsta rap. This predisposition even extends to social science research: researchers aren't busy wiring Shakespeare viewers up to electrodes and measuring their penile tumescence or their galvanic skin responses to the violence or misogyny there. The violence of high culture seems not to have effects on *its* consumers, or rather, no one bothers to research this question, so we don't hear much about how *Taming of the Shrew* expresses contempt for women, or watching *Medea* might compel a mother to go out and kill her children; when a South Carolina mother did drown her two kids in 1994, no one suggested banning Euripides. When Lorena Bobbitt severed husband John's penis, no one wondered if she'd recently watched Oshima's *In the Realm of the Senses*, the Japanese art film where a male character meets a similar bloody fate. Is that because the audiences of Euripides and Oshima have greater self-control than the audiences of pornography and other low culture, or is this a class prejudice that masquerades as the "redeeming social value" issue?

The presumption that low cultural forms are without complexity is completely embedded in media effects research. I was quite startled to read that one of the country's leading pornography researchers routinely screens the notorious sexploitation movie *I Spit on Your Grave* as an example of sexual violence against women, then measures male audiences for mood, hostility, and desensitization to rape.[8] But as anyone who's actually seen this movie knows, it's no simple testimonial to rape. This is a rape-*revenge* film, in which a female rape victim wreaks violent reprisal against her rapists, systematically and imaginatively killing all three, and one mentally challenged onlooker—by decapitation, hanging, shooting, and castration. Film theorist Carol Clover, who does see low culture as having complexity, points out that even during the rape sequence, the camera angles force the viewer into identification with the female victim.[9] If male college students are hostile after watching this movie (with its grisly castration scene), who knows *what* it is they're actually reacting to? Antiporn activists are fond of throwing around data from social science research to support the contention that pornography leads to violence, but this research is so shot through with simplistic assumptions about its own materials that it seems far from clear what's even being measured. (Or how it's being measured: data collection in sex research based on sexual self-reporting is so frequently unreliable and plagued with discrepancies that researchers resort to cooking the numbers to make them make sense: the general population apparently doesn't report on its sexual experiences in ways that translate into neat statistical columns.[10])

If pornography, too, is laden with complexity and meaning, and even "redeeming value," then the presumption that only low culture causes "effects" starts to look more and more like a stereotype about its imagined viewers and their intelligence, or their self-control, or their values. Pornography isn't viewed as having complexity, because its *audience* isn't viewed as having complexity, and this propensity for oversimplification gets reproduced in every discussion about pornography.

Raising these loathsome issues of class also offers another way of thinking about the current social preoccupation with pornography. This intensified focus on regulating and suppressing the lowest of all low things comes just as the legacy of Reaganomics has been fully realized, as gaps in U.S. income levels between high and low ends of the social spectrum have become the widest in the industrialized West, as middle-class wages are dropping, as the lower classes are expanding *and* becoming increasingly impoverished.[11] A new social compact is being negotiated by the right, with an intensified ideology of distinctions, as those at the bottom end of the class structure (the homeless, the welfare classes, minimum-wage workers) are nonchalantly abandoned to their fates. Shifts in economic ideology require a retooled social conscience, and arguments about culture are one place these new forms of consent get negotiated—and this is the subtext of what's come to be known as the Culture Wars.[12]

Current economic realignments may seem far afield from pornography. But pornography is a space in the social imagination as well as a media form . . . interestingly, the issue of pornography is never very far away from any political argument about culture: it's been an explicit focus of these culture debates the right has been waging over the last ten years [ca. 1996]. What do the Culture Wars stage but a duel between the canon (imagined as the high thing) and pornography (clearly, the low)? Wherever arguments in favor of elite culture are made, they seem unable to resist invoking pornography (or its kissing cousin, masturbation), to represent the dangerous thing that has to be resisted. What this means, of course, is that pornography ends up being spoken about more and more frequently, and becomes ever more culturally indispensable.

NOTES

1. Hunt, *The Invention of Pornography* (Cambridge, Mass.: MIT Press, 1993), 9–45.

2. On the relation of spanking to rhythm, specifically to poetry, see Eve Kosofsky Sedgwick, "A Poem Is Being Written," *Representations* (Winter 1987).

3. Adam Phillips, *On Kissing, Tickling and Being Bored* (Cambridge, Mass.: Harvard University Press, 1993), 9–11.

4. The first quote is in "The Dissolution of the Oedipus Complex" (1924), the second is in "On the Universal Tendency to Debasement on the Sphere of Love" (1912). Both essays can be found in Sigmund Freud, *On Sexuality* (New York: Penguin, 1977).

5. Elias, *The History of Manners* (New York: Pantheon, 1982), 129–169.

6. See Raymond Williams, *Keywords: A Vocabulary of Culture and Society* (New York: Oxford University Press, 1976), 264–266. Elias also has much to say about taste throughout *The History of Manners*.

7. Gunshot wounds are the second leading cause of accidental death in the country after auto accidents, and these deaths have increased by 14 percent over the last ten years. There were 38,317 gunshot deaths in 1991. "Guns Gaining on Cars as Bigger Killer in U.S.," *New York Times*, January 28, 1995.

8. Edward Donnerstein and Daniel Linz, "Mass Media, Sexual Violence and Male Viewers: Current Theory and Research, *American Behavioral Scientist* 29 (May–June 1986), 601–618.

9. Carol Clover, *Men, Women and Chain Saws: Gender in the Modern Horror Film* (Princeton: Princeton University Press, 1992), 139. Clover makes an extended analysis of *I Spit on Your Grave*; I borrowed the term *rape-revenge film* from her.

10. The problem seems to be that men overreport and women underreport sexual activity. In a widely publicized University of Chicago sex survey, 64 percent of male sexual contacts can't be accounted for—or rather, could be accounted for only if in this survey of 3,500 people, 10 different women each had 2,000 partners they didn't tell researchers about. To solve this problem, one statistician suggested eliminating from the data all respondents who reported having more than 20 sex partners in their lifetime; she found if she eliminated all people who said they had more than 5 partners in the last year, the data made more sense. David L. Wheeler, "Explaining

the Discrepancies in Sex Surveys," *The Chronicle of Higher Education*, October 27, 1993, A9. This sounds less like crunching numbers than inventing them.

11. Keith Bradsher, "Gap in Wealth in U.S. Called Widest in West," *New York Times*, April 17, 1995, cites new studies reporting that the wealthiest one percent of Americans now own nearly 40 percent of the national wealth, that the gap between rich and middle classes widened throughout the 1970s and 1980s, just as the new planned welfare cuts and tax breaks for the wealthy will further widen that gap and further impoverish the poor.

12. I've been much helped in thinking about the specifics of current economic shifts and their relation to cultural distinction-making by Roger Rouse's "Thinking Through Transnationalism: Notes of the Cultural Politics of Class Relations in the Contemporary United States," *Public Culture* (Winter 1995): 353–402.

Current Directions

Henry Jenkins

"He's in the Closet but He's Not Gay": Male-Male Desire in *Penthouse Letters*

Two couples get snowed in together.[1] After several bottles of wine, they begin to snuggle together near the fireplace. One thing leads to another and they decide to play a new board game that requires participants to engage in sex acts together. After a series of progressively more heated encounters, the two wives end up going down on each other while the amazed guys stand around and watch. Then, the evening takes an unexpected turn.

> "Do you like what you saw?" Melissa asked after her breathing had slowed down.
>
> "Wow," I said. "I never would have dreamed that you and Jennifer could give us such a show."
>
> "Well," said Jennifer, "the show isn't over yet."
>
> "What do you mean?" Michael asked.
>
> "We want to watch you two do each other," Jennifer said.
>
> "Are you crazy?" Michael asked.
>
> "We want to watch you guys suck each other's prick," Melissa said.
>
> With that, they pushed Michael and me onto the floor. When we landed, Michael's prick was inches from my face. Pre-come leaked out of the tip.
>
> "Go ahead," Melissa said. "Taste it. Please. For me. I want to watch you do Michael with your mouth."
>
> I was so hot at that time, I probably would have done anything Melissa asked. I stuck out my tongue and licked the drop of precome off the tip of Michael's cock. It was a little salty but not bad . . . Melissa took my hand and placed one of my fingers inside her cunt, coating it with her honey. Then she told me to stick the finger inside Mike's ass. . . . When we were finished, the girls came over and thanked us for our little show.

When I first read this scenario in *Penthouse Letters*, my jaw just about hit the floor. I was doing research on "slash," a form of fan erotica, produced and circulated predominantly by women and depicting male television characters having sex with each other.[2] The initial research pondered why straight women got off imagining two men making love. While male interest in female-female scenarios was well established, the reverse situation was less discussed. When I first read this scenario, my first interest was in this acknowledgment that women might desire to watch two male bodies entangled.

And then it sunk in! What was this fantasy doing in a mass market men's magazine in the first place? Wasn't the expression of female homoerotic fantasy really a way to make queer scenarios safe for "straight" male readers?

Since then, I have discovered that male-male[3] scenarios are commonplace in *Penthouse Letters*. In many cases, women are depicted as encouraging, begging, facilitating, and even providing the lubrication for encounters between men. After the fact, they are depicted as offering approval and acceptance for a pretty big step off the straight and narrow. Such a framing provides a context for the male reader (straight, bi, or otherwise) to "safely" engage with an erotic fantasy that took him someplace he "never" imagined going before. After all, we often fantasize about things that we would never act upon and even if we were to act upon such fantasies in reality, they wouldn't really alter our sexual identities. Lots of straight men "experiment" with gay sex and besides, lots of women find it hot. Let's call it what it is—plausible deniability.

We should be surprised that these stories exist at all within what remains a homophobic culture. Most writing about straight male pornography more or less takes for granted that, as Thomas Waugh claims, there is a "rigid taboo on intermale sexuality." So, what are we to make of the persistence of such fantasies in *Penthouse Letters*?[4] Has that taboo become softer, maybe even flaccid, since Waugh's essay was published in 1985, or has male-male desire always been an influence on "straight" porn?

In this essay, I want to look more closely at scenarios in *Penthouse Letters* that deal with male-male sex, hoping to understand what such letters have to tell us about the always unstable relations between straight and queer sexualities. As I do so, I am going to be examining the conventions that shape the publication and their relationship to earlier forms of erotic writing. In many ways, *Penthouse Letters* is anachronistic—in its reliance on words when most contemporary pornography is visual, in the ways it borrows the letter as a narrational device from earlier epistolary fictions, and in the sense that it embraces something of the libertine sexual ideology of its eighteenth- and nineteenth-century predecessors.

Male-male desire is more deeply embedded within the conventions of pornography than most accounts have acknowledged. One reason that this aspect of pornography has received such little attention has been the focus of most scholarship on visual and audiovisual pornography. In the closing section, I consider what happens when *Penthouse Letters* is adopted for video. In watching pornography, we are often so taken with its seeming lack of inhibitions that we overlook what it doesn't show. Examining print-based pornography allows us to see a different set of genre conventions, which operate according to a different sexual logic and constructs a different relationship with its consumers. I am hoping that recognizing the open acknowledgment of male-male desire in literary porn may make us more conscious of its arbitrary absence in audiovisual porn.

Reading *Penthouse Letters*

Initially, the "letters" appeared alongside other letters of comment in the front section of *Penthouse* magazine or, later, in *Penthouse Forum*. The letters were represented as a space where readers could share their erotic fantasies and experiences. Over time, the letters became so popular that the company spun off their own publication, *Penthouse Letters*, which includes more than a hundred scenarios each month. Here, the letters became longer, more vivid, more crafted, and more diverse. These letters are also periodically reprinted in books and for a short time in the early 1990s, the company produced video versions (more on this later).

Here's how the content is described in the front matter of one of the *Penthouse Letters* books:

> Each letter gives you a very descriptive, blow-by-blow (pun intended), detailed encounter as told by the people who lived them. Sex comes to life with each turn of the page. . . . We're confident there's something for everyone. Who knows, you may even find enjoyment in places you never thought to look before.[5]

And then on the back cover:

> You'll thrill to the good fortune of those willing to share the most lurid details of their sexual exploits. Hear readers of the world's most uninhibited and provocative lifestyle magazine talk about sex at its wildest and its hottest in every possible combination and in every imaginable position.

First, this blurb characterizes the content as "real life" rather than fantasy. The magazine presents these letters as if they came from actual readers. Another book jacket pushes the reality claims of the letters further: "You can't make this stuff up! Nowhere is fact more stimulating, more satisfying, and more real than fiction than in the letters to *Penthouse*. Every word is guaranteed true. . . . Checking out other people's mail has become everybody's second favorite turn-on."[6] To maintain the blurring between fact and fiction, each section ends with a call for submissions. For example, here's the invitation following a selection of letters called "Girls & Girls, Boys & Boys": "The letters above are from men and women who have enjoyed the pleasures of same-sex encounters. Is there a similar tale in your personal history of erotic highs? Then let your story be told."[7] The letters include cryptic acknowledgments of the individual contributors and their hometowns (Y.L., Minneapolis, Minnesota), although for many of the more transgressive letters, the name and address are "withheld." It is widely believed, however, that most, if not all, of the letters, are pure fiction, written by inhouse or freelance writers or that minimally, submitted letters undergo dramatic revision to make them consistent with the magazine's fairly well-established conventions. I am treating these letters as fictional and thus subject to genre analysis rather than as ethnographic evidence of *Penthouse* readers' real world sexuality, but to be honest, I can't be 100 percent sure and that's part of the fun.

Second, the magazine stresses diversity. While there is "something for everyone," not every scenario will appeal to every reader. The magazine is a kind of omnibus of sexual possibilities, even though letters tend to be clustered by common themes or fantasies, such as "Crowd Scenes," "Flying Solo," "Domination & Discipline," "Head & Tail," or "Someone's Watching."

Third, *Penthouse Letters* is about transgression and risk-taking. These "sophisticated" scenarios will take readers places they never "thought to look before." To arouse us, each scenario must be "edgy" but not step outside the reader's comfort zone. What the magazine depicts is subject to legal restrictions, which shift due to the unpredictability of local case law. Yet they are also subject to the limits their readers place on the kinds of scenarios they are willing to entertain.

While the promise is "every possible combination," in practice, some combinations recur and others are pushed to the margins. Sometimes, only mild elements of male-male desire enter stories otherwise focused on heterosexual fantasies. Other times, a single letter may appear in a section devoted to various kinks, such as "Different Stokes" or "Carnalcopia." In other cases, there may be a cluster of such scenarios, sometimes mixed with female-female scenarios in a section such as "Girl Meets Girl, Boy Meets Boy" or standing alone under headings like "A Gay Place" or "Suck-A-What?" In many cases, sex between men is limited to mutual masturbation or oral contact, while some letters explore anal penetration. There are many steps forward and backward, as the magazine circles around the problem of representing same-sex desire. Whatever is going on here, it is nothing as simple as a linear progression toward more and more openness in dealing with queer content. If anything, every step into nervy territory is met in the following issue with a hasty retreat back into the safety zone.

The View from the Closet

Before one starts to see the blurring of reality and fantasy in *Penthouse Letters* as another example of postmodernism, keep in mind that a similar claim of authenticity for fictional material surrounded the earliest novels, which often presented themselves as collections of letters or diaries that accidentally fell into the hands of their authors. In *The Rise of the Novel*, Ian Watts suggests the "erotic" possibilities writers like Samuel Richardson achieved through the literary device of intimate and unintentionally exposed correspondence: "The letter form . . . offered Richardson a short-cut, as it were, to the heart and encouraged him to express what he found there with the greatest possible precision, even at the cost of shocking the literary traditionalists. As a result, his readers found in his novels the same complete engrossment of their inner feelings and the same welcome withdrawal into an imaginary world vibrant with more intimately satisfying personal relationships than ordinary life provided."[8]

Although tame by modern standards, Richardson took advantage of what Watts calls a voyeuristic perspective to offer a more intimate glimpse of human sexuality. The use of a first-person voice constructed an unusually close identification between readers and characters, while the writer seemingly removed himself as an intermediary. Referring to *Pamela*, Watts explains, "Richardson's impersonal and anonymous role allowed him to project his own secret fantasies into a mysterious next room: and the privacy and anonymity of print placed the reader behind a keyhole where he, too, could peep in unobserved and witness rape being prepared, attempted and eventually carried out. Neither the reader nor the author were violating any decorum: they were in exactly the same situation as Mandeville's virtuous young woman who exemplified the curious duality of public and private attitudes to sex."[9] Watts describes a different kind of epistemology of the closet than has occupied most queer theorists. He notes that in most Georgian homes, there was a closet or antechamber just outside the bedroom. It was here that most letters were written and most novels were read—tantalizingly close to the bedroom and cut off from other spheres of daily activity. Here, Richardson's readers could become voyeurs not simply to the characters' bedroom activities but also to their subjective experiences as they shared those events with an intimate or reflected upon them in their diaries.

While less inventive than Richardson in exploring the potentials of this form, the *Penthouse Letters* depend on a similar pleasure in watching what people do in their bedrooms and having access to their intimate thoughts. These early epistolary novels often involved multiple characters engaged in correspondence with and about each other. Whom the letter addressed (and what degree of risk of exposure its writing involved) gave these fictional letters much of their charge. *Penthouse Letters*, on the other hand, usually publishes stand-alone letters, offering us only one perspective on the represented actions. While Richardson's letters were private correspondence, these letters are clearly understood as public confessions addressed to other *Penthouse* readers. Only rarely does the magazine examine the motives that might lead the writers to publish such accounts. For example, one letter concludes, "But, Mickey, if you read this (and I'm sure you will), look for the bulge the next time I massage you. Yes, it's there for you."[10] For the most part, they contain no such intimacies, functioning to introduce private sexual experience into the public sphere of magazine readers. These readers are often assumed to include not simply men but also couples; a constant theme is the idea that men and women might use the magazine to open up franker conversations about their erotic desires.

The letter format restricts our understanding and perceptions of the depicted events to what can be known to a single participant. Some writers play with the erotics inherent in not knowing everything that occurred. In "The Party Was a Drag Until They Played the Sex Game, but Who Was His Partner?" the narrator finds himself the "winner" of a sex game.[11] The other party guests blindfold him and then "everybody—men and women"—draw cards to see who will give him a blow job. Unable to see who draws the magic card, he fixates on the risks and possibilities of this situation: "Since there were two guys and three girls, I figured there was a forty percent chance I was about to receive a blowjob from a man. But then I wondered—would Mike really agree to suck my cock? Would Albert? For that matter, I wasn't too sure any of the women would either. But then everybody was pretty drunk now, and after all, rules were rules." As the scene unfolds, the author describes his giddy confusion as multiple people stroke and suck his penis: "A minute later, I felt a big hand rubbing my dick. It felt nice. I tried to think who had big hands. Was it a guy? Then I felt a warm mouth wrap itself around my fully erect cock. It felt great. But who was it?" In the end, the identity of his lovers remains a mystery to us, allowing both the author and the reader a certain degree of plausible deniability. As the scenario climaxes, the writer confesses, "I shot the biggest load of my life into what I have to believe was a female throat." Such an effect may only be realizable in the print medium.

Even in the absence of such overt play with subjectivity, the restricted narration shapes the erotics of reading these letters. Often, the letter writer is female, inviting the magazine's male readers to imagine what sex feels like from the other side of the wet spot, describing, for example, the experience of penetration: "I was beyond ecstasy. I couldn't think anymore. I lost all ability to function—I could only feel and smell sex. I could feel dicks in me, hands and mouths on me, legs and bellies touching me. I felt Frank's body hair on my face and the slick smoothness of Rick's chest on my back. And, oh my god! The delicious smell of sex—the freshness of Frank's deodorant and soap and the sexy aroma of Rick's cologne, all mingled with the smell of their sweat and my pussy juice."[12] While masculinity is heavily marked here, the femininity of the narrator surfaces only in the final words of this passage, allowing male readers who are so inclined to imagine themselves making love to all of those men.

Even in those letters narrated by men, the author spends a great deal of time thinking and talking about the genitalia of any other man involved in the scenario. In a letter aptly titled, "He's in the Closet But He's Not Gay, He's Watching His Wife Do Her Lover," the writer describes this action: "I had a perfect view of Harry's cock penetrating my wife through the slats of the closet door . . . With each stroke he pulled his cock almost all the way out and then jammed it all the way back in, his balls slapping against her asshole as he did."[13] The author is at least as interested in the movement of his friend's cock as he is in his wife's responses. Of course, the image of the man observing from the closet links us right back to Watt's comments about Georgian architecture!

At least one letter writer seems to be self-conscious of the homoerotic implications of these descriptions.[14] A husband and wife agree to try to arouse each other without physical contact between them. The husband cheats by introducing another man in the action, who can touch her without breaking that particular set of rules, and then narrating the action, giving both participants encouragement: "He's got his cock in your hands now, Helen. It's big and really hard. I bet you wouldn't mind sucking on that for a while, would you?" In the process, he becomes strongly identified with his wife's contact with the other man's body as well as fascinated in monitoring and shaping the man's physical responses: "I saw his ass clench five or six times as he shot his load." The author masturbates while watching the scene unfold, laying down on the floor to get a closer look. Here, we have the classic formulation of the fantasy where the author gets to play all the parts—the man, the woman, and himself as spectator.

A Slippery Slope

As this example suggests, the persistent fantasy of sharing spouses or watching another man make love with your partner presents plenty of opportunities for subtle or not so subtle male-male contact. From here, the slope is not only slippery; it is well lubricated. Each scenario involves escalating risks and greater transgressions.

The stakes grow even higher when two men make love to the same woman. While letters that involve two women and one man almost always incorporate some form of female-female contact, many letters involving two men and a woman go to great lengths to keep the men separate. But, this is not always the case. One scenario consistently returns to the homoerotic.[15] As the two men shed their clothes, the narrator explains, "This was the first time I was completely naked in the same room with a guy except at the gym or when I was in the army. I wasn't sure how to feel." His wife alternates licking both of their cocks, with the result that "my cock frequently rubbed against Brad's." As he is giving his wife head, he looks up as Brad's "cock appeared in front of my face, heading for Sandy's pussy" and he continues to lick her. As he explains, "I was so excited, I didn't care that I was licking Brad's cock at the same time." She then insists that they both enter her at once, which produces unfamiliar sensations: "I moved in behind Sandy and eased my cock in her spit-lubricated asshole, feeling Brad's cock rub against mine through the thin membrane separating us." By the end of the scenario, the author is forced to acknowledge that his pleasure was as much in making love with Brad as it was with sharing Sandy: "As I pulled out, I watched my come run onto Brad's balls and mix with his. I have no desire to be with another man, but this was very hot." The woman's role here is reduced to a "thin membrane" that separates the two men, keeping them less than one inch inside hetrosexuality.

The ways the exchange of women solidify homosocial bonds has been a common theme in feminist literary criticism, but seldom is the theme played out with such a literal-mindedness.[16] The women in these stories seem to relish being a vestal that mediates between men. This concept surfaces perhaps most dramatically in scenarios that involve "sloppy seconds," a fantasy that often involves direct contact with the other man's fluids. In various letters, one sees descriptions of kissing a woman shortly after she has given another male partner a blowjob, feeling the warmth and liquid inside her vagina, or licking out all of the deposited substance. In one letter, a man's hunger for more and more "cum" convinces him to hire out his wife as a prostitute so she can harvest a regular supply.[17] The wife willingly goes along with the plan since her sexual appetite cannot be satisfied by only a single man, thus giving a thin veneer of female empowerment.

From here, it is only one small step further to scenarios where the woman acts as a guide and coach while an inexperienced man learns to satisfy his male partner. As the title of one scenario explains, "Thanks to His Girlfriend, He Now Enjoys the Best of Both Worlds."[18] Even when the woman doesn't initiate male-male sex for her husband, there is a good-natured acceptance, as suggested by another title, "That's Odd—My Husband Never Sucks Cock at Home."[19] In one letter, a husband and wife both agree to enact the other's fantasy—in both cases, the fantasies involve watching their partner make love to someone of the same sex.[20] When the man is forced to make good on his agreement, the woman takes a hands-on approach: "Donna brought Tom closer and guided my hand to his dick. . . . She placed her hand over the back of mine and guided it. She started moving my hand slowly, meanwhile bragging about how big his cock was and how good it tasted to her. She brought my other hand up to feel his balls. They were hot and felt odd. . . . After a few seconds, she removed her hand from mine and placed it on the back of my head. She guided it in the direction of Tom's cock, with my mouth positioned near the head." Throughout, the writer disclaims any direct interest but claims to be doing so only to fulfill his wife's fantasy. The climax of the scene comes not when Tom comes but rather when the husband and wife kiss: "I felt closer to her at that moment, when we were sharing another man's come, than I had in a long time."

Here, as in so many of these letters, the long-standing convention of female-female scenes is used to make male-male contact more acceptable. If so often in porn female-female encounters are staged like an erotic dance for male spectators, male-male contact can be understood in very much the same way—as something men do to satisfy the women in their lives. One female character explains, "Men who aren't afraid to touch each other turn me on."[21] And, as these scenarios become better established and thus more tame, the women urge the men toward greater intimacy. In one letter, the wife dares her husband, "I want to see you two fuck! Are you man enough to take it in the ass?"[22]

The Structure of Reassurance

Just as feminist critics have argued that female-female scenarios in porn devalue lesbianism by turning it into heterosexual foreplay, these letters may be said to do the same for gay sex. Yet, here is where the concept of plausible deniability enters the picture. If these letters were truly meaningless to the male readers, they would not exist at all. These letters are designed, in part, to satisfy the curiosity of men who have previously seen themselves as primarily if not exclusively straight. The heterosexual references serve as reassurances that they can entertain such fantasies and still be straight. In some senses, this structure preserves heterosexual privilege but from another point of view. It expands the fluidity of sexual desire, making homosexuality something that is no longer unthinkable. By lowering homophobic panic, such stories create a context where straight men can feel more comfortable with a broader range of sexual identities and experience—at least through their fantasy lives.

In one scenario, a woman comes into the room to find her husband making love to another man. At first, she is angry and confused, forcing him to have anal sex with her using a dildo to see if she can either work it out of his system or share some of the fun. In the process, she realizes that his male-male dalliances do not damage what the two of them have together. The letter concludes, "It seems Sami no longer cares if John and I get it on. In fact, she wants to hide in the closet the next time we do it. I just hope she comes out to play when the action gets hot!"[23] In another, a wife arranges for her husband to get a massage. As the male masseur rubs warm oil into his body, the husband gets turned on and one thing leads to another. To his surprise, he looks up after he climaxes to see his wife standing in the corner. At first, he can't read her response, but then she offers him reassurance: "I now saw that the flush on Christine's face was unmistakingly sexual excitement. This made me feel better as I turned my attentions to the fleshy firmness of Donald's prick."[24] Gay sex is so much more fun when your wife approves!

In the absence of reassuring women, the letter writers often feel compelled to separate sexual acts from sexual identities. Homosexuality becomes something you do, not necessarily something you desire, and almost never part of whom you are. In "The Only Singles Bar He'll Ever Need is Right Between His Legs," the narrator dismisses any meaning the sex act might have other than narcissistic pleasure: "I don't know if your readers will understand this or not, but I don't really have sexual feelings for Joel, no more than I have true sexual feelings for my hand, or for the cantaloupe I jerked off into once at college. I lust after women. I love women. But I also love the feeling of having my hard cocks rubbed, licked or stimulated to orgasm, and I guess it doesn't matter who's doing it. As long as I get off, that's the only important thing."[25] Another letter takes the opposite perspective, seeing sexuality as the logical extension of all forms of emotional attachment:

"First I would like it to be known that I am not gay; in fact, I don't even think I'm bi. I simply have this uncontrollable desire to be intimately close with very good friends, male and female."[26] Either way, whom you have sex with has little or nothing to do with how you conceive your own sexuality. As in the punchline of so many dirty jokes, this isn't what it looks like.

This refusal to label one's sexuality runs through these letters. In a few cases, the narrators ascribe some form of "bi" curiosity to themselves. In most cases, the writer has had little or no previous male-male experiences. The other participant may be gay, but the narrator rarely is. One can see this denial of previous experience as a way of restoring at least temporarily the experience of being a virgin within a body of literature that assumes the protagonists have a long sexual history. Yet, in many cases, it is also a denial of accountability, even a denial of agency. In one improbable letter, a businessman is tricked by a dominatrix to have sex with her boyfriend: "In a sense, it sort of relieved me of the responsibility for what was happening."[27]

In her book of men's erotic fantasies, *Men in Love*, Nancy Friday argues that perhaps the most persistent fantasy involves being released from the responsibility of initiating sexual contact.[28] She argues that in a world where male sexuality has been viewed in ever more problematic terms, men feel ever more anxiety about initiating sexual interactions. Here, the writer often asserts not only that what happened wasn't premeditated but that they have had no prior same-sex fantasies. In a surprising number of the scenarios, sex is initiated while the protagonist is asleep or semi-asleep, with the man getting caught up in a moment of passion as they regain consciousness. The persistence of game scenarios where the random luck of the draw forces two protagonists together or of scenarios involving massage that justify the man's decision to undress and allow another man to have physical contact with him suggest other ways that these stories enable a kind of passive slide into homoeroticism.

A Helping Hand

Friday suggests that straight men's fantasies about gay sex often represent a nostalgic return to a culture of boyhood that allowed a range of accepted forms of male-male contacts precisely because they were seen as sexually innocent: "Goosing each other in the shower, mutual masturbation in the movies, reading dirty books and magazines together when there are no adults around—it's all horsing around, breaking the rules—that's how boys are."[29] Many male fantasies, she suggests, begin with memories of boyhood play carrying over into the adult world. The *Penthouse Letters* often involve the reuniting of boyhood friends for adult sexual encounters. Yet, current child pornography law limits reference to childhood sexuality. It is a wink-wink fiction in all letters that no one ever has sex before their eighteenth birthday. The result is, in this case, incongruous with forms of sexual contact that Friday associates with preadolescence being fondly recalled as occurring in some magic moment after their eighteenth birthday but before they faced sexual taboos. The aptly titled "Rites of Passion, Rites of Spring, Rites of Initiation" begins with this confession: "Growing up together, my best friend Steve and I shared many experiences. When we turned eighteen, these included masturbation. This slowly came to a head as the summer before college wore on. Sometimes, when I was over at Steve's house, we would read his *Penthouse* magazines and beat off." When he visits his friend, Steve, in his college dorm, he discovers that Steve likes to have sex with his roommate. As he confesses to his boyhood friend, soon to be lover, "I always did like to watch you shoot your wad."[30]

These boyhood forms of male bonding surface in other stories that depict men exchanging pornographic stories, working out, sharing rooms and seeing each other step out of the shower, or going skinny dipping together. As one letter matter-of-factly concludes, after a detailed description of mutual oral stimulation around the campfire, "We give male bonding a new meaning. We couldn't be closer friends."[31] In one such story, two businessmen get turned on as one recounts a heterosexual erotic movie he had watched in his room the night before: "Craig's erotic video tale was driving us out of control as well. We had stripped our suits off, and now loosened our ties and unbuttoned our shirts, exposing our hairy chests to the wind." Pulling his penis out of his pants, Craig tells him, "Dude— we're too hot not to play this out."[32] While anonymous sex is frequent in straight scenarios in *Penthouse Letters*, it is much less common in these male-male scenarios. These men count on the help of a good buddy to get them over the hump and into homoeroticism. The title of one such story concisely sums up this basic plot: "Old Friends Meet, Talk About Old Times, Suck a Little Cock . . ."[33] Often scenarios dealing with chance reunions with boyhood friends create a "now or never" context, where having such short time together, they have one and only one chance to fulfill those long-denied fantasies.

Managing Homophobia

Women's slash scenarios often dramatize homophobia as a means of intensifying the emotions that surround the movement from homosocial to homoerotic desire. By contrast, the *Penthouse* letters most often downplay homophobia, depicting the slide into same-sex interplay in matter-of-fact terms, another part of the structure of reassurance that allows such stories to exist. As one writer explains, "I thought, what the hell? I opened my mouth and took the first cock in my life."[34] The sexual intensity of these first-time experiences can be profound. As another letter writer describes it, "He put his hands on my waist and our pricks touched. It felt like a bolt of electricity running through my body."[35] Yet, the participants experience little or no emotional turmoil, seeing the experience as "natural" and pleasurable. Several letter writers suggest that they knew "instinctively" what needed to be done, having received blow jobs from women or having penises themselves.

Of course, in some cases, hints of underlying anxieties surface even as the writer seeks to reassure us about the normality of what he has experienced: "We lay on the bed in a 69 position for several minutes, both of us silently working up the courage to bring our cocks and mouths together."[36] There's nothing politically correct about another narrator's perspective, "For all you guys out there who think homosexuality is just for queenie hairdressers, I want to tell you that you're absolutely wrong. Sexual contact with another human being, no matter what the gender, is a very precious thing. I am 'straight' whatever that means, but I am glad to have had that experience. It stirred me from muscle to marrow, and I'll never forget it."[37] And in a few cases, the encounters force men to overcome deep-seated distastes over the concept of homosexuality, as suggested by the title of one such scenario, "Lifelong Fear of Queers Starts to Crumble In the Back Row."[38] Another letter critiqued the hypocrisy of an outspoken queer basher who likes to get anonymous blowjobs in the "glory hole" of the local adult bookstore.[39] And a third letter poignantly began with the writer's fearful confession, "If anyone around here even suspected I like men, they'd probably lynch me, so I do my best to be discreet about my proclivities."[40]

If homophobia is rarely overtly present, that does not mean that homophobia plays little role in shaping the content. We have already seen the persistent need for female approval and sanction of male-male sex, as well as a range of other strategies designed to give male readers plausible deniability for their enjoyment of these scenarios. While *Penthouse* letters dealing with heterosexuality often take great pleasure in public exposure and exhibitionism, male-male scenarios often require more covertness. Consider how many different ways the writer of this scenario seeks to mask his conduct: "I had asked him to come to the back of my house, which overlooks vacant land, so he would be less likely to be seen by nosy neighbors. . . . I stood up and drew the living room drapes. . . . I spread a large bath towel on the living room floor and lay down on my back."[41] Such precautions are rarely present in heterosexual scenarios, nor are the condoms that figure prominently in a number of the same-sex scenarios. While none of the male-female scenarios ever raised the prospect of sexually transmitted diseases, several male-male scenarios reassure readers that both men had been tested for AIDS before they got into bed together.

To be fair, some of these fears—and the stereotypes about homosexuality they embody—are set up precisely so that they can be dispelled. Another story begins with equally tentative participants: "When we got to his place, he pulled the blinds and sat on his bed. Without a word we took off our shirts, shoes, and socks, and sat there looking, but not looking, at each other, with our pants on but unzipped." Yet, the intensity of their subsequent encounter overcomes any anxiousness, as the young law student wants to come bursting out of the closet: "The entire Bar Association could have walked in at that moment and I wouldn't have cared."[42]

On the other end of the spectrum, there are stories that portray male-male contact purely in terms of degradation. One such story opens with a man's confession that his dick is too small to satisfy his wife. He grants her permission to take in male lovers and he gradually gets drawn into participating in the action—first as a voyeur and then as someone who tongue-washes their genitals before and after sexual contact. Step by step, we watch him get stripped of his manhood until he spends the rest of his life dressed in women's clothing, wearing makeup and toe polish, and waiting on his wife and her lovers all day.[43] Such extreme degradation stands out because it is so rare in the scenarios I have examined. For the most part, male-male contact gets integrated into "healthy" relationships, bringing about a greater equality between man and woman who now share one more thing in common—their love of sucking cocks.

Return to Pornocopia

Carol Queen and Lawrence Schimel have coined the term *pomosexual* to describe the breakdown of established categories of sexual identity in recent years: "The 'pomosexual' . . . may not be tied to a single sexual identity, may not be content to reside within a category measurable by social scientists or acknowledged by either rainbow-festooned gays or by Ward and June Cleaver. Pomosexuality lives in the space in which all other non-binary forms of sexual and gender identity reside—a boundary-free-zone in which fences are crossed for the fun of it, or simply because some of us can't be fenced in. It challenges either/or categorizations in favor of largely unmapped possibility and the intense charge that comes with transgression."[44] For Queen and Schimel, then, pomosexuality may be the most radical sexual category of all—the category that refuses categories, the sexuality that observes no constraints. Such a concept makes sense when talking about the politically self-conscious and avant-garde sexual practices they describe but I am finding it difficult, given all of the hesitation, equivocation, reassurance, and denial in *Penthouse Letters*, to read these scenarios in such revolutionary terms. And I have some difficulty accepting the largely ahistorical belief that pomosexuality represents a departure from all previous forms of sexual identity. The ongoing discourse of "sexual revolution" that has run through these mass market men's magazines since their inception has created a context where erotic fantasy can be valued on its own terms and where readers are perhaps more receptive to scenarios that draw them away from the sexual mainstream. They have thus found a way to expand their conception of heterosexuality to encompass at least some forms of sex between two men.

However, such fantasies have a longer history that does not fit comfortably within the postmodern framework constructed by Queen and Schimel. Just as the narrational structure of the letters imitates, albeit in a more simplified form, the rhetorical structures of the early novel, the scenarios also build upon generic structures borrowed from earlier forms of erotic literature. In *The Other Victorians*, Steven Marcus examines the nature and functions of pornography within mid-nineteenth-century England, and finds there many of the same situations and the same contorted logic found in *Penthouse Letters*. These earlier erotic writings often took the form of personal confessions, journals, or diaries recording the protagonist's sexual exploits, making it difficult to tell what, if anything, was based on real experience as opposed to pure fancy. Writing about *My Secret Life*, a multivolume autobiography of a self-proclaimed "libertine," Marcus writes, "In middle age the author seems to pass through an increase in homosexual tendencies; or to phrase it another way, as his experimentation and freedom of impulse enlarge, he naturally goes in for certain homosexual experiences. . . His homosexual experiences are not 'direct': he almost always has them in concert with a woman so that the woman is there to mediate, as it were, between himself and the other man. . . . He now conceives the desire to have coitus with a woman immediately after another man has had her. Sometimes he desires to see the two in coitus, sometimes he does not. Always, however, he desires to copulate with a woman in another man's semen."[45] Marcus argues that the fantasy of sharing a woman in a threesome represented "the final threshold in pornography" since it was "the last form in which male homosexual play is still disguised in heterosexual activities."[46]

While relatively little overtly and exclusively homosexual material survives from the period, male-male contact was common in porn novels, especially in orgy sequences, which are shaped by what he describes as "a general pansexualized vision."[47] Marcus uses the evocative term *pornocopia* to refer to that "pansexualized" vision. As Victorian pornography reaches its climax, there is often an episode or episodes where all the rules governing normalized sexual relations break down: "All men in it are always and infinitely potent; all women fecundate with lust and flow inexhaustibly with sap or juice or both. Everyone is always ready for anything, and everyone is infinitely generous with his substance. . . . No one is ever jealous, possessive or really angry."[48] Pornocopian narrative equates male-male contact with a general loosening and transgressing of sexual boundaries—the transcending of heterosexuality seen as the ultimate example of someone pursuing pleasure without inhibitions. As a set of generic conventions, however, such stories follow mathematical logic: the action continues until a full range of sexual permutations has been performed.

Consciously or unconsciously, *Penthouse Letters* evokes Marcus's analysis when they label a recurring section of the magazine *carnalcopia*, which contains stories about the most cosmopolitan forms of sexual experimentation. One orgy scenario, aptly named "Bisexual Blowout," concludes with the narrator's somewhat clinical summary of the intense weekend, "I drifted off to sleep in bed with Maggie, Erica, and Tom. Together we spent the next four days sucking and fucking in ever imaginable combination. . . . My exhibitionistic, voyeuristic and bisexual tendencies were all fulfilled."[49] Here's how another letter described a group grope session: "Someone began stroking my cock, but I was too busy watching my beautiful Frannie being fucked by this big stud to take much notice. . . . The hand on my cock had been replaced by a warm, wet mouth. Looking down, I saw that Hans had his lips wrapped around my shaft. He glanced up at me, winked, and then went back to work on my rigid rod. . . . Looking around, I saw that there was a lot of indiscriminate sexual activity going on. Some of the guys were intently watching their buddy fuck Frannie while stroking their own cocks, others were lending a hand or a mouth to the pleasuring of each other. . . . What a day!"[50]

In pornocopia, sex follows its own logic. As Marcus writes, "it is always bedtime."[51] As sensation builds upon sensation, the narrator is so overwhelmed by the experience and spectacle of abundant pleasure that he can literally become indifferent to the gender of the hand(s) stroking him. Marcus similarly stresses this "tendency to abolish the distinctions between the sexes" within Victorian pornography: "clitorises become penises, anuses are common to both sexes, and everyone is everything to everyone else. Yet this everything is confined strictly to the relations of organs, and what is going on may be described as organ grinding."[52]

Pornocopia represents a form of sexuality that, for the most part, only exists through fiction—a particular kind of pornographic space that gives greater license to the imagination of readers and writers alike than they were apt to enjoy in the real world. Because this utopian fantasy exists "no place" (the literal meaning of utopia), what happens there has no impact on one's real world sexual identity. It remains, as Marcus suggests, simply "organ grinding." As is often said about Las Vegas, what goes on there, stays there.

Even so, in almost every orgy scenario in *Penthouse Letters*, gay sex is treated as at once the ultimate transgression and the penultimate pleasure. Sexual acts get organized so that each represents one step farther from normative sexuality. Within that hierarchy, male-male sex represents one step beyond having sex with more than one partner at once and one step beyond female-female sex. In almost every case, however, the final act is heterosexual, suggesting a return to normality, a retreat from the outer limits into something that is seen as more rewarding. With pornocopian fantasy, then, gender breaks down, only to be restored, making the world safe for heterosexuality once again. As always, plausible deniability is maintained and a structure of reassurance dispels any lingering aftertaste. Even within fantasies that are about shattering all limits, there are, after all, limits.

What is titillating about the ambiguous status of all of these letters, diaries, and personal confessions may be the possibility that someone, somewhere, has found themselves in this Brigadoon of erotic desire and carried something back alive into the real world. Such pornography represents the erotic branch of Todorov's the Fantastic, where the reader's relationship to the described event fluctuates between belief and disbelief, with only a "thin membrane" separating the two.[53]

What's Missing from This Picture?

Both Watts and Marcus argue that this epistolary structure could only operate this effectively within literary texts. Watts sees the privacy that surrounded the act of reading as enabling the transgression of norms about what could be discussed in public, suggesting that Richardson could not have entered the closet so fully were he to have created works for the stage. Making such scenarios visible would have made them too public and making them public would have rendered them too literal. There is something in the ambiguities printed texts create that enables a different kind of sexual fantasy.[54]

And that helps to explain why such scenarios, hidden in plain sight in one of the most commercially accessible adult publications, have been all but "invisible" in discussions of pornography in its audiovisual forms. To be sure, there are films explicitly marked for bisexual audiences that enable a similar play with sexual orientation and there are plenty of scenarios in gay porn that center on the seduction of straight men, but within straight porn, male-male sex is literally the missing act, even as female-female sex is omnipresent.

We need look no further than *Penthouse*'s own efforts to produce pornography for the mainstream video market. In the early 1990s, the company released a series of videos based on *Penthouse Letters*—*Forum Letters Volume 1* (1993) and *Forum Letters Volume 2* (1994). The package promises us the "wild ride of sensual experiences" already well known to the readers of the magazine: "These are the kinds of titillating and fulfilling adventures that have inspired thousands of readers to share their most intimate exploits with us. Vividly retold in our sexy, sensuous style, little is left to the imagination with these letters to *Penthouse*!"

Well, actually, now that you mention it, rather a lot is left to the imagination here. The videos operate according to very different norms of representation than can be found in the magazine itself. While the fantasies described here would be in the "mainstream" of print pornography and thus can be sold to the mass market, they are nowhere to be found within the videos. To be fair, across the two videos, there are only eleven scenarios represented, and it would be possible to select eleven stories out of the magazine itself that contained none of the kinds of situations discussed above. By contrast, four of the eleven scenarios include representations of female-female sex. There are also none of the other kinks, such as discipline and punish, crossdressing, or even ménage à trois, which are regularly treated in the magazine. And, oh yeah, being a softcore video, there is no representation of the erect male penis. In fact, the penis itself remains off-screen almost entirely. While references to bodily fluids are central to the magazine scenarios, they are never depicted and only rarely referenced in the video adaptation. There are only two scenarios that involve more than one man—in one, a patient connected to a heart monitor watches his roommate have sex with the nurse, silhouetted through the curtain, and in the other, two men swap wives in scenarios that involve a large hot tub and two lawn chairs, both situations allowing them to remain several yards apart at all times. In this second scenario, the men cuddle with their spouses afterward but there is no suggestion here that they do anything that would bring them into direct contact with the other man's bodily fluids. There are several scenarios that involve voyeurism but men are allowed only to watch two women having love. Even male autoeroticism is present only by suggestion in one scenario involving phone sex: the man remains fully dressed, though his facial expressions and bobbing head suggests that something may be going on well below the frame. It would be hard to overestimate how systematically the videos dismantle all of the contexts that led us along that slippery slope toward homoeroticism.

Except on its packaging, the videos never claim these scenarios are based on real experiences. Indeed, given the glossy production values, the soft-focus photography, and the overinflated, overmadeup and overcoiffed women featured, there is nothing here that suggests any ties to the real world whatsoever.

Some residuals of the letter format remain here. Most of the segments begin ritualistically with "Dear Penthouse" and first-person narration is used throughout. Often, in an audiovisual format, the voice-over narration is purely redundant ("I grabbed him and kissed him"). And in many cases, the lyricism, which adds an extra layer of sensuality to the print descriptions, stands in stark contrast to what we are seeing. The narrator may describe "a mind-clouding climax" while the viewer sees only a mechanical and passionless performance. This is most striking in one of the few segments to give us even a fleeting glimpse of the penis. As the narrator exclaims, "Just when I thought he was going to enter me. . .", the man depicted on screen remains totally flaccid. Perhaps unintentionally, the images pull us away from the frenzied excitement and "boundless" pleasures of pornocopia toward something much more mundane and down to earth. Because the videos were shot without sync sound, the voice-over narration provides the only human sounds, adding to the impression that the depicted action is hermetically sealed off from its viewers. The narrator may tell us that "her grunts and groans were like music to my ears," but those sounds are not to be heard. The voice-over does serve an important function in intensifying the action, describing in words what is not directly depicted on the screen, which, includes, pretty much anything that happens below the belt. The only erections here are described ("a mighty oak in my hand," "his turgid manhood") and not depicted on screen and the same might be said of the descriptions of cunnilingus ("his tongue flicking against my quivering pussy like a humming bird") that remain blocked from view. Here, the spoken narration is frequently more explicit than the images, suggesting once again that words offer greater latitude for erotic expression.

There is a much more elaborate play with narration in the videos than is common in the magazine. Several segments have both a male and a female narrator. In "The Paint Job," a man is reading a woman's diary of her sexual exploits—with a female voice narrating the sex and the male voice commenting on the feelings the text provokes. In "Mystery Caller," the male narrator receives a series of explicit phone messages from an anonymous woman working in his office, sending him off a series of daydreams about what it would be like to have sex with various co-workers. In many cases, it would seem that this dual narrational structure was created to solve the problem of having a male protagonist show too much (or even any) interest in the genital activities of another man. Contrast, for example, this segment from "The Big Switch" as a man describes his wife making love with another man with other such passages from the magazine quoted earlier: "Watching my wife in the heated embrace of another man was incredibly exciting. The expression on her flushed face mirrored the pleasure she was deriving from Dan's tongue on her aroused sex. I could hear soft whimpers of delight tumble from her lips." The focus is entirely on her response to the lovemaking; nothing remains that would suggest male interest in the other man's body.

In many cases, the narrator has little or no direct sexual experiences. The narrator may watch others having sex from some distance, separated from them by a wall of glass, as in "The Window Washer" or through the lens of a camcorder in "Maid to Order," but the story ends with only the meager hope that they may someday join the action. While the magazine scenarios rarely included segments explicitly marked as fantasy, the video ones often mark off the depicted actions as unfulfilled fantasies. Perhaps the goal was to make the protagonist more like the viewer, someone who gets off thinking about or watching others have sex, but Brecht would be hard pressed to design pornography that was more systematically distancing from the viewer.

Whereas the magazine promises us infinite diversity in infinite combinations, the sex depicted on screen is carefully contained. One can argue that the producers have made a conscious decision to avoid the magazine's more risky content and go softcore in order to get their work into video stores that might not be willing to circulate more explicit content. Yet, this does not explain fully why such scenarios are outside the mainstream onscreen, while the print magazine can be sold in convenience stores and airport newsstands around the country. There would seem to be a limit to the flexibility of male heterosexual fantasy. Perhaps some possibilities can be entertained within the mind's eye as long as one doesn't have to watch them actually depicted on screen. Whereas print porn shows an almost infinite capacity for deniability, audiovisual porn literalizes what it depicts. Here, a man sucking another man's penis is exactly what it looks like, nothing more and nothing less.

NOTES

1. "Snowbound, Two Couples Find More Than Enough Ways to Keep Warm," *Penthouse Letters*, November 1993, 85–87.

2. Henry Jenkins, *Textual Poachers: Television Fans and Participatory Culture* (New York: Routledge, 1990); Shoshanna Green, Cynthia Jenkins, and Henry Jenkins, "'The Normal Female Interest in Men Bonking': Selections from the Terra Nostra Underground and Strange Bedfellows," in Henry Jenkins, *Fans, Bloggers and Gamers: Exploring Participatory Culture* (New York: New York University Press, 2006). Initially, slash was discussed as straight women's fantasies about gay sex. More recent accounts have complicated both sides of that description, seeing the fantasies as produced and circulated among women of varied sexualities, and defining the construction of same-sex relationships only sometimes as gay.

3. I am using the somewhat awkward phrase *male-male* rather than *queer*, *gay*, or *bi*, because the meaning of these fantasies—and their relations to the sexual identities of the characters and of their readers—is very much what is under investigation here.

4. Thomas Waugh, "Men's Pornography: Gay vs. Straight," *Jump Cut* 30 (1985): 30–35.

5. The Editors of Penthouse Magazine, *Letters to Penthouse XIII* (New York: Time Warner, 2001).

6. The Editors of Penthouse Magazine, *Letters to Penthouse IV* (New York: Time Warner, 1994), front matter.

7. *Penthouse Letters*, November 1993, 55.

8. Ian Watts, *The Rise of the Novel* (Berkeley: University of California Press, 1957), 195–196.

9. Ibid., 199.

10. "The Object of His Desire Gets the Massage, But Not the Message," in The Editors of Penthouse, *Letters to Penthouse V* (New York: Time Warner, 1995), 282.

11. "The Party Was a Drag Until They Played the Sex Game, but Who Was His Partner?" *Penthouse Letters*, June 2003, 22, 24.

12. "Happy Birthday to Me—and To You and The Stud Who Came With You," *Penthouse Letters*, March 1994, 42–50.

13. "He's in the Closet But He's Not Gay, He's Watching His Wife Do Her Lover," *Penthouse Letters*, July 2001, 46, 48.

14. "Couple's Hands-Off Policy Results in Many an Explosive Encounter," *Penthouse Letters*, December 1991, 61–62.

15. "His Superhot Girlfriend Is Still Really Hot For His Best Friend," *Penthouse Letters*, October 2001, 58.

16. Gayle Rubin, "The Traffic in Women: Notes Towards a Political Economy of Sex," in *Toward an Anthropology of Women*, ed. Rayna Reiter (New York: Monthly Review Press, 1975); Eve Kosofsky Sedgwick, *Between Men: English Literature and Male Homosocial Desire* (New York: Columbia University Press, 1985).

17. "His Favorite Dessert Is Sloppy Seconds, but Only if He Can Lick the Plate," *Penthouse Letters*, November 1993, 58–61.

18. "Thanks to His Girlfriend, He Now Enjoys the Best of Both Worlds," *Penthouse Letters*, October 1998, 86.

19. "That's Odd—My Husband Never Sucks Cock at Home," *Letters to Penthouse V*, 43.

20. "She Makes His Fantasy Come True, and He Honors His End of the Deal," *Penthouse Letters*, October 1998, 48.

21. "He and His Nudist Neighbors Do 'Whatever Feels Good and Right!'" *Penthouse Letters*, March 2001, 104.

22. "On the Eve of Their Double Wedding, They Celebrated With a Five Way Orgy," *Penthouse Letters*, May 2000, 85.

23. "Two Heads are Better Than One—And That's Just the Dildo!" *Letters to Penthouse V*, 275–278.

24. "When It Comes to Masseurs He Learns He Prefers a Monsieur," *Penthouse Letters*, March 1995, 6–7.

25. "The Only Singles Bar He'll Ever Need is Right Between His Legs," *Penthouse Letters*, November 1993, 42–44.

26. "After Much Frustration, He Finally Got His Man," in The Editors of Penthouse Magazine, *Letters to Penthouse VI* (New York: Time-Warner, 1996), 200–203.

27. "Businessman Skewered in Texas Bondage Motel Beef Barbecue," *Penthouse Letters*, January 1989, 10.

28. Nancy Friday, *Men in Love* (New York: Dell, 1980).

29. Ibid., 359.

30. "Rites of Passion, Rites of Spring, Rites of Initiation," *Penthouse Letters*, July 1996, 10.

31. "Three Guys Get Away Into the Woods and Come Back Transformed," *Penthouse Letters*, March 1994, 84.

32. "Put Two Pumped-Up Businessmen in a New Ferrari and Anything Can Happen," *Penthouse Letters*, October 2001, 33.

33. "Old Friends Meet, Talk About Old Times, Suck a Little Cock . . ." *Penthouse Letters*, November 1993. 40.

34. "It was Halloween in San Francisco, And His Wife Had a Bet to Collect," *Penthouse Letters*, July 2001, 144.

35. "From Strictly Ballroom to Dirty Dancing in One Easy Lesson," *Penthouse Letters*, November 1993, 38–40.

36. "His Marriage is Behind Him, But So Is A New Route to Pleasure," *Letters to Penthouse V*, 291–294.

37. "Air Force Hunk Takes Randy Lieutenant on Fanciful Flight," *Letters to Penthouse VI*, 215.

38. "Lifelong Fear of Queers Starts to Crumble In the Back Row," *Letters to Penthouse V*, 289–291.

39. "Holier-Than-Thou Glory-Hole Aficionado Doesn't Practice What He Preaches," *Letters to Penthouse VI*, 233.

40. "Masseur Teaches Neophyte The Ins and Outs of the Business," *Letters to Penthouse VI*, 227.

41. "He was Faithful to His Wife Until He Fell Hard for A Coworker—Named Walter," *Letters to Penthouse XIII*, 121.

42. "Future Lawyers Forego the Glory Hole and Look Into Each Other's Briefs," *Letters to Penthouse V*, 262–265.

43. "He Found His Destiny As Servant and Then Maid to His Wife and Her Lovers," *Penthouse Letters*, June 2004, 7.

44. Carol Queen and Lawrence Schimel, "Introduction," in *Pomosexuals: Challenging the Assumptions about Gender and Sexuality*, ed. Carol Queen and Lawrence Schimel (San Francisco: Cleis, 1997).

45. Steven Marcus, *The Other Victorians: A Study of Sexuality and Pornography in Mid-Nineteenth-Century England* (New York: Basic, 1964), 174.

46. Ibid., 234.

47. Ibid., 261.

48. Ibid., 273.

49. "Bisexual Blowout," *Penthouse Letters*, March 1994, 56.

50. "Sunning in the Greek Isles: How Swede It Is!" *Letters to Penthouse VI*, 161.

51. Marcus, *The Other Victorians*, 269.

52. Ibid., 275–276.

53. Tzvetan Todorov, *The Fantastic: A Structural Approach to a Literary Genre* (Ithaca, N.Y.: Cornell University Press, 1975).

54. We see this problem when one considers the roles that photographs play in *Penthouse Letters*. The magazine sprinkles erotic and semi-explicit photographs through its pages, often

with little or no effort to link what we are seeing in the images with what we are reading in the text. This indifference to context reached its absurdity when images of straight sex were scattered throughout the sections devoted to same-sex fantasies, perhaps as another way of reassuring heterosexual readers, perhaps as a way of preventing their illicit fantasies from being exposed to anyone who stumbled upon them pawing the glossy pages. In more recent years, there have been images of two naked men frolicking together included in relevant sections of the magazine, though such images are no where near as explicit as the current norms in depicting male-female or female-female sex.

Chuck Kleinhans

The Change from Film to Video Pornography: Implications for Analysis

In Paul Thomas Anderson's dramatic feature on porn filmmaking, *Boogie Nights* (1997), the initial half of the film closes during a 1979 "end of the decade" party at the home of director Jack Horner (Burt Reynolds), who aspires to make quality porn films that people want to see for the story as well as the sex. Amid the partying, a new figure shows up, Floyd Gondolli (Philip Baker Hall), the money man behind the operation to announce that the future of the business is in video production. Horner resists, adamant that he makes film art. But in the second half, in the 1980s, Horner is making fast, cheap videos that he knows are crap, aware that he sold his aspiration for a quick buck. While dramatically condensed for narrative effect, the film shows the remarkable economic, technical, and aesthetic change that video brought to the porn world.[1]

In the 1980s a drastic change took place in U.S. commercial, moving-image pornography. The previously dominant form, the dramatic feature-length theatrical film, almost disappeared as home videocassette pornographies overwhelmed the market. This development was concurrent with changes in the sociopolitical environment, such as a new wave of sexual image censorship, changes in sexual practices and ideologies due to the AIDS crisis, and the increased public visibility of previously stigmatized sexualities such as sadomasochism. Contextual and technological changes produced a new set of conditions for analyzing porn, which now demands new forms of analysis.

This essay serves as a preface to a full consideration of the phenomenon. Adequate data simply does not exist for a complete study. Here, to illustrate the significance of the project for contemporary media and cultural studies, I develop two general areas: a description of the institutional change from film to video porn, and a discussion of the critical problems in advancing an analysis. My general argument is that economic and industrial changes affecting financing, production practice, and diffusion are the dominant factors in pornographic texts' changes during this period. Others have attributed change to other causes: stylistic innovation (using familiar art and literary history concepts), the imperatives of authorship (the need for makers to change and grow), and presumed close correspondence with changes in social consciousness. (My primary reference throughout is heterosexual pornography; however, from limited research, I'm reasonably sure that the same general conditions apply to gay male pornography.)

Of course, economic influences do not operate alone or as simple prime movers or even as determinations in a last instance that never comes. But economic elements are present and must be accounted for as, in this case, the leading factor in a set of interrelated determinations. Both by training and experience, I tend to approach the study of media initially through a close study of individual texts. But pornography—texts intended (in production and consumption) for sexual arousal—obviously raises, in a distinct way as part of the analysis, questions of individual and collective audience response. In addition, one of the most common strategies in historical, social, and generic media analysis is to relate changes in form or content within a temporal sequence of texts to social factors. This is an especially appealing strategy (in the case of commercial pornography) both by those who want to condemn it and by those who want to defend it. Pornography as social pathology remains a recurrent trope in analysis. I address these questions in my conclusions.

From Film to Video

Maybe the Golden Age [in the 1970s] was a rare moment where X tried to mimic Hollywood. Now the videos are like TV shows instead of movies.
—Actor Joey Silvera, quoted in Oliver and MacDonell 1987, 30)

A current commonplace in discussions of heterosexual porn claims that the video product is not only different from film, but aesthetically and erotically inferior to it. A consumer guide's editor sums up the situation circa 1990:

> While technology has advanced to the point where the shot-on-video format has overtaken film—and become almost more appealing to a new generation of carnal consumers—the essence of erotic filmmaking has been reduced to its most basic form. Feature adult videos are produced for a few thousand dollars, often shot in one day, and released within a month, only to be rapidly forgotten. Plot has been replaced with premise, the seven sex scenes per movie norm of a few years ago has been cut down to five couplings, with budgets prohibiting the once expected orgy scene. Running times now tend to be just over an hour, while video box covers often incorrectly state them as up to half-an-hour longer. . . . With the advent of home video, it seems that adult movies have been with us forever. Part of that, of course, has to do with the way time has accelerated in America, so that last month's erotic release might well have been created ten years ago. The modern eye reacts rapidly to shortened messages, especially if

they are evocative. What this all means to the porn movie buff is more emphasis on the visual and sexual imagery, and less thought given to established
filmmaking philosophy. (Stone 1990)

An industry gossip column repeats the charge more dramatically:

> The worst news of the year [1989] was the "project X" video shoot where Stal-
> lion Productions attempted to make 100 feature porn videos in one month.
> After two weeks, fifty or so movies completed, production halted never to begin
> again. Talent and four technical crews worked day and night, never receiving a
> penny in salary. All the movies have been sold and released with the perform-
> ers getting screwed twice! . . . More and more cheap product continued to flood
> video stores with major manufacturers forced to lower prices to keep up with
> fly by night video vendors selling inferior quality product for less than five dol-
> lars wholesale. . . . The consumers voice some sort of complaint by renting and
> buying less than in previous years. (Anonymous, 1990, 54)

How did such a situation evolve? To answer this question we must turn
to a discussion of the economic basis of commercial porn, understanding that after
government censorship restrictions, market conditions are primary in influencing production. In the 1950s, 60 to 70 theaters nationally, mostly in large urban
areas, showed soft-core films. In the 1960s, driven by simple economics existing
burlesque houses converted completely to film, or had "nudie cuties" replace the
traditional live music and comedians who filled in between the strippers.[2] In the
early 1970s, following the Supreme Court's ruling that local community standards
should set the norm, thus changing local censorship laws, essentially legalized
hardcore—explicit genital sexuality. In the 1970s a peak of 780 theaters regularly
showed hard-core films.[3] A typical budget of $100,000 to $150,000 paid for the production of a feature-length drama shot on 35mm film. By about 1983, approximately 120 new features were available every year. Given the standard practice of
a weekly double bill, with a rerun in the B spot, only 52 new films a year were
needed by any one theater. Of course more were produced, and theaters did compete within markets, but the lowest-rank theaters simply ran and reran old features. In 1983 there were about 100,000,000 customers for 763 theaters with a
total gross of $364,000,000 admissions (Friend 1984, 23).

But things were already changing:

> the video companies such as VCA and Caballero would typically advance
> $40–60,000 for the video rights to a theatrical porn film. Then roughly two
> years ago [1986] they stopped making offers—they decided they could do four
> shot-on-video programs themselves for the cost of video rights to a single the-
> atrical film. These programs are shot in a single day, with no theatrical value,
> [director Chuck] Vincent notes. (Cohn 1988, 3, 26)

In the 1990s, a budgeting rule of thumb assumed two video features could be made
for about $15,000, and that involved a two-day shoot, including cast and crew

salaries, equipment rental, and postproduction editing costs (thus producing a feature and its sequel at the same time).

In the 1980s the videocassette recorder entered the home market in a big way. In 1978 150,000 households had VCRs. In 1980 1 percent of U.S. households had VCRs; by the decade's end 70 percent of all households had them—a rate of introduction that exceeds any other consumer communication appliance, including phone, record player, radio, TV, and color TV to that time. At the time of the major 1979–1980 introduction of VCRs, they cost over $1,000. By the end of the decade the cost was down to about $200 for a simple model. In the mid-1990s it was common in a middle-income household to find children's bedrooms with their own TV and VCR. By 1997 85,500,000 households had VCRs. The introduction of DVD players around 1997 bolstered by cheap Asian electronics production has been even more spectacular, with 2005 seeing players available for about $30 retail.

Early on, competing formats (Beta and VHS) and Hollywood film industry reluctance to release films on tape (video being initially perceived as product that competed with theatrical exhibition) produced a limited rental product. Commonplace wisdom in the video business assumed most early purchasers of VCRs were significantly motivated to purchase the device to see pornography at home.[4]

The effect on theatrical porn was profound. By 1987 there were only about 250 theaters (a loss of over 500 venues in 5 years) and the numbers were declining. Distributors had trouble collecting from theaters, subdistributors went bankrupt, and the former percentage-of-house arrangement was replaced by flat rates as low as $100 per week. By 1987 or so, couples left the theatrical market completely (especially significant in the "quality" suburban theaters, such as the California Pussycat chain). Furthermore, some urban theaters in marginal neighborhoods were lost due to zoning changes and the exercise of eminent domain, moves often linked to property values increasing due to gentrification. (Women Against Pornography in New York City had free rent from real estate developers in the 1980s for their storefront operation giving horror show tours of the 42nd Street porn district.) Most of the remaining theaters began to convert to video projection, simultaneously "plexing" into several screens per theater.

However, the X-rated rental market swelled to an estimated 100,000,000 rentals in 1987: this was the same number of rentals as admissions to adult theaters four years earlier. Nationally by 1990, it was assumed that 20 percent of a typical video store's gross was from adult tapes (and 20 percent from children's tapes). These estimates seemed to be borne out in the floor and shelf space allocations in those stores that carried X-rated material.[5]

While theaters declined, overall production increased drastically. By 1987, 400 new video features a year were produced, only 40 of them shot on film. (With the release of older films on tape, compilations, and such, about 1,500 new releases appeared each year.) And through video rental and sales, overall availability of adult "movies" increased nationally and for individual consumers. In the late 1980s one mail-order adult-video distributor, Excalibur, advertised that it stocked 9,000 adult titles.

On the exhibition end, theatrical viewing lost out to home viewing (with the significant exceptions of those who did not have privacy for home viewing, although they could still choose peep show viewing—now updated to video viewing—and gay men's theaters that maintained an ongoing importance as meeting places). Women Against Pornography campaigned especially against theatrical pornography at the same moment it was disappearing. Their organizing had virtually no effect on neighborhood video store porn, which typically in the United States consists of a physically segregated display or rental/sales in adult-only stores.

On the production end, film lost out to tape because film is more expensive than video. Video equipment rents for less than film equipment, and it doesn't require the investment in film stock, processing, work print, answer print, audio tape, and sound mixing. By convention and with some basis in reality, film demands highly trained personnel: director of photography, cameraman, magazine loader, lighting crew, two sound people, and, later, specialists for film editing and sound mixing. In contrast, video allows shooting with a smaller crew, with less training. Also, video requires no elaborate post mix if you put live voice on one track and add music to other track later while fading out unwanted sound on the voice track.[6]

There is a significant exception to the video trend: shot-on-film is a selling point, particularly with a "name" director such as Andrew Blake, known for classy production values, and stars who enhance home video diffusion. Film also helps in the foreign theatrical market, which remains strong in Hong Kong, Japan, and Southeast Asia. And it is also a plus for cable distribution (which typically involves recutting as softcore). In the 1990s some video packages prominently displayed a "shot on film" banner to assert quality. And "shot on Betacam SP" becomes another such marker as tapes shot on VHS or digital camcorders multiplied.

For shot-on-video, one- to two-day production is the norm, and the product is increasingly like reality TV rather than dramatic film. In terms of dramatic narration, a simple skit structure replaces dramatic scripting.

> "Back in the early '80s, the going rate for an adult film script varied from $1,500 to $5,000. With the advent of videotaping around 1985, producers either stopped using scripts or stopped paying for what constituted a script. It was considered too expensive since the budgets for these tapes were so low," [Rick] Marx recalls. (Cohn 1988, 3)

The narrative in porn features tends to move "back" to the more aesthetically primitive stag film or episodic series. Similarly, the acting changes from a style that calls for more character development and some psychological realism to a skit or cartoon-style simplicity. A related factor is actor pay. In the mid-1980s some female stars asked for and got $1,500 to $2,000 a day (men get about half of what women make). With lowered budgets, quick and short shoots without extensive rehearsals or scripts to memorize became the norm.

In the mid-1980s some of the skilled theatrical porn directors found they could bail out of the business and find work shooting low-budget dramas for the product-hungry cable TV market. Their experience allowed them to make fairly slick, quickly produced, low-budget drama on film. Thus *Boogie Nights*'s Jack Horner could have joined the new immigrants trained in Eastern European film schools in making erotic thrillers, muscle-driven action pictures, and cop and private eye pursuits for direct-to-video or direct-to-cable release.

These tendencies become even more exaggerated in the 1990s with the advent of "gonzo" porn. This documentary subgenre typically uses improved small video cameras and desktop, small-format video editing. The camera is often hand-held by the protagonist, who is often also the male star, and the tapes often feature episodes with "amateur" female talent (i.e., previously unknown untrained actors), though they usually seem to be professional sex industry workers. Producer-stars such as Ed Powers, John "Buttman" Stagliano, Ben Dover, and Rodney Moore have recognizable serial product lines.[7]

Among other production changes, the central location became different. Formerly, in the 1970s, New York City was a significant site (using a cinematic and production design style that in many cases could be arguably called New York University–style), as was San Francisco (San Francisco State University–style).[8] Both styles used exteriors prominently, and the urban location becomes a significant part of story line. Larger-budget films often used sound stages and some period pieces were produced with appropriate sets and costumes. In early 1980s and with the shift to video, greater Los Angeles became the dominant center of production. (Although the business always supports some local productions, and imports.) After 1986 due to police restriction following the Traci Lords affair,[9] production changed to the San Fernando Valley, outside LA County. It is now predominantly in the Valley, and due to police and legal restrictions on outdoor location shooting of porn, it is shot almost exclusively indoors. The typical set is a Valley bungalow or townhouse, or sometimes office or warehouse space, furnished with rental furniture. Even transportation transition shots are omitted. Screen talent wear their own off-the-rack clothing until they strip down.

In the early 1990s, major control of distribution (by far the most profitable part of the business) was vested in three companies: Essex, VCA, and Caballero. To avoid legal entanglements (censorship, vice, etc.), distributors purchase from independent producers and no longer finance production. Because of this, there is more competition among producers, who face most of the legal trouble, and therefore they often omit their name from the product/package (Stone 1990).

Video sales are a high-volume, low-expense business, with virtually no warehousing costs and little capital needed. There are some direct market mail order sales to rental stores and to consumers. This has opened the space for some entrepreneurs to end-run the usual distribution business. (The key examples are Femme, the feminist porn company, and various amateur and specialty lines.) At the consumer end, video rentals are more significant in marketing than video sales. In video rental stores, adult tapes usually rent for the same fee as new-release mainstream features. While the neighborhood mom-and-pop video stores of the early 1980s have been squeezed out by the national chains, those that remain can compete in part because the chains do not carry hardcore (though they do carry softcore such as "erotic thrillers" of the *Body Chemistry* series, and cable packages such as episodes of *Red Shoe Diaries*, etc.).[10] Such local rental outlets maintain their niche by offering a substantial variety and frequent addition of new titles. Hard-core porn is always a staple of adult stores that typically offer peep show viewing, sex toys and clothing, and sexual novelties.

With video sales the general pattern (that developed in the 1980s) is that retail cost drastically changes from $70 to $100 per feature-length tape, circa 1980, to $35 to $40 for new releases, $15 to $25 for basic features in 1990, with some discounters going lower. But this varies somewhat: the cost of specialty videos (sadomasochist, transvestite, transsexual, etc.) remains high because the niche market will bear it. In general in terms of retail sales and rentals, the consumer now has a wide range of tapes available. The market is much like the former porn magazine market: differentiation by length of tape, production quality, star presence, and topic/narrative/fetish diversity. In addition, porn tapes are seldom copy-guarded, and can be easily duplicated with two VCRs, thus making personal ownership relatively economical.

Both rental and sales face significant pressures from local laws and the cultural climate. Thus Mormon Utah and parts of the Baptist South do not have hardcore, and some suburban jurisdictions keep it at bay. But hardcore is usually available in nearby localities—the urban core and adjacent states.[11] Furthermore direct-market sales avoid local laws, and parcel delivery services avoid any tangles with U.S. mail regulations. Beyond that, in a frequently traveling nation, hardcore can be purchased elsewhere, like fireworks, and used locally. And most large hotel chains offer highly profitable pay-per-view porn, even in the most conservative locales.

The VCR isn't the only significant technological change affecting moving-image porn. The vast expansion of cable, and more recently satellite-dish service, has also provided a range of pornographies. Cable/dish services typically offer some pay-per-view hardcore (usually without close-up details of penetration or male ejaculation). Premium channels, requiring an additional monthly fee beyond the basic cable/dish service (and without commercials except for their own service), such as Showtime, present softcore nightly (full nudity, no erections, simulated intercourse). HBO frequently presents sex with a documentary beard (*G-String Divas*, *Real Sex* and the like). The Internet provides an additional home porn source. On the Internet, while still images and written porn are extensively available from both individual and commercial sites, at present moving-image hardcore material is available only from commercial sites with a pay-per-view requirement (a credit card, presumably available only to adults) after an initial "teaser." Streaming video downloads escape all local government attempts at control.

Implications for Analysis

Linda Williams, in *Hardcore: Power, Pleasure, and the "Frenzy of the Visible,"* develops her analysis of post-1970 pornography using the model of the dramatic fiction feature, beginning with *Deep Throat.* Her pioneering genre discussion comparing feature porn with musical comedies in the chapter, "Generic Pleasures: Number and Narrative," is followed by chapters elaborating this comparison. She deals with sadomasochism narratives, considering sequels to earlier successful films, and the Femme feminist porn. Williams is careful to warn against reading her sample as a narrative of progress (Williams 1989, 268). However, at a deeper/implicit level, the argument's structure reads the historical sequence as generic development, with a conclusion speculating on the Femme films demonstrating a new aesthetic responding to a female presence among makers and audiences.[12] Many readers take up her argument about pornography duplicating dominant habits of interpretation in art history, literature, and media studies. Williams's argument is careful and guarded, but her readers have often ignored the warning. If one only follows her sequential, close textual analyses of exemplary works, it is easy to project a progressive teleology on the genre.[13]

Williams's analysis also vastly privileges feature-length, dramatic narratives shot on film with a traditional script, and classical film narrative style, made by relatively accomplished directors trained in such filmmaking. Researched and written in the early and mid-1980s, the discussion rests on assumptions that now often must be reversed because of the shift to video and quasi-documentary that I outlined above. Even tracing the most aesthetically/erotically accomplished hard-core work of the 1990s such as that of Andrew Blake, we find Blake's films display a non-narrative spectacle that approximates the high-gloss upscale porn of *Penthouse* magazine. All show, no story.

In terms of porn analysis, understanding the transience of a "Golden Age" of X-rated features means revising basic assumptions. Now a comprehensive understanding has to come to terms with the vastly widened spectrum of sexual imagery—ranging from R-rated movies to exclusively adult videos—and with the realities of actual marketplace circulation and use. In terms of titles, the dominant, hard-core, heterosexual porn today displays quasi-documentary, episodic scenes or a casual skit structure rather than a developed narrative. Where framed with a story, the narrative offers only the slightest pretext for the sexual episodes that follow. Character and acting are minimal; display and activity predominate. Analyst John Champagne called for replacing textual analysis with a sociology/ethnography of porn places and use. I find his fieldwork excellent, but I don't agree that we should discard textual studies. Rather, they need to be more firmly grounded in an understanding of reception and the realities of diffusion, especially institutional ones. The goal should not be simply to construct a canon of film/video porn. We need to understand pornography's full social and cultural significance, including its most marginal and disreputable areas.

Williams concludes by arguing for the then-new Femme group of videos, specifically refuting Andrew Ross's criticism that they may be too sentimental, pretty, "feminine," to be erotic. She projects that the presence of women as makers and consumers of porn may significantly change the field. However, fifteen years later, we can see that Williams's (and many others) optimism regarding feminist effects on the field has not worked out. Commercial hard-core porn's center of gravity has not changed. Softcore has developed in a subgenre of "couples porn" videos, and a considerable expansion of soft-core erotica, often combined with Harlequin-type fantasies or the thriller genre available in video store rental and cable/dish premium channels. The strongest hard-core "feminist" presence seems to be in a subgenre of "girl-girl" porn that features all-female casts in lipstick-lesbian settings. These works include the *Girl World* gym series or *Where The Boy's Aren't* series, and the raunchier "strap on a dildo" subgenre. More obviously feminist work tends to the arty margins; it exists, and is hard-core, but does not seem to have a significant market share. Femme has produced a new feature every year or two, such as Candida Royalle's *Revelations,* a distopic future fable that approximates independent U.S. or European narratives.[14] Other examples of feminist interest fit more clearly into the artworld and subculture scene, such as the Blush lesbian videos, or the *Real San Francisco Lesbians* series, or the films of Monica Treut, or video artist Shu Lea Cheang's dramatic sci-fi porn feature *I.K.U.* (2000).

The problem of critics' wishful thinking becomes especially acute in dealing with very contemporary cultural work. The investigator is "invested" in the emerging or cutting-edge development. Consequently, what makes innovative porn interesting and gives the analyst the emotional impulse to pursue the study—the phenomenon's newness and its potential—can easily be overanticipated in analysis.[15] Similarly, offbeat directors such as Rinse Dream or F. X. Pope are more interesting because they vary from the norm; their unusual films seem more useful for textual analysis whereas the inept or banal leaves the textual critic little new to say.

A related problem occurs when the critic desires to see variation from the norm as more transgressive than it may be. David James makes a notable and strong argument that amateur porn (made by untrained couples, exchanged with other couples, but also available commercially) can offer a form of cultural resistance; his argument is similar to those of Laura Kipnis on certain porn magazines and subgenres.[16] Yet many currently available "amateur" tapes (many of which seem to be shot by a more expert camera person) for the most part don't simply document activity, but they follow the pace and norms of commercial hardcore in terms of costume, changing sequence of positions and activities, groaning for the camera, and so on. In everything but (usually) the relative physical/cultural attractiveness of the men, they imitate or even aspire to the dominant commercial norm rather than subvert it.

Since very little reliable information is available about the porn sector, another recurrent problem emerges when critics use speculation in place of actual data, or use dubious "facts." For example, Linda Williams quotes a *Time* magazine article that 40 percent of video porn rentals are by women (Williams 1989, 231). I have seen this figure cited repeatedly (often to argue that women are interested in porn, that it is not only of interest to men, that not all consumers are men, that women form a substantial part of the hardcore market as opposed to the days of theatrical hardcore, etc.), and heard it referred to in discussions (most recently on a panel at the Society for Cinema and Media Studies in 1998). However, the initial source, *Adult Video News*, is a newsletter monthly for video store owners who carry porn. I must say that this figure is so far off the mark—based on my own experience and informal interviews with other porn consumers, store owners, managers, and employees—that I find it totally unbelievable. Four percent seems a far more likely figure (or perhaps 14 percent—I surmise that *Time* got the figure from a phone interview, so perhaps it was misheard). People in the humanities often don't have any experience or training in working with statistics or questioning nonscholarly sources. How anyone ever arrived at this figure remains unexplained. Is it just a guess by an editor? Is it based on polling? Of what kind and of what population? How reliable is this source? (A rival guide, *Adam Film World*, occasionally promotes itself by indicating its competitor guides obviously have a bias favoring their advertisers). Further, even the 40 percent figure doesn't indicate if these women are alone, in female couples, or in heterosexual couples when they rent. Williams herself expresses some skepticism toward the figure, allowing that women often do most of the shopping.

The point is that this statistic has circulated precisely because so few statistics are available, and "40 percent" seems like hard data. Similarly, figures on the actual size of the porn industry circulate without any explanation of the source or method, or the numbers are credited to obviously self-interested sources such as the FBI or other police agencies (interested in inflating the "danger" to get more appropriations), or to the industry itself (interested in seeming more prominent, and thus more respectable), without any further confirmation, or real explanation of what falls under the category "porn": softcore and hardcore? print, video, and pay-per-view? Internet porn? phone sex? strip clubs and topless bars? just the entertainment or also the liquor sales? How would we measure soft-core erotica on HBO and Showtime?[17]

We also need to be aware that the purchase of pornography and its circulation in capitalist exchange are strongly governed by larger economic trends. When general print advertising practices changed in the 1970s, *Playboy* lost major revenue. It was widely known within the industry that the recession of the late

1970s and early 1980s decreased overall sales and profits, driving some publications and outlets out of business. Whatever else it is, people pay for porn out of expendable income, and for the consumer hard times mean less porn or making do with cheaper versions or using the "same old" again rather than buying the new model.

Examining the "research" done for the 1986 Federal Commission on Pornography (the Meese Commission), any experienced analyst could easily conclude that this work was ill-conceived, prejudiced in advance, and patently biased in many cases, as well as being poorly funded. At the same time, a resurgent right in U.S. politics, in both the executive and legislative branches, has created immense barriers to any kind of sex research, especially funding for investigation. Normal social science interviewing and U.S. Census research has been off limits, since the Christian right finds any questioning intrusive and clearly does not want real information on sexual practices to exist or circulate. The right assumes research on sexuality validates what it considers "perversions." That this level of ignorance about social-sexual realities could be validated in the middle of the AIDS crisis and the appearance of new life-threatening sexually transmitted diseases marks the vicious meanness of these politics. Similarly, developing any information about youth's porn use and the information they gain from it is completely impossible. The chief U.S. public health official in the Clinton administration was forced to resign when she simply mentioned that children might masturbate. This lacuna in sex research occurs at the same time we've seen porn vastly more available to youth, especially females, in the home environment. My own informal questioning about this to teens whose parents agree to let me ask (my network of friends, relatives, acquaintances), teachers, and those eighteen years old and over (about their earlier experience) leads me to surmise that most teens and many middle school preteens in the United States, male and female, have the opportunity to view at least some hard-core video porn, though some (usually more religious or conservative) choose not to.[18]

Pornography is an extreme generic form; as such, it presents challenges to notions that are too generalized to deal with its specifics. As a renegade genre and one without any clear production standards, one can find examples of almost anything within it. With over one thousand new titles per year, feature-length, heterosexually aimed "films" on video provide too big a collection for close textual analysis or social science content analysis, even if some archive could provide any consistent collection of the output (unlikely in times of censorship and fear). Yet over time, the field of moving-image pornography does change. Once more noticeable as an innovation, in the late 1980s, bisexual tapes (homosexual male as well as girl-girl and heterosexual coupling) now seem to not be in fashion or have much of a presence in rental/sales. After causing a certain sensation when first introduced, transsexual themes and characters seem to have found a definite but very limited place in the market. Within the gonzo subgenre, for a couple of years in the early 2000s, several producers began a "footsie" cycle with the female partner's feet being used to stimulate the man's penis, and often ending with ejaculation on the foot. But whatever novelty or untapped market this aimed at seemed to dry up quickly. Pro-am (professional and amateur screen talent together, as in the gonzo tapes) goes through phases as well, with a late 1990s vogue for black women who are or portray street prostitutes, as well as blacks joining the perennial cheerleaders or college girls. (Though in my experience, the African American genres are more available in racially diverse Chicago stores than in Oregon, with its minuscule black population.) One obvious question is, who views? Is it primarily across racial lines, staring at the Other, or is it within racial/ethnic boundaries? Does such viewing differ? How? The point is that we don't have any reasonable assessment of the variety of and changes in pornography, much less a theory to explain how fashion functions within this market.

I've tried to broadly sketch some of the institutional context over the past twenty-five years of commercial moving-image porn and to indicate some problems for further research and thinking in this area. These problems are largely pragmatic ones, but ones that seriously shape knowledge in the area. The cultural study of pornographic images and practices needs to advance by overcoming these limits on research. The subjectivity and personal interest that often motivates initial work in cultural studies needs to be balanced by an awareness of the technological, institutional, social, and economic aspects of the topic being investigated.

NOTES

Earlier portions of this essay were presented at the Screen Conference, Glasgow, 1992; the Marxist Literary Group Institute on Culture and Society, University of Oregon, 1991; and the Society for Cinema Studies, Washington, D.C., May 1990.

1. While Anderson and others I quote clearly hold to the idea of a "Golden Age" of porn films and a decline with video, my own aim is simply descriptive. I think that these pornographies are basically different, and I'm not concerned here with an evaluation, be that artistic or erotic.

2. The story is told anecdotally in McNeil, and in a comprehensive scholarly analysis in Schaefer's 1999 book on the history of exploitation films and his forthcoming history of porn films.

3. Some films had breakout success and achieved short-run status in regular cinemas, some were shown in midnight screenings, and so on. Jon Lewis provides a detailed analysis of the effects of hardcore on the mainstream industry.

4. In his otherwise comprehensive monograph on the VCR, Frederick Wasser devotes only a few pages to X-rated tapes (2001, 92–94).

5. Throughout the 1980s small local "mom-and-pop" video stores served most of the retail sector while various chains were being established (Blockbuster, West Coast, Hollywood, etc.). Eventually competition by the chains, who offered ample availability of the newest releases, drove most small stores out of operation. Desperately trying to hold onto some market share, the family operations often expanded their porn section, while Blockbuster famously advertised itself as endorsing family values and not carrying any X-rated material. But, in fact, with time it carried softcore.

6. By the late 1980s even music was cut in a cost-saving move.

7. Lehman (1999) describes Powers's product.

8. In contrast to the extremely conventional Hollywood studio formulas that dominated the University of Southern California, NYU favored a more independent style, echoing a long

tradition of New York City production (e.g., Engel, Kubrick, Cassavetes, Woody Allen, Spike Lee). SFSU was also looser in style, often documentary in approach, and, in the 1970s, heavily shaped by the local counterculture lifestyle and ethos. Talent image complemented the visual style: New York City included stylish "native New Yorker" types such as Veronica Hart, zaftig Annie Sprinkle, Latina Vanessa Del Rio, caustic, wiry Bobby Astyr, hairy Jewish Ron Jeremy, and so on. San Francisco featured Faye Dunaway double Annette Haven, Asian-exotic Linda Wong, and a plethora of hippie chicks, as well as the original incarnation of John Holmes, New York City transplant Joey Silvera, and Paul Thomas. 1980s-era Los Angeles featured blonde athletic bodies such as Ginger Lynn, Shauna Grant, and others with notable body modification (implants, labia trims, etc.), as well as gym and tan spa guys such as Peter North.

9. In three years Lords became a major star, with her own production company, but it was discovered she was underage (eighteen) and had worked with a fake identification for this period. All of her films were withdrawn (or her segments were deleted) except for one made after she was eighteen. Subsequently she appeared on talk shows indicating she renounced her hard-core work and moved over to low-budget independent work.

10. Juffer (1998) details female consumption of softcore. Martin's dissertation (1999) analyzes made-for-cable and direct-to-tape soft-core thrillers.

11. For example, traveling on Interstate 80, one can pick up porn in Evanston, Wyoming, an hour from Salt Lake City, and then travel across Utah to find porn available again on the Utah-Nevada border.

12. The second edition expands the final discussion with considerations of gay/lesbian and other pornographies, and her ongoing work has produced a variety of views of new developments, such as explicit sex scenes in some European features.

13. Personal observation of classroom and academic conference discussion, and discussions with colleagues.

14. See Peter Lehman's extended analysis in this volume, which includes an additional commentary on Williams's argument.

15. This problem crops up in some of the graduate student essays in Williams (2004).

16. James's argument is complex and nuanced, especially in its reprinted form in the context of a series of essays on cultural resistance in the margins, as is Kipnis's. A reductionist summary is unfair, and in the case of Kipnis has been used by some to dismiss her work without engaging the issues she raises.

17. Fairly reliable sources: Lane (2000) and Anonymous (2005).

18. I examine how legislative attempts to control child pornography reveal changing attitudes to defining sexual boundaries in Kleinhans (2004).

WORKS CITED

Anonymous. "Notables." *Adam Film World Guide* (June 1990): 54.

———. *Porn Industry Facts.* 2005. www.Court TV. Available at www.courttv.com/archive/onair/shows/mugshots/indepth/hollywood/facts1.html, accessed March 22, 2005.

Champagne, John. "'Stop Reading Films!': Film Studies, Close Analysis, and Gay Pornography." *Cinema Journal* 36, no. 4 (1997): 76–97.

Cohn, Lawrence. "Pornmakers Surface in Mainstream." *Variety*, March 9, 1988, 3, 26.

Friend, Lonn M. "Porn-Film Maker Cecil Howard." *Chic*, January 1984, 22–24, 26, 28, 36.

James, David E. "Hardcore: Cultural Resistance in the Postmodern." In *Power Misses: Essays across (Un)Popular Culture*, ed. David E. James, 215–229. London: Verso, 1996.

Juffer, Jane. *At Home with Pornography: Women, Sex, and Everyday Life.* New York: New York University Press, 1998.

Kipnis, Laura. *Bound and Gagged: Pornography and the Politics of Fantasy in America.* New York: Grove, 1996.

Kleinhans, Chuck. "Virtual Child Porn: The Law and the Semiotics of the Image." In *More Dirty Looks: Gender, Pornography, and Power*, 2nd ed., ed. Pamela Church-Gibson, 71–84. London: British Film Institute, 2004.

Lane, Frederick S. *Obscene Profits: The Entrepreneurs of Pornography in the Cyber Age.* New York: Routledge, 2000.

Lehman, Peter. "Ed Powers and the Fantasy of Documenting Sex." In *Porn 101*, ed. James Elias et al., 359–366. Amherst, N.Y.: Prometheus, 1999.

Lewis, Jon. *Hollywood V. Hard Core: How the Struggle over Censorship Saved the Modern Film Industry*. New York: New York University Press, 2000.

Martin, Nina K. "Encountering Soft-Core Thrills: Gender, Genre, and Feminism in the Erotic Thriller Film." Ph.D. diss., Northwestern University, 1999.

McNeil, Legs, and Jennifer Osbourne. *The Other Hollywood: The Uncensored Oral History of the Porn Film Industry*. New York: Regan/HarperCollins, 2005.

Oliver, Doug, and Allan MacDonell. "Fuck Films in Flux: The Slimes They Are a-Changin'." *Hustler*, August 1987, 26–28, 30, 38, 94.

Ross, Andrew. "The Popularity of Pornography." In *No Respect: Intellectuals and Popular Culture*, ed. Andrew Ross, 171–208, 53–58. New York: Routledge, 1989.

Shaefer, Eric. *"Bold! Daring! Shocking! True!": A History of Exploitation Films, 1919–1959*. Durham, N.C.: Duke University Press, 1999.

———. *Massacre of Pleasure: A History of the Sexploitation Film, 1960–1979*. forthcoming.

Stone, Jeremy. "Untitled Editorial Introduction to 'Reviews.'" *Adam Film World Guide* (March 1990): 67.

Wasser, Frederick. *Veni, Vidi, Video: The Hollywood Empire and the VCR*. Austin: University of Texas Press, 2001.

Williams, Linda. *Hardcore: Power, Pleasure, and the "Frenzy of the Visible."* Berkeley: University of California Press, 1989.

———. *Hardcore: Power, Pleasure, and the "Frenzy of the Visible."* 2nd ed. Berkeley: University of California Press, 1999.

———, ed. *Porn Studies*. Durham, N.C.: Duke University Press, 2004.

Marjorie Heins

Sex and the Law: A Tale of Shifting Boundaries

"I know it when I see it." This famous phrase, from the pen of Supreme Court Justice Potter Stewart in a 1964 obscenity case,[1] accurately summarizes the relation between American law and sexually arousing art and entertainment. For despite many attempts over the years, courts have not been able to come up with a precise definition of criminally punishable obscenity—or with a persuasive explanation of why it should be suppressed.

The First Amendment to the U.S. Constitution states unequivocally that "Congress shall make no law . . . abridging the freedom of speech,"[2] but since at least the middle of the nineteenth century, it has been assumed in legal circles that obscenity is an exception to this broad First Amendment guarantee. When, in the 1960s and early 1970s, civil libertarians finally began to challenge the assumption, the Supreme Court—albeit by a narrow margin—rejected their arguments.

But where did the presumed exception to the First Amendment for obscenity originate? How has it evolved in the 170-plus years since Congress passed its first anti-obscenity law? More broadly, how do politics and culture affect laws censoring sexual expression? What other ways, outside the criminal penalties of obscenity law, have government officials found to control or regulate erotic speech? And why do some of them continue to do so, in the face of ever-more sexual explicitness all around us?

What is Obscene? The Elusiveness of Obscenity Law

Virtually since the dawn of civilization, governments and dominant religious institutions have suppressed expression that they considered threatening to their hegemony. Not surprisingly, then, the main targets of censorship—at least until modern times—were subversive or blasphemous speech: threats to government and organized religion, respectively. Sexual information (or misinformation), bawdy tales, songs, jokes, and pictures were, for the most part, not objects of institutionalized concern.

Historian Philippe Ariès notes a change in Europe around the end of the six-teenth century, when "certain pedagogues . . . refused to allow children to be given indecent books any longer."[3] By the middle of the eighteenth century, this notion of childhood sexual innocence led to anti-masturbation hysteria in Europe and America, and fueled early attempts to censor sexually arousing art and literature.[4]

But it was not until the nineteenth century that this obsession with pos-sible corruption of the young—especially sexually curious adolescents—along with urbanization, increased literacy, and anti-vice movements fused to create the political will for widespread suppression of sexual ideas. The first federal obscen-ity law in the United States, passed in 1842, authorized the Customs Service to confiscate "obscene or immoral" pictures. (It did not define these terms.) Earlier in the century, a few states had prosecuted books or illustrations with sexual con-tent, also without any precise legal definition of what constituted "obscene or immoral" expression.

There was not much concern at the time with defining obscenity or try-ing to distinguish it from words or pictures that policy makers did not think needed to be banned. "I know it when I see it" seemed to be the prevailing view even then, and arguments by the early free-speech crusader Theodore Schroeder that the First Amendment protects all creative expression, whether high- or low-brow, did not make any headway in U.S. legislatures or courts.[5]

In 1868, the English courts did come up with a definition for criminally punishable obscenity, in the famous case of *Regina v. Hicklin*. The *Hicklin* stan-dard, which American courts soon adopted, turned on whether "the tendency of the matter charged as obscenity is to deprave and corrupt those whose minds are open to such immoral influences, and into whose hands a publication of this sort may fall."[6] The publication at issue in *Hicklin* was an anti-clerical pamphlet, *The Confessional Unmasked*, which described the sometimes lurid details of Catholic confession.

What was likely to "deprave and corrupt" vulnerable minds according to this new legal standard? This was anybody's guess, but by the end of the nine-teenth century in the United States, "anybody" was most often Anthony Com-stock, a grocery clerk-turned-social activist who, by virtue of sheer zeal, a fine sense of timing, and an obsession with sexual matters, became America's chief censor after he persuaded Congress to expand the federal obscenity law in 1873. This new "Comstock Law" barred sending through the mails not only "any obscene, lewd, or lascivious book, pamphlet, picture, print, or other publication of vulgar and indecent character," but also "any article or thing designed or intended for the prevention of contraception or procuring of abortion."[7]

Armed with this broad language and deputized as a special agent of the Post Office, Comstock proceeded, during the forty-odd years of his reign as head of the New York Society for the Suppression of Vice, to seize and destroy thou-sands of books, magazines, illustrations, and contraceptive advertisements and devices. Arrests and prosecutions only occasionally led to appellate court decisions, and when they did, the courts followed the *Hicklin* definition of obscenity: would the material charged as obscene "suggest impure and libidinous thoughts in the young and inexperienced"—that is, would it tend to "deprave and corrupt" impressionable youth?[8]

Some judges did question *Hicklin*'s underlying assumption—that the law's censorship standard should turn on what society deems inappropriate for a vulnerable child. New York's Judge Learned Hand, for example, wrote in a 1913 case involving a "girl of the streets" novel called *Hagar Revelly*, that American authors, publishers, distributors, and readers should not be forced to "reduce our treatment of sex to the standards of a child's library in the supposed interest of a salacious few."[9] But Hand refused to dismiss the prosecution because he felt bound by existing law.

The American legal and cultural establishment was not yet prepared to follow Learned Hand, but by the 1930s, at least in the relatively enlightened precincts of New York City, some judges did repudiate the *Hicklin* standard. The two major cases involved a sex education pamphlet called *The Sex Side of Life*, written by birth control activist Mary Ware Dennett for her teenage sons, and the literary *succès de scandal*, James Joyce's *Ulysses*, the subject of an obscenity case after federal officers refused to allow it through U.S. Customs. (Of course, underground copies had been circulating for years among the *cognoscenti*.)

Dennett's obscenity conviction was reversed by the U.S. Court of Appeals in New York in 1930. The appellate judges acknowledged that "any article dealing with the sex side of life and explaining the function of the sex organs is capable in some circumstances of arousing lust," but said it did not follow that youngsters should be left "to grope about in mystery and morbid curiosity" because of obscenity law. Instead, they seemed to suggest, the legal standard should be whether the information is conveyed in "clearly indecent" terms.[10]

In the famous *Ulysses* decision three years later, federal judge John Woolsey cleared Joyce's sprawling novel of obscenity charges. After a close reading, Woolsey said, he found the work more "emetic" than "aphrodisiac," and therefore unlikely to "stir the sex impulses or to lead to sexually impure or lustful thoughts" in the average person—"what the French would call *L'homme moyen sensuel*."[11] (Perhaps Woolsey did not read *Ulysses* in the proper spirit.) The court of appeals affirmed, in a decision that repudiated the *Hicklin* "deprave and corrupt" standard, and replaced it with an obscenity definition that focused on whether, "taken as a whole," the "dominant effect" of a work on the average person is libidinous.[12]

Although this was an improvement over *Hicklin*, the appeals court in the *Ulysses* case did not question the presumed social necessity for some sort of exception to the First Amendment for true pornography—that is, expression whose prime effect is sexual arousal. And outside the jurisdiction of the federal court of appeals headquartered in New York, *Hicklin* remained the obscenity standard in much of America throughout the first half of the twentieth century. Indeed, the New York State courts in the 1940s condemned as obscene *Memoirs of Hecate County,* a volume of short fiction by the country's leading literary critic Edmund Wilson.[13]

So matters stood until the Supreme Court finally confronted the issue in 1957. The case involved a work with some claim to serious value—the erotically themed literary quarterly *American Aphrodite.* But its purveyor, Samuel Roth, was a notorious pornographer, and the Court, in a memorable opinion by Justice William Brennan, upheld Roth's obscenity conviction. Brennan wrote that even though sex is "a great and mysterious motive force in human life" and "a subject of absorbing interest to mankind through the ages," sexual materials that have a predominantly "prurient" appeal to the average adult, and that utterly lack "redeeming social importance," are not protected by the First Amendment.[14]

The *Hicklin* standard was now history. American courts for the next sixteen years struggled to apply Brennan's "utterly without redeeming social importance" formula to the volumes of sexual art and literature that could now, at least arguably, be made available to American readers. Henry Miller's *Tropics* and D. H. Lawrence's unexpurgated *Lady Chatterley's Lover* were among the works that were freed from official censorship in the wake of the *Roth* decision.[15]

Some observers at the time thought the end of obscenity law was just around the corner, but their optimism proved unfounded. In 1973, the Supreme Court revisited obscenity law, and in five cases decided on the same day, announced a new obscenity test that would allow local communities to set their own censorship standards and that would relieve prosecutors of the difficult burden of proving that a work charged as obscene utterly lacked redeeming social value. The leading case in the 1973 quintet, *Miller v. California,* defined constitutionally unprotected obscenity with a new, three-part test:

- Does the material depict or describe specific sexual or excretory activities or organs in a "patently offensive manner?
- Would the average person, applying "contemporary community standards," find that the material, taken as a whole, appeals predominantly to a "prurient" or morbid interest in sexual or excretory matters?
- Does the material, taken as a whole, lack "serious literary, artistic, political, or scientific value"?[16]

Interestingly, by this time Justice Brennan, author of the 1957 *Roth* decision, had come to the conclusion that judicial efforts to articulate a meaningful, legally comprehensible definition of "obscenity" are doomed to failure. "Although we have assumed that obscenity does exist, and that we 'know it when [we] see it,'" Brennan wrote in one of the four companion cases to *Miller v. California,* "we are manifestly unable to describe it in advance except by reference to concepts so elusive that they fail to distinguish clearly between protected and unprotected speech."[17] But Brennan's was the dissenting view, and *Miller*'s ambiguity-laden three-part definition remains the test for legally punishable obscenity in America.

There is still, of course, endless confusion in public debate over the use of the term *obscenity*, and its relation to *pornography* and *erotica*. Only *obscenity* has a specific legal meaning; *pornography* and *erotica*, by contrast, are subjective terms whose meaning is very much in the mind of the beholder. One person's pornography can clearly be another's erotica, and vice versa. Some commentators think of pornography as depicting hard-core sexual acts and erotica as more suggestive and less explicit. Both genres, in common parlance, are distinguished by their consistent ability to provoke sexual arousal. But both are completely legal and constitutionally protected forms of art and entertainment in the United States—unless, judged by the standards of a particular community, they meet the three-part *Miller v. California* obscenity test.

If this sounds vague and confusing, it is. But there is one advantage to the Supreme Court's variable and subjective definition of obscenity in *Miller*: its almost infinite flexibility. That is, as "contemporary community standards" change, the law evolves as well. Although in theory, neither judges nor juries—and certainly not police officers and prosecutors—should be deciding what is so "patently offensive" or lacking in ("serious value" as to be censored (the First Amendment, after all, was designed to protect unconventional and, indeed, offensive speech), in practice, the decisions of judges, juries, police, and prosecutors all reflect changing societal attitudes toward sex and sexual expression.

Thus, in the thirty-plus years since *Miller*, and despite continuing cries of alarm from culturally conservative advocacy groups such as Morality in Media or Concerned Women for America, pornography has become a massively profitable industry in the United States; sexually explicit material is produced and distributed outside the commercial pornography industry by amateurs and publishers of personal web sites; sex talk is pervasive on nonprofit listserves; and obscenity prosecutions have been sporadic and unpredictable. In most parts of the country, sexual materials that would almost surely have been suppressed as obscene (and thereby forced underground) a half-century ago are widely available, in media ranging from videos and magazines to pay-per-view hotel room offerings and the Internet.

This does not mean that purveyors of pornography have nothing to fear from obscenity law today. Both state and federal prosecutors are political animals and will initiate proceedings when they deem it advantageous to do so; and even artists who explore sex without pornographic intent are sometimes told by local officials to remove their work from display or risk criminal charges.[18] But as a practical matter, legal controls on sexual expression in America today take primarily indirect, noncriminal forms. The consequence is a highly schizophrenic contemporary culture in which the rawest of sexual information thrives alongside a climate of moralizing and relentless child protection rhetoric.[19] The cognitive dissonance resulting from such cultural contradictions might well astonish a visitor from Mars—or Europe, for that matter.

Indirect and Noncriminal Controls on Sexual Expression

Zoning, Pasties, and G-Strings

Zoning of adult entertainment, and bans on nude dancing, are two prominent, closely related forms of control. As the relaxation in "contemporary community standards" over the past quarter-century made obscenity convictions of porn video store owners or the proprietors of nude dancing establishments difficult to obtain in many communities, local officials began to use restrictive zoning to limit entertainment venues that they could not ban entirely. Often, the hope was to drive them out of business, or if not, at least consign them to undesirable and inaccessible parts of town.

Singling out one form of expression for restrictive zoning, however, is a form of "content discrimination"—that is, adverse treatment based on the content or subject matter of speech. And content discrimination is presumptively forbidden by the First Amendment. To finesse this difficulty, the Supreme Court, in a 1986 case called *City of Renton v. Playtime Theatres*, invented a legal fiction called the "secondary effects" doctrine. The Court said that restrictive adult zoning is not *really* content discrimination, because even though the businesses to be regulated are admittedly identified based on the content of their wares, the regulators are not motivated by hostility to sexual expression. Instead, the regulators are concerned with "adverse secondary effects": they want to prevent the seedy atmosphere, low property values, and crime associated with red light districts from infecting the wholesome parts of town. In the words of Justice William Rehnquist (writing for the Court in the *Renton* case), the city's

> "predominate [*sic*] concerns" were with the secondary effects of adult theaters, and not with the content of adult films themselves. . . . [This] is more than adequate to establish that the city's pursuit of its zoning interests here was unrelated to the suppression of free expression. The ordinance by its terms is designed to prevent crime, protect the city's retail trade, maintain property values, and generally "protec[t] and preserv[e] the quality of [the city's] neighborhoods, commercial districts, and the quality of urban life," not to suppress the expression of unpopular views.[20]

Why pretend that adult zoning is not "content-based," as the Court did in *Renton*, rather than simply admitting that it is, and then finding that the discrimination is justified anyway because of "adverse secondary effects"? The reason has to do with "levels of scrutiny" under the First Amendment. Because content discrimination is usually equivalent to censorship—by definition, it is aimed at particular expressive content—government officials have to meet a high burden of proof in order to justify it. In the case of adult zoning, though, municipalities tend to rely either on seat-of-the-pants judgments about adverse effects, or on debatable empirical studies that often are not even done in their own communities. It was in order to relieve municipalities of the rigorous burden of proof needed to justify content-discriminatory regulations that the Supreme Court in *Renton* pretended that the zoning law was content-neutral.

The "secondary effects" doctrine, although a transparent fiction, thus functions as permission for municipalities to discriminate against expression that is considered tawdry or immoral but that can no longer be suppressed entirely. It serves the purpose of reconciling society's increasing tolerance for sexual entertainment with persisting taboos and inhibitions against ideas and images that are often raw, crude, arousing, disturbing, or, at the very least, widely thought inappropriate for children to see.

A similar set of legal rules has arisen to control erotic dancing. Amusingly, much of the legal debate has centered on whether municipalities and states can, consistent with the First Amendment, ban totally nude entertainment by requiring that dancers wear pasties and G-strings.

As early as the 1970s, the Supreme Court recognized that nude dancing is a form of expression and thus has First Amendment protection.[21] In a 1990 case challenging an Indiana anti-nudity law, the appeals court judge and prolific author Richard Posner went further: dance, Posner wrote, in an opinion striking down Indiana's application of its law to a nude dancing club, is an ancient art form that "inherently embodies" the expression of emotions and ideas. "The raw communicative power of dance," Posner went on, "was noted by the French poet Stephane Mallarmé who declared that the dancer 'writing with her body . . . *suggests* things which the written work could *express* only in several paragraphs of dialogue or descriptive prose.'"[22]

But the Supreme Court soon put a stop to such effusions. On Indiana's appeal of the Posner decision, a slim majority of five justices ruled that the state's requirement of pasties and G-strings is constitutional, and does not significantly impair the expressive power of erotic dance. Justice Rehnquist's "plurality" opinion (stating the Court's judgment but without a majority of justices agreeing to its reasoning) asserted that nude dancing is "only marginally" protected by the First Amendment. Justice David Souter concurred (a choice he would later regret), on the dubious ground that the presumed "adverse secondary effects" of nude entertainment are sufficient justification for states to require minimal coverings on dancers.[23] As another justice, John Paul Stevens, later noted: "To believe that the mandatory addition of pasties and a G-string will have *any* kind of noticeable impact on secondary effects requires nothing short of a titanic surrender to the implausible."[24]

As these conflicting opinions suggest, the Supreme Court was not able to agree on a legal rationale for allowing cities and states to require pasties and G-strings. Nineteen years after the Indiana case, four justices used the secondary effects rationale—which Souter, its former champion, now protested—to uphold another minimal-coverings requirement, this one the brainchild of city officials in Erie, Pennsylvania.

In this Pennsylvania case, the Court's reasoning was even less persuasive than before. In the legal understatement of the decade, Justice Sandra Day O'Connor, writing for a plurality of four justices, admitted that, "to be sure, requiring dancers to wear pasties and G-strings may not greatly reduce [adverse] secondary effects."[25] But she upheld Erie's requirement anyhow.

Justice Antonin Scalia's concurrence in this Pennsylvania case at least had the virtue of intellectual candor. Scalia asserted that society's "traditional judgment" that nude dancing "*itself* is immoral" is sufficient justification for banning it: no First Amendment analysis is necessary.[26]

What is missing in Scalia's approach, though, is an acknowledgment that applying anti-nudity laws to ballets or other upscale theatrical offerings would, at the very least, raise serious First Amendment problems. In these "brie and chablis"-laden venues, requiring performers to wear pasties and G-strings would be an obvious affront to artistic freedom. Total nudity is, after all, the whole point of the clothing-free scenes in *Equus, Salome, Hair, Oh, Calcutta,* and many other productions.[27] It is thus hypocritical—indeed, discriminatory—to require pasties and G-strings in less upscale locales, as the dissenting justices in the Supreme Court's nude dancing cases pointed out.[28]

Public Spaces and Public Funds

Other noncriminal restrictions on sexual expression—measures that do not ban it but do limit its availability—involve public exhibition spaces for art and public funds. At least since 1989, when federal legislators and religious conservatives made headlines by attacking the National Endowment for the Arts (NEA) for funding "pornography" (in that instance, the photographs of Robert Mapplethorpe), there has been tremendous political resonance to the argument that whatever the First Amendment may protect, surely the taxpayers' money should not be used to support sexually explicit expression.

The Supreme Court in essence accepted that argument—or, at least, *sub silentio* recognized its political force—when, in 1998, it upheld a 1990 law that directs the NEA to consider "general standards of decency and respect for the diverse beliefs and values of the American public" when awarding grants. This case, brought by the famed "chocolate-smeared woman," Karen Finley, three other sexually provocative performance artists, and the National Association of Artists' Organizations, challenged the "decency and respect" directive as a form of unconstitutional "viewpoint discrimination" (a highly suspect subcategory of "content discrimination"). But the Supreme Court majority rejected their argument, explaining that

> any content-based considerations that may be taken into account in the grant-making process are a consequence of the nature of arts funding. . . . Although the First Amendment certainly has application in the subsidy context, we note that the Government may allocate competitive funding according to criteria that would be impermissible were direct regulation of speech or a criminal penalty at stake. . . . Congress may "selectively fund a program to encourage certain activities it believes to be in the public interest."[29]

The Court did hedge its bets in the *Finley* case, first, by insisting that the "general standards of decency" criterion is merely advisory, not mandatory; and second, by reiterating a rule it had articulated in earlier funding cases, that "even in the provision of subsidies, the Government may not 'aim at the suppression of dangerous ideas.'" Thus, "if the NEA were to leverage its power to award subsidies on the basis of subjective criteria into a penalty on disfavored viewpoints, . . . we would confront a different case."[30]

As the dissenters in *NEA v. Finley* pointed out, however, the "decency" criterion, even though phrased as simply something the NEA must "consider," could be ignored by the agency only at its peril. It was also having documented chilling effects on artists seeking government grants. *Finley* is thus best understood as a case in which the Supreme Court majority, well aware of the political precariousness of federal arts funding, found a way to sustain the constitutionality of the decency clause by—as Justice Scalia wrote in a typically pungent concurrence—"gutting it."[31]

Moving from government funding to the availability of government-owned space for artistic expression, we see a similar political dynamic at work. Provocative artists—and sometimes, not very provocative ones—who address sexuality or even simple nudity in their work are often denied public display space. Under the Supreme Court's convoluted "public forum" doctrine, citizens are entitled to equal, nondiscriminatory access to government property for expressive activity, if the property has been customarily used that way—for example, art displays in the lobbies of public buildings or theatrical productions at municipal auditoriums. The problem arises most often where a town official chooses an art exhibit or delegates the job to a local curator, but then someone complains that one or more works in the show are offensive, "pornographic," inappropriate for children, or a form of "sexual harassment." The offending works are removed; official "no nudity" policies frequently follow.

A typical example comes from Tennessee, whose Arts Commission announced in 2002 that no depictions of human nudity are permitted in its gallery space. This was a surprise to the artist whose work precipitated the newly discovered policy; according to one report, while preparing an exhibit of his work for the Commission's gallery in 2002, artist Ernie Sandidge was told that TAC policy prohibited artworks featuring nude figures. When he protested on First Amendment grounds, the Commission responded: "The TAC Gallery is not a designated public forum opened for exhibitions by all groups. Rather, the Gallery is a limited public forum with restrictions on the selection of works exhibited. One of the . . . restrictions placed on all exhibits in the Gallery is no nude figures."[32]

Although the artist and the National Coalition Against Censorship protested, no lawsuit, or change in policy, resulted.

When, on occasion, these conflicts do make their way to court, judges tend to reason backward from the result they want, based on their reaction to the art in question. If they are liberal in their aesthetic tastes and do not find the art particularly offensive, they will often find that the venue is a "designated public forum," and that, accordingly, city officials violated the First Amendment by censoring the work. If, on the other hand, the judges deem the work highly provocative or otherwise inappropriate for a public space, then they usually find that no "designated public forum" is involved, so that, absent a showing of "viewpoint discrimination," government officials have discretion to exclude it.[33] The results may make sense politically, but they end up marginalizing sexual expression by keeping it out of public view.

Schools, Universities, and Libraries

Schools, universities, and libraries also receive government support—indeed, public schools and libraries are government agencies—and here, too, feared political reaction to government funding for provocative expression often causes constitutionally protected and important art and information with sexual content to be marginalized. A striking example is the federal Children's Internet Protection Act (CIPA), passed in 2000, which mandates that all schools and libraries receiving e-rate discounts or federal aid for Internet connections install a "technology protection measure" (that is, a filter) on all computers, for adults and minors alike.[34]

Although the law requires only that the filters block "visual depictions" that are "obscene," "child pornography," or "harmful to minors," in fact, no filter can make these legal distinctions. On the contrary, as a detailed opinion by a three-judge federal court striking down CIPA found, leading filtering products erroneously block tens of thousands of useful, nonpornographic web pages, even at their narrowest, "adult" or "sexually explicit," settings. The judges gave numerous examples of this chronic overblocking, from a Knights of Columbus site, misidentified by Cyber Patrol as "adult/sexually explicit," to a site on fly fishing, misidentified by the "Bess" filter as "pornography."[35]

On appeal, however, the Supreme Court reversed the district court and upheld the constitutionality of CIPA. Chief Justice Rehnquist, writing for a plurality of four justices, reasoned that filtering the Internet is no different from selecting library books for purchase, and that since discretionary choice is an element of both processes, neither libraries nor the Internet access they provide qualify as "public fora." Moreover, Rehnquist said, because government is providing funds for Internet access, it has discretion to determine the scope of the information allowed. To the extent that erroneous blocking of "completely innocuous" sites raises a constitutional problem, he added, "any such concerns are dispelled" by a provision in CIPA giving librarians authority to disable the filter upon request from an adult.[36]

Three justices dissented. They emphasized that the broad, often irrational censorship imposed by filters undermines the fundamental principle of libraries—free and open access to all sorts of ideas. Given the uncertainty, delay, and disincentives inherent in the law's discretionary disabling provision, they thought it a poor substitute for unfettered Internet access. Justice Souter objected, moreover, to Rehnquist's description of Internet filtering as equivalent to library book selection; it is actually more akin, he said, to "buying an encyclopedia and then cutting out pages with anything thought to be unsuitable for all adults." Justice Stevens's dissent protested that censorship is not necessarily constitutional just because it is a condition of government funding, especially when, as in libraries, funded programs are designed to expand citizens' access to a wide range of expression.[37]

But the lesson of the CIPA case is that the First Amendment is a highly malleable concept when applied to conditions on government funding. When the expression sought to be restricted is sexual, the Supreme Court is inclined to give legislative restrictions a wide berth. Add to that political reality the almost inevitable use of "child protection" as a justification for the law and, as the CIPA case illustrates, restrictive measures will sometimes be upheld even where they apply to adults.

Where restrictions are imposed in the public school setting, the child protection rationale is even more potent. In school censorship cases, moreover, pedagogical theories emphasizing intellectual freedom and open inquiry often clash head on with views of the educational function that lean toward inculcation of moral values and proper conduct. Thus, although the Supreme Court long ago acknowledged that students do not "shed their constitutional rights to freedom of . . . expression at the schoolhouse gate"[38]—the case involved black armbands worn to protest the Vietnam War—when youngsters' speech is less clearly political, and especially when it is sexual, the Court has given school administrators wide latitude to punish, censor, and suppress.

No case better illustrates this phenomenon than *Bethel School District v. Matthew Fraser*, which reached the Supreme Court in 1986. Young Matthew Fraser had the impudence to deliver a student government campaign speech loaded with sophomoric sexual innuendo at a school assembly; his humor included such subtle metaphors as a description of his candidate as "a man who takes his point and pounds it in" and "who will go to the very end—even the climax, for each and every one of you." Rejecting Fraser's claim that his subsequent punishment violated the First Amendment, Chief Justice Warren Burger explained that "vulgar and lewd" expression undermines the public schools' basic mission of teaching "the habits and manners of civility"; moreover, "by glorifying male sexuality and in its verbal content," Fraser's speech "was acutely insulting to teenage girl students."[39]

The Court majority thus combined its distaste for the vulgar with a sexist paternalism that even some of the other justices could not stomach. As Stevens wrote in dissent, Matthew Fraser "was probably in a better position to determine whether an audience composed of 600 of his contemporaries would be offended by the use of a four-letter word—or a sexual metaphor—than is a group of judges who are at least two generations and 3,000 miles away from the scene of the crime."[40]

"Harm to Minors" and the Federal Communications Commission's "Indecency" Regime

As should be clear by now, "harm to minors" remains, a half-century after the Supreme Court rejected the *Hicklin* standard, a powerful force in many areas where sexual speech, and certainly sexually *arousing* speech, is regulated. One prime example is the politically driven censorship scheme that applies to radio and television broadcasting. Ever since 1978, when the Supreme Court approved the Federal Communications Commission's (FCC's) sanctions against a radio station for airing "indecent" speech—comedian George Carlin's hilarious monologue on the "seven dirty words" that one could presumably not say on radio—this agency of the U.S. government has had the power to censor vulgar terms, sexual innuendo, and anything else it considers indecent on the airwaves. The power extends only to broadcasting, not to cable TV, video, the Internet, or print media. The FCC's definition of indecency—expression "that describes, in terms patently offensive as measured by contemporary community standards for the broadcast medium, sexual or excretory activities or organs"[41]—is almost identical to the "patent offensiveness" prong of the Supreme Court's obscenity test; but significantly, it omits the other two requirements: that the speech be "prurient" and that it lack "serious value." This gives the FCC free rein to censor anything it considers "patently offensive" on the airwaves, no matter what its value as art, commentary, or political satire.

In the 1978 case of *Federal Communications Commission v. Pacifica*, the Supreme Court approved the FCC's indecency standard in a decision that turned largely on the perceived need to protect minors from coarse language such as Carlin's. Justice Stevens wrote a plurality opinion explaining that even though Carlin's monologue is clearly protected by the First Amendment, censorship is justified because broadcasting "invades" the home and is "uniquely accessible to children, even those too young to read." Besides, Stevens said, the FCC was not *banning* indecent speech but simply channeling it to late-night hours when children are unlikely to be listening. Justice Lewis Powell wrote a concurrence asserting that vulgar speech "may have a deeper and more lasting negative effect on a child than on an adult."[42]

In the years since *Pacifica*, the FCC's indecency regime has been as variable as the political winds. Until 1987, enforcement was lax, as long as broadcasters avoided the "seven dirty words." Pressures from the religious right in 1987 triggered a change: now, the FCC announced a "generic" test for patent offensiveness that would embrace sexual innuendo and double entendre along with taboo words. Of the three broadcasts the commission cited in this 1987 announcement, two came from noncommercial radio: a KPFK-Pacifica reading from a play about homosexuality and AIDS, and a punk rock song played on a student radio station. (The third was a Howard Stern show.)[43] Given the massive dominance of commercial over noncommercial radio, this disproportionate condemnation of nonmainstream broadcasting suggests the same kind "ethnocentric myopia" that Justice Brennan had noted nine years earlier, dissenting in the *Pacifica* case: "In our land of cultural pluralism, there are many who think, act, and talk differently from the Members of this Court, and who do not share their fragile sensibilities. It is only an acute ethnocentric myopia that enables the Court to approve the censorship of communications solely because of the words they contain."[44]

Indeed, in the first years of the twenty-first century, the FCC was still using its subjective "patent offensiveness" standard to condemn nonmainstream, countercultural expression such as the song "Your Revolution," by feminist rap artist Sarah Jones.[45]

The FCC's indecency regime is probably America's best-known instance of a government agency imposing mainstream values of sexual and linguistic propriety in the presumed interest of protecting youth. But the criminal law is also used for this purpose. After the Supreme Court finally made clear in 1957 that the obscenity standard for adults could not, constitutionally, turn on what might be thought inappropriate for a child, states began to enforce separate "harmful to minors" laws that use the basic obscenity definition, only modifying it for youth. The legal standard, under these criminal laws banning sale or distribution to youngsters of "harmful to minors" material, thus turns on whether the book, picture, or magazine in question is "patently offensive," "prurient," and lacking in value *for minors*.[46] Only in the 1980s did a few courts even consider whether the First Amendment rights of older minors—teens age sixteen or seventeen, for example—are infringed by laws criminalizing the distribution to them of books or magazines that their community thinks inappropriate for kindergarteners.[47]

"Harmful to minors" law (sometimes called "*Miller* lite" or "obscenity lite") is obviously driven by powerful concerns about children's vulnerability, impressionability, and need for proper socialization. To a large extent, adult anxieties about the possibly harmful psychological effect of sexual explicitness or other highly charged media content on the tender sensibilities of youth are a projection of their anxieties about possibly corrupting effects on society as a whole.

And although cultural standards about what is inappropriate for minors differ around the globe (and indeed, in many parts of the United States), most societies do attempt to limit the material available to youth.

A final category of censorship justified in the name of child protection is, of course, the law that has developed to suppress child pornography. Child pornography and "harmful to minors" laws are often confused, but their rationales—and the legal standards that govern them—are miles apart. While "harmful to minors" laws regulate what expression youngsters are able to read, see, or listen to, and thus focus on their *minds*, child pornography laws are aimed at protecting them from physical harm, and thus focus on their *bodies*. Actual sexual exploitation of minors is thus the fulcrum of child pornography law; and in theory, at least, where a child has been used sexually in the making of a photograph or film, "patent offensiveness" "prurience," and "serious value" are irrelevant. And conversely, paintings and drawings that do not use child models, and sexually graphic writings about youngsters, might be found obscene if they meet the three-part *Miller* test, but they cannot constitutionally be covered by child pornography laws because they do not exploit actual children.

In practice, however, deciding what qualifies as child pornography can often be as difficult as deciding what is "patently offensive" or "prurient" for purposes of the obscenity test. The problem is particularly acute where simple nudity is targeted: numerous cases have arisen in which overzealous prosecutors or social workers have deemed parents' or artists' innocent nude photos to be child pornography—with frightening and often heartbreaking consequences for the family involved.[48] The legal standard turns on "lasciviousness," which, obviously, is often in the eye of the beholder. As law professor Amy Adler has pointed out, the law's close scrutinizing of child nudes for elements of lasciviousness may have the perverse effect of further sexualizing children's bodies and fomenting rather than squelching pedophilia.[49]

Child pornography laws, moreover, have become increasingly draconian. While simple possession of obscenity in one's home—as opposed to public display, distribution, or sale—is constitutionally protected based on principles of personal freedom and privacy,[50] simple possession of child pornography is often harshly punished. (Prison terms under federal law can be up to fifteen years.[51]) The rationale is that *demand* must be suppressed in order to discourage production, which physically damages minors. Empirically, that may or may not be true. Certainly, harsh penalties do not seem to have suppressed pedophilia or inhibited the popularity of child pornography, which thrives online.

The Internet

Which brings us, of course, to the Internet. It has changed everything, at least in terms of any individual community's—or even country's—ability to enforce its view of acceptable sexual expression. Not only are state or local "community standards" meaningless in cyberspace, but laws banning "indecent" or "harmful to minors" expression, which assume the ability of retail clerks and movie ticket-sellers to distinguish minors from adults, and to provide questionable material only to the latter, would have the effect online of doing just what obscenity law used to do in the days of *Regina v. Hicklin*—that is, consign all of us to the sand-box. Indeed, Congress's first attempt to suppress sexual Internet speech, the 1996 Communications Decency Act (CDA), was struck down precisely because it would have reduced "the adult population" to reading and viewing "only what is fit for children."[52]

The CDA was also constitutionally deficient because it imposed criminal penalties based on the broad FCC "indecency" standard, thereby chilling vast quantities of valuable cyberspeech. Indeed, despite the rhetoric of child protection that runs through the Supreme Court's decision in the CDA case, the justices recognized that a great deal of potentially "indecent" speech, from safer sex information to the Carlin monologue that some of them condemned in *Pacifica*—and that is now available on countless web sites—might well *not* be psychologically damaging to youth.

Congress tried to correct this problem of "overbreadth" in the CDA with a second Internet censorship law, the Child Online Protection Act (COPA). COPA substituted for the CDA's broad indecency ban the "harmful to minors" or "obscenity lite" standard for censoring cyberspace. But the problem of distinguish youthful cybersurfers from older ones remained, and the government's proposed solution—a "good faith" defense to criminal prosecution for Internet speakers who install adult ID screens and the like—is unacceptable to artistic Web publishers, nonprofit groups, and providers of safer sex information, among others, who wish to make their content freely available, cannot afford adult ID or credit card technology, or simply do not want to self-identify as pornographers.[53]

Symbolic Politics and Shifting Boundaries

In the face of these daunting enforcement problems, and despite its post-9/11 focus on suppressing terrorism rather than sex, the George W. Bush administration nevertheless began in 2003 to revive the war on pornography. The impetus was not only Attorney General John Ashcroft's own cultural and religious conservatism, but the ever-present "politics of porn": pressures from the religious right, including complaints of lax enforcement under the previous (Clinton) administration.

Thus, Morality in Media in 1998 asked its supporters "to contact their U.S. Senators to urge an inquiry into the record of the U.S. Attorneys in their states" on obscenity enforcement; and the following year, representatives of Family Friendly Libraries and the Family Research Council complained that President

Clinton had broken his campaign promise of "aggressive enforcement of federal obscenity laws."[54] By late 2003, the Bush administration Justice Department, working with local U.S. attorneys, could report twenty-one federal obscenity convictions. The Baptist News Service quoted Morality in Media:

> Vigorous enforcement of federal obscenity laws came to a somewhat abrupt halt in 1993, right around the time when the Internet was getting ready to take off. In large measure because of a lack of federal obscenity law enforcement, the Internet is now saturated with Web sites peddling hardcore pornography, resulting in untold numbers [of young and old] being lured into sexual addictions. The harm done by pornography shows up in failed marriages, rape, sexual abuse of children, sexually transmitted diseases and abortion. Curbing traffic in illegal obscenity will reduce the number of such tragedies and the need for government programs to deal with them.[55]

Whatever truth there might be in any of these charges (there is no empirical proof of adverse effects from the age-old genre of pornography),[56] it is probably fantasy to think that even a highly aggressive campaign of criminal prosecution will make a significant dent in the quantity of erotica available online. (For one thing, much of it originates abroad.) But this remains a potent symbolic issue for the right—and for some elements of feminism as well—and a relatively easy way to appease an important constituency of the Bush administration.

As Morality in Media's comment suggested, the religious right had by this time adopted much of the rhetoric of anti-pornography feminism, going back to the heyday of law professor Catharine MacKinnon and writer Andrea Dworkin in the 1980s. (MacKinnon and Dworkin coauthored a model anti-pornography ordinance that was held unconstitutional in 1985.[57]) Indeed, the alliance of cultural conservatives with this wing of feminism goes back to the Meese Commission on Pornography investigations of the late 1980s. Sexuality scholars along with anti-censorship and "sex-positive" feminists contested the claims of MacKinnon/Dworkin supporters. But the rift weakened the women's rights movement, and the focus on pornography diverted political energy from actual, rather than symbolic, efforts to stop rape, domestic violence, and sex discrimination.[58]

Ironically, while these political forces continue to contend, pornography has now entered the academy as a legitimate field of study (hence this volume, among others). The Motion Picture Association of America's movie rating system, which forces producers and directors to reduce the sexual charge of their works or else risk the dreaded NC-17 rating, also has the paradoxical effect of further eroticizing taboo content. And the "harm-to-minors" argument for censorship, whose origins lie in powerful cultural anxieties and taboos surrounding *sexuality*, has reemerged as the theme of highly charged political attacks on *violence* in popular culture. (One recent book is even called *Saving Our Children From the First Amendment*.[59])

All of this debate and discussion may be healthy, but what tends to be missing is an acknowledgment of the importance, for adults and minors alike, of art, literature, and accurate information about sexuality, that "great and mysterious motive force in human life." In the midst of an ever-more sexually explicit culture, the U.S. government has myopically adopted an ideologically driven "abstinence-only-until-marriage" philosophy of sex education, and promoted it with the large infusions of federal funding that state health and education officials, even if they know better, find difficult to resist.[60] As a result of this and other inhibitions on providing comprehensive sex education, American children and teenagers are considerably more ignorant about sexuality than their counterparts in other Western societies. Masturbation—the desired outcome, after all, of much pornographic reading and viewing—is still a taboo subject not only in the classroom but in much of the mainstream media.

Meanwhile, the boundaries on what sexual expression is acceptable, for adults or minors, continue to shift. Sexuality and sex censorship remain hot political issues, as they have been since the days of *Regina v. Hicklin*.

NOTES

1. *Jacobellis v. Ohio*, 378 U.S. 184, 197 (1964) (Stewart, J., concurring).

2. Technically, the First Amendment only prohibits Congress from passing laws that abridge free speech. Indeed, all of the Bill of Rights originally applied solely to the federal government, with states bound only by their own constitutions. By the middle of the twentieth century, though, the Supreme Court had applied almost all the basic protections of the Bill of Rights to the states.

3. Philippe Ariès, *Centuries of Childhood* (New York: Vintage, 1962), 103.

4. See Marjorie Heins, *Not in Front of the Children: "Indecency," Censorship, and the Innocence of Youth* (New York: Hill & Wang, 2001), 18–23.

5. See Theodore Schroeder, *"Obscene" Literature and Constitutional Law* (New York: privately printed, 1911); David Rabban, *Free Speech in Its Forgotten Years* (Cambridge: Cambridge University Press, 1997).

6. *Regina v. Hicklin*, 3 Queens Bench 360, 362 (1868).

7. An Act for the Suppression of Trade in, and Circulation of, Obscene Literature and Articles of Immoral Use, c. 258, §2, 17 Stat. 598, 599 (1873) (carrying over some language from the 1865 Post Office Act, c. 89, §16, 13. Stat. 504, 507 (1865)). The federal obscenity law has been amended many times; it is now codified at 18 U.S. Code §1461.

8. For example, *United States v. Bennett*, 24 F. Cas. 1093, 1101–04 (Cir. Ct. S.D.N.Y. 1879); see *Not in Front of the Children*, 32–33.

9. *United States v. Kennerley*, 209 Fed. Rep. 119, 121 (S.D.N.Y. 1913).

10. *United States v. Dennett*, 39 F.2d 564, 568 (2d Cir. 1930).

11. *United States v. One Book Called "Ulysses,"* 5 F. Supp. 182, 183–85 (S.D.N.Y. 1933).

12. *United States v. One Book Entitled Ulysses by James Joyce*, 72 F.2d 705, 706–07 (2d Cir. 1934).

13. *People v. Doubleday & Co.*, 297 N.Y. 799 (1947), affirmed by an equally divided Court, 335 U.S. 848 (1948).

14. *Roth v. United States*, 354 U.S. 476, 483–87 (1957).

15. *Grove Press v. Gerstein*, 378 U.S. 577 (1964) (*Tropic of Cancer*); *Grove Press v. Christenberry*, 175 F. Supp. 488 (S.D.N.Y. 1959), affirmed, 275 F.2d 433 (2d Cir. 1960) (*Lady Chatterley*). See Edward de Grazia, *Girls Lean Back Everywhere: The Law of Obscenity and the Assault on Genius* (New York: Random House, 1992).

16. *Miller v. California*, 413 U.S. 15, 24 (1973).

17. *Paris Adult Theatre I v. Slaton*, 413 U.S. 49, 84 (1973) (dissenting opinion of Justice Brennan).

18. See, for example, the incidents described by the National Coalition Against Censorship's Arts Advocacy Project, www.ncac.org/projects/artsadvocacy.html (last visited January 10, 2006); Steven Dubin, *Arresting Images* (New York: Routledge, 1992), 170–190 (describing uproar over exhibition of erotic images by Robert Mapplethorpe, including obscenity prosecution of Cincinnati Contemporary Arts Center and its director).

19. The reference here is to rhetoric emphasizing the perceived need to protect minors simply from exposure to sexual information and ideas. The conceptually distinct question of child pornography, which turns on the need to protect minors from actual sexual abuse, is discussed later in this chapter.

20. *Renton v. Playtime Theatres, Inc.*, 475 U.S. 41, 49 (1986) (quoting the federal district court decision). In 2002, the Court revisited adult zoning and "secondary effects"; its decision in *City of Los Angeles v. Alameda Books, Inc.*, 535 U.S. 425 (2002), followed *Renton* but made the city's burden of justification even lighter. Justice Anthony Kennedy wrote a concurrence in which he acknowledged that designating adult zoning regulations as "content-neutral" is "something of a fiction." *Id.* at 447.

21. *Schad v. Mount Ephraim*, 452 U.S. 61, 66 (1981); see also *Doran v. Salem Inn, Inc.*, 422 U.S. 922, 932 (1975) ("the customary 'bar-room type' of nude dancing may involve only the barest minimum of protected expression").

22. *Miller v. Civil City of South Bend*, 904 F.2d 1081, 1087, 1085–86 (7th Cir. 1990) (*en banc*) (emphasis in original) (no source is given, but the quotation comes from Mallarmé's *Selected Prose Poems, Essays, and Letters*, trans. Bradford Cook) [1956], reprinted in *What is Dance? Readings in Theory and Criticism*, ed. Roger Copeland and Marshall Cohen (New York: Oxford University Press, 1983), 111–115.

23. *Barnes v. Glen Theatre, Inc.*, 501 U.S. 560, 565 (1981) (plurality opinion); *id.* at 580 (concurring opinion by Justice Souter). Souter's *mea culpa*, acknowledging that to defend a law on the basis of adverse secondary effects, municipalities ought at least to present some evidence, came nineteen years after *Barnes*, in *City of Erie v. Pap's A.M.*, 529 U.S. 277, 310 (concurring and dissenting opinion of Justice Souter).

24. *City of Erie v. Pap's A.M.*, 529 U.S. 277, 323 (2000) (dissenting opinion of Justice Stevens).

25. *City of Erie v. Pap's A.M.*, 529 U.S. at 301 (plurality opinion).

26. *City of Erie v. Pap's A.M.*, 529 U.S. at 310 (concurring opinion of Justice Scalia).

27. See Marjorie Heins, *Sex, Sin, and Blasphemy: A Guide to America's Censorship Wars* (New York: New Press, 1993; 2nd ed. 1998), 95–115 (describing use of full nudity in *M. Butterfly, Marat-Sade, Dr. Faustus, Tannhäuser*, and other works).

28. *Barnes v. Glen Theatre, Inc.*, 501 U.S. 560, 593 (1981) (dissenting opinion of Justice White) (quoting *Salem Inn, Inc. v. Frank*, 501 F.2d 18, 21 n.3 (2d Cir. 1974)); *City of Erie v. Pap's A.M.*, 529 U.S. 277, 327–30 (2000) (dissenting opinion of Justice Stevens).

29. *National Endowment for the Arts v. Finley*, 524 U.S. 569, 585, 587–88 (1998) (quoting *Rust v. Sullivan*, 500 U.S. 173, 193 (1991)). The author was co-counsel for the plaintiffs in the *Finley* case.

30. *National Endowment for the Arts v. Finley*, 524 U.S. at 587 (quoting *Regan v. Taxation With Representation*, 461 U.S. 540, 550 (1983)).

31. *National Endowment for the Arts v. Finley*, 524 U.S. at 600 (dissenting opinion of Justice Souter); *id.* at 590 (concurring opinion of Justice Scalia).

32. Christina Cho, Kim Commerato, and Marjorie Heins, *Free Expression in Arts Funding: A Public Policy Report* (New York: Free Expression Policy Project, 2003), 38–39, available at www.fepproject.org/policyreports/artsfunding.pdf (last visited January 10, 2006).

33. See, for example, *Hopper v. City of Pasco*, 241 F.3d 1067 (9th Cir. 2001) (ruling that city officials had created a "public forum" at city hall for the display of art); *Lebron v. National RR Passenger Corp.*, 69 F.3d 650, modified, 89 F.3d 39 (2d Cir. 1995) (rejecting public forum argument for the large display space in New York City's Pennsylvania Station); *Henderson v. City of Murfreesboro*, 960 F. Supp. 1292 (M.D. Tenn. 1997) (holding that city hall exhibit space was a "designated public forum"); *Claudio v. United States*, 836 F. Supp. 1219 (E.D.N.C. 1993), affirmed without opinion, 28 F.3d 1208 (4th Cir. 1994) (finding no public forum in federal building lobby).

34. Public Law 106–554, §§1(a)(4),114 Stat. 2763, amending 20 U.S.C. §§6801 (the Elementary and Secondary Education Act); 20 U.S.C. §§9134(b) (the Museum and Library Services Act);

and 47 U.S.C. §§254(h) (the Universal Service Discount, or e-rate, provision of the Communications Act).

35. *American Library Association v. United States*, 201 F. Supp.2d 401, 431–48 (E.D. Pa. 2002), reversed, 123 S.Ct. 2297 (2003). On the flaws in Internet filters, see David Sobel, ed., *Filters & Freedom 2.0* (Washington, D.C.: Electronic Privacy Information Center, 2001); Christina Cho, *Internet Filters: A Public Policy Report* (New York: Free Expression Policy Project, 2001), www.fepproject.org/policyreports/internetfilters.html; Free Expression Policy Project, *Fact Sheet on Internet Filters*, www.fepproject.org/factsheets/filtering.html (both last visited January 10, 2006).

36. *United States v. American Library Association*, 123 S.Ct. 2297, 2304–09 (2003). Justices Anthony Kennedy and Stephen Breyer wrote separate opinions concurring in the judgment upholding CIPA. Both relied on the "disabling" provisions as a way for libraries to avoid restricting adults' access to the Internet. Kennedy emphasized that if libraries fail to unblock, or adults are otherwise burdened in their Internet searches, then a lawsuit challenging CIPA "as applied" to that situation might be appropriate. *Id.* at 2309–12 (2003) (concurring opinions of Justices Kennedy and Breyer).

37. *United States v. American Library Association*, 123 S.Ct. at 2317 (dissenting opinion of Justice Souter); 2321–22 (dissenting opinion of Justice Stevens).

38. *Tinker v. Des Moines Independent School District*, 393 U.S. 503, 506 (1969).

39. *Bethel School District No. 403 v. Fraser*, 478 U.S. 675, 681 (1986) (quoting, on "habits and manners of civility," Charles & Mary Beard, *New Basic History of the United States* (1968), 228); *id.* at 683 ("by glorifying male sexuality"); 687 (concurring opinion of Justice Brennan) (quoting the speech).

40. *Bethel School District No. 403 v. Fraser*, 478 U.S. at 692 (dissenting opinion of Justice Stevens).

41. *Pacifica Foundation*, 56 FCC 2d 94, 97–98 (1975). Carlin's monologue, broadcast in 1973 on WBAI-Pacifica radio in New York, was a commentary on taboos surrounding "seven dirty words" that, Carlin rightly predicted, could not be spoken on the public airwaves. For background on the *Pacifica* case and the origins and subsequent fortunes of the indecency regime, see *Not in Front of the Children*, 89–136.

42. *Federal Communications Commission v. Pacifica Foundation*, 438 U.S. 726, 749 (1978) (plurality opinion); *id.* at 757–58 (concurring opinion of Justice Powell). The decision was 5–4; Justice Brennan wrote in dissent: "surprising as it may be to some individual Members of this Court, some parents may actually find Mr. Carlin's unabashed attitude towards the seven 'dirty words" healthy, and deem it desirable to expose their children to the manner in which Mr. Carlin defuses the taboo surrounding the words." *Id.* at 770 (dissenting opinion of Justice Brennan).

43. Public Notice, *New Indecency Enforcement Standards To Be Applied to All Broadcast and Amateur Radio Licensees*, 2 FCC Rcd 2726 (1987); *Pacifica Foundation*, 2 FCC Rcd 2698 (1987); *Regents of the University of California*, 2 FCC Rcd 2703 (1987); *Infinity Broadcasting*, 2 FCC Rcd 2705 (1987).

44. *Federal Communications Commission v. Pacifica Foundation*, 438 U.S. at 775 (dissenting opinion of Justice Brennan).

45. *In the Matter of the KBOO Foundation*, File No. EB-00-IHD-0079, DA 01–1212 (May 14, 2001), www.fcc.gov/eb/Orders/2001/da011212.doc (last visited January 10, 2006). In 2003—nearly two years after its indecency ruling that essentially barred Jones's song from radio, and in the face of a lawsuit from Jones—the FCC reversed itself, now finding that although this was "a very close case," the rap was not indecent because "on balance and in context," the sexual descriptions were "not sufficiently graphic to warrant sanction." *In the Matter of the KBOO Foundation*, DA 03–469 (Feb. 20, 2003), www.fcc/gov/eb/orders/2003/DA-03–469A1.html (last visited January 10, 2006). See Marjorie Heins, "The Strange Case of Sarah Jones," January 24, 2003, www.fepproject.org/commentaries/sarahjones.html; Free Expression Policy Project, "News: FCC Declares *Your Revolution* not Indecent After All," February 20, 2003, www.fepproject.org/news/sarahjones.html (both last visited January 10, 2006).

46. In *Ginsberg v. New York*, 390 U.S. 629 (1968), the Supreme Court upheld a criminal law that used the "harmful to minors," or "variable obscenity," standard; see *Not in Front of the Children*, 71–74, 121–122.

47. In a few such cases, the courts recognized that First Amendment rights of teens could be compromised by "harmful to minors" laws, and accordingly interpreted such laws narrowly so that they would not apply to sexual material or erotic works with serious value for "a legitimate minority" of "older, normal (not deviant) adolescents." *Virginia v. American Booksellers Association*, 236 Va. 168, 173–75 (1988); see also *American Booksellers Association v. Webb*, 919 F.2d 1493 (11th Cir. 1990).

48. See, for example, *Arresting Images*, 137–141, 174–175 (describing prosecution of Cincinnati museum for showing child nudes by Robert Mapplethorpe, among other cases); web site of Marilyn Zimmerman, www.umich.edu/~ws483/Zimmerman.html (last visited January 10, 2006) ("like too many feminist photographers in recent years, [Zimmerman] found herself on the front lines of the culture wars when she battled censors who claimed that photographs of her three year old daughter in the bathtub and at her birthday party could be child pornography and she should be prosecuted. In 1993, her home and office at Wayne State University were raided by Detroit police who had been tipped off by a janitor claiming that a contact sheet 'looked like porn' to him. The prosecutor's investigation ended after a nationwide response from artists, curators and scholars attested to Zimmerman's significance as an American artist and educator, and to the historical context for works of art that have shown nudes, including children").

49. Amy Adler, "The Perverse Law of Child Pornography," 101 *Columbia Law Review* 209 (2001). The Supreme Court first created an exception to the First Amendment for child pornography in *New York v. Ferber*, 458 U.S. 747 (1982). In 2002, it struck down Congress's attempted expansion of the federal child pornography ban to cover computerized "virtual" child pornography images, precisely because it could not be shown that any real children had been sexually abused in their production. *Ashcroft v. Free Speech Coalition*, 535 U.S. 234 (2002). The government had argued that computer graphics and morphing techniques make it too difficult for prosecutors to prove that an actual child was used.

50. *Stanley v. Georgia*, 394 U.S. 557 (1969).

51. 18 U.S. Code §2252, §2252a (penalties for possession of child pornography).

52. *Reno v. American Civil Liberties Union*, 521 U.S. 844, 875 (1997). The line originally comes from *Butler v. Michigan*, 352 U.S. 380, 383 (1957). The author was co-counsel for the plaintiffs in *Reno v. ACLU*.

53. A federal appeals court initially invalidated COPA on the ground that the statute's reliance on "community standards" to regulate cyberspace would permit the most puritanical communities, by choosing to initiate prosecutions, to set the censorship standard for the entire nation. *American Civil Liberties Union v. Ashcroft*, 217 F.3d 162 (3d Cir. 2000). But the Supreme Court reversed, and sent the case back for further consideration. *Ashcroft v. American Civil Liberties Union*, 535 U.S. 564 (2002). Whereupon, the court of appeals again struck down the law—or, to be precise, issued a preliminary injunction in an opinion strongly suggesting that the law was unconstitutional. *American Civil Liberties Union, et al. v. Ashcroft*, 322 F.3d 240 (3d Cir. 2003). This time, the Supreme Court affirmed. *Ashcroft v. American Civil Liberties Union*, 124 S.Ct. 2783 (2004).

54. Morality in Media, "Clinton Administration Prosecutes Six Obscenity Cases in '97," *Conservative News Service*, October 19, 1998, www.conservativenews.org/Culture/archive/CUL19981019b.html; Janet LaRue and Karen Gounaud, "Few Obscenity Cases Prosecuted Even As More Kids Use the Web," letter to *Sacramento Bee*, March 13, 1999, www.fflibraries.org/Speeches_Editorials_Papers/LaRueGounaudKnightRidderColumn3-13-99.htm (last visited January 10, 2006).

55. Robert Peters, president of Morality in Media, quoted in Erin Curry, "Obscenity Prosecution Featured in Congressional Resolution," Baptist Press News Service, December 2003, www.crosswalk.com/news/religiontoday/1147544.html (last visited January 10, 2006; see also Jan LaRue, "DOJ Releases List of 'Obscenity Prosecutions During This Administration,'" Concerned Women for America, December 18, 2003, www.cwfa.org/articles/5022/LEGAL/pornography/ (last visited January 10, 2006); Jake Tapper, "Politics of Porn: Justice Department Launches Long-Anticipated War on Obscenity," ABC News, August 28, 2003, www.stevegilliard/blogspot.com/2003_08_29_stevegilliard_archive.html (last visited January 10, 2006).

56. See, for example, the brief filed by four sexuality scholars' organizations in the COPA case: Brief *Amici Curiae* of the Society for the Scientific Study of Sexuality, et al., in *Ashcroft v.*

American Civil Liberties Union, S.Ct. No. 00–1293 (Sept. 20, 2001), www.fepproject.org/court-briefs/ashcroft.pdf (last visited January 10, 2006).

57. *American Booksellers Association v. Hudnut*, 771 F.2d 323 (7th Cir. 1985), affirmed mem., 475 U.S. 1001 (1986).

58. The literature on both sides of the feminist pornography debate is vast; see, for example, Catharine MacKinnon, *Feminism Unmodified* (Cambridge, Mass.: Harvard University Press, 1987); Andrea Dworkin, *Pornography: Men Possessing Women* (New York: Plume/Penguin, 1981); Nadine Strossen, *Defending Pornography* (New York: Scribner, 1995); Feminists for Free Expression Web site, www.ffeusa.org/ (last visited January 10, 2006); Nan Hunter and Sylvia Law, Brief *Amici Curiae* of Feminist Anti-Censorship Task Force et al. in *American Booksellers Association v. Hudnut*, No. 84–3147 (1985), published in 21 *Michigan Journal of Law Reform* 69 (1987–88).

59. Kevin Saunders, *Saving Our Children From the First Amendment* (New York: New York University Press, 2003). The literature on "media effects" is vast; see, for example, Free Expression Policy Project, "Issues: Violence in the Media," www.fepproject.org/issues/violence.html; and the bibliography in Free Expression Policy Project, "Media Violence Fact Sheet, www.fepproject.org/factsheets/mediaviolence.html (both last visited January 10, 2006).

60. The 1996 welfare reform law included an obscure provision that provides for federal funding of "abstinence education" if it meets an ideologically driven, medically inaccurate eight-part standard, including teaching that "sexually activity outside of the context of marriage is likely to have harmful psychological and physical effects." Personal Responsibility and Work Opportunity Act of 1996, §912, codified at 42 U.S. Code §710; see *Not in Front of the Children*, 145–148.

Nina K. Martin

Never Laugh at a Man with His Pants Down: The Affective Dynamics of Comedy and Porn

The scene unfolds as Dr. Seymour Love (Jamie Gillis) and a flight attendant discuss his future flight arrangements near the cockpit. Seymour is on his transatlantic journey to turn the ingénue prostitute Misty into the infamous "Golden Rod Girl" in *The Opening of Misty Beethoven* (Henry Paris, 1975):

> FLIGHT ATTENDANT: I can confirm your return on that date.
>
> SEYMOUR: That's wonderful.
>
> FLIGHT ATTENDANT: The destination is NY and its first class? Which part of first class—sex or non-sex?
>
> SEYMOUR: Sex.
>
> FLIGHT ATTENDANT: First class, sex, non-smoking, or first class, sex, smoking?
>
> SEYMOUR: Uh, first class, sex, non-smoking.
>
> FLIGHT ATTENDANT: Are you a fucker or only interested in a little head?
>
> SEYMOUR: Just a little head.
>
> FLIGHT ATTENDANT: Very good. That's 3 seats, Cascade Flight 111, destination New York, first class, sex, non-smoking, no special meal, interested in a little sex, and a lot of pleasure. Happy landings!

Shortly thereafter, a series of libidinal events occur that would seem startlingly unfamiliar on your average commercial flight, but merrily absurd in this classic porn film. Another flight attendant confirms the order of one gentleman for "one dinner, a brandy, 2 blowjobs, and a headset," and the man politely complains that he has only received one blowjob and no brandy. Another flight attendant immediately arrives to remedy the situation. Meanwhile, Misty is visited in first class by a woman who sits next to her and starts caressing her, but is interrupted during cunnilingus by a flight attendant, who quietly tells the woman that she cannot be in first class without a reservation, even if she is the pilot's wife.

As these high flying maneuvers occur, I hear a rumble of laughter repeatedly circulate through the small screening room where my graduate students and I watch *Misty* for the seminar I am teaching on body genres. Henry Paris's classic retelling of *Pygmalion* is the first film of three I will show, and I am delighted that my students are relaxed and enjoying the film instead of nervously tittering or being silently horrified at the explicit images represented onscreen. This 1970s example of heterosexual hard-core porn, masterfully discussed in Linda Williams's book *Hard Core*, is riddled with gags, verbal puns, and a completely hilarious montage of Misty "training" with Seymour, sporting a track suit and pigtails as she works through her exercises, culminating in successfully getting three servants off simultaneously. Further, an absurd libidinousness permeates the entire film as Seymour and his lusty friend, Geraldine, are constantly sipping champagne while being serviced by the various servants in their employ. The mingling of humor and sex seems effortless, and in the analysis of bodily affect, the dynamics between the genres—comedy and pornography—seems curiously unexplored.

The Body Convulsed in Ecstasy and Laughter

> *Visually, each of these ecstatic excesses could be said to share a quality of uncontrollable convulsion or spasm—of the body "beside itself."*
> —Williams, "Film Bodies," 269

My interest in the affective dynamics of comedy and porn was not only stimulated by my students' positive response, but also through Linda Williams's close analysis of what she deems "body genres"—melodrama, horror, and pornography—and their affective relationship to both spectatorial pleasure and gender representation. For Williams, porn films are meant to stimulate arousal, as pent-up tension convulses ultimately in release—orgasm. Similarly, melodrama and horror also produce specific bodily responses in the spectator—tears and screams respectively. Williams argues that since these genres maintain an affective relationship to the spectator's body, they are looked upon as "low" genres, due to the excessive sensation and emotion they produce (Williams, "Film Bodies," 270). Comedy can also produce excessive bodily responses, placing the spectator "in the throes of a mild seizure we call laughter" (Gutwirth 1993, 9). While, as Williams clarifies, comedy may not produce a bodily mimicry of the characters onscreen (who usually react in a deadpan manner), the success of the comedy genre is still measured by bodily response—as it is in pornography (Williams, "Film Bodies," 270). Laughter and orgasm share both the building of tension and the body convulsed. As John Bancroft explains in his discussion of selections of sex and humor from the Kinsey Institute,

> Darwin drew the analogy between tickling the body, which makes us laugh in almost reflex fashion, and "tickling the imagination with a ludicrous idea." The theoretical approach that probably takes us closest to this basic mechanism sees laughter as the response involved in the release of pent-up tension, with humor the mood state associated with this release. (Bancroft 2002, 7)

Further, in both orgasm and laughter the body experiences a form of defenselessness and physical vulnerability, as the person lets down her or his guard entirely, in laughter with "eyes streaming, chest heaving" (Gutwirth 1993, 11).

Both comedy and pornography are also situated in the realm of spectacle, and as Laura Mulvey has pointed out, spectacle works against narrative development and "freezes the flow of action" (Mulvey 1999, 63). With comedy, as Steve Neale and Frank Krutnick explain, "it is difficult to use [jokes, wisecracks, and funny lines] as a springboard for narrative development. They are instead much more suited to constructing or marking a pause or digression in the ongoing flow of the story" (Neale and Krutnick 1990, 48). The dialogue between Seymour Love and the flight attendant in *The Opening of Misty Beethoven* provides a good example. Ultimately, the narrative momentum follows Misty's journey toward sexual expertise; the brief discussion regarding flight reservations is not necessary to the story, and virtually halts the narrative's drive as the jokes and puns are told. Similarly, physical humor such as pratfalls also emphasizes spectacle and creates a pause in the film's narrative, focusing on a vulnerable body and often stimulating the bodily response of laughter.

In pornography, the spectacle onscreen is the naked, sexual body, usually in close-up, explicitly displayed. Williams reiterates the spectacular nature of pornography in her book-length exploration of the subject, *Hard Core*, emphasizing that the conventions of porn require that "the bodies within the film frame come so close that their means of relation is no longer looking but touching," and this spectacle in turn halts pornography's narrative drive (Williams, *Hard Core*, 71). Still, she is equally invested in exploring the narratives of porn films, suggesting that their alternating structure of narrative and sexual number, where the spectacle of sex seems to be bracketed from the narrative, is similar to the structure of the Hollywood musical, with its spectacles of song and dance embedded in the film's narrative (Williams, *Hard Core*, 130–152). Her analysis of *Misty Beethoven* certainly supports this assertion as the sex numbers are integrated within the narrative but nevertheless delineated through their sheer spectacular nature.

Still, not all porn scholars agree with Williams's reliance on comparing porn with Hollywood narrative film, and I believe that the successful intermingling of comedy and porn, and the subsequent mixing of narrative and spectacle apparent in some of 1970s hardcore, is dependent on an historical understanding of screening and exhibition practices. Peter Lehman, for instance, takes issue with her discussion of spectatorship in relation to some of the classic porn films she explores, suggesting that classical Hollywood spectatorship does not apply. He points out that "in the 1970's, for example, when many of the films Williams analyzes were being shown exclusively in 35mm theaters, most spectators entered the theaters randomly, without the usual regard for the starting time of the feature" (Lehman, "Twin Cheeks," 47). Indeed, while Williams outlines some of the differences between stag films and theatrical features, she does not initially address the genre's subsequent changes as porn moved to different exhibition venues. In what seems to be an answer to this criticism, Williams adds in her epilogue to the expanded paperback edition that when shifting to a theatrical venue, "this comparatively public, mixed-company viewing situation presumed a much greater suppression of visceral response than that of the gregarious, but much more private secret museum [of the stag film]" (Williams, *Hard Core*, 296). The important shift hinges on the presence of a public audience.

The influx of home viewing technology in the last twenty-five years has not only changed the exhibition space of porn, but the structure of its narratives as well. Now that the viewing situation is often private (in the home) and frequently individual (by oneself), the purposes of hardcore are more masturbatory and also highly interactive as the spectator has control over the watching and manipulation of specific scenes; the films have subsequently become less narrative-driven and far more episodic. As Joseph Slade explains in analyzing John Leslie's porn films from the 1980s and 1990s,

> the plots in a pornographic film do not matter. They are just enabling devices to permit the sex to take place. They are continuously destroyed anyway by the intrusion of sex, which still so shocks our sensibilities that we forget the story. Sex gives weight to bodies, and removes the ordinary necessity for characterization. (Slade 1997, 141)

Certainly porn narratives have become less complex over the last two decades, and I would suggest that the humor that was part of 1970s hardcore was not only dependent on the public audience that saw those films, but has also lost its intermingling within a larger narrative form. Whereas for Neale and Krutnick, "comedy seems especially suited to hybridization" because laughter can be inserted in most other genres without disturbing their generic conventions, in most contemporary pornography, humor proves far too disturbing (Neale and Krutnick 1990, 18). Comedy and pornography seem to have grown increasingly incompatible.

Pornography Is No Laughing Matter

The fact remains, however, that the porn industry's humorous titling of many of its films basically consists of isolated, single jokes. Most porn films, however witty their titles, are not comedies and involve little or no humor (Lehman, "Twin Cheeks," 48).

Pornographic representations are deeply invested in seriousness, and much of porn's lack of humor relates to cultural understandings of patriarchal power, a power that is rigorously maintained by equating the sight/site of the penis with awe. Porn conventions emphasize not only the size of the penis, but its requisite, and often perpetual hardness. Peter Lehman has pointed out in his study of penis-size jokes that the conspicuousness of a large male organ is an essential component of what Freud sees as the visual drama of sexual difference (Lehman, "Penis-size Jokes," 44–45). Certainly, any insertion of laughter and levity in regards to the penis smacks of derision, and implies inadequacy. Porn foils any notions of inadequacy by utilizing conventions that maintain *awesome* representations of the penis, whether through close-up "meat shots" (genital penetration) or the ubiquitous "money shot" (visible ejaculation). The awesomeness of the penis in heterosexual porn is further emphasized by the repeated use of the "facial" at the close of virtually every sex number, where the male star ejaculates on the woman's face, and she appears to writhe ecstatically at his display.

Another way that porn retains its serious tone is by fiercely separating any comedy or funny bits from the actual performance of the sex numbers. As Marcel Gutwirth explains, "laughter is rigorously incompatible with awe. Awesomeness and absurdity are two distinct perspectives: we cannot encompass them simultaneously" (Gutwirth 1993, 17). The shift from laughs to sex is usually distinguishable by the increased aural presence of background music, almost complete lack of dialogue, and frequent moans of pleasure on the part of the actors. For instance, in the porn comedy/parody *Austin Prowler* (Jim Powers, 1999), a nurse is enlisted to pull superagent Austin out of deep freeze in order to defeat the evil Dr. Pussy (who just moments before also came out of deep freeze, seemingly stuck in the 1970s, discussing bands like the Bay City Rollers). In order to get Austin his "mojo" back, a nurse addresses the camera, stating she'll give him "CPR," and the other nurse then also turns to the camera and states, "I'd say she's a woman of many skills." Ba-dum-bum. A protracted sex number beginning with fellatio then begins, where the only sign that Austin is still in character is his occasional "Oh baby" and "Yeah, baby." No more jokes or wisecracks are present as the actors perform the sexual number with serious intensity; the comedy is distinct from the sex, maintaining the awe and drama surrounding the representation of the penis. Joseph Slade quotes exploitation director Roberta Findlay as likening hardcore porn to opera: "You have the opera story, but then everything stops when the soprano has to sing. It's the same thing in sex films. The story goes on, then it stops, then they have to screw" (Slade 1997, 115). As in opera, no one laughs while the aria is underway—opera conventions demand this respect. The penis demands its own form of respect.

Porn conventions perpetuate the visual drama of the penis by maintaining standards aligned with documentary evidence; sex numbers and performances are not simulated, but "real," actual events captured by a camera and revealed through the money shot. As Williams explains, "the genre has consistently maintained certain clinical-documentary qualities at the expense of other forms of realism and artistry that might actually be more arousing. We might call this latter feature the principle of maximum *visibility*" (Williams, *Hard Core*, 48). The successful depiction of the sex unfolding is not only established by conventional graphic close-ups, but also a necessary disavowal that the characters having sex are *performing*; for "the successful performance—of sex or song and dance—depends on the number's seeming not to *be* a performance but to arise naturally and spontaneously from the sexual desires of the performing couple" (Williams, *Hardcore*, 145). Nevertheless, any implied spontaneity is only an illusion, part of the temporal fantasy structure that is intrinsic to the construction of porn. For Williams, porn "attempts to posit the utopian fantasy of perfect temporal coincidence: a subject and object (or seducer and seduced) who meet one another 'on time!' and 'now!' in shared moments of mutual pleasure" (Williams, "Film Bodies," 279). Even though this utopian simultaneity appears unexpected, the sex number is precisely choreographed and ritualized; the scene's ending in a money shot fulfills expectations and verifies, with visible evidence, that the sex act is not simulated, but real.

Comedy, instead, is dependent upon the element of surprise, and the unexpected is what stimulates the sudden burst of laughter. Comic scholar Jerry Palmer defines comedy's surprises as "Peripeteia"—the moment when the fortunes of a character are suddenly reversed (Palmer 1987, 39–40). Sharing similarities with horror (another body genre, according to Williams),

> surprise is the point at which the spectator's position is most at stake—the point at which the physical articulation of affect (in the form of laughing or screaming) is more likely to occur. The spectator's laughter, specifically, marks in each instance the restoration of superiority and power. (Neale and Krutnik 1990, 80)

In opposition to porn's temporal utopian spontaneity, both horror and comedy suggest a temporality that is "too early." The notion of surprise and the unexpected in porn produces a loss of the superiority and control invested in the penis, resulting in the horrible reality of premature ejaculation. Conversely, any planned setup of a gag or a joke in a comedy film often fails to elicit laughter, for, as Gutwirth explains in quoting humor scholar A. J. Chapman,

> subject laughter is diminished in quantity and quality whenever there is a hint, however subtle, that it is an expected behavior. Laughter is choked off by the slightest inroad on its spontaneity. Unexpected is also unforeseen: unguarded against, on the one hand; on the other, unprepared for. (Gutwirth 1993, 103)

Another way in which porn is markedly different from comedy is through the necessary close identification porn spectators have with the bodies onscreen—an identification that is intrinsically part of all so-called body genres. This closeness to the image is replicated through a lack of aesthetic and intellectual distance that might be undermined by the revelation of self-conscious performance or artifice. While porn undeniably veers from the narrative illusionism common to theories of spectatorship surrounding classical Hollywood cinema, the genre does rely heavily upon coded conventions of realism that are rigorously maintained. These conventions involve the concealment of artifice, and even though actors may look directly at the camera in ways that do "not threaten to collapse the sealed-off world of the fiction" as Peter Lehman rightly claims, nevertheless the fiction of spontaneous, endlessly satisfying sex must persist (Lehman, "Twin Cheeks," 51).

On the other hand, comedy frequently revels in its status as fiction, knowingly nodding toward an implied audience and emphasizing a divergence from common realities and experiences through the use of exaggeration and seemingly impossible incongruities. Neale and Krutnik contend that

> with comedy laughter "disrupts" the "passively consumed" dramatic illusionism and one is pulled away from the world represented on the screen and is united with other spectators as part of an *audience*. And as comedy frequently calls attention to its status as fiction the spectator is more aware that he/she is watching a *film* rather than looking into a "realistically" constructed world. (Neale and Krutnik 1990, 149)

Certainly, when laughter erupts in a theater, not only does the film acknowledge its artifice but also acknowledges the presence of other spectators. Any kind of close identification with the image or character onscreen shatters (while porn's frequent viewing by an audience of *one* serves to sustain the spectator's closeness). As Gutwirth asserts, "The function of laughter is clear: it consists in breaking up this at-one-ness with things, this communion with the real" (Gutwirth 1993, 85).

So, it would seem that comedy and pornography, while both aligned with spectacle and a spectator's bodily response, are fairly opposed to each other in structure and intention. Despite comedy's easy melding with other genres such as horror or the Western, comedy would appear to undermine radically the conventions that sustain porn's emphasis on phallic superiority and control. Nevertheless, there *are* award-winning porn comedies, however few, that have been produced in recent years, and their success relies upon their ability to parody not only Hollywood films and television but also the conventions of the porn genre themselves.

The Power of Parody

As Peter Lehman argues, the sheer amount of parodied porn titles available and continually produced says more about porn's "ugly stepsister" relationship to the

Hollywood industry than it reveals about porn's interaction with humor and comedy (Lehman, "Twin Cheeks," 45–54). Truly inspired titles such as *Black Cock Down*, *Bonfire of the Panties*, *Done in 60 Seconds*, *Finding Nympho*, *Frosty the Blowman*, *Hairy Pooper and the Sorcerer's Bone*, *Lawrence of a Labia*, and *Ordinary Peepholes* do not retain a connection to their parodied text beyond their title (The Greatest Porn Parodies Ever). Still, there are those films that not only depend upon a target text, but are also genuinely funny. For Neale and Krutnik, "parody is a special case. In contrast to generic hybrids, which combine generic conventions, parodies work by drawing upon such conventions in order to make us laugh" (Neale and Krutnik 1990, 18). In a sense, porn parodies do not undermine the conventions of porn but *solidify and reify* these conventions by highlighting their ubiquitous presence. Porn parodies acknowledge a particular type of audience, usually those well-versed in porn and porn conventions; the possibility of "getting" the parody is actually dependent upon the spectator's familiarity with porn. As Dan Harries outlines in his detailed exploration of film parody, "the viewer needs to have some familiarity with the target text in order to appreciate the parodic activity" (Harries 2000, 25). Further, porn parodies, in their continued address to heterosexual male spectators, tend to parody male-identified genres, such as science fiction. (The Sex Trek series, a blatant rip-off of "Star Trek" is a noteworthy example.)

One very recent parody that relies heavily on an audience's association with a film's target text is Antonio Passolini's *The Ozporns* (2003), a parody based on MTV's reality series *The Osbournes*, which stars real-life former rocker Ozzy Osbourne, with his wife, Sharon, and kids, Jack and Kelly. The parody is striking in its portrayal of Izzie, Sherri, and their kids, John and Fiona, in that Izzie is a dead-on imitation of Ozzy, from his incomprehensible British accent, laden with expletives, broken sentences, and trailing thoughts, to the man's odd, brain-dead shuffle around his Los Angeles home, painstakingly stumbling over the most mundane tasks (such as taking out the garbage). Like MTV's reality series, *The Ozporns* oscillates between captured candid moments of the family with talking head interviews of the show's main characters; these interviews provide the majority of the film's humor such as when Izzie utters bizarre statements such as "I like little kittens and things," or when Sherri's assistant, Sarah, describes a typical day with Izzie: "He almost fell down the stairs. He wanted to roll around in broken glass. He wanted to grill the Pomeranian on the rotisserie. He wanted to stick a live fruit bat up his ass, and that was all in the first day." The "fruit bat" episode, continually reiterated throughout the parody, actually refers to a notorious event in Ozzie Osbourne's past when he bit the head off a live bat. The humor of this repeated joke is dependent on the spectator knowing about this actual past occurrence.

The Ozporns also takes concentrated jabs at the industry and the genre by having Izzie's son, John, become a porn film producer, starting a production company called "Soggy Pants Video" (unlike the reality show, in *The Ozporns*, Izzie's kids are in college, and therefore, legal). Shortly thereafter, John (and the spectator) receives a lesson in remedial porno as female star Chloe first explains, and then demonstrates, a DP (double penetration) scene. Sherri even goes so far as to rent out the living room as a porn set; Izzie initially balks at the use of his home for adult entertainment until he finds out how much money he is getting paid. During one sex scene of two couples on the living room floor, Izzie is allowed to handle the video camera, where he proceeds, quite humorously, to shoot close-up images of his own feet. In another scene, when Izzie is about to have sex with Sherri's assistant, Sarah, Izzie is told to put on a condom because VCA (the company that produced *The Ozporns*) wants him to, to which he replies, "Fuck VCA." The film ends with a parody within a parody, as Ozzie (played by director Antonio Passolini) arrives home to confront Izzie and the rest of the cast that are currently shooting in his home.

The structure of parody, and its knowing play with generic conventions, appears to allow a mixing of comic and porn elements that diverges from the clear and apparent separation of humor and sex common to most porn films and porn comedies; this mix depends upon the sending up and acknowledgment of porn conventions, maintaining strict differences from standard Hollywood fare (Peter Lehman astutely points to porn's remarkably different conceptions of plot and character in his analysis of the Clouseau porn parody *A Shot in the Mouth 2* [Lehman, "Twin Cheeks," 52–53]). Nowhere is this play with porn convention more apparent than in Jim Enright's *Hung Wankenstein* (2000), a parody of Mel Brooks's *Young Frankenstein* (1974), which is incidentally a spoof of the old Universal horror films. Much of *Hung Wankenstein*'s success and humor relies upon the comic acting talents of Randy Spears and Evan Stone, a comic buddy team of male porn stars that are common to many porn parodies, especially most of Jonathan Morgan's porn comedies such as the two-and-a-half-hour long *Space Nuts* (2003) and the equally ridiculous *Hercules* (2001). Spears plays William Wankerstein, the reluctant heir to the Wankerstein fortune, a mild-mannered veterinarian whose business currently suffers from an unfortunate incident with a sheep. When he arrives at his ancestral castle, Scheisswasser, he is met by the expected cast of characters, including Frau Schtupper, his manservant, Egon, and Inga, the lovely female milkmaid/assistant. His heritage, of course, requires him to fix the monster, played by Stone, who unfortunately suffers from an abnormally small penis; with Egon and Inga's help during a hilarious surgery filled with all sorts of interesting spare parts, the monster is outfitted with the proper organ for a porn film (represented by Evan Stone's "real" penis).

Hung Wankenstein's most humorous moments, though, are the ones that parody both filmmaking and the porn genre, to the point where sex scenes are sometimes interrupted to play on the parody. For instance, as the good veterinarian is about to celebrate with his devoted nurse his change in fortunes (with a blowjob), the messenger returns to interrupt the scene by exclaiming, "Dude. Dude. What are you doing? You're wasting so much valuable screen time right now." Spears quickly looks at his watch and leaves the room. Still, the nurse is not finished with the scene, and demands sex from the messenger, crying, "I'll be damned if that cheap production manager is going to pay me for just dialogue. So, let's go!" Later, as William retires for the night, he hears childish giggling coming from within the walls of the castle. Following the sound, he encounters two women half-naked on a big bed. The following dialogue occurs:

WILLIAM: What are you doing?

INGA: Obligatory lesbian scene.

WILLIAM: No, that's not what I mean. Who are you?

INGA: I am Inga and this is Petra.

WILLIAM: And you are here because . . . ?

PETRA: We are nine pages into the script, and we need more sex.

WILLIAM: Oh.

Later, as William and Inga sit down to what appears to be a plastic turkey dinner, every sentence uttered is followed by the obviously fake sound effect of a thunder and lightning storm, repeatedly exaggerated until William finally cries, "This place is driving me mad! This endless storm is driving me mad, mad, I tell you!" Finally, in a blatant acknowledgment of the film's implied audience, a flashback reveals that the last "evil" Dr. Wankenstein was none other than everyman porn star Ron Jeremy.

The humor involved in *Hung Wankenstein* is also explicitly sexual, as required for the interweaving of explicit pornographic sex scenes. William and Egon gain entrance to a secret passage (behind a bookcase) leading to the laboratory when Inga inserts a dildo into her vagina; the bookcase rocks violently back and forth as Inga proceeds to masturbate on camera, in close-up. When it comes time to find a penis for the monster, William and Egon visit the organ depot, where wide arrays of sizeable dildos are displayed. When the power goes out during the crucial operation, Inga saves the day by performing a hand job on the monster, rendering him erect! Further, once the monster possesses his monster penis, he cannot stop playing with himself or using it on the lovely Inga. In the end, Inga and Mel (the monster) move to Chatsworth, California, so that Mel can become a great porn star. William is not devastated, for he has a female "bride" on hand to keep him from being lonely, and the film ends as happily and satisfactorily as porn could end—orgasms for all.

Both *The Ozporns* and *Hung Wankenstein* indicate that porn films can transgress the rigid rules and generic conventions required that separate sex and humor, but both films are funny because they make fun of, while simultaneously acknowledging, their necessary conventions; no changes are made in the fundamental structure of porn. As Harries explains regarding film parodies in general,

Transgression therefore straddles the boundary, but does not move beyond it. Transgression is the act of violating rules, yet only barely crossing the limits of the prescribed boundaries. To move beyond such limits (and to totally violate the macro-codes of the social structure) is to subvert. (Harries 2000, 128)

While porn parodies do point out some of the ridiculousness of the genre's conventions, such as porn's reliance on the penis as a sight/site of visual drama and awe, they do not transform the genre through the presence of laughter. As Nicole Matthews asserts in her discussion of comedy's gender politics, "There is a long-standing tradition of seeing laughter as shaking the foundations of power" (Matthews 2000, 14). Perhaps the insertion of laughter into the world of porn could undermine patriarchal power as well.

Medusan Laughter and the Transformation of Porn

Isn't laughter the first form of liberation from a secular oppression? Isn't the phallic tantamount to the seriousness of meaning? Perhaps woman, and the sexual relation, transcend it "first" in laughter?

—Irigary 1985, 163

In Kathleen Rowe's compelling analysis of women and comedy entitled *The Unruly Woman*, she suggests that comedy, especially when wielded by women, can unsettle and undermine, as women proceed to make "spectacles" of themselves that exceed the boundaries of what is deemed appropriately feminine. She uses the examples of Miss Piggy and Roseanne Barr to point out the connections to be made (as Freud has already done) between laughter and aggression (Rowe 1995, 7). Rowe's text crucially argues that comedy and laughter could be considered a feminist weapon that deconstructs and "dismembers," so to speak, patriarchal power and authority. She uses the words of feminist critic B. Ruby Rich to make this essential point:

[Rich] . . . advocates the feminist potential of the "Medusan film," a type of film about sexuality and humor. She argues that comedy should not be overlooked as weapon of great political power, which women should cultivate for "its revolutionary potential as a deflator of the patriarchal order and an extraordinary leveler and reinventor of dramatic structure. (Rowe 1995, 8–9)

Rich's mention of the "Medusan film" is a reference to Helene Cixious's polemic essay "The Laugh of the Medusa," which encouraged women "to take up arms and invent a new kind of women's writing, *ecriture feminine*, which will liberate women's voices from their repression and oppression. Cixous's vision of the end of this repression of femininity is suffused with laughter" (Matthews 2000, 24–25).

While Cixous has been criticized for an investment in feminine essentialism, she most importantly suggests that women's voices in writing, and by extension, film-making, can be seen as a liberating force in the fight to undermine patriarchal power. Some of the changes wrought in the porn industry have occurred as porn actresses such as Veronica Hart and Candida Royalle have moved behind the camera, paralleled by the increasing accessibility of porn at female-oriented sexual emporiums such as Good Vibrations in San Francisco and Eve's Garden and Babes in Toyland in New York City—all providing porn films recommended by female staff members via the Internet.

Still, the presence of a female director does not necessarily guarantee a challenge to heterosexual porn's phallocentric conventions, as an analysis of Veronica Hart's porn comedies reveals. Both *Sinful Rella* (2001) and *Booby Trap* (1999) contain an unprecedented amount of sexual numbers in films that clock in at under two hours. Both films contain nine total sex scenes, which seldom vary from the formula of blow job, straight sex, anal sex, money shot facial, except when the rare cunnilingus scene occurs, or the less rare double penetration. The humor in *Sinful Rella* is also not as integrated into the sex scenes as in other, male-directed porn parodies. As Sinful Rella despairs of ever going to the ball, she is visited by her "fairy godfather," who continuously takes offense at being called a "fairy," and whose every line is followed by a chorus of canned laughter on a laugh track. There is no laughter in the scene that follows, though, as the young woman gleefully performs fellatio on her godfather while being doubly penetrated by two coachmen; the scene ends with three money shots.

When Sinful Rella goes to the ball and meets the prince, she starts to give him "the best blowjob" in the land, but is interrupted when the clock strikes midnight; alas, she must run home immediately before her carriage turns into a Honda Civic (which it does, to her disgust). The prince, left unsatisfied, is brought another woman as a substitute, and demands that his valet find this mysterious woman through testing blowjobs (as opposed to the usual glass slipper). The valet then finds and tests the wicked stepmother, the daughter, and finally finds Sinful Rella, and brings her to the prince. In a scene that flies in the face of feminist politics, Sinful Rella insists that the prince marry her in order to achieve his desires, and as soon as the ceremony finishes, the final sex scene occurs, with the princess exclaiming, "I knew someday my prince would come" as she giddily enjoys her final money shot facial. Porn conventions such as the strict delineation between narrative and number, ubiquitous meat and money shots, and an inordinate emphasis on fellatio certify that Hart's work may play on the female-oriented fairy-tale genre, but certainly does not alter the structure of porn or its relationship to humor.

Hart's *Booby Trap* (1999) plays like a spy spoof, with two doctors, Dr. Goodhead (Nina Hartley) and Dr. Shaft (Dale Da Bone), who create two femme-bots (porn stars Vicca and Nikita) to go undercover as spies in order to find the mole in their agency. Most of the humor in the film regards the behavior of the two femme-bots, who constantly seem to need adjustments to their hardware. The camera pans over an array of props used to situate the film as a comedy—*The Dummies Guide to Making Robots* is nestled next to some Barbie dolls, a child's paint set, and a *Plastic Surgery Made Easy* textbook. In the opening scene, Dr. Shaft teaches them how to perform fellatio with brightly colored dildos; the femme-bots amusingly keep thrusting the dildos into their foreheads instead of placing them in their mouths. Shortly after, Dr. Shaft decides that the women should use his body for practice, and the first sex scene occurs; the humorous situation rapidly disappears as the two femme-bots are clearly represented as experienced porn stars. Most of the film's other laughs consist of very brief verbal and visual puns—Agent Lotta Wad thinks that bugs are "six legged insects" instead of surveillance devices, Nikita uncovers bogus American secrets such as "Elvis is Alive and Well," and Chief Hard-on, who has an obsession with adhesive bandages, turns out to be the "mole" because he is covered with moles. These funny lines and wisecracks are necessarily brief, as this film, too, has nine explicit sex scenes, which again are fellatio-dominated with repeated money shots. Hart's work, while occasionally amusing, never veers from the conventional focus of heterosexual hardcore on the penis, especially through multiple come shots.

Veronica Hart's films defy Linda Williams's hopeful assertion that due to the influence of women filmmakers, the requisite money shot or come shot is waning—that "one day this law may be looked back on, like the convention in westerns of good guys in white hats and bad guys in black, as an archaism no longer viable in the representation of sexual pleasures" (Williams, *Hard Core*, 116). Still, there are female porn directors invested in changing porn's phallocracy. Candida Royalle's films intentionally distinguish themselves by adding "a female voice" and "a woman's touch" to a field crowded with mostly male directors (Candida Royalle's Femme). Since 1984, Royalle's Femme productions have produced over fifteen films, but *Stud Hunters* (2003) is one of the first to link humor explicitly with sex. In a recent interview about the film for www.eros-guide.com, Royalle herself admits that "I just think it's not easy to do humor and eroticism effectively" (Sexy Spreads). One of the dangers, especially for a woman director, is that humor can come at the expense of men, for, as John Bancroft explains, some sexual humor "focuses on the absurdity of the human genitalia. Here the man is at a distinct disadvantage" (Bancroft 2002, 10). Peter Lehman outlines this problem in his work on penis-size jokes told by women in film. He states,

> Women's jokes are certainly based on "obscene exposure," and they are motivated by aggressiveness and satire. They do so not out of frustrated desire for the body but out of revenge. These jokes speak more of a desire to get back at men than a desire for men. (Lehman, *Running Scared*, 112)

Indeed, delicacy is required in order to represent women laughing *and* desiring in the regimented world of porn. Royalle effectively represents an erotic realm where men are both amusing and desirable objects for women in *Stud Hunters*.

The film was inspired by an interview that Royalle did for Candice Bergen's Oxygen Network television show; the episode wanted to show the director "at work" and gave her space to host a casting call for her latest erotic film. (Sexy Spreads) Royalle, upon reviewing the footage, thought, "What a riot this is! Let's do a movie all about a director looking for the next great stud and show people how funny casting can be!" (Sexy Spreads). The film begins with director Carla Divine (Alexandra Silk) and her star, Giselle Lorngette (Ava Vincent) arriving in New York to attend a casting call for over fifty "studs" eager to be the next star in one of Divine's "erotic" movies (with a background theme song that cries "C'mon, drop your pants—here's your big chance"). The film represents a wide variety of men of different ages, races, and sizes, but most are showing their nonerect penises for female perusal. One man asks, "I wonder if she's going to want a come shot. I've been saving all week!" One man refuses to take his clothes off for the audition *and* the film. Another man is a virgin, and thought that the film would be a good way to get experience. Another is at the wrong audition, mistakenly believing he is at a call for the musical version of *A Streetcar Named Desire*. Yet another man rambunctiously yells, "Yo! Where's the free pussy? Who do I fuck?" with gusto.

During the casting call (which encompasses almost the entire film), actual male porn stars such as Brian Bishop, Johnny Dannon, Marcus Oralius, and Grego also audition, and then venture off with the star (Vincent), a horny casting assistant, and an aggressive female reporter to experience what Divine calls "the casting couch." These interludes occur humorously to Divine's dismay, as she is constantly losing future studs and assistants to various sex scenes. The amusing casting call, combined with the women who desire some of the auditioning "studs," provides a way of subtly and gently undermining the superiority and focus of the phallus, literalizing Irigary's suggestion that, "Perhaps if the phallocracy that reigns everywhere is put unblushingly on display, a different sexual economy may become possible" (Williams, *Hard Core*, 116).

Royalle is not above making fun of herself, as well as smartly tweaking some of the more cherished porn conventions. Upon arriving at the warehouse the women are using for the casting call, Carla Divine (a stand-in for Royalle) is disgusted to find a bare mattress in the middle of the gray, concrete room. She comments that it must be "the leftover dregs from some sleazy porn shoot." She repeatedly insists, haughtily, that she is making an erotic film, not pornography, and is met by a group of cheering women (including Royalle herself) clamoring for "good porn" as opposed to "bad porn." Divine also explains that her film will contain "no icky come shots," even though Jennifer, the casting assistant, quietly states that she likes them (and there are no money shots in *Stud Hunters*). Giselle, the star, is shown reading Voltaire, and states that she only wants to "get married and make babies." Later, when Giselle and Brian Bishop claim they are "in love," Brian states Giselle cannot be in the film, because "I don't want my wife in porn movies," to which Carla replies, "What about the 150 films she's already been in!"

Of course, everyone is having sex *but* the director, until she finally receives her revenge, getting all four of the studs to herself in a landmark orgy scene where each man is intent on pleasuring her.

Royalle's *Stud Hunters* does veer from some more typical porn conventions beyond a lack of money shots. The film only has four explicit sex scenes, and while there are one or two meat shots, the film mostly utilizes full body representations, a great deal of kissing, and high production values that emphasize flattering lighting and cinematography. The sex scenes are still distinct from the comedy moments, yet there are frequent cuts during sex not only to Karla's exasperated "where is everyone??" but also to an actual coitus interruptus, where Rod exclaims, "Hey, I didn't get off!" to which Jennifer replies, "Well, neither did I!" There is even one, incredibly brief scene showing two studs sexually together in one room—a scene rarely shown in heterosexual porn. Still, Femme productions films are known for their attempts to appeal to women and couples specifically. When asked of her views on female-driven porn, Royalle replied,

> I don't think [women are] doing it much differently than the guys. They have heavy-handed distributors standing over them telling them what to do, enforcing the "formula," demanding cum in your face shots. Some like it. My friend Veronica Hart, a wonderful director, does more female-friendly movies, but admittedly does them much harder than me, because she likes it that way! (Sexy Spreads)

Royalle makes two important points here: product is influenced by formula and what sells, and women directors are subject to those rules. Likewise, porn pleasures are often personal and subjective, even if they are influenced by the dictates of the market. While Hart's films are undeniably harder than Royalle's, both directors are restricted by conventions that limit the potential for a subversive transformation of porn—porn films that do not take themselves quite so seriously.

The Radical Potential of Laughter

I hope you agree that there's nothing more fun than mixing a healthy dose of humor with sex!

—Candida Royalle, Candida Royalle's Femme

While some of Royalle's viewers may agree with her, the contemporary porn industry as a whole is relatively devoid of this particular mixture of genres, despite a few successful porn parodies on the market. Affectively, the dynamics between the two genres do seem contentious, especially when a genre so invested in the male ego and the penis could be undone by the laughter of a woman. Still, as porn continues to grow more accessible and mainstream, and successful foreign art films such as Lars Von Trier's *The Idiots* (2001) and Catherine Breillat's *Romance* (1999) feature both penetration and cross-over porn actors (Rocco Sifreddi), the genre still has the potential to change. The explicit "romantic comedy" genre still seems to be untapped—a genre that is often light-hearted, certainly about sex, and could provide a place for Medusan filmmaking. *The Opening of Misty Beethoven*, in fact, is a precursor for this genre manipulation, as it ostensibly plays with the narrative of *My Fair Lady* (George Cukor, 1964) and countless other derivative *Pygmalion* rip-offs. What makes *Misty* unique, beyond its historical placement in the golden era of porn and its accompanying theatrical screenings and audience attendance, is the film's integrated humor and pervasive libidinousness—the film never takes itself too seriously. As in most romantic comedies, the guy gets the girl, or in this case, Misty gets Seymour, and the romance culminates in a final, climactic scene: in a Hollywood film, at the altar, in a porn film, in bed. Still, the true ending of *The Opening of Misty Beethoven* is very telling. The final scene closes on Misty, dressed in business attire, leading a "training session" for other burgeoning lovers. As the camera follows her across the set of Seymour's much used room, the camera comes to rest on Seymour, naked except for a dog collar, quietly reading a book, content, as Misty runs the show. Certainly taking sex less seriously could be a positive move for all genders, and perhaps it is time to let in a little laughter.

WORKS CITED

Bancroft, John. "Sex and Humor: A Personal View." In *Sex and Humor: Selections from the Kinsey Institute*, ed. Catherine Johnson, Betsy Stirratt, and John Bancroft, 5–12. Bloomington: Indiana University Press, 2002.

Candida Royalle's Femme. www.royalle.com. Accessed June 10, 2004.

Gutwirth, Marcel. *Laughing Matter: An Essay on the Comic*. Ithaca, N.Y.: Cornell University Press, 1993.

Harries, Dan. *Film Parody*. London: BFI, 2000.

Horton, Andrew. "Introduction." In *Comedy/Cinema/Theory*, ed. Andrew Horton, 1–21. Berkeley: University of California Press, 1991.

Irigary, Luce. *The Sex Which Is Not One*. Trans. Catherine Porter. Ithaca, N.Y.: Cornell University Press, 1985.

Lehman, Peter. "Twin Cheeks, Twin Peeks, and Twin Freaks: Porn's Transgressive Remake Humor." In *Authority and Transgression in Literature and Film*, ed. Bonnie and Hans Braendlin, 45–54. Tallahassee: University of Florida Press, 1996.

———. *Running Scared: Masculinity and the Representation of the Male Body*. Philadelphia: Temple University Press, 1993.

———. "Penis-size Jokes and Their Relation to Hollywood's Unconscious." In *Comedy/Cinema/Theory*, ed. Andrew Horton, 43–59. Berkeley: University of California Press, 1991.

Matthews, Nicole. *Comic Politics: Gender in Hollywood Comedy After the New Right*. Manchester: University of Manchester Press, 2000.

Mulvey, Laura. "Visual Pleasure and Narrative Cinema." In *Feminist Film Theory: A Reader*, ed. Sue Thornham, 58–69. New York: New York University Press, 1999.

Neale, Steve, and Frank Krutnik. *Popular Film and Television Comedy*. London: Routledge, 1990.

Nelson, T.G.A. *Comedy*. New York: Oxford University Press, 1990.

Palmer, Jerry. *The Logic of the Absurd*. London: BFI, 1987.

Rowe, Kathleen. *The Unruly Woman: Gender and the Genres of Laughter.* Austin: University of Texas Press, 1995.

"Sexy Spreads: Candida Royalle." Eros-Guide, San Francisco. www.eros-guide.com/articles/2003–08-26/candida. Accessed June 10, 2004.

Slade, Joseph W. "Flesh Need Not Be Mute: The Pornographic Videos of John Leslie." *Wide Angle*, 19, no. 3 (1997): 115–148.

"The Greatest Porn Parodies Ever." www.hal9000.inetstrat.com/parodies.html. Accessed December 9, 2003.

Williams, Linda. "Film Bodies: Gender, Genre, and Excess." In *Feminist Film Theory: A Reader*, ed. Sue Thornham, 267–281. New York: New York University Press, 1999.

———. *Hard Core: Power, Pleasure, and the "Frenzy of the Visible."* 2nd ed. Berkeley: University of California Press, 1999.

José B. Capino

Asian College Girls and Oriental Men with Bamboo Poles: Reading Asian Pornography

What Makes Asian Pornography Asian?

Unlike the marginalia of porn—scat from Western Europe, lactating and pregnant women, granny fetishists, and bestiality—which are frequently lumped together under a single, nameless column on the shelves of mom-and-pop adult video stores, Asian-themed videos command their very own section.[1] But while this category is assuredly vibrant and long lived, the precise configuration of traits and elements that define it is decidedly elusive.

The inventory of "Asian porn" includes films imported from Asia or, as in the case of the Vietnam-era fantasy *She's My Little Fortune Nookie* (1997), supposedly set there. Some videos earn their spot on the shelf by promising exotic Asian-style sex, ranging from the hackneyed Oriental massage to the intriguing "Menage-a-Thai," to the unique erotic stylings of "the extremely kinky Deanna" who, in *Oriental Oddballs 2* (1994), "takes her teeth out and gums David to pleasure." Videos that traffic in Asian themes—like *The Twin Peaks of Mount Fuji* (1996), about a nymphomegalomaniac who "wants the formula for a secret love potion in order to rule the world"—also end up on the same rubric. That said, the chief defining characteristic of Asian porn is decidedly the "race"—or more accurately, the racial category—of the performers. While it may seem as if the legibility of race is a precise touchstone for defining a category or genre, it is, in truth, quite unstable and problematic.

Marking bodies racially, and its converse of using racialized bodies to draw the boundaries of a category, are unwieldy enterprises. The co-presence of Asians and Caucasians is but one issue: one runs into problems with videos like the football gangbang classic, *I Can't Believe I Did The Whole Team* (1995), a non-Oriental themed tape topbilled by an Asian actor (Annabel Chong) but populated by a predominantly non-Asian cast. The same goes for *The World's Biggest Gang Bang* (1995), also featuring Ms. Chong who, this time, services almost 300 men. Despite Ms. Chong's record-setting superhuman feat and her considerable star appeal, her video is rarely found on Asian shelves.[2] The race of individual stars is equally problematic, especially when one considers biracial porn stars such as Asia Carrera. But more to the point, "Asian" is not really a race—in fact, you'll count at least three discrete "races" among the peoples of Asia—but a category of race favored by the West despite its arbitrary combination of physiological and geographic criteria. Thus, Sammy Gee, described in a videotape boxcover as "the hottest Polynesian on any US campus," satisfies the criterion for Asianness even though, geographically speaking, she should not. (She would, of course, fit into the racial category "Asian and Pacific Islander" that the U.S. government prefers for immigration, census, and affirmative action purposes.)

Complicating things further, the race of performers like Ms. Chong is layered over with the discourse of their nationalities or ethnicities. Often noted on video boxcovers (i.e., "China sluts," "Thai Lady Boys") and in the diegesis of the videos, these ethnic or national markings fracture both the subgenre and its singular criterion by making distinctions between race and geographic origins. The effect of these markings on the genre of Asian porn—if we were to consider it a genre, and pornography, a mode of cinema—is a concomitant division of the rubric into even smaller units, each one behaving like an unstable subgenre. Those subgenres of nationalities and ethnicities promise its spectators specific physiognomic traits, a repertoire of types and roles (e.g., Japanese geishas and Vietnamese war brides), or what Richard Fung calls "sexual associations" (e.g., "a person could be seen as Japanese and somewhat kinky or Filipino and 'available'").[3]

This atomization of Asian porn into corresponding racial and geographic subcategories, when inevitably confounded by the additionally divisive introduction of fetishes, results in dizzying permutations of bodies, roles, fantasies, and sexual skills, the sheer number of which threatens to explode the category or genre.

But just as race is the central problematic of Asian pornography, it is also in many ways, the logic that animates its production. For Asian porn as, I argue in the rest of this essay, is not simply porn *with* Asians but porn that is specifically preoccupied with the problem—or mystery—of Asianness. A close look at both the structure of Asian porn videos and the discourse of their boxcovers reveals that they are driven by a profound curiosity with Asian bodies and an intense preoccupation with generating permutations of interracial sex. This predilection is, in several ways, consistent with colonial desire's residual structures that resurface out of Asian porn's evocation of the figures of colonial encounter and, more important, of the historical and political resonances of Asian and Caucasian sexual relations. This particular explication of Asian porn constitutes the bulk of my argument. It is, however, only one way of reading; toward the end of the essay, I offer several alternative perspectives for studying this cultural object. For purposes of discussion and illustration, I refer at length to a couple of videos (one gay, one straight) and, in passing, to several others that may represent the bulk of Asian porn circulating in the United States during the writing of this essay. Because of the nature of the arguments I wish to build, most of these videos were chosen from the corpus of Asian porn made in the United States, though I occasionally reference several videos that originate in Asia.

A Pornography of Race

Composed of two words, *Asian pornography* misleadingly indicates a conceptual division between the two terms or elements. But as with all forms of "ethnic pornography," these two terms are deeply imbricated, effecting not only the more obvious racialization of pornography but also a pornography of race. It aspires to nothing less than making Asianness pornographic.

Consider, for instance, how Asian porn obsessively catalogues the sexual uses of racial markings and racialized bodies. The blurb for *Asian Persuasion* (1993) lures audiences with the promise of a "sticky explotion [*sic*] on the Chinese girl's face." Here the ritualized spattering of ejaculate on a sexual partner's face—a routinary moment in straight pornography often referred to as a "facial"—is proffered as a racialized act, distinguished by the ethnicity of the face, the implied "Oriental" submissiveness of the figure that performs it, and the polyvalent image of "stickiness" that is associated less with the absent ejaculator than with the unfortunate recipient of his load (stickiness is, after all, stereotypically Asian, linked to such Oriental matters as sticky rice and sticky, humid weather). With the proliferation of such "ethnic facials," the Chinese face enters the imaginary of white desire as the ideal surface for spattering with ejaculate. This same logic explains the surprisingly all-too-logical juxtaposition of race and pornography in such expressions as "All-Asian, All Anal" (the subtitle of the video *Vivid Raw 2*, 1999) or Suzi Suzuki's title of "Asian Anal Queen."

This imbricated sexualization and racialization of Asian porn is, more-over, hyperbolized, in keeping with one of pornography's key aesthetic strategies. It involves a hyperbolization of racialized and sexualized bodies that is consistent with what Mikhail Bakhtin would describe as "grotesque."[4] In the following blurb, the women in the video *Asian Lesbos 2* (1996) are characterized by an excess of eroticism and Asianness that arguably teeters on absurdity: "those slant-eyed, fun loving, cunt licking, clit sucking sweethearts of the Orient." Similarly, in box covers of gay Asian videos, the body parts of Asian men are hyperbolically racial-ized and eroticized by their inordinate feminization. *Asian Cuties 1* (1998) adver-tises "sweet hairless buns with lots of hardcore action" while *Asian Studs 5* (1997) peddles the somewhat impossible idea of "young muscular Asian bodybuilders" that also happen to be "silky smooth." A blurb for *Asian Dreams 3* (1999) is more succinct: "See: cutest, smoothest, sweetest." Predictably enough, nothing is more racialized, sexualized, and relentlessly inflated than the sex organs of Asian performers. The blurb for *Over 18 Video Magazine 2* (1997), for instance, orientalizes porn star Lynn's labia as "silky sleeves" which, the box cover claims, she "dreams" of stuffing with "a huge American cock." Another blurb, from *College Video Virgins 25: Asian Academics* (n.d.), draws a comparable image within a narrative context: "Momiko: She is getting all A's and she's proud. The first year of college was rough and this is her celebration. She spreads her Asian cunt open, the cutest beaver. Like a princess, her dark pussy oiled and wet anyway." As for Asian penises, the blurb for the gay video *Asian Persuasion* (1997) is similarly both crass and creative: "How about smooth, supple chested men giving you their eager Far East cocks standing firm in sweet scented nests of jet black hair?" The image of strange and aggressive Oriental members conjured by the phrase "eager Far East cocks" is matched by another blurb's hyperorientalized and hypersexualized characterization of "golden hard cocks," rendering the stereotypical Asian man's yellowness and his often unacknowledged sexual potency in extreme. Here we observe that the racialization and sexualization of Asianness are hyperbolized equally and together.

The preoccupation with isolated, disembodied, hyperbolic body parts—predictably belonging to what Bakhtin refers to as the "lower stratum of the body"—is clearly an attempt not only to come to terms with and to represent the excess of Asian sexuality but, perhaps more accurately, to represent Asian sexuality as excess.[5] One may thus find in the one-line catalogue blurb for *Oriental Sluts Vol. 6*—"Boiling Asian Pussy Juice"—an image of Asian sexuality as both inexhaustible and insatiable. While the inflation of sexualities and races is common to pornographic objects, the magnitude of such practices in Asian pornography is decidedly atypical. For while bodies of female African Americans, for instance, are described in box covers as "caramel" or "brown sugar" and their genitals characterized by epithets of enormity, Asian bodies are sexualized so conspicuously in practically every element of porn videos: plot, dialogue, performance, music, and mise-en-scène.

Take just one episode from the "Asian edition" of *Over 18 Video Magazine 2*. Here, Al Miller, a white guy in punk attire, acts as gonzo interviewer to Racquel Lace, a short and tan "Japanese" woman sporting a shiny gold robe and the swept up, secured-with-a-chopstick hairdo associated with geishas. After introducing Racquel and reminding her that "You don't speak very much English," he announces his purpose: "So, uh, anyways, uh, we're here and I'm just trying to find out a little bit about the Asian culture . . ." He opens up the woman's robe to reveal her breasts, which he then squeezes playfully before remarking: "What a culture you've got in there." He then proceeds to goad a definition of culture out of her. "I'm just trying to find out what it is that you like to do," says Al. Without waiting for Racquel to respond, he continues talking dirty: "Maybe, uh, I dunno . . . do you maybe like to suck dick?" As she proceeds to service him orally, his speech gets ugly: "Boy, I love you cocksucking Asians.

You like that? I love it when you little Asian girls are sucking dick! I love it when you Asians suck cock that way!"

While it is hard, indeed unwise, to take Al's chauvinism and racism seriously, it is worth noting that the episode—from narrative to costume, performance to dialogue—revolves around the conspicuous and relentless pairing of race and sexuality, racialized genitals and their "Oriental" activities. Here Al jokingly but nonetheless *literally* equates Asian culture with Racquel's breasts while also explicitly associating race with sexuality and identifying the (inter)racial aspect of the act as the ultimate source of sexual pleasure. Her desirability as a fellatrice rests upon her Asianness while her being Asian makes her give good head.

Residual Structures of Colonial Desire

Asian porn's preoccupation with racialized, sexualized, and hyperbolized bodies is consistent with a dominant trope identified by Robert J. C. Young in the various discourses of colonialism. The fascination with "uncontrollable sexual drive of non-White races" and the fantasy of "people having. . . interminable, adulterating, aleatory, illicit, inter-racial sex" litters the myriad texts—political, scientific, and literary—of colonial regimes."[6] For instance, many of the concerns about bodies, sexualities, and racial boundaries expressed in Asian porn also permeate the language of antimiscegenation law. They also appear in travel guides, fill primers on health and public sanitation, and litter the reports of colonial ethnologists. Young points out that this obsessive attention to the "countless motley varieties of interbreeding. . . an every-increasing *mélange*, 'mongrelity,' of self-propagating endlessly diversifying hybrid progeny: half-blood, half-caste, half-breed, cross-breed. . ." fuels what he calls the "colonial desiring machine."[7] As with Al Miller's vacillation between attraction and disgust toward Racquel Lace, colonial desire spans the gamut of feelings between desire and repulsion and is therefore, to use Homi Bhaba's term, decidedly *ambivalent* in nature.[8] While the notion that Asian porn films are underlined by residual colonial erotics may seem obvious, I venture that it is productive from a historical perspective. Asian porn videos obsessively resurrect figures of interracial romance from the cultures of colonialism: the GI and the prostitute, the vampy Oriental spy and the obsessed Caucasian lover, the impoverished Asian woman and her older white benefactor. Indeed, not only do colonial fantasies of old supply today's Asian porn with a catalogue of scenarios to enact and expand; they also furnish the animating logic for the production of such fantasies. For as Young argues, the paranoid and compulsive enumeration of the many permutations of interracial sex and their progeny evinces a voyeuristic logic: a pleasure, both manifest and latent, in imagining its inexhaustible plenitude, its fecundity of "frenzied, interminable copulation, of couplings, fusing, coalescence *between races*."[9]

This logic is lodged within the very structure of Asian porn videos, which I would characterize as picaresque because they often move across multiple scenarios and cycle relentlessly across myriad (though mostly stereotypical) figures and variations of Asian sexuality. This itinerant tendency is evident in the plot of *Over 18 Video Magazine 2*, a representative example of Asian porn. The video follows Al Miller as he prowls the streets of greater Los Angeles to conduct gonzo-style interviews with Asian women. In the first episode, Al finds a Suzi Suzuki who, though Japanese in real life, sports a black silk Kung Fu attire and practices tai-chi moves. He introduces himself as a "special style monkey, uh, crane, tiger, Kung Fu master" and proposes to teach her "some special Kung Fu moves." These "moves," as executed by Miller's male assistant, include "tongue exercises" and "finger exercises." Suzuki reciprocates with fellatio. The second episode alters the sex play, the stereotype, and the scenario. As rock music blares in the background, Kimmy Ji, looking a lot like Pamela Anderson, saunters into a modern kitchen, climbs to the sink, crouches over it, and douches herself. An attractive white stud, Tommy Gun, enters and asks what she is doing. In a highly affected, tiny voice, she explains: "This is an ancient Asian custom of douching in a sink. That's how Asians do it. It's been a custom for centuries and centuries." The stud administers cunnilingus and fucks her on top of the chopping board before giving her a facial. The third episode returns to a first-generation American immigrant, this time in the person of a Filipino college student (Lynn). Although—or precisely because—she admits to having a boyfriend "back in Seattle," the temporary host of the show (Ken Glide) takes her home for a quickie. In this particular episode, fellatio is the sex act in focus. As soon as the two find some privacy—in the stairwell of a well-appointed house—the man sternly orders her to "get on your knees and suck my dick," after which he pushes her into a corner and shoves her face into his crotch. The usual sex routines follow, punctuated by the leitmotif of the woman's body being gently slammed against solid surfaces (the steps, the walls, the railings), and the numerous shots of considerable length showing the innermost regions of her tattooed vagina. The scene ends with a variation on the oral-facial dynamic, this time with the man slapping her face with his penis. The fifth and final episode, which I discussed earlier in this essay, revolves around an encounter between Al and Racquel, who claims she is from Japan but is dressed in a Chinese silk robe.

Gay Asian pornography also exhibits the same obsessive attention to permutations of interracial sex and thus also employs the picaresque structure we find in straight Asian porn. In the case of *Secret Asian Man* (1984), told in four episodes and set in two Asian countries and two American cities, the variations are even more dramatic than those of *Over 18 Video Magazine 2*. The first episode, a modern gay take on the geisha scenario, features a Chinese bellhop who seduces an older American businessman in a Japanese-inspired Hong Kong hotel. After seeing the white man's penis, passport, and family pictures (in that order), the bellhop offers the businessman a Japanese bath: "A shower is good for the body; the bath is good for the soul." The bellhop then blatantly solicits him: "Well, they say, once you have an experience with an Asian, you don't go away from them." The second episode, a throwback to 1950s teen films, takes place inside a big Chevy convertible parked on an overlook, with tree branches and a full moon hovering above. Two young men, one white and one Asian American, both supposedly "straight" and preppy-looking, wax nostalgic and make love the night before the Asian guy leaves town for college. In the third episode, the figure of the treacherous Oriental femme fatale is reincarnated in the form of a Filipino masseur (dressed in a Chinese silk robe) who is commissioned by a silver-haired, cowboy hat–wearing American businessman to liquidate a fellow American. The masseur's attempt to strangle the white man with a rubber hose fails after he is physically and sexually dominated (i.e., fucked in the ass) by his burly would-be victim. In the fourth episode, a professorial-looking middle-aged white man comforts the homesick Thai exchange student he is hosting by extending him sexual favors.

The variations between the four episodes occur on several registers, encompassing different locales, nationalities, ages, figures of both Asians and Caucasian homosexuals, permutations of sex acts, and shifting structures of dominance, among many others. There is a sex worker and a servant, a houseguest and a buddy. Two are scheming natives, one is a bashful FOB (fresh off the boat) émigré, while another looks like a second-generation American. Two solicit sex, one consents, another seduces. These overlapping and criss-crossing fugues of Asianness, interracial couplings, and gay sex create the impression of an inexhaustible plenitude, a pornotopia that hails the normative white male spectator with visions of the endless satisfaction of his desires.[10] This impression of richesse that Asian pornography provides is keyed to pornography's economy of desire which, for both aesthetic and entrepreneurial reasons, seeks the relentless implantation of perversions and generation of fantasies.

The parade of bodies in sexual congress simultaneously caters to the multifarious configurations of desire that exist in the market while also further stimulating—no, driving—the unremitting production of sexualities and identities among performers and spectators/consumers. In this sense, yet another aspect of Asian porn ties deeply into the colonial project and the mechanisms of colonial desire for, as Robert Young argues, colonialism "originated, indeed, as much as an exchange of bodies as of goods, or rather of bodies as goods."[11] The commercial logic—the traffic of bodies—embedded at the crux of colonial desire works in such a way that the number of sexualities produced and serviced by Asian porn registers a compounded pleasure that is simultaneously (and interchangeably) erotic and economic.

The pleasure of Asian porn's plenitude is intensified by the compulsory sexual availability of virtually all the Asian figures within the diegesis of video pornography. Practically every scenario bestows the illusion of unlimited economic and sexual power upon the white male figure. This is easily apparent in the videos we closely examined. In *Over 18 Video Magazine 2*, Al Miller wields his microphone, penis, and potty mouth to subdue and pounce upon his subjects whose inferior social status is marked by their racialization, purportedly inadequate language skills and grotesquely servile sexual roles. With the sole exception of the Asian American preppy in *Secret Asian Man*, the rest of the Asian figures in the video are clearly encoded as sexually available because of their class and their attraction to white partners: the exchange student who seduces his benefactor, the killer masseur whose ploy is botched when he gets literally fucked, and the bellhop who visibly lusts after the white businessman's material and biological goods. One also observes this marked power differential in other videos, including for instance, *Asian Persuasion*, in which a band of Asian pool cleaners render service to their white boss as both manual and sexual laborers. Here we see how the term *sexual availability* succinctly expresses the inseparable economic and sexual registers of colonial desire.

This skewed power differential depicted in the diegesis of Asian porn points to a corresponding dynamic in their mode of production. To constitute fantasies about the total satisfaction of white desire, the predominantly white male producers of Asian porn not only fabricate Asian figures but also deploy and (de)form Asian bodies that are receptive to such purposes. In this sense, one might think of Asian porn in the same way that Karla Rae Fuller sees "yellow-face" (a performance practice in which Asian roles are played by white actors) as a means by which Asians are "managed" or controlled by white impresarios in the practices of embodying, performing, and projecting images of Asianness.[12] By commanding performances of race, the makers of these videos not only require sex acts and servile roles but also engage in the symbolic management of unwieldy "foreign" bodies as well as the translation and marshalling of "alien" desires.

From the perspective of Asians and Asian American performers, these performances of Asianness are just one of many ways by which their identities are (re)produced in late capitalist, white androcentric society. To be sure, they are not without agency in this practice and are decidedly complicit in constructing their "Asian" selves (more on this in the next section) but their lot is quite problematic. A blurb from *Temple of Love* (1995) hints at the kind of hairsplitting predicament involved here: "These little jaded little fortune cookies wonder, do we have slanted slits? So they go looking for cute little Asian asses, to check cunt geometry, and eat a little Asian pussy as well. They taste the chopsticks of a few buff dudes while they are at it. Follow the adventures of these geisha harlots as they suck and fuck the Confusian way." The blurb suggests an interesting scenario where the performers end up being confused about their own "Asianness." It is thus the female Asian porn actor's unique dilemma to figure out and define exactly how an "Asian pussy" must look and behave.

Reading Alternatively

To be sure, any sort of analysis that systematically factors out the transgressive nature of pornography would not only be humorless but also foolhardy. While my explication of Asian porn above might as well—though it really shouldn't—fall in line with critiques of racial representation that bemoan the subjugation and exploitation of minorities, it is truly more concerned with articulating the economy of desire that underpins both the form and content of Asian porn. In the remainder of this essay, I would like to propose several alternative readings by considering elements and registers of Asian porn that I have otherwise ignored.

First, I wish to call attention to the reflexivity that permeates Asian porn. One may begin by reading the bawdy, ridiculous, and carnivalesque humor of the boxcover blurbs as a cue of reflexivity. Consider, for instance, this write-up for *Harry Horndog's Amateur Oriental Orgasms 1* (1992):

> Sex-crazed amateur felines from the Far East take command in this ode to decadent desires. Very wet n wild Japanese, Chinese, Thai & Filipino women perform lesbian, anal, double penetration and other sexual acrobatics with their lovers—exclusively for you.

Notice how the references to a performance indicate the artifice and excess of the blurb's own characterization of the video's subjects as "sex-crazed amateur felines" and "very wet n wild." A similar positioning of the spectator outside the video's diegesis and a reflexively excessive marking of the subjects may also be observed in the blurb for another video, *Asian Bombshells Vol. 1*: "These hot Asian sluts love to fuck and suck. They love to get creamed in the ass by their papa sans. China sluts love to suck clits of Asian whores. They suck big boners while we watch." Self-awareness also characterizes performances by both white and Asian actors in Asian porn. In *Over 18 Video Magazine 2*, Al's constant adlibs about the absurdity of the video's scenarios reinforce his tongue-in-cheek acting and the video's self-reflexive gonzo interview set-up. We see this at work most notably in the fourth episode, as Al pokes fun at Suzi when she reappears in the video as a different character. On reencountering her, he deadpans: "I was just interviewing your sister, the ninja." To which she replies, quite ashamed: "Actually, we, uh, twin sisters." In addition to this, Al's campy adlibs constantly poke fun at the video's unredeemed Orientalism as when, having convinced Suzi to come to his place, he promises to "light some incense. Maybe put the Buddha statue out and do some stuff." He subjects even his own practice of gonzo porn to self-reflexive humor. During his interview with Racquel Lace, he quips, after playfully squeezing her breasts: "It seems like you understand what the interview is all about. . . . Well, I'm gonna pull my dick out and let you interview it. What do you think of that?" He whips out his penis and offers it to Racquel, who happily accepts the offer: "Hmmmm, I like!" Later, he instructs her to remove her underwear before saying, with tongue in cheek cruelty, "I think you'd do a much better interview with your panties off."

Self-reflexive distanciation is also achieved in Asian porn through strategies of camp performance, and is especially heightened when Asian actors are camping along. This is the case with some of the better performers like Suzi Suzuki who are so adept at winking through their Orientalist spiels. Suzi ably exorcises the tension created by Asian porn's unabashed racism with her playful banter.

In the scene in which, as Kung Fu master, she has sex with a white guy named "Hop Hopper," she camps it up by offering coyly to administer fellatio ("Can I try my tongue technique to you?") and spouting ridiculous Oriental-themed porn clichés ("Oh, you've got a great sword!"). When, after some time, her partner tells her "it's time for some sword-in-the-hole technique," she gamely finishes him off "doggie style" before deadpanning: "So this is brown belt?. . . Ooooh, this is brown belt, huh? Do you think I can graduate?" Instead of playing dupe or drugged-out whore, Suzi clearly shows that she is merely riding along with the gimmick, taking the racism and condescension in stride and contributing actively—and gleefully—to her own "Orientalization."

Camp performance, by calling attention to its artifice, denaturalizes Asianness, revealing it—to use Judith Butler's term—to be performative.[13] But camp, which admittedly requires some sophistication, is not the only means by which Asianness is unmasked as a performance. The excessive Asian markings (the cheongsams, chopstick-secured hair buns, exaggeratedly slanted eyeliner marks), artificially broken English, the practice of playing different nationalities (especially with famous actors whose nationalities are well known), and even the Orientalizing screen names they adopt (e.g., Pearl Essence, China Moon, Asia Carrera) produce a similar effect of heightened artificiality.[14] The result is a sort of Oriental drag: Asianness by dress-up. Moreover, these tactics of distanciation have the potential to push Asianness into the arena of pornography's distinct mode of role-playing. In this case, Asian drag degenerates into Asianness-as-drag, making Asianness function like the complex of sex roles, assumed/performed identities, subcultural expressions, and gender reconfigurations that comprise such porn cinema personas as dominatrices, daddies, leatherfolk, nymphomaniacs, slaves and masters, and the like. In short, Asianness itself becomes an act. The rolf of Asianness, unlike that of the dominatrix, is *still* one that is assigned on the basis of a performer's skin color and national origin: Asianness requires an inordinate amount of submission and humiliation on camera. There is no question that it is racialized both within the diegesis and outside it. But I think it's productive to transcend strategically the overdetermined discourse of racism and to ponder alternative ways of reading such politically confrontational objects as Asian porn. Accounting for the possibilities, and not just the constraints of role-playing as it operates within the transgressive space of Asian pornography, is one of several ways to go about it.

Yet another alternative is to read symptomatically the converse of white desire, which we might tentatively (and awkwardly as well as problematically) refer to as "Asian desire." We might look at how the Asian characters' sexual desires are articulated within the diegesis of the videos, as when the pool boys in *Asian Persuasion* visibly and verbally lust after their white boss and take turns "doing" him and each other. Alternatively, the impromptu statements and involuntary kinesthetic responses of Asian actors while in the thrall of coitus evince less legible but nonetheless perceptible ways by which both the desires and pleasures of Asian figures are encoded.

One might also profitably consider the exact converse of American-made Asian porn's encoding and construction of white desire, best observed in Asian-made Asian porn films with or without Caucasian figures. *Sex Tours of Bangkok* (1993), a porn travelogue addressed to white spectators, tries to represent the figure of the white sex tourist even without a Caucasian body at its disposal: a very fair-skinned, presumably South Asian male torso takes its place as the recipient of erotic pleasure from the native women. The video generates multiple scenarios of pleasuring the white tourist, thus offering a construct of white desire from the other side of the power divide. These images of whiteness, which may well be considered as visions of an eroticizing return gaze, are sobering reminders of the white man's own vulnerability in his pursuit of interracial sex with Asians. As videos like *Sex Tours of Bangkok* enumerate the attractions, sensations, and expenses that await the white tourist, it becomes clear that the terms of interracial sex with Asians—whether imagined or otherwise—do not always favor them and that their "desire" is as much a product of their own imagination as it is of the machinations and titillations of those who traffic in Asian bodies and Oriental fantasies.

The absence of the white spectator's Caucasian proxy in all-Asian videos (i.e., with all-Asian casts) such as the *Asian Studs* series provides an even more dramatic means of witnessing the construction of both white and Asian desire. With all Asian bodies performing both the Oriental self and the white man's Asian proxy, these videos telegraph white desire through a process akin to possession. What this entails is, of course, a difficult and woefully imprecise method of reading the performers' bodies, especially at those moments when the dominant male figure romances his partner (whether male or female) and enacts his unquestioned preeminence. The pronounced and subtler shifts as the dominant figure plays both the native/Asian and the White man's racialized proxy registers as a dramatic impersonation of power (and its equally compelling removal), reminiscent of Jean Rouch's ethnographic documentary *Les maîtres fous* (1958), in which black peons enter into a trance and channel the spirits of Africa's former white colonizers.

Finally, it is possible to read Asian porn against the grain of the feminist and critical race theories typically employed to characterize it as a bad if not utterly irredeemable object. The rhetoric of this line of criticism holds that persons of color are doubly violated in pornography, as Cowan and Campbell point out in their content analysis of interracial moving-image pornography. "Women are dominated but Black women are particularly dominated. Men are shown as sex machines, but Black men are particularly so," they conclude, after counting instances of aggression ("penis slapping," "name calling"), racism ("using a racial name, playing ethnic music in the background"), submission ("performing *fellatio* while kneeling, facial ejaculation"), and shots of the large penises attributed to black men ("if the female character was projected as unable to span the length of the penis with both hands").[15] Phyllis Klotman, in her content analysis of vintage pornographic comic books, makes a similar conclusion, finding that racialized figures have "the least status and . . . the most denigrated." This line of criticism also enumerates the figures of eroticized Asians in video pornography, as in the case of Richard Fung, whose famous analysis of Asians in gay video porn singles out "the egghead/wimp" and "the Kung Fu master/ninja/samurai" as the most prevalent types represented.[16]

Instead of making an attempt to interpret Asian or interracial porn's fantasies, studies like those of Fung and Klotman focus on protesting the representational violence they inflict. Fung is particularly—but not very imaginatively—critical of the way Asian porn "narratives privilege the (White) penis while always assigning the Asian the role of bottom . . . [thus conflating] Asian and anus."[17] While I appreciate Fung's polemic, I think it strategically leaves out numerous videos that exclusively feature Asian men stroking themselves or romancing each other. Apart from organizing the sexual spectacle almost exclusively around the presentation of Asian penises, these videos decidedly position the white male spectator as "bottom" or voyeur. In fact, my viewing experience tells me that, based on the singular criterion of who occupies the top/bottom position, the power differential between Caucasians and Asians in gay porn is dramatically less problematic than in straight porn, where one would be very hard pressed to find Asian men romancing white women. But before we make too much of this observation and apply the same hopelessly reductive criterion to such videos—and thus end up speculating about how comparatively unphallic or pornographically untelegenic Asian penises might be in the eyes of porn makers—I wish to suggest that the absence of Asian men means much more than, say for instance, American society or the porn industry's judgment of them as sexual failures. If anything, I think their absence points to what Linda Williams identifies as larger structural limitation of pornography as an apparatus fundamentally controlled by white men: its inability to cater to and represent the desire of white women, including those who fancy Asian men. Because pornography for women is still a niche market, straight Asian porn for women is consequently and deplorably scarce.[18] The case of other minorities, particularly African Americans, appearing in interracial sex scenes is a different matter altogether. You'll find such scenes mostly in straight porn produced for a predominantly male audience, placed there to cater to the white man's fantasy of a white slut who is "degraded" by her sexual relations—being "ravaged"—by a black man.[19]

Ironically, it is the most obvious, superficial reading of these videos that critics like myself engage in the least—and it's fitting that I close this series of readings precisely with such a reading. I propose that Asian porn be read not only as a transcript of perverse and oppressive eroticism but also, for starters, as a love letter to interracial sex.

Asian porn is, after all, sought mostly by those who desire or are at least curious about sexual contact and romance with Asians of all sorts and stripes. It would be naïve to think that the spectators of Asian porn simply replicate in real life the "demeaning" and "oppressive" scenarios suggested by the videos; that, for instance, they would act on the conviction that the drizzling of ejaculate on the face or the bosom of a lover is the ultimate sign of affection and gratitude. The images of interracial coitus generated by Asian porn are bound to be, at the very least, polyvalent. Moreover, I'd like to take my analysis a bit further and suggest that the kind of control being exercised in Asian porn is not only confined to the realm of the symbolic or the virtual. Because I think of moving-image pornography not just as a representation of sex but an actual way of having sex—sex with and through the cinema—I see the very fact of Asian porn's continual popularity as a rubric or genre as a sign of progress in racial relations while also an ugly emblem of racism and colonialism's residual structures of power and desire.[20] While the emplacement of interracial love between Asians and Caucasians (along with the other transgressive practices of sexuality) within the pornographic domain may seem to others an unfortunate marginalization, I can't bring myself to ignore the value of Asian porn's sustained contribution in making such "love" visible.

NOTES

The author thanks L. S. Kim, Chuck Kleinhans, John Labella, and Peter Lehman for helpful comments on this essay.

1. Sometimes, the rubric *specialty* is assigned to the section containing porn's marginalia. *Adult Video News* (AVN), the trade publication of the adult video industry, uses this category as well but for a very wide range of materials.

2. Perhaps it is in recognition of this problem—particularly in relation to practical issues of commercial appeal and audience expectation—that Internet vendors specifically point out in their web catalogues that *Dollar and Yen* (1994), which features a cast of both Asians and Caucasians, "is not all oriental."

3. See Richard Fung, "Looking for My Penis: The Eroticized Asian in Gay Video Porn," in *How Do I Look: Queer Film and Video*, ed. Bad Object-Choices (Seattle: Bay, 1991), 145–160.

4. See Mikhail Bakhtin, *Rabelais and His World*, trans. Hélène Iswolsky (Bloomington and Indianapolis: Indiana University Press, 1984), especially 308–367.

5. In *Rabelais and His World* (318), Bakhtin suggests a metonymic function to the grotesque body: "Actually, if we consider the grotesque image in its extreme aspect, it never presents an individual body; the image consists of orifices and convexities that present another, newly conceived body." The grotesquely sexualized and racialized genitals in Asian porn signify not just the excessive sexuality of the entire bodies to which they belong but also of the entire "race."

6. Robert J. C. Young, *Colonial Desire: Hybridity in Theory, Culture and Race* (London and New York: Routledge, 1995), 181.

7. For an insightful discussion of sexuality and race (and class and gender) in colonial cultures, see Anne McClintock, *Imperial Leather: Race, Gender and Sexuality in the Colonial Contest* (New York and London: Routledge, 1995).

8. Bhabha develops his concept of ambivalence most thoroughly in "Of Mimicry and Man: The Ambivalence of Colonial Discourse," in *The Location of Culture* (London and New York: Routledge, 1994), 85–92.

9. Young, *Colonial Desire*, 181.

10. In *Imperial Leather* (22), Anne McClintock coins the related (and more amusing) term "porno-tropics" to describe how "Africa and the Americas had become . . . a fantastic magic lantern of the mind onto which Europe projected its forbidden sexual desires and fears."

11. Young, *Colonial Desire*, 181.

12. Karla Rae Fuller, "Hollywood Goes Oriental: Cauc/asian Performance in American Cinema" (Ph.D. diss., Northwestern University, 1997).

13. Judith P. Butler, *Gender Trouble: Feminism and the Subversion of Identity*, 10th anniversary ed. (New York: Routledge, 1999).

14. Cowan and Campbell use the term *racial names* to refer to both screen and diegetic names. See Gloria Cowan and Robin Campbell, "Racism and Sexism in Interracial Pornography: A Content Analysis," *Psychology of Women Quarterly* 18 (1994): 323–338. In an interview for an Asian American magazine, Suzi Suzuki discusses the practice of switching between nationalities in porn, noting that it is common practice for "Filipinos [to] become Japanese" in porn because the latter are in much shorter supply in the industry. See Eric Nakamura, "Suzuki Samurai," *Giant Robot* 14 (Summer 1999): 50.

15. Cowan and Campbell, "Racism and Sexism," 328–329.

16. Fung, "Looking for My Penis," 148.

17. Ibid., 153.

18. The paucity of straight porn starring Asian men was underlined by the guerilla gesture of Asian American Studies professor Darrell Hamamoto, who produced the still-unreleased *Skin to Skin* to fill this dearth and make a statement about Asian American masculinity.

19. Thanks to Peter Lehman, the editor of this book, for calling my attention to some of the arguments about the "underexposure" of Asian penises made in Linda Williams's latest anthology, *Porn Studies*, which was still in press when I finished this essay. Lehman's summary of these arguments, and his own suggestions about other issues that could be raised in this regard served as the bases of my treatment.

20. In *The Address of the Eye: A Phenomenology of Film Experience* (Princeton: Princeton University Press, 1991) Vivian Sobchack makes a strong case for an understanding of the cinema as a "sensing and sensual" subject and object of vision. By extending her argument, we may imagine how it is possible to have sex *with* the cinema.

Daniel Bernardi

Interracial Joysticks: Pornography's Web of Racist Attractions

Pornography revenues—which can broadly be construed to include magazines, Internet Web sites, magazines, cable, in-room hotel movies, and sex toys—total between 10 and 14 billion dollars annually. This figure, as New York Times *critic Frank Rich notes, is not only bigger than movie revenues; it is bigger than professional football, basketball, and baseball put together. With figures like these, Rich argues, pornography is no longer a "sideshow" but "the main event."*

—Linda Williams

For one thing we cannot afford to take a libertarian approach. Porn can be an active agent in representing and reproducing a sex-race status quo.

—Richard Fung

In an essay published in 2002, "Cyborgs in Cyberspace: White Pride, Pedophilic Pornography, and Donna Haraway's Manifesto," I simultaneously embraced and critiqued Donna Haraway's "A Cyborg Manifesto: Science, Technology, and Socialist Feminism in the Late Twentieth Century."[1] Like so many other poststructural leaning scholars, Haraway greatly informed my thinking about both the possibilities and the limits of critical theory to address the power of mediating technologies. "Her cyborg is a poetic vision and socialist plan for action," I wrote, "a manifesto of the highest signifying order." And yet I critiqued this paradigm-breaking theorist's "blasphemous" and "ironic" metaphor as strikingly naïve and implicitly binary for its subtle reliance on a notion of gender that gives the mothers of cyborgs the benefit of the doubt, condemns their fathers en masse for structuralizing the past, and neglects the myriad ways in which all people, at least in the United States, are represented by and live under the coercive power of whiteness.

Under the blasphemous notion of "hate," "Cyborgs in Cyberspace" associated Jeff Black's neo-Nazi website, Stormfront.org, with racialized and quasi-pedophilic pornography linked to Persiankitty.com. I saw in these sites the persistence of a form of whiteness that rests tenaciously on the degradation of people of color—adults and children alike. "Hollywood films and television, not to mention the more disturbing texts of the pornography industry," I continued, "are claiming cyberspace as their own and bringing with them a history that still requires rigorous critical confrontation despite new paradigms." My point was not to call for the rejection of the cyborg metaphor—on the contrary, I believe it is an imaginative tool for critical activism—but to suggest that models for critiquing systems of oppression such as racism in new media often fail for lack of historical, textual and ideological specificity. There is a history to the articulation of race online, a history that requires a persistent critical intervention that refuses belligerently to take the side of a gender, theoretical possibility or line of scholarly debate.[2]

I am sure most film and television scholars would agree with my overall assessment of Stormfront.org, as the so-called white pride site explicitly advocates white supremacy. Black's whiteness is an easy target, not unlike the whiteness in the blackface of D. W. Griffith's *The Birth of a Nation* (1915). In the classic American film, Griffith uses cinematic techniques to tell an epic story about the threat reconstructed blacks pose to white children, white women, and white patriarchy. Disloyal former slaves and their mulatto offspring represent the worst of Americankind, a dark evil that uses interracial sex as a tool to undermine and threaten a righteous nation. In the knick of time, the Ku Klux Klan ride in parallel action to rescue whiteness and a divine America is reborn. Stormfront.org uses the Celtic cross, racist cartoons, colorful adjectives, and interactive platforms such as chatrooms to tell a similar story in real time. And not unlike the real space-time Klan's historic use of *The Birth of a Nation* as propaganda to recruit new members to its brand of terrorism, particularly in the 1930s and 1940s, Black uses the stuff of the Web to attract surfers to his terrorizing fantasy. Putting aside for the moment the fact that too many film scholars elect not to teach or write about the racist elements of Griffith's masterpiece, preferring to excuse or ignore them in favor of stressing the film's artistic impact on the development of classical Hollywood narration,[3] most scholars would agree that constructing the Klan as heroes in cinema or on the Web equates to racism. *The Birth of a Nation* and Stormfront.org may be many things, and they are certainly different in form and content, coming about in different moments in the development of mass media, but they both contribute hateful forms of race to American popular culture.

I am not sure the majority of scholars that study pornography would agree with my overall assessment of that "dirty" genre. After all, Stormfront.org is explicitly about race; pornography is explicitly about sex. Of course, "antiporn" scholars such as Catharine Mackinnon and Andrea Dworkin see pornography as hate speech, engaging the genre critically.[4] Believing that it leads to violence against women and rape, they have in fact called for its censorship. Yet these scholars are not concerned with the specificity of race or, conversely, the diversity of gender formations. Engaged in polemics more than facts, Mackinnon and Dworkin neglect to think through the weaknesses of their methodology. They fail, for instance, to provide concrete evidence for the argument that watching pornography leads men to rape women. As Cynthia Toolin jests pointedly:

the stereotype of an unwashed, unshaven older man reading sexually explicit texts in his dingy apartment and then rushing *off* to rape the first unsuspecting woman he can find in an unlit park is inaccurate. So too would be the nervously giggling man who lures a ten year old girl away from the swing set in the playground to a garbage littered alley to fondle her after seeing "baby pictures," and also the teenager who finds his father's cache of dirty pictures, and then succumbs to the unknown pleasures of black mesh stockings, garter belts and leather whips.[5]

Toolin's point is that, contrary to the essentializing and unsubstantiated conclusions drawn by antiporn scholars, we are not all duped by pornography into committing violent acts against women and children. Mackinnon and Dworkin also fail to consider the tools available to people interested in fighting the ideological aspects of pornography, such as media literacy and education. To avoid rape, they conclude, the government must censor pornography. Linda Williams, perhaps the most well-known "radical sex feminist" scholar writing about the virtues of pornography, retorts: "We come away from her article (MacKinnon) with the impression that it is pornography that we must fight, not rape."[6] Williams, Toolin, and others argue that men and women enjoy pornography in ways that do not lead to horrific acts of violence, and I agree. One need only watch the genre with a critical but open mind to know that, like Hollywood film and television, it offers spectators a great deal of complexity, even humor, like it or not.

In the spirit of Haraway, paradigm-breaking radical sex scholars like Williams are against misogyny, racism, and child pornography as much as they are against censorship. With telling insight, they open up for analysis the artistic and subversive dimensions of pornography. Making comparisons to classical Hollywood genres, for example, Williams argues that men and women share in the pleasure and sexual liberation offered by pornography. For Williams, men in pornography are not always already involved in the exploitation and degradation of women. Instead, pornography subverts Victorian notions of sex by facilitating complex forms of pleasure. Showing us that pornography is not strictly about or for men in the same way that melodrama is not strictly for or about women,[7] Williams and other radical sex scholars do not see pornography as a form of hate speech and, as such, do not call for its censorship.

Yet as a discourse that reflects and refracts popular culture, it is hard to believe that pornography escapes the wrath of the Republic's hateful color line. Radical sex feminists seem unwilling to address the facts of racism, and in fact ignore or excuse racist elements in favor of arguing against positions held by their antiporn counterparts. Hence, although I agree with many aspects of the radical sex position on pornography, specifically its resistance to censorship in favor of a more sophisticated understanding of the genre, at the same time I find it problematic that their argument about the genre's aesthetic and subversive elements comes at the expense of its hegemonic articulations. Until her recent anthology, *Porn Studies*, which I discuss later, Williams has all but ignored the role race plays in pornography.[8] Her pioneering book, *Hard Core: Power, Pleasure, and the "Frenzy of the Visible,"* fails to mention the function of race, let alone of whiteness, in the genre.[9] Laura Kipnis's highly engaging study, *Bound and Gagged: Pornography and the Politics of Fantasy in America*, invokes but does not discuss in depth the role of race in pornographic fantasies.[10] Other books, such as Drucilla Cornell's *Feminism and Pornography* and James Elias et al.'s *Porn 101: Eroticism, Pornography, and the First Amendment*, not to mention Williams's recently published anthology, *Porn Studies*, relegate race to underdeveloped sections.[11] These books tend to ignore whiteness, and thus the force behind the color line, while focusing on one color, usually black, as if it stands for all colors.

When it comes to the question of race, the radical sex position on pornography is too extreme. Complex texts can include stereotypes and myths that work diligently against resistant or enlightened readings. Pleasure can be motivated by and lead to troubling practices. Watching pornography is not likely to lead to physical acts of violence such as rape, but it might lead to the perpetuation—or ignorance—of violent ideologies such as racism. One can critique the misogynist, racist, and homophobic aspects of pornography, call for media literacy, without advocating censorship or aligning with moral zealots. What we need, in short, is the Aristotelian version of a cinephile's golden mean, where critical analysis lies between two academic vices: excessive polemics on the one hand and deficient ideological analysis on the other.

Assuming pornography does not escape the prevalence of racism in American society, even in the absence of colorful bodies and interracial intercourse, we might ask: what is it about this genre, critical theory, or scholarly interests that facilitates this degree of oversight? What is it about race that complicates and undermines the application of various principles of critical theory to the study of pornography? In a world fraught with media complexity and expansive methodologies, why can't media scholars nonetheless call a spade a bloody shovel?

There are, of course, many reasons for the lack of attention to the question of race in studies of pornography, and none of them should be summarily explained away as racist. I do not think these scholars, and certainly not Williams, the author of an insightful book on race in the media, *Playing the Race Card: Melodramas of Black and White from Uncle Tom to O. J. Simpson*, are racist. These kinds of ad hominem charges do no good, and actually distract from what should be the focus of metacritical studies: paradigms and disciplinary trends. As I see it, race poses far too many problems for a methodology and academic agenda focused on proving and predicting complexity in artistic and popular texts, diversity among audiences, the counterhegemony involved in open sexual expression, and the failing of arguments steeped in moral turpitude. The problem lies in the predictive failings of critical theory and the application of several of its principles in the context of disciplinary interests.

Williams and other radical sex scholars put the carts of contemporary theory and disciplinary interests before the horses of historical and textual evidence.

The radical sex analysis of pornography's complexities and pleasures neglects the ideological dimensions of complexity and pleasure. The result of seeing popular cultural as complex, pleasure in texts as ambiguous, spectators as diverse and empowered, sex as a topic for open expression, leads these scholars to essential-izing and naïve conclusions about race. Particularly telling is the assumption that, because black men and white women get pleasure from interracial pornography, a pleasure long repressed in our society, neither the text, the woman, nor the black man participates completely in racism. Their mutual pleasures open up emanci-patory and masturbatory possibilities, leading to semiotic resistance and critical change. Yet as I see it, radical sex scholars let white women and black men off the ideological hook. As Amy Allen explains, they "conflate empowerment with resistance, which means that they fail to recognize that we might be empowered to act in various ways that actually uphold or reinforce existing relations of dom-ination and subordination rather than subvert or undermine such relations."[12] Although women have clearly been repressed and oppressed, and that fact requires sustained scholarly attention, should we not address the fact that white women have participated in the oppression of people of color? Why are we not talking about how white women benefit from the American color line? For that matter, haven't men of color participated in racism and even found pleasure in doing so? Haven't some even benefited from it? Whiteness is a ubiquitous formation, an embodied historical discourse, that has remained superior throughout our history and into the present, and thus the study of it, like the study of pornography and other forms of popular culture, should not exclude a race, gender, or genre despite otherwise critical and laudable goals.

We have little evidence outside of theory to predict how spectators of pornography will interpret and incorporate racism in pornography, save for the fact that we know masses of them continue consuming it faster than they con-sume "professional football, basketball, and baseball put together." We do, how-ever, have access to a great deal of evidence for the diverse and complex ways volumes and volumes of pornographic texts draw upon and perpetuate volumes and volumes of racist attractions. Side-stepping the ideology of race-in-and-about-the-text because spectators are not dupes is not unlike side-stepping and conse-quently ignoring the profound and determining role racism plays in the narrative integration that makes *The Birth of a Nation* an important film. To quickly but gently tug at her pigtails, Williams is absolutely right when she writes: "As a cul-tural form that is 'as diverse as America,' pornography deserves both a serious and extended analysis that reaches beyond polemics and sensationalism."[13] I would add paradigmatic pitfalls and academic agendas to the list of what scholars should reach beyond.

In the rest of this essay I hope to show that the meaning of race in online pornography, "money shots" and "meat shots" notwithstanding, is far too famil-iar to ignore: a racialized attraction that reduces people of color—be they gay, bisexual, straight, and transsexual—to abnormal or hyperfeminized body parts and phenotypes while constructing interracial sex as fetishistic perversions for the "pleasure" of spectators coded as white—male, female, straight, or gay. Using as my guide (without allegiance to them) some of the theoretical principles that make up poststructuralism, and even some that can be found in structuralism, I hope to illustrate why the history of racism online is best described today as a familiar form of hate speech. To do so, I focus on a network of sites on one of the Internet's more popular pornographic portholes, *Greenguy Link O'Rama*.[14] *Greenguy Link O'Rama* brings to the study of pornography unique forms of articulation, from hypertext aesthetics to interactivity. As a popular network of dirty words and images, it also brings with it a history full of hate.[15]

The Persistence of Ideology

Before addressing the specificity of race on *Greenguy Link O'Rama*, I should point out that, as Allen's work attests, there is debate among radical sex scholars. They don't all think alike. Peter Lehman, for example, takes aim at Williams's emphasis on narrative in pornography, concluding she overextends the comparison with classical Hollywood and, in the process, neglects a full consideration of the visual qualities of the genre. "For better or worse [and I think for better]," he writes, "pornography really is dirtier than Williams acknowledges."[16] Lehman likens the dirty images found in pornography to exhibitionist attractions found in early cinema, arguing that "the hard-core feature's diegesis has little or nothing to do with its display of sexual attractions."[17] The visualization of hard-core sex is what matters most in pornography. Lehman's work, then, returns the study of pornography to the subject of sex, bringing with it a clear sense of how the genre's hard-core attractions are worthy of rigorous textual analysis irrespective of narrative integration. As I show later, racial-sexual attractions comprise the stuff of online pornography; narrative is present, but it is not the featured element.

Constance Penley links pornography to "white trash" sensibilities, agreeing for the most part with both Williams and Lehman yet extending the discussion to include the problem of class:

> It would be more accurate to say that both popular forms (of pornography) are fundamentally based in a kind of humor that features attacks on religion [and, later, the professional classes], middle-class ideas about sexuality, trickster women with a hearty appetite for sex, and foolish men with their penises all in a twist—when those penises work at all.[18]

Penley emphasizes the resistant aspects of pornography, particularly class-based interests that make a "spectacle of masculinity." In doing so, she proves the genre's ideological dimensions warrant critical scrutiny. Yet Penley's work begs the question, what happens when a man or a woman of color is involved in the spectacle of sex? How about transsexuals of color? Penley does not address these questions, and as a consequence fails to define fully what she means by white, claiming simply: "A Southern white child is required to learn that white trash folks are the lowest of the low because socially and economically they have sunk so far that they might as well be black."[19] Implicitly subsuming race under class, and thereby creating an ahistorical hierarchy that reduces race to the determinacy of class, Penley forgets that it actually takes someone that can pass as white to make such a claim—a claim that ignores the semiotic fact that poor whites can and do pass as white, thereby accessing many of the privilege structures that go with what George Lipsitz calls the "possessive investment in whiteness," while both rich and poor blacks, not to mention other men and women of color, cannot.[20] Indeed, the metaphor she employs to link poor whites to poor blacks, "they have sunk so far," suggests that people who pass as white can rise again to the top. Coloreds remain forever at the bottom, the real-time lowest of the low. Thus, although Penley's work opens up the radical sex position to the question of class, it says little about race in general or whiteness in particular.

Several scholars have addressed the specificity of race in pornography. Interestingly but perhaps not surprisingly most of this work comes from scholars focused on gay pornography, a subgenre especially concerned with outing diverse forms of sexual expression. In "Looking for My Penis: The Eroticized Asian in Gay Video Porn," Richard Fung offers up one of the more persuasive studies of race in pornography, stating with telling clarity: "It is not the representation of the fantasy that offends, or even the fantasy itself, rather the uniformity with which these narratives reappear and the uncomfortable relationship they have to real social conditions."[21] Fung argues that "Asian and anus are conflated" in gay pornography featuring Asian American characters, revealing a clear textual pattern that can be linked to a history of Orientalist representations.[22] Absent in these films is Asian-Asian sex. Asian men in gay pornography tend to have anal sex exclusively with white men on top; in other words, Asian bottoms serve the desires of penetrating white men. For Fung, this clear and persistent pattern shows that gay pornography tends to be "reframed from a white perspective." In an interview published alongside the essay, Fung concludes: "I also feel that one cannot assume, as the porn industry apparently does, that the desires of even white men are so fixed and exclusive."[23] Like white women and straight white men, the interests and desires of real-time gay white men are more complex and diverse than gay pornographic texts encourage.

Kobena Mercer has offered a multifaceted analysis of race in "pornography." Mercer published two principal studies of Robert Mapplethorpe's photography, specifically his nude photographs of black men. Looking at famous Mapplethorpe works of art such as *Man in Polyester Suit* (1980), his initial position addresses the racist aspects of the image in relation to what Franz Fanon recognizes as white attempts to define the black man as a threatening penis that must be contained and controlled.[24] In this study, Mercer's position is similar to that of

Fung's in arguing that Mapplethorpe's images "fix" the spectator in the "ideological subject-position of the white male subject."[25] The artwork is racist.

In the second study Mercer performs a "180-degree turn" and concludes that there is a great deal of ambiguity to Mapplethorpe's photographs of nude black men. The spectator is not fixed in whiteness. The artwork isn't really racist; it's subversive. The articulation of ambivalence in the photographer's art, he writes, "can be seen as a subversive deconstruction of the hidden racial and gendered axioms of the nude in dominant traditions of representation."[26] Grounding his analysis in contemporary critical theory and artistic traditions, he goes on to explain:

> One might say that what is staged in Mapplethorpe's black male nudes is the return of the repressed in the ethnocentric imaginary. The psychic-social boundary that separates "high culture" and "low culture" is transgressed, crossed and disrupted precisely by the superimposition of two ways of seeing, which thus throws the spectator into uncertainty and undecidability, precisely the experience of ambivalence as a structure of feeling in which one's subject-position is called into question.[27]

In the second study, then, Mercer sees a great deal more contradiction and uncertainty in Mapplethorpe's images of black men with relatively larges penises, arguing that this textual pattern leads spectators of the photographer's "high art" to question their relationship to the "low art" of race. It turns out that the spectator is not fixed in the subject-position of the white male.

For all its critical insights, which are plenty, Mercer's revision reads forced. He, too, puts the cart of theory, in this case Foucaultian notions of authorship and power, as well as an alliance with the art and gay communities, before historical, textual, and ideological evidence. Although it is quite possible for a spectator of Mapplethorp's photographs to walk away uncertain and undecided, even ambivalent, about the artistic image of the black man's flaccid penis framed by polyester, it is also quite possible that he or she, black or white or other, gay or straight, will not. For that matter, what exactly absolves the articulation of ambivalence of the potential to perpetuate racist ideologies? The qualities of the art, specifically the framing of the man's uncircumcised penis penetrating a headless body, are clearly centered, like many other images of black men in Western culture, on the constructed primitiveness of its iconographic blackness. The subject's foreskin is associated visually and metaphorically with the cheap polyester suit, a suit that engulfs the man but not his penis, cutting off the head that symbolizes civilization to reveal the embodied qualities of a mysterious dark continent. There is no fast or easy way around it: however else it might be read or intended to be read, however beautifully it manipulates photographic techniques and artistic contradictions, whether you want one inside you or hanging on a museum's wall, Mapplethorpe's black male is reduced to Fanon's penis.

Although questioning Mercer's assumptions about popular culture, Williams ultimately agrees with his revised position. As I noted earlier, the author of *Hard Core* addresses the representation of race in pornography in an essay published in *Porn Studies*, "Skin Flicks on the Racial Border: Pornography, Exploitation, and Interracial Lust." "Mercer's argument," she writes, "evades, but also evokes, the important question of whether the phobic fetishization that once fixed Fanon is still present in the new desiring fetishization." She goes on to acknowledge the fact that pornography contains fetishistic scenes of race, of large black penises penetrating white vaginas, but that these scenes "work in the service of fueling a pleasure that has become more complex, a pleasure that serves more than the white former masters."[28] To cross the sexual line in black and white, returning to what was once repressed, reveals that sex-race transgression is both possible and pleasurable. For Williams sexual-racial differences in pornography, like images of sex in general, now serve a subversive function. "It would seem," she continues, "that what is involved instead is a complex flirtation with the now historically proscribed stereotype operating on both sides of the line. Thus the very taboos that once effectively policed the racial border now work in the service of eroticizing its transgression."[29] The assumption here is one of progression: pornographic art and film, presumably like society, have progressed in the way they represent interracial sex to the point at which, like Mercer, "one's subject-position is called into question." A poststructural claim, the evidence apparently lies in polysemic texts produced and received in the post "separate but equal" space-time of multiculturalism.

Williams's analysis is thoughtful and rigorous, but like Mercer's second study seems to say more about critical theory and the current state of pornography studies than it says about race. Her application of critical methodologies coupled with an uncomfortable commitment to the radical sex perspective forces Williams to assume that race has progressed because interracial sex is no longer repressed, thereby neglecting in almost circular fashion the complex ways whiteness maintains hegemony across U.S. history. She also neglects the degree to which different forms of racism inform the color of race in pornographic texts. Interracial sex is not simply black and white. In fact, Williams sidesteps the role black women play in the representation of interracial relationships, bypassing a line of criticism advanced by Alice Walker: "where white women are depicted in pornography as 'objects,' black women are depicted as animals. Where white women are depicted as human bodies if not beings, black women are depicted as shit."[30] Should we conclude that Walker's analysis is too narrow or are black women no longer depicted as animals and shit? Moreover, Williams ignores the fact that interracial relationships involve more than black men and white women. What about the growing corpus of pornographic texts featuring Asians, Asian Americans, and Latino/as? Is pornography not raced by these attractions and narrative elements? What about the fact that Native American men and women seem to be completely absent from pornography? How does their absence structure the meaning of race in-and-about pornographic texts?

Looking at the representation of race from multiple angles, the color spectrum of the U.S. color line, including its absences, leads one to make an argument that is far less optimistic. Contrary to Williams's position, I think it is important, even crucial, to charge these pornographic works with racism. Doing so does not necessarily mean all of its producers, directors, stars, and fans are racist or that the text themselves are without a degree of socially redeeming value. It doesn't mean its spectators will run out and burn crosses, lynch, and engage in rape. It means the texts are racist. Once we agree on this critical point, we are able to turn to more fundamental questions: How do racist representations and myths mutate across mediums, genres, and time to find their way into and out of pornography? What is it about sex that attracts race? What is it about race that attracts sex? How can scholars combat racism in pornography without falling into polemics or preaching? What tools are available to us as we challenge racism in the dirty genre, and how do those tools simultaneously help and hinder our work?

Racist Marketing

I cannot answer all of these questions in this essay, but I can begin the process of confronting the articulation of race on *Greenguy*. The website functions as a network of pornographic material, a self-marketed "link-o-rama," available to anybody with an uncensored connection to the Web.[31] Designed to attract spectators to go deeper into "The Porn List" while capitulating to the legalities of the Web, the opening view offers a virtual plea: "Please, if you're over the age of 18, just go in & have fun enjoying the free XXX porn links." And, in fact, much of the pornographic material ultimately linked to this site is "free," in the sense that a patient spectator can click through the labyrinth of links, careful to bypass colorful banner ads with embedded links, to find libraries of soft-core and hard-core pictures and streaming video clips. Capitalism is, of course, advancing in online pornography, as "free" links, images, and video clips, like television advertisements, are designed to attract spectators to pay sites and other commercial activities such as an "Adult Super Store," where the spectator can "Buy DVD & VHS Movies, Adult Toys & Novelty's, Porno Magazines & Much, Much More!"

Greenguy Link O'Rama's network of links is divided into several categories, or subgenres, ranging from "Amature Sex" to "Wet Women Sex." When the spectator clicks on a category, a page of banner ads and links appear under various headings: (1) Pay Sites with Free OR $1 Trials, (2) Pay Sites, (3) AVS Sites, (4) Recommended Free Sites, (5) Free Sites, and (6) Other Lists. Under each heading are the links to affiliated websites, several residing on servers across the globe, which is where, after a few more clicks of the mouse, you will be presented with dirty pictures and movies. Because I am interested in the Web as a mass medium available to all sectors of the population—young and old; local and global—and because I did not want to use my credit card to purchase access to pornography, concluding I would not be reimbursed for the expense, I studied free links, images, and videos.[32] In some ways *Greenguy Link O'Rama* is similar to a cable television channel: as long as you pay your monthly Internet Service Provider (ISP), your cable bill, you will have access to a flow of pornographic speech, images, and streaming videos designed to capture your attention in order to sell more of itself, its products, and popular ideologies.

The marketing of race on *Greenguy Link O'Rama* is primarily achieved through the naming of both subgenres and links to affiliated sites. The producers of the network are adept at using colorful words, phrases, and metaphors to attract spectators to "click here." You can find Black Porn, tagged "It's all pink inside," as well as Asian Porn, Interracial Porn, Latina Porn, and India Sex. Specialty links include Interracial Mature, where characters age fifty or older engage in sex with each other or with a teen; Gay Ethnic, which almost always signifies a white man and a man of color; and "Interracial Lesbian-Hunnies Loving Pussy Tasting And Sextoys." This is similar to other forms of pornography. As Alice Mayall and Diane Russell note: "People of color fall into the special interest category, other examples of which are rape, bondage and sado-masochism, anal sex, sex with children, large breasted women, and sex between women."[33]

Click on a category and you are taken to a page of links described in unambiguous terms.[34] Under Black Porn, which offers more than 150 separate links under the Free Sites heading, the spectator is offered anything but a poverty of options: "Ghetto Pussy Pounding—Clips Of A Ebony Couple Doing The Nasty Stuff," "Ebony Sluts Fucked—Vids Of Some Black Chicks Doing Some White Cocks," and "Ghetto Bitch—Ebony Babe Exposes Her Big Tits And Pink Pussy Over Here On Two Pages," and the like. Under Asian Porn, which offers almost as many links, typical descriptions are written to entice spectators interested in exotic options: "Oriental Exotics—Two Spiffy Pages Of Kinky Asian Chicks," "Exotic Island Girl Sucks Cock—2 Pages Of An Island Babe Sucking Cock," and "Exotic Asian Pussy Exposed—Two Pages Over Here Of This Fresh Thai Cutie Posin." Offering more than 150 links, the Latina Porn category markets women as food: "Spicy Latina Slut—Two Good Pages Of This Busty, Redheaded Latina Gettin Some Manmeat," "Mexican Girl Needs Gringo—This Hot Chica Is In Need Of Some Gringo Enchilada Over Here," and so on. Among the ninety-one sites linked under India Sex, Orientalist metaphors entice the spectator to click through "Discover Indian Pussy—Couple Pages Of This Indian Looking Woman Posing Nude" and "Indian Interracial Fuckfest—An Indian Chickybabe Is Gettin Some Action Over Here From A Blonde Dude." Finally, links under Interracial Porn play to the street: "White Ghetto Booty—Pics Of A Horny Ass White Chick Doing A Huge Black Cock" and "She Loves Black Cock—Two Pages Featuring A Ho Sucking A Big Black Cock Over Here." At times playful, even self-consciously irreverent, *Greenguy Link O'Rama* nonetheless relies on denotative categories and links with connotative references to race to create and satisfy consumers interested in virtually transgressing the sex-color line.

On *Greenguy Link O'Rama* "interracial" almost always signifies black men "doing" white women. Forming society's collective fear of and prurient interest in black sexuality, black men in these sites are consistently marketed by a racialized economy of scale. They are sold as "big" or "long" or "massive" or "huge" or "gigantic." They are described as "pounding," "ramming," "drilling," and "nailing" white "whores" and "sluts." White women are worked on by punishing verbs, and subsequently defined for their interracial transgressions by adjectives and nouns, key words, that cast them as dirty: "Interracial Teen-Series Pics Of Big Cocked Black Guys Fucking White Sluts," "Hot Cuckold Threesome—A Couple Of Pages Of This White-Trash Wife Gettin Some Black Mamba," and "Hardcore Interracial Sex—Skinny White Whore Gets A Taste Of Her First Big Black Cock." Most of these links sell the opportunity to see a white woman with several black men simultaneously, "one in every hole," rhetorically constructing black men as a pack of sexual predators. Sites include "Blonde Slut Group Fucked—Couple Pages Of This Blonde Getting Fucked By A Few Black Guys," "Gangland Victims Movie—Some Super Interracial Group Sex Movies Over Here," and "Gangbanged German Slut—Pics Of A Busty Blonde German Babe Taking On 4 Black Studs."

When an interracial site includes another color, the woman is often Asian and the men white, black, or both. Black men "split" and "gag" all women; Asian women willingly submit to all forms of male desire and sex. "Interracial Gangbang—Great Shots On 2 Lovely Pages Of This Asian Girl Sucking And Fucking A Black & White Dude" and "China Girl Fucked—An Asian Honey Getting Plugged By Big Fat Black Cock" are representative examples. Asian men are never seen with white or black women. As Orientalism literally and figuratively dictates, Asian women stand in for all of Asia. And your garden variety sex act is not sufficient; anal sex and faces splattered with ejaculate dominate the Asian point of sale. Of the 388 links under the Interracial Porn category, for example, several sold white men sodomizing Asian women, including "Asian Anal Sex—Two Pages Of A Slutty Asian Babe Taking A Big White Cock Up Her Ass & A Load On Her Face," "Asian Anal Amateurs—Two Pages of Some Asians Getting Ass Fucked Here," and "Asian Anal Pics—Two Pages Over Here Of This Eurasian-Lookin Chick Gettin Hammered." A couple feature Asian women with black men, such as "Asian Swallows Black Cock—2 Pages Of A Slutty Asian Babe Taking On A Black Guy" and "Asian Fucky Fucky—Two Pages Of This Ordinary Asian Gettin A Length Of Black Mamba." In all cases, Asian women are sold as willing to do anything to please non-Asian men.

In the few sites that feature white men and black women, the point of sale involves the woman, described using animal metaphors, being gagged and humiliated by the man. Links are described as "Face Fucked Bitches—Couple Pages Of Some Ebony Women Getting White Man To Cum On Their Faces" and "Ghetto

Gaggers—Shots Of Some Black Chicks Doing White Cocks." And like most women in online pornography, black women enjoy the pleasure white men take in their degradation. Their sexual servitude is a labor of lust: "Jizz In Ebony Mouth—Two Hummer Pages Of Some Black Chick Enjoying Some White Cock," "Hot Interracial Babe—Two Pages Over Here Of This Back Floozie Suckin On White Meat," and "Face Fucked Bitches—Couple Pages Of Some Ebony Women Getting White Man To Cum On Their Faces." White men are not rapists. They merely deliver sexual punishment to black women that entice them to do so, yet another ideology dating back to the days of slavery. White women, of course, are constructed similarly, as sites feature them sodomized and splattered with ejaculate. Yet this is the dominant way black women are sold: animals freely bound and whitewashed.

Even in the absence of colorful nouns and adjectives race structures the marketing of online pornography. In the Cheerleader Porn category, not a single site lists an Asian, black, or Latina.[35] And the spectator's expectations are not challenged or undermined by the lack of denotative references to color in these links, as there are no cheerleaders of color—black, brown, red, or yellow—on any site linked to *Greenguy Link O'Rama*'s Cheerleader Porn. The spectator can count on the network's marketing campaign, as there are only "blonds," "redheads," "Coeds," "Sluts," and "Teens"—all in white. When it comes to color on Cheerleader Porn, denotation is not required. Color is excluded. Instead, whiteness is represented through various connotative code words involving hair and petit parts. Cheerleaders, as symbols of beauty and youth, as paragons of beauty in the American imagination, are always already white.

The segregated structure of online marketing is perhaps most clear in links that feature "barely legal" or "teen" characters. Racially coded with implicit and explicit references to puerile orifices, white teens in the Teen Porn category are sold as innocent, almost angelic, yet ready and willing to be deflowered. We are offered, for example, "Teen Tender Penetration—Shots Of A Teen Hottie Getting Freaky With A Toy," "Sweet Teen Kitten—2 Pages Of A Sweet Teen Showing The Good Parts," "Natural Teen Virgins—Three Sweet Pages Of A Coed Posing For Ya," and "Playful Blonde Teen—Sweet Pics Of Blonde Coed Posing In Her Dorm Room." Some links are more explicit in their use of metonymic figures, such as "Pigtails and Braces," "Innocent Faces & Tight Places," and "Happy Teen Valley." Braces and pigtails, innocent faces and valleys of happy teens function as synecdoche for sex with otherwise "pure" and always white girls. These and similar links pander to a popular stereotype of teens as good but naughty, happy to be trained, implicitly connecting white girls with discourses of beauty, innocence (only to be soiled by an older man), and sexual curiosity. To be sure, "white" teens are sold for their sexual parts, but at the same time the fetishization is marked by discourses that are otherwise considered "positive" in dominant culture (e.g., pure, innocent, angelic). These girls are not colored by race; they are the essence of it. They are not colored by violence; they are treated gently if firmly.

When a Teen Porn link is marketed by color, the color and its role in the ensuing representation are unmistakable: "Two Black Cocks for Redhead—2 Pages Of Pics Of This Young Redhead Taking On 2 Big Black Cocks," "Double Black Trouble—2 Pages Of A Slutty Teen & Her Big Clit Lips Taking On 2 Big Black Studs," and "Deep Interracial Double Fuck—2 Pages Of A Big Cocked Black Guy Banging 2 White Teens." Black men provide the most virulent threat and subsequent pleasure sources in interracial articulations of teen sex. When with a black man, white teens, like their more mature counterparts, are almost always "bitches," "sluts," and "hos"—a pattern that dates as far back in America's racial color line to Griffith's representation of reconstruction. As Gloria Cowan and Robin R. Campbell surmise: "It is also possible that in pornography, Black men are used to punish erring White women and reduces their status."[36] One site, "My Dad Thinks I Am Still A Virgin," promises: "Not After He Sees These Pics Of His 19 Year Old Daughter & A Big Cocked Black Guy." Black men—not Asian, Native American, or Latino men—are used to excite the viewer's desire in the descriptions of these sites. Their ideological role is to promise the punishment of naughty white teens and their overprotective fathers. At the center of the pleasure in this punishment is the white male, who remains present ideologically even if absent from the mise-en-scène. Contrary to Williams, it is this "fixed" desire that we see in black dicks with white vaginas, a prurient mix of racism and misogyny.

We see a slightly different pattern, though no less white, in sites marketed to viewers interested in gay pornography. There are thirteen gay categories on *Greenguy Link O'Rama*: (1) Gay Webcams; (2) Gay Video; (3) Gay Twinks ("College age gay males only in this one"); (4) Gay Solo; (5) Gay Mature; (6) Gay in Uniform; (7) Gay General; (8) Gay Fetish; (9) Gay Big Cock; (10) Gay Bears; (11) Gay Amateurs; (12) Gay Sex; and (13) Gay Ethnic. Race is thus segregated to a specific subgenre, Gay Ethnic, making the marketing of men of color on *Greenguy Link O'Rama* an exotic fetish in ways that are similar to the marketing of men and women of color in straight pornography on the network's link-o-rama. In fact, although you might find a link selling men of color in a subgenre not "ethnic," such as Gay Video, it is extremely rare. In the cases when race is present, the link notifies you in the same denotative way it does in straight categories: "Interracial Gay Sex-Two Pages Over Here Of This Ebon Dude Gettin Some White Schlong." There are a few images of men of color under the Gay Twinks category, the metonymic equivalent of Teen Porn, that are not marked as colorful in some way, suggesting, unlike its straight counterpart, race is more easily passed unmarked in sites that feature youthful gay men. These "college age" men are always Asian and Latino; black men are not associated with the fetish of youth in any link. Asian and Latino men are like white teen girls, feminized as bottoms for the dominating desire of white men.

The marketing of race in gay categories is restricted to Gay Ethnic, where we find mostly black men with relatively large penises engaged in sex with white men. There are few instances of black men engaged in sex with other black men or posing by themselves, but here too we read familiar stereotypes: "Black Thug Posing—A Hot Black Hunk Is Over Here Strippin And Showin Off His Schlong," "Black Muscle Stud—Solo Muscular Black Man Strips Naked In 3 Series Pages," and "Black Man Booty—A Homeboy Loves Having A Dick In His Butt And One In His Mouth." By putting these sites under Gary Ethnic, *Greenguy Link O'Rama* envisions a white spectator that will see all colors as specialty items whether or not interracial sex is involved. There are no sites that feature black men engaged in sex with Asian men or Latinos, let alone sites featuring sex between Asian men or between Latinos. To be gay is to be white. To be a gay person of color is to be a source of white male desire and pleasure. In one way, then, gay sites are more segregated than straight sites; in all ways they are linked intimately to the articulation of race in straight pornography.

Racist Attractions

Satisfying *Greenguy Link O'Rama*'s demographic, the representation of race in these links is reduced to phonotypical signifiers: from "exotic" skin colors to the size, shape, and "nature" of racialized genitalia, breasts, and buttocks. What we see in the representation of interracial sex, in the actual images and video clips, is a pornographic version of eugenics: race reduced to manufactured sizes and shapes, phenotypes linked to a form of difference defined by an invisible norm, racial myth in the service of white desire, all functioning as fetishistic evidence for the superiority—the pleasure—of whiteness. People of color on *Greenguy Link O'Rama* are reduced to their exotic sexual organs, a form of fragmentation and fetishization that emphasizes historical constructed differences in race that ultimately dehumanize people of color.[37] They are, as Walker suggested about black women in pornography, "animals" and "shit." At the same time, this discourse positions people of color as worthy of a voracious consumption. Their body parts might not be "normal," but they are definitely exotic, edible, and perishable. In fact, it is their constructed difference, the apparent abnormality, that facilitates desire, a Hegelian desire that ultimately defines whiteness as normal, ugly, and perverse. While we may or may not have a reduction in various forms of material racism in the twenty-first century, ideological racism remains powerful, mutating with time and across mass media to ensure the virtual hegemony of whiteness.

The evidence lies in the marketing of race, as I have tried to show, as well as in the representation of race in the free pictures and video clips found in the network's affiliated sites. For example, most images of black women reveal a hyperbolic emphasis on butts in ways the reduce them to Walker's shit: "Sweet Black Asshole—This Brown Sug-Babe Is Gettin A Workout Over Here," "Ebony Booty

Juice—Two Pages Of Some Hot Ebony Action," and "Black Ass Pussy—Some Shots Over Here On Two Pages Of Black Flesh Posin," among many others. Conflating vagina with anus, the representation of black women in this way dates to slavery, when Europeans and European Americans conceived of Africans and African Americans as deviant, an ideological construction that validated their perverse sense of normality and subsequent supremacy. A clear example dates to London in the early nineteenth century, where apparently a woman from South Africa, Sartlee (Sarah) Baartman, marketed as the "The Hottentot Venus," was exhibited as a sort of freak show for the enlightened justification that Europeans are superior and African female sexuality abnormal, out of control, and thus in need of being controlled. The Hottentot Venus became a standard among art critics to illustrate the monstrosity of black female sexuality against the norms of white beauty, a pattern we consistently see represented on affiliates of *Greenguy Link O'Rama*.

Latina representations are betwixt and between black and white, food and shit, slavery and segregation. The Latina's proscribed anatomical difference is described and constructed using food metaphors: "Saucy Latina's Facial Wash—2 Pages Of This Tiny Titted Plump Latina Babe Getting Fucked & Facialed," "Spicy Cum Lover—2 Pages Of A Latina Amateur Taking A Couple Facial Cumshots," and "Sweet Latina Booty," to name only a few. Fast, high in fat, Latinas are also cute little animals, rodent-size dogs, and oversexed in every way. In my original study, I found an image of a Latina with the dog from the Taco Bell ad placed in front of her crotch. The ad, I argued, "reveals not only the racism in on-line pornography but that on-line pornography takes advantage of the racism in traditional media to sell its texts—even if for a joke." In the ad, Latina sexuality is ready for anything—even a dog (which, to drive the point home, is depicted with an erection). And this is the case today, as "trashy" Latinas are associated with fast food and depicted as desperate for white dogs. Little has changed.

Like the representation of black women, but seemingly capitalizing on the obsession with the star discourse surrounding Jennifer Lopez, images linked to *Greenguy Link O'Rama* reflect popular culture's obsession with Latina butts. Examples include "Sexy Brazilian Ass—Pics Of A Sexy Brazilian Slut Getting Dirty Fixing A Car," "Bubble Butt Latina Babe—Pics Of A Latina Babe Sucking & Fucking A Stranger," and "Tasty Latin Butt—2 Pages Of A Latina Babe Sucking & Fucking Her Man," to name just a few. Even Latino/as transsexuals cross over; they, too, are obsessively represented with "large" fetishistic butts. Moreover, the vast majority of anal-oral pictures and movies involve Latino men and white women, Latinas, Latinos, and transsexuals. If, as Fung suggests, Asian men are equated with the anus, Latina/os are a bigger and "nastier" version of that trope.

What we see in these images is the systematic and persistent reduction of the Latina to what amounts to a hyperbolic ass, overflowing and always ready for public penetration. One site reads: "She Wants It In The Anus—2 Pages Of An

Amateur Latina Sucking A Big Cock & Taking It Up The Ass." As Frances Negrón-Muntaner, writing about cross-over star Jennifer Lopez, critiques: "A big Latin rear end is an invitation to pleasures construed as illicit by puritan ideologies, hetero-normativity, and the medical establishment through the three deadly vectors of miscegenation, sodomy, and a high-fat diet."[38]

There are, of course, racial-specific patterns to these articulations. Not all colors are constructed in the same way—"all ass," high fat, fast food—suggesting again that the articulation of race in online pornography is mindful of history. Asian body parts are hyperbolically feminized in ways that rely upon Oriental myths and stereotypes to affect pleasure: "A Tiger In Bed—2 Pages Of This Petite Asian Babe Getting Naked In Bed," "Sweet And Sour Pussy—This Asian Babe Sure Loves To Spread It Wide," and "Amateur Asian Flower—Some Nifty Shots Over Here Of Some Amateurish Gash In The Kitchen." Dissected by the camera lens, Asian women are showcased for the "irregular" but delicate orifices. They are positioned in such a way that manufactured differences are obsessively erotized for a white consumption strung out on Orientalist myths. *Greenguy Link O'Rama* surfers are offered: "Tiny Asian Twats," "Petite Asian Pussy," "Oriental Exotics," "Katsumi's Asian Surprise," "Hot Chinese Babe Opens Pussy," "Fortune Pussy," "Far East Beaver," and the like. Most are designed in "chop stick" font with a mix of clichéd symbols and metaphors from various Asian countries, allowing the spectator to experience a homogenized Far East in English from the comforts of home.

In Orientalism, according to Edward Said, Asians are constructed as exotic, childlike pleasure sources for an insatiable and perverse colonial appetite.[39] West doesn't meet East; West consumes East's men, women, and children. Orientalism is a Western opiate, a drug that has everything to do with myth. Unlike white teens, where the focus is on the exposed parts, the vaginas and penises of Asian teens are neither always visible nor necessary to the myth-reproducing goals of the site's making campaign. Their sexual parts are less important than the way the characters are framed by a discourse that cherishes "smooth," "bald," and "shaved" "orientals." In several images on the Gay Ethnic sites, we see gay house-boys feminized in the same way Asian girls are fetishized: as smooth Oriental bod-ies ideal for the quasi-pedophilic desires of whiteness.

We are more likely to see white penises penetrating young Asian mouths, vaginas, and anuses than Asian penises penetrating anything Asian. Like video and cinematic pornography in the United States, Asian men rarely have sex with Asian women and never with other Asian men. Searching for the heterosexual Asian penis is as difficult a venture as searching for the Asian penis in gay pornog-raphy. In fact, Asian women are with black men more than they are with Asian men. There are also more sites featuring Asian women with dildos than Asian women with Asian men. There are more Asian women with other Asian women than with Asian men. And most of the pornography featuring Asian men with Asian women involves Japanese characters, exports of Japan, hardly the diversity of Asia. We do not see, for example, Chinese, Island, Korean, Thai, or Vietnamese men, despite the fact that we see lots of Chinese, Korean, Island, Thai, and Vietnamese women. When Japanese men are shown having sex with Asian women, their heads are often cut off; the point of focus is the smooth skin and submissive facial expression of the Asian woman. And while the woman is often shown in deep pleasure, it is all too often difficult to determine what exactly is producing that pleasure. As I noted, we don't see the Asian penis.

Asian women on *Greenguy Link O'Rama* function as virtual sex tours for white men around the Internet world. These spectators can see and masturbate to almost any exotic act they want without the fear of breaking "American" laws, social castration, or the effort it takes to leave the country (let alone the house or office). At the same time, they market real-time sex tours: "Asian Adventure Movies—Vids Of A Asian Babe Getting Some Hot Cock," "Bangkok Meatwad Suckers—Couple Super Pages Of Some Asian Hardcore Action," "Thai Street Walker—A Couple Of Pages Over Here Of This Raunchy Thai Chick Gettin Two Schlongs," "Japanese Blowjob Girls—2 Pages Of Sexy Asian Babes Sucking Cock," "Korean Hottie Gagging—Dandy Vids Of This Asian Getting Fucked By Two Guys," among many others. All feature white men on sexual vacation with Asian girls, bonding over their sexual exploits, an exotic exploration with a patriotic dose of homoerotic-inspired racism. These men are eroticized watching each other, other men, sometimes groups of other men, exploit Asian women as tourist attractions of the sexual kind, displacing desires in a way that allows them to see each other in action. In one series of images, a young woman is branded with the American flag on her shirt, which is positioned in the mise-en-scène parallel to two white crotches belonging to men giving the thumbs-up sign—unpatriotic images of America that all too often are sold nationally and globally as patriotic. Later in the picture story, she takes both men in almost every way imaginable, always smiling for the camera as if to lure other men to the tour. She is as docile and submissive as she is young, exotic, and willing. The two white men, thumbs-up American-style, sell themselves to other white men interested in white men on an Asian sex tour—a mix of homoerotic and Orientalist disire to be sure.

Although black men do not participate in too many Asian sex tours, we see an awful lot of black penises on *Greenguy Link O'Rama*. Black men, as Fanon tells us, are not represented as men: "the Negro is eclipsed. He is turned into a penis. He *is* a penis."[40] For Fanon, black men are not just aestheticized as colored. Rather, their difference, the darkness of their foreskin in the case of pornography, is constructed to represent savagery and primitiveness, the danger of the jungle and "goin' ghetto." They become animals, a common racial slur, that need to be controlled for the benefit of a miscegenated mix of fear, labor, hate, and desire. And one should not be too surprised; size is the essence of black male sexuality on the network. Black men are shot in ways that elongate their penises, drawing attention to the threat posed by their blackness and thus supporting their sexual and economic use-value if properly, though only momentarily, tamed. These men are fixed, literally and metaphorically caged, by the size of their penises or, rather, by the way their penises are constructed visually and rhetorically segregated in white spaces. Emancipatory imaginations notwithstanding, there is little for the spectator to desire in these texts except for the trappings of the black man's monstrous sexual part. As Isaac Julien remarks about video pornography: "I see a fixing of different black subjects in recognizable stereotypes rather than a more dialectical representation of black identities, where a number of options or fantasy positions would be made available."[41]

"In pornography," writes Alice Walker, "the black man is portrayed as being capable of fucking anything . . . even a piece of shit. He is defined solely by the size, readiness and unselectivity of his cock."[42] And this is the case on *Greenguy Link O'Rama*, where the story of black sexuality is anything but passionate or self-controlled. Blackness is associated with "deviant" and "perverse" forms of sexuality. This includes black women; they, too, are represented as willing to "fuck anything." A visible frenzy of interracial fornication, the representation of African Americans in links under Midget Sex category is particularly telling. Blacks are extreme sexual deviants, animalistic and monstrous, and the evidence lies in both their genitalia as well as their inability to control their sexual appetite for other malformed freaks. This is not to say that diverse forms of sexual expression are always racist. What makes these images racist is the way in which they are coded: to emphasize and enhance freak-show stereotypes that have a very long history in white cultures. The hate in these images is not located in the fantasy or the sex itself, but, as Fung noted about Asian men in gay pornography, in the uniformity with which they reappear. These are semiotic sexual freaks that were born even before Griffith's *The Birth of a Nation*.

The association with "deviant" forms of sexuality is most clear in *Greenguy Link O'Rama*'s Shemale Nudes and Shemale Sex categories. Even more so than other sites, perhaps because gender norms are so clearly challenged in these subgenres, body parts are dissected and emphasized for their grotesque realism. But here, too, we see constructions that are racialized in ways consistent with the representations of men and women of color across pornography. Many of these sites contain a diverse range of racial options: "Black Tranny Buttfuck—Two Pages Of This Black Tranny Enjoyin A Suck," "Assfucked Asian Ladyboy—2 Pages Of An Asian Shemale Getting Fucked," and "Brazil Shemale Group Sex—2 Saucy Pages Of Some Wild Ass Tranny Action." Yet unlike every other category on *Greenguy Link O'Rama*, these subgenres integrate Asian, black, Latino, and white transsexuals in numerous sites without the need to market the color of the characters. Diverse in profound ways, shemales are already colored by prurient difference and perverse identities. Shemales of color need not be sold in ways different than their white brothers/sisters.

Black transsexuals are represented with large penises, and many shots of them are framed such that the male sex organ is both centered and grotesque. And, like black women, a great deal of visual attention and rhetorical naming centers on Baartman-like butts. Asian shemales, on the other hand, are represented as smooth, "bald," and childlike—just like their men and women, straight and gay, counterparts seen in Asian Nudes, Asian Porn, and Gay Ethnic categories. They are the repressed conflation of the Asian house boy and the geisha coming into being in unnatural light. Representative examples include "Asian Tranny Girl," "Asian Trannies Tities," "Asian Pantyhose Trannies," "Asian Ladyboys" and "Beautiful Asian Ladyboys." Latino/a transsexuals are represented in ways similar to straight Latinos and Latinas. In one series, "Tgirl Island Whores," the representation of shemales includes emphasis on large butts and anal-oral sex, standard racist tropes involving Latina/o pornography.

In these *Greenguy Link O'Rama* linked sites race is sold as an oddity, a deviant object worthy of fetishization but in need of punishment, ideological and literal, analogous to other oddities and ideological freaks like midgets and transsexuals. All virtual turns lead to the white male at the joystick of pleasure. In other words, these sites are not for Asian men and women seeking pornography online. They are not for Latino/as or Native Americans. Although all spectators may or may not enjoy Shemale Nudes and Shemale Sex, or Midget Porn for that matter, the marketing, representation, and story of these "freaks" is the story of race in the service of white fear and fantasy, pain and pleasure, hate and lust.

Scholars engaged in the study of pornography must work diligently to reveal the whiteness in-and-about the genre's text. As Mercer argues: "Paradoxically then, for all our rhetoric about 'making ourselves visible,' the real challenge in the new cultural politics of difference is to make 'whiteness' visible for the first time, as a culturally constructed ethnic identity historically contingent upon the disavowal and violent denial of difference."[43] This is perhaps most obvious in interracial bisexual sex, where several white males are pleased by the same black and white female types. What we have in every instance is black men and white women serving in anticipation and rapture the white man's desire, arousal, and eventual ejaculation. The centrality of whiteness does not begin or end with interracial bisexual encounters, however. It can also be seen in scenes involving anal sex of all shapes, colors, and preferences. In far too many cases, from the past and today on *Greenguy Link O'Rama*, the recipient of white male sexuality endures great pain despite finding whitewashed desire pleasurable.

In other cases whiteness is difficult to see, seemingly "invisible" as Richard Dyer theorizes.[44] But like popular culture, whiteness is alive and clicking in pornography. We need only focus our critical eyes in the direction of history, ideology, and signification. As one "smoking gun" image demonstrates, pornography offers a white way of looking. The black man is headless; he sees nothing. He is simply the size of his large penis, emphasized by the outstretched hand of the white woman. Her whiteness is hyperbolic, bleach blonde, an iconic balance. She is a paragon of American beauty impressed by what she is about to take in her mouth. In the background, in the mirror, we see a white man looking on, perhaps the person taking the picture, the auteur, crouched forward in anticipation. This blowjob is for him and his spectators. Like Mapplethorp's *Man in a Polyester Suit*, the picture says "more about the white male subject behind the camera than they do about the black men whose beautiful bodies we see depicted."[45] The scene takes place in the bathroom, rhetorically linking the act that is about to be performed with urination, defecation, and cleaning up. Interracial sex is dirty, "shit," and requires one to clean up immediately afterward. This is not intimacy or affection, even mutual desire or sexual expression. It is not, dare I say, love. This is semiotic hate, the history of mediated whiteness, and the opposite of love. This is not truly open sex. This is sex open to white eyes. This is not multiculturalism. This is colorized hate.

Toward a Conclusion

Pornography, like "high" art and popular culture—for that matter, like conservative, liberal, and radical spectators, men and women, people of color and people that pass as white—engages in overt and implicit, complex if not always explicit, forms of racism. Indeed, when it comes to the representation of race—black, brown, red, white, yellow; gay, straight; transsexual—pornography today is very much about yesterday's ideology of hate. The hate involving racialized pornography online is both similar to and different from the hate involving pornographic films, videos, and Hollywood in general. Online pornographers often upload to servers material from sources originally produced in magazines and video, thereby turning the libraries of dirty scenes and images into an international interactive mass medium. Their old images and videos facilitate meaning production in cyberspace. These images also form the stylistic model for new material, pornography made especially for the rich Internet market.

Criticizing pornography for perpetuating "hate speech" is a blasphemous act for a scholar against censorship. Calling a text "hateful" can easily be read as closing it off to alternative or resistant readings. It can be seen as oversimplifying the complexity of texts. The fact remains, however, that pornography, like cinema and television and popular culture in general, engages in articulations of race easily described as hateful. These articulations might be implicit, connotative, and even naturalized, but they are fundamental parts of the text. This does not mean we should censor pornography, any more than we should censor *The Birth of a Nation*. We simply need to focus on it, address it critically with an eye toward media literacy, as the articulation of race in pornographic texts require rigorous and sustained scholarly attention despite the radical future predicted by certain principles of critical theory, the intellectual call for a more nuanced and careful understanding of the genre, or the corollary fact that women get pleasure from and are thus empowered by dirty images.

NOTES
———

This essay originally included a number of pictures taken from the web pages I critique, the most "explicit" being samples of Robert Mapplethorpe's work. I agreed to my editors' request to remove them, but I'm uncomfortable with that decision. Have we undermined or even contradicted our arguments about pornography by removing the images? For any number of reasons pornography is an important subject of analysis. Since images function as evidence in support of arguments, shouldn't academic books on pornography include relevant images that are not otherwise considered illegal? Isn't this especially the case with images on websites, as web masters often change and delete images on a daily basis? How can scholars test the veracity of my arguments without access to the evidence? Academic publishers have valid reasons for not wanting to publish pornographic images, so these questions aren't so easily answered. In the future I hope to hold or take part in an academic workshop on the problem. Pornography has a long way to go before it is accepted alongside the musical and slapstick genres as a worthy subject of scholarly scrutiny, and what's most important is that the discussion continue.

Notes to epigraphs: Linda Williams, "Porn Studies: Proliferating Pornographies On/Scene: An Introduction," in *Porn Studies*, ed. Linda Williams (Durham and London: Duke University Press, 2004), 2; Richard Fung, "Looking for My Penis: The Eroticized Asian in Gay Video Porn," in *How Do I Look: Queer Film and Video*, ed. Bad-Object-Choices (Seattle: Bay Press, 1991), 147.

1. Daniel Bernardi, "Cyborgs in Cyberspace: White Pride, Pedophilic Pornography, and Donna Haraway's Manifesto," in *Reality Squared: Television Discourse on the Real*, ed. James Freidman (New Brunswick, N.J.: Rutgers University Press, 2002); Donna Haraway, *Semians, Cyborgs, and Women: The Re-invention of Nature* (London: Free Association, 1991).

2. For an excellent case study of the intersection of sex, race, and Cold War anxiety in comics positioned as pornographic, see Andrea Friedman, "Sadists and Sissies: Anti-pornography Campaigns in Cold War America," *Gender & History* 15, no. 2 (August 2003): 201–227.

3. For more on this subject, see Clyde Taylor, "The Re-Birth of the Aesthetic in Cinema," in *The Birth of Whiteness: Race and the Emergence of U.S. Cinema*, ed. Daniel Bernardi (New Brunswick, N.J.: Rutgers University Press, 1996), 15–37.

4. Several of the articles I am referencing are reprinted in *Feminism and Pornography*, ed. Drucilla Cornell (Oxford, U.K., and New York: Oxford University Press, 2000).

5. Cynthia Toolin, "Attitudes Toward Pornography: What Have the Feminists Missed?" *Journal of Popular Culture* 17, no. 2 (1993): 168.

6. Linda Williams, "Porn Studies: Proliferating Pornographies On/Scene: An Introduction," in *Porn Studies*, ed. Linda Williams (Durham and London: Duke University Press, 2004), 8.

7. As Williams explains: "In both cases I have resisted some of the more gendered reactions to both, especially the assumption that melodrama is an inherently feminine form designed for women and that pornography is an inherently masculine form designed for men. While initially useful, neither of these views is adequate or productive of deeper understanding of these forms. Indeed, conventional attitude toward both have contributed to my own sense of distances from orthodox feminist film and media study." Linda Williams, "Why I Did Not Want to Write This Essay," *Signs: Journal of Women in Culture and Society* 30, no. 1 (Autumn 2004): 1269.

8. Linda Williams, ed., *Porn Studies* (Durham, N.C., and London, U.K.: Duke University Press, 2004).

9. Linda Williams, *Hard Core: Power, Pleasure, and the "Frenzy of the Visible,"* 2nd ed. (Berkeley and Los Angeles: University of California Press, 1999).

10. Laura Kipnis, *Bound and Gagged: Pornography and the Politics of Fantasy in America* (Durham, N.C.: Duke University Press, 1999).

11. Cornell, ed., *Feminism and Pornography*; *Porn 101: Eroticism, Pornography, and the First Amendment*, ed. James Elias et al. (Amherst, N.Y.: Prometheus, 1999).

12. Amy Allen, "Pornography and Power," *Journal of Social Philosophy* 32, no. 2 (Winter 2001): 521. On page 522 Allen goes on to note: ". . . one general lesson we can learn from the pornography debate is that an adequate feminist analysis of power needs to be expansive rather than reductive; it needs to illuminate different modalities of power, including power-over, power-to, and power-with."

13. Williams, "Porn Studies," 6.

14. Link-o-rama.com, January 14, 2005.

15. I don't mean to suggest that *Greenguy Link O'Rama* represents all forms of pornography online; only that it represents a pervasive and popular network of pornographic links that draws upon a history of otherwise familiar ideologies, discourses, and tropes.

16. Peter Lehman, "Revelations about Pornography," this volume.

17. Ibid.

18. Constance Penley, "Crackers and Whackers: The White Trashing of Porn," this volume.

19. Ibid.

20. George Lipsitz, *The Possessive Investment in Whiteness: How White People Profit from Identity Politics* (Philadelphia: Temple University Press, 1998).

21. Richard Fung, "Looking for My Penis: The Eroticized Asian in Gay Video Porn," in *How Do I Look: Queer Film and Video*, ed. Bad-Object-Choice (Seattle: Bay, 1991), 157. Christopher Ortiz offers a similar though much less developed analysis of Latinos in gay pornography: "Hot and Spicy: Representation of Chicano/Latino Men in Gay Pornography," *Jump Cut* 39 (1994): 83–90.

22. Publishing some thirteen years after Fung's essay, Nguyen Tan Hoang discovers a similar pattern in pornography featuring a "top" Asian actor, Brandon Lee. He writes: "For although his (Brandon Lee) work does invert the passive houseboy-bottom paradigm critics like Fung have protested against, this new and improved 'positive image' of the Asian American top comes about at the expense of relegating other Asian men to the same old, tired, objectified position of unassimilable, forever bottomhood. Though the Asian penis has been found, there are only a few inches of it to go around, or it comes to resemble another white pink dick, tinted yellow." Nguyen Tan Hoang, "The Resurrection of Brandon Lee: The Making of a Gay Asian American Porn Star," in *Porn Studies*, ed. Williams, 238. See also Daniel Tsang, "Beyond 'Looking for my Penis': Reflections on Asian Gay Male Video Porn," in *Porn 101*, ed. Elias et al., 473–478. In this volume José B. Capino challenges some of the positions held by Fung, but nonetheless concludes that "practically every scenario in Asian pornography bestows both economic and sexual power upon the white male figure." See "Asian College Girls and Oriental Men with Bamboo Poles: Reading Asian Pornography," this volume.

23. Richard Fung, in *How Do I Look*, ed. Bad-Object Choice.

24. Frantz Fanon, *Black Skin, White Masks* (London, U.K.: Paladin, 1970), 120.

25. Kobena Mercer, "Imaging the Black Man's Sex," in *Photography/Politics: Two*, ed. Pat Holand et al. (London: Comedia Methuen, 1987), 61–69.

26. Kobena Mercer, "Skin Head Thing: Racial Difference and the Homoerotic Imaginary," in *How Do I Look*, ed. Bad-Object-Choice, 177. For the original essay, see Mercer, "Imaging the Black Man's Sex."

27. Ibid., 187.

28. Linda Williams, "Skin Flicks on the Racial Border: Pornography, Exploitation, and Interracial Lust," in *Porn Studies*, ed. Williams, 279.

29. Ibid., 286.

30. Alice Walker, *You Can't Keep a Good Woman Down* (New York: A Harvest/HBJ Book, 1981), 52.

31. Link-o-rama.com, January 14, 2005.

32. The Pay and Recommended Free Site links tend to take the viewer to places that require an exchange of cookies that involve viruses and spyware pop-ups, which is also why I'm leaving their analysis to future work.

33. Alice Mayall and Diane Russell, "Racism in Pornography," in *Making Violence Sexy: Feminist Views on Pornography*, ed. Diane Russel (New York and London, U.K.: Teachers College Press, 1993), 167–178.

34. Given the fact that *Greenguy Link O'Rama* is a clearinghouse of pornographic material, it is likely that the number of sites noted in this essay, per section, will have increased by the time of publication.

35. As of April 15, 2005.

36. Gloria Cowan and Robin R. Campbell, "Racism and Sexism in Interracial Pornography: A Content Analysis," *Psychology of Women Quarterly* 18 (1994): 326.

37. For more on the fragmentation and fetishization of race in online pornography, see Don Heider and Dustin Harp, "New Hope or Old Power: Democracy, Pornography and the Internet," *Howard Journal of Communication* 13, no. 4 (2002): 285–299.

38. Frances Negrón-Muntaner, "Jennifer's Butt," *Aztlan* 22, no. 2 (Fall 1997): 188.

39. Edward Said, *Orientalism* (New York: Vintage, 1979).

40. Fanon, *Black Skin, White Masks*, 70.

41. Isaac Julien, quoted in Richard Fun, "'Looking for My Penis'" 164.

42. Walker, *You Can't Keep a Good Woman Down*, 52.

43. Mercer, "Skin Head Thing," 206.

44. Richard Dyer, *White* (London: Routledge, 1997).

45. Ibid., 171.

Marty Klein

Pornography: What Men See When They Watch

Is porn good or bad?

> That's not what this is about.

Are you saying that no man ever struggles with porn?

> No, of course not.

Are you saying that no man ever develops unrealistic ideas from watching porn?

> No, some do.

Are you saying that porn never shows awful stuff?

> No, although the overwhelming majority shows completely happy, consensual encounters.

So is porn good or bad?

> That's not what this is about.
>
> But we can agree that porn is not a love story.

Pornography is not forced on the 50 million Americans who consume it regularly. Each day, the public votes with its dollars, its feet, and its eyes, and the vote is clear: an extraordinary number of people enjoy looking at sexually explicit material. According to filings with the Securities and Exchange Commission, Americans spend more money on porn each year than on movie tickets and all other performing arts *combined*.[1]

The U.S. government and other forces that are trying to limit or eliminate various pornographic options claim a myriad of nasty (and unproven) consequences of viewing porn: they imagine it leads to antisocial behavior; is "addictive;" destroys viewers' abilities to relate to real partners; undermines consumers' morality, spirituality, and self-respect; leads to disrespecting women; and encourages degenerate sexual desires.

The implication of these stark predictions is that the act of consuming pornography is fundamentally hostile and done with a complete lack of consciousness. Is that really true? A key aspect of America's culture war is that consumers and nonconsumers simply don't see or imagine the same things when they consider porn. That's why there's such a disparity between what nonviewers predict and what viewers experience. And this is why nonviewers can never prove their apocalyptic assertions, but instead rely on isolated anecdotes, raw emotion, and alleged "common sense."

The Problem with "The Problem with Porn"

There's something almost always missing from the common critiques of pornography: the voices of actual consumers. Tens of millions of men and women make porn a perennial winner in America's ongoing economic referendum, freely spending, according to Forester Research in Cambridge, Massachusetts, $10 billion for the industry's products every year.[2]

But these adults have been relegated so far to the margins of polite society (and political effectiveness) that no one is apologetic about excluding them from the decision-making processes that affect them. Despite all the discussion about what rights porn producers should have, virtually no one talks about the rights of porn consumers. Policy makers, morality groups, and the media all seem perfectly willing to speculate about the results of porn consumption—without consulting consumers.

By contrast, the main cultural narrative about pornography almost exclusively involves its alleged victims (identified, variously, as porn actresses; wives; all women; pathetic male consumers; at-risk children; the entire society). These critiques omit (in fact, contradict) the experiences of tens of millions of satisfied, repeat customers. That fact alone should make us suspicious of the relentless criticism.

So one major problem with "the problem of porn" is that, other than histrionically described "victims," it references no real people—only caricatures of consumers, with imagined experiences and assumed consequences, unsupported by scientific, clinical, or law enforcement data. One would never suspect that these people are actual husbands, brothers, fathers, and sons (and, lest we forget, girlfriends, sisters, and mothers) with lives, feelings, and loving relationships.

This critique also assumes that porn consumers are involved in an esoteric sideshow, a clandestine activity on the fringe of society. On the contrary—pornography is America's conventional entertainment. Do sports appear to be mainstream? Americans spend more on porn than on tickets to all professional baseball, football, and basketball games *combined*, says *The New York Times*.[3] The Internet? It now features almost 2 *million* porn sites.[4] Porn is the number one Internet destination of American men ages eighteen to thirty-four—50 percent more than music sites or ebay, four times as much as travel services such as airline and hotel reservations, says the *Times*.[5] And men don't stop the day they turn thirty-five.

As we shall see, the conventional critique of porn collapses when applied to such a ubiquitous activity. By contrast, the present analysis is a more useful, plausible explanation of the omnipresent male use of sexually explicit imagery.

The Conventional Critique of Pornography

Porn's conventional critics perceive erotic displays literally, forgetting that porn is theater, which of course has subtext.[6] If critics actually watch (critics always claim to be nonconsumers, although every month it seems yet another one is caught with porn films and a hooker), they will observe fellatio and cunnilingus, penis-vagina intercourse in every imaginable position, penis-anus intercourse, fingers in every orifice, orgasms in both sexes, both genders touching themselves for pleasure, and sex involving more than two people at a time. In the overwhelming majority of pornography, virtually everyone is depicted as feeling intensely happy.

Critics then draw conclusions about the meaning of what they see, transmuting presentations of pleasure into suffering, and of mutuality into oppression. Critics see women doing things they believe no woman would do voluntarily, and therefore see coercion and humiliation. Since critics don't perceive depictions of women's pleasure as pleasure, but rather as twisted male fantasy, they can't see mutuality, only women pleasuring men; therefore they see only servicing and degradation. Critics see women participating in sex with people they don't "love"; since critics can't imagine women choosing to do so, they see objectification.[7]

To put it another way, conventional critics see men doing things they believe men want to do (having wild sex), and women doing things they don't believe women want to do (having wild sex). Thus, critics see men being coercive, and women being victims.

In taking what they see literally, critics also reduce every image to a single dimension. Critics assume, for example, that viewers watching a woman involved in fellatio simply perceive her as someone providing oral sex and nothing more. She isn't a partner, a playmate, an accomplice in transgression, a self-confident woman, a sexually motivated person—just someone giving head.

The conventional critique of pornography is rooted in a specific narrative: fear and danger. It assumes that male sexuality is inherently dangerous, and that women are inevitably its vulnerable, powerless targets. It asserts that pornography proves that men want to control women; that porn's consumers derive pleasure from seeing women as hapless; and that male fantasies of enthusiastic female sexuality prove that women are in danger from barely concealed male misogyny. Critics then use this critique dialectically as "proof" that porn leads to violence, and as evidence that society needs laws limiting sexual expression in order to protect women from the male tendency to degeneracy.

There are many, many problems with this view of the porn experience and its consequences, however:

- It doesn't match what actual consumers say.
- It doesn't account for the large number of couples who watch porn.
- It doesn't account for gay or lesbian porn.
- The massive levels of social disruption it predicts don't exist.

- The implied grimness doesn't match the lighthearted experience of most viewers.
- The obsessiveness of most critics doesn't match that of most viewers.

Also, the critique doesn't account for porn's huge audience. Despite the imperfections of American society, most men are not violent or out of control; they're mostly just trying to raise their kids, do their jobs, and make their relationships work. According to the FBI, the number of child molesters and rapists in America is a tiny, tiny fraction of the number of men who watch erotic films each month.[8] It's simply foolish (and contrary to our everyday experience) to imagine that most of America's 50 million porn consumers hate themselves, fear intimacy, disrespect their wives and girlfriends, or enjoy women's pain. It's similarly foolish to imagine that none of these men watch *Spider Man* or *The Sopranos* or *The Good, The Bad, & The Ugly* with the tools of irony, metaphor, interpretation, and iconography. Those that do surely use those same tools when they're watching *Bra Busters in Berlin.*

Finally, most consumers of erotic material don't believe that viewing the stuff has awful effects; men don't go around telling each other, or their kids or younger brothers, "don't use porn because it will mess up your life."

So let's look at what consumers experience when they consume. This will involve an entirely different way of conceptualizing the viewing experience.

The Subtexts of Pornography

Like all media portrayals, pornography is about more than itself. The consuming of any cultural product is an active, constitutive process; both the entire genre of pornography, and each individual example, offer a narrative. This is what actually keeps viewers coming back. But this narrative is apparently invisible to most nonviewers. When critics talk about porn in simplistic, literal terms, they have missed the form's narrative. They have not interpreted or decoded what porn presents or describes, and thus, they miss the complex psychological experience and rewards that its messages offer. Those experiences and emotional payoffs are, nevertheless, real to consumers.

When nonviewers take pornography literally instead of decoding it, they're being uneducated critics of consumer behavior. Their literal critique is akin to thinking that W. C. Fields was simply promoting drinking, or that the Beatles were primarily about long hair, or that teens use cell phones constantly because they really do need to make all those phone calls to their friends. This naivete violates the most basic principle of sociocultural analysis: all media must be decoded before they can be properly understood and critiqued.

Unfortunately, those with the primary legitimacy for defining and critiquing pornography—morality groups, religious authorities, conservative feminists, law enforcement officials—continue to be uninterested in this kind of decoding. Their agenda, rather, is to show how sexually explicit imagery is a vehicle for debauchery and male domination of women. Viewing erotic materials literally is one of their fundamental strategies in accomplishing this. Like consumers of *Seinfeld*, *The Three Stooges*, *Our Town*, and *Madame Butterfly*, however, consumers understand pornography's conventions, and translate them effortlessly and automatically.

Most viewers understand that these conventions—the outside-her-body ejaculation ("money shot" or "cum shot"), the instant vaginal orgasms, the lack of kissing, the sex in physically uncomfortable positions—exist for narrative reasons more important than the literal depictions. Most viewers know that erotic videos don't portray sex the way it usually is (almost no one over twenty-five has sex at the beach more than once; most women aren't having sex with other women). Viewers know that characters' various actions, words, and choices are expressions of desire, self-acceptance, and empowerment. They know that porn involves unrealistic situations (pizza delivery man knocks on door and is greeted by naked women demanding sex), rare bodies (nine-inch penises), and symbolic moments (woman hoping her partner ejaculates on her face). Like these, most of porn's conventions represent extreme desire, responsiveness, disinhibition, and competence.[9]

Viewers of other movie forms use the same decoding process when watching unrealistic scenes. In action films, careening car chases represent danger and sociopathic defiance of rules; in the *Rocky* series, the hero gets brutally beaten but somehow gets on his feet and resumes fighting, a trope expressing courage and toughness; Zorro repeatedly taunts his community's aristocrats and police into pursuing and finding him, telling us that this is a man with not only confidence but moral decency at his core. Only those distracted or frightened by careening cars, spurting blood, and humiliated authority would be unable to glimpse these representations. Porn's critics seem so distracted by sexual depictions that they can't see past them to its conventions.

People use erotica to become aroused, and so its characters are simply vehicles for choices that arouse consumers. As expressions of erotic archetypes, their individuality is not salient. Viewers are not invited to empathize with who characters are, but rather with characters' desire, lack of inhibition, and belief in the importance of sexuality and fulfillment. This does *not* "objectify" those characters; rather, it focuses on a deeply human part of them. What are the subtexts of pornography's consistent, coherent presentation?

First, that such a sexual environment is possible; second, that wanting such an environment is reasonable; third, that any rules that restrict it are arbitrary. These messages give viewers encouragement to seize hold of and shape their own sexual experience without having to depend on socially defined sources of erotic power or redemption—such as love, marriage, beauty, procreation, or youth.

Pornography offers a narrative of validation—of the viewer's eroticism, of deliberately focusing on (and even enhancing) desire, of the possibility of mutual male-female satisfaction, of the viewer's vision of a world of erotic abundance, playfulness, and self-acceptance.

Finally, porn's narrative challenges the traditional sexual economy of heterosexual men and women—that women are supposed to control men's access to sex, and trade this access for nonsexual things (such as childcare, intimacy, affection), rather than having sex for their own satisfaction.

Is everyone watching *Snow White Does the Seven Dwarfs* aware of these narratives, these subtexts that offer reassurance and comfort? Certainly not. Similarly, we know that many viewers of *Star Trek*, *Airplane!* and Shakespeare miss the existential themes, parody, and political commentary. No matter—seen or not, themes and subtexts still influence audiences unconsciously. Just as gravity works whether people believe in it or not, the subtexts of sexually explicit films affect viewers whether they're aware of them or not. That's why viewers keep coming back. Ironically, the conventional critics of porn agree—they just misunderstand what those subtexts are, and what their impact is.

Subtext: Abundance

Regardless of content, the most straightforward narrative of pornography is erotic abundance. In the world that porn depicts, there is more than enough of everything, including an environment in which eroticism is its own justification. This abundance includes:

- abundant desire (both male and female)
- abundant responsivity (nothing is conditional)
- abundant privacy (if people want it)
- abundant time (and the willingness to spend time sexually)
- abundant erections
- abundant breasts, vulvas, mouths, and buttocks
- abundant orgasms (of both genders), easily created
- abundant erotic connection (rendering preparation unnecessary)
- abundant erotic expertise (eliminating performance anxiety)
- abundant female self-acceptance

This is the ultimate erotic fantasy of most viewers—not actress A or B, not position A or B, but a world of erotic surplus in which all choices are possible, the desire for these choices is validated, and the acceptability of desire and the wholesomeness of eroticism is validated over and over. This is a profound vision—spiritual for some, healing for some, reassuring for some, supportive despite past trauma or current despair for some.

In the world of sexual imagery, not only is there enough of what's wanted, but everyone *assumes* there will be enough. Such confidence is another aspect of abundance. There is nothing for anyone to be anxious about—all expectations are positive, and virtually all are fulfilled. For people who lack it, this sense of erotic confidence is a huge prize. In this regard, men are more emotional about sex than many people imagine. Men may talk about tangible representations of abundance— enormous breasts, gallons of ejaculate, perfectly tight vaginas—but such things are merely approximations of the feelings that they want to have. These include relief, confidence, relaxation, acceptance, trust, and the absence of anxiety.

That's why the average viewer doesn't generally want to replace his *partner* with a porn star. Rather, he wants to replace the *feelings* in his bedroom with the feelings portrayed in pornography. Instead of being undermined by the inhibitions, self-consciousness, fear of losing control, and arbitrary tabooing of various body parts that Americans learn so well, he dreams of the lush validation that seems built into the very fabric of the world depicted in porn. This is a perspective from which conventional psychotherapy and couples counseling, and their clients, would benefit greatly.

It's true that self-acceptance, erotic confidence, and enthusiasm are not qualities that every person possesses. But they are qualities that most women (indeed, most people) can, if they wish (and not every woman does), develop more of—unlike the extraordinary physical beauty (and youth) of professional erotic actresses to which most women cannot realistically aspire.

In fact, many men value pornography's portrayals of female desire and self-acceptance so much that their standards of actress attractiveness are broader than the conventional ideals of the media and fashion industry. There are porn actresses popular today who are obviously in their forties and fifties, such as Juliet Anderson, Seka, and Nina Hartley. With the niche marketing of porn sites, it's now easy to find sites that feature women who aren't young and conventionally beautiful— as long as they are portrayed as enthusiastic about sex. On the other hand, very few Hollywood films or TV shows can boast sexy forty-five-year-old women. Interest in older subjects is so common that contemporary pornography has jargon for such depictions: "mature," "granny porn," and "MILF" (mothers I'd like to fuck).

And so the common female anxiety that watching erotica encourages men to crave unrealistically beautiful women and devalue normal-looking women is, although understandable, misplaced.[10]

Subtext: Permission

Consumers also decode what they see as permission—to experience, accept, and lose themselves in their own idiosyncratic eroticism. In this sense, pornography is primarily about the viewer, not about whatever it portrays. This permission is a fundamental meta-message of each porn film, photo, and story, as well as of the genre, whose very *existence* legitimizes desire and arousal.

This is similar to the permission people feel from watching cooking shows—to desire food, to spend time creating food, to prioritize and enjoy eating. The actual dish portrayed on a given episode is a minor character in the larger text.

And so viewers see porn actresses portraying characters who accept their bodies, their desire, and their power to participate in (and even create) their own fulfillment. Viewers value this much more than a specific actress's looks or specific behaviors. Such particulars are like the day's recipe on a cooking show; the portrayal of a sexually self-accepting woman is the real payoff of watching. An actress and her behavior may enable a viewer's arousal, but it is the validation of the viewer's erotic vision that keeps him returning. This validation makes the viewing experience larger than a simple masturbatory outlet; after all, people can simply close their eyes and imagine whatever they like while masturbating. As in partner sex, the orgasm that generally ends masturbatory sex may feel good physically, but it is a mere highlight in a larger psychological erotic tapestry.

Subtext: Validating Male Eroticism

American culture is conflicted about male desire: it says male desire is inevitable, but that it can be satisfied in conventional marriage only rarely. It says that a man who expects to have his desire satisfied is unrealistic—but that any man without this desire isn't a real man. Thus, our culture says that to be a man is to be sexually frustrated. By depicting a world of abundance in which male eroticism is valued, erotic imagery challenges this horrible, Sisyphean destiny.

Pornography says that men are attractive not as a function of being rich, famous, handsome, or smart, and not even because they're sexually adequate, but because they desire sex and women, and accept their desire. This is what many men yearn for—to have their desire seen in the positive way they see it themselves.

Pornography also depicts a world in which that desire *can* be satisfied, because the typical obstacles of the real world are missing. There are no constraints of time, privacy, fatigue, or health. There is no erotophobic culture to contradict. And there are no (arbitrary) limits set by partners, who might be self-conscious, self-critical, anxious, or inhibited. When men watch porn, they're able to imagine "yes, that's how I would be without the obstacles I normally face." This enables men to feel sexually normal even if they're watching activities that they'll never actually experience.

Many heterosexual men believe that some or most of the scarcity in real-world sex is unnecessary—that it is primarily enforced by women who have learned to fear sex and their bodies. In contrast, pornography portrays a world in which men don't have to expend any erotic energy to get a partner, overcome her shame, or convince her to be sexual; porn's sexual experiences don't begin, as real-life sex often does, with one or both partners having to demean themselves as an entry fee into eroticism. Thus, porn-sex can be (vicariously) enjoyed in a heightened way.

Subtext: Undermining the Sexual Economy

Most heterosexual men bemoan this sexual economy, though they rarely use that term. They observe how, instructed, supported, and defended by the dominant culture, women learn to see their sexuality as a precious commodity that men will pay (financially and otherwise) to get access to. Women *appear* to gain power as a result, but it comes at the cost of seeing their sexuality as something for *them*. Both men and women suffer from this arrangement; even worse, each gender typically blames the other for the problems institutionalized by this destructive gender-role system.

This cultural arrangement leads to the traditional fear that if women were to claim and enjoy their sexuality for themselves, they would lose their power in relationships (This is another aspect of the insulting concept of male-female relationships so prevalent among critics of porn.). As an alternative, porn imagines a world in which male-female power is equal, because male and female sexual desire are equivalent. It's a world in which sex is not a problem between men and women, because women have *claimed* their erotic power. As their partners, men are thus more powerful too—not *over* women, but *with their partner*, situationally, as they no longer have to pay for access to the formerly scarce female sexual interest. (In the traditional sexual economy, erotic access fees involve paying for sex with nonsex activities, such as child-rearing, domestic chores, unwanted recreation, or sharing feelings.)

In pornography, men are able to consume the scarce commodity of female eroticism in ways that they aren't supposed to consume it in their nonporn daily life. While viewing porn, men can consume beauty in a direct, enthusiastic fashion, and shamelessly acknowledge their interest as blatantly sexual. In such a world, no one's afraid of male sexuality; there's plenty of interpersonal power for everyone, so no one has to hoard it or barter it.

In this (artificial) environment, a viewer can be himself without fear of inadvertently offending someone. As in strip clubs, this is not simply a pleasure, but a relief.

Telling the Truth

Despite the many ways in which American media and culture obsess on sex, gender, consent, and perversion, American society is built upon simplistic, superstitious, anhedonic, fear-and-danger based conceptions of eroticism.

In such a culture, many obvious sexual facts are denied, tabooed, and distorted. Examples of these include: virtually all children masturbate; virtually everyone has sexual interests; most people fantasize sexually, primarily about "inappropriate" partners or activities; and most people are curious about others' bodies and sex lives.

Pornography tells a variety of truths about sex and gender that some segments of society want to limit or eliminate. These truths are far more important than the enhanced breasts, abnormally big penises, and casual group sex that are staples of the genre (which when taken literally, are porn's lies). These truths include:

- Anyone can feel and be sexy.
- Nothing is inherently nonsexual or nonerotic.
- The only rules in sex are arbitrary.
- Many, many people love sex.
- The erotically "nasty" can be life-affirming.
- Even "nice" people enjoy "nasty" fantasies.
- In sex, neither intercourse nor orgasm is everything (e.g., experiencing others' desire is a central part of eroticism, and is not fungible with other erotic vehicles such as perfect body parts).
- Focusing on sexuality is itself legitimate.
- Women (and men) who feel secure in their dignity and admit that they love sex can enthusiastically "submit" erotically, because they don't fear judgment (others' or their own).

These truths, of course, defy America's dominant paradigm about sexuality. Consumers of pornography regularly visit an erotic world quite different than the traditional one—in which external rules are important, there are clearly identifiable sexual and nonsexual body parts, "nice" and "nasty" eroticism are clearly distinguishable from each other (and different, nonoverlapping groups of people indulge in each), and eroticism is dangerous if people don't control their arousal.

The truth that porn tells is that all people have the option of conceptualizing their sexuality any way they like. Social norms regarding age and beauty, religious norms about godly and ungodly sex, personal fears about acceptance, cultural myths about the human body—all of these are ignorable; none are inevitable. Each of us can triumph over the ways social institutions attempt to control our sexual experience and expression.

Ironically, this paradigm of pornography's truths is what sex therapists try to get couples to understand and install in their own lives. These professionals know that the keys to satisfying sexual relationships are self-acceptance and self-empowerment, not losing a few pounds, buying flowers, or going away on vacation.

Porn's subtexts of abundance and validation are as responsible for contemporary cultural resistance as its explicit presentations of sexual activity.

Pornography's Truths as Subversive

And why does our culture resist these truths? Because the revolutionary implications of empowering people sexually challenge the cultural status quo. Pornography does this without even portraying sex exactly as most people experience it.

Pornography is an admission that people feel, imagine, and do what they do. In a culture committed to both hiding and pathologizing (and therefore shaming) sex as it really is, this admission isn't "polite." It's subversive.

Erotica challenges fundamental, accepted ideas about sex, gender relations, and the role of sexuality in daily life. It reveals men to be even more interested in sex than suspected—which is culturally shocking, because pop wisdom says men are always thinking about sex and are completely captured by it. Porn reveals that indeed, many men are profoundly interested in desire, lust, transcendence, and erotic partnership. That's much larger and more significant than simply "thinking about sex all the time."

Ultimately, pornography's truths are subversive because they claim that people can empower themselves and create their own erotic norms. Political structures just hate when ideas or cultural products empower people. This is the recurring lesson of Copernicus, Guttenberg, Margaret Sanger, Lenny Bruce, and Timothy Leary.

In the conventional fear/danger model, the genders are adversaries. Pornography helps reconcile the war of the sexes, as it contains no adversaries. In it, everyone shares the same interests: passion, unselfconsciousness, pleasure, mutuality, and so on. Porn's undermining of the conventional scarcity-themed sexual economy is one of its most radical features. This is one reason it attracts political opposition.

The massive popularity of pornography, and its consistent themes of female lust and male-female mutuality, testify to men's pain about the conventional sexual economy. Taking porn on its own terms would require society to acknowledge this pain; such a cultural challenge makes pornography subversive.

Amateur Pornography as Truth

A new way in which pornography tells the truth even more radically is amateur porn, which has exploded via the democratic frenzy of the Internet. More than a million people across the globe are now photographing themselves during various sexual activities, uploading these photos onto personal and commercial websites, and inviting the entire computerized world to enjoy them.[11] They know that viewers will use their photos as part of masturbation or partner sex; for some amateurs this thought is a key part of the experience.

In contrast to most commercial pornography, common features of amateur porn include:

- a wide range of bodies, including ordinary and even conventionally unattractive ones
- a wide range of ages, including adults conventionally considered way past the prime of their attractiveness or sexuality
- a mostly unproduced physical environment (poor lighting, composition, etc.)
- a heightened sense of mundane reality (shots with unkempt kitchens or kids' toys in the background; scenes filmed in Motel 6, etc.)
- a sense of humor and even parody

Despite containing all of these challenges to conventional porn, amateur porn supports (and, for some consumers, even enhances) the valued subtexts under discussion. Its very existence confirms many of the arguments about narrative, subtext, and emotional validation made here. Conventional criticism of pornography would not predict amateur porn's popularity. These criticisms assert that the supernatural beauty of actresses is central, that the desultory domination of actress by actor is crucial, that the spectacular genital friction portrayed is what viewers most envy and desire.

Amateur pornography turns these assumptions upside down. There are no actresses, only real women. These women aren't pretending to be excited, they *are* excited. They aren't flaunting impossibly perfect bodies, they are enjoying their bodies as they are—some of them gorgeous, many of them imperfect and attractive, some . . . well, let's say their enthusiasm is more appealing than their form. Virtually all the women in amateur porn share that quality—enthusiasm. They are really, yes really, enjoying themselves: the activities, the violation of taboos, the exhibitionism. Clearly, there's no coercion here.

In contrast to the typical nonconsumer criticism, our analysis of porn's attraction and value *would* predict and *can* explain why amateur porn is such a rapidly growing genre. If the keys to porn's popularity are validation of the viewer's vision of erotic abundance, female lust, and the reasonableness of erotic focus, a viewer can experience those even more intensely when this validation comes not from actors but from real people. Rather than actors *implying* that the viewer isn't alone, amateur photos show real people *proving* the viewer isn't alone.

How much more inspiring is an actual lusty woman than an actress portraying a lusty woman? How much more validating is a group of average-looking people exhibiting themselves, contrasted with a group of actors pretending that real people do sexy things? How much more fellowship does a viewer experience when seeing real people participating in an actual erotic community, compared with seeing actors implying a community that must be inferred and never actually seen?

Epilogue: Beyond Porn

It would be nice if people could get more of their eroticism validated by a range of social institutions, such as schools, churches, medicine, psychology, government, and the media. But forces of great power and wealth are committed to limiting how much that will ever happen in America. To the extent that such change does occur, it would be less necessary for people to get away from "real life" to get erotically validated.

It would be nice if more people validated their own eroticism without help from pornography. This would involve creating an erotically validating life, for which most Americans currently lack the sense of entitlement. Most people don't realize they already have nearly everything they need to create sexual intimacy and pleasure—and don't need to be younger, more physically attractive, crazier, more experienced, or more skillful.

It would be nice if people were so self-accepting, uninhibited, erotically focused, and (consensually) opportunistic that porn offered very little. It would then be considered like a beautiful landscape—enjoyable, but not a challenge to a dominant paradigm. It would be nice if pornography weren't valued for its subtext of validation and abundance, because that had become a common human experience.

In such a culture, what people would see when they watched porn would be just porn—fantasies, dreamscapes, theater. It would have no subtext, because viewers would have all that validation already. And then a pretty woman, or cunnilingus, or a moan, would just be a pretty woman, cunnilingus, or a moan.

Just like porn's critics, with neither understanding nor irony, complain about now.

NOTES

1. As quoted in Frank Rich, *New York Times*, May 20, 2001.
2. Nielsen/Net Ratings, September 2003; *Adult Industry Today*, published by AVN; Forester Research, Cambridge, Massachusetts, October 23, 2000, as quoted by Frank Rich, *New York Times*.
3. As quoted in Frank Rich, *New York Times*, May 20, 2001.
4. *New York Times*, March 29, 2004.
5. *New York Times*, March 29, 2004.
6. See Linda Williams, *Hard Core* (Berkeley: University of California Press, 1989).
7. See Andrea Dworkin, *Intercourse* (New York: The Free Press, 1985); Catherine MacKinnon, *Only Words* (Cambridge, Mass.: Harvard University Press, 1993).
8. Rape statistics from *Crime in the U.S.* published by the U.S. Department of Justice, 2002; child molestation figures from *Statistical Abstracts of U.S.*, published by the U.S. Department of Health and Human Services, 2003.
9. Of course, any problem with porn consumers taking porn literally could be solved via comprehensive sex education, whether via school or popular literature. See Michael Castleman, *Great Sex* (Emmaus, Pa.: Rodale, 2004).
10. At least some of women's anxiety about not being sexually attractive enough for their men reflects the popularity of "women's magazines" like *Cosmopolitan* and *Vogue*, which fea-

ture images of female beauty that are far more homogeneous (and unattainable) than heterosexual pornography.

11. A single such "amateur" site, voyeurweb.com, gets over 2 million hits per day. Including its bulletin boards and video site, it features new photos and video clips from over one hundred contributors worldwide each day. Even accounting for some duplication, that's over thirty thousand unique individuals or couples posting pictures of themselves each year—on this site alone.

Contributors

DANIEL BERNARDI is an associate professor in Film and Media Studies and Chicana and Chicano Studies at Arizona State University. He is the editor of *The Birth of Whiteness: Race and the Emergence of U.S. Cinema* and *Classic Hollywood, Classic Whiteness*, and the author of *Star Trek and History: Race-Ing Toward a White Future*.

JOSÉ B. CAPINO is an assistant professor of English and Cinema Studies at the University of Illinois, Urbana-Champaign. He writes about colonialism and film, nonfiction cinema, and the representation of sexuality in moving images.

JOHN ELLIS is a professor of media arts at Royal Holloway, University of London. He is the author of *Seeing Things: Television in the Age of Uncertainty* (I. B. Tauris, 2000) and *Visible Fictions* (Routledge, 1982) as well as numerous articles in journals such as *Screen* and *Media Culture and Society*. Between 1982 and 1999 he was a full-time TV producer, running Large Door Productions, which made documentaries on cinema and cultural issues, including Angela Carter's last work "The Holy Family Album."

MARJORIE HEINS is the director of the Free Expression Policy Project (www.fepproject.org) and the author of *Not in Front of the Children: "Indecency," Censorship, and the Innocence of Youth* (Hill and Wang, 2001).

HENRY JENKINS is the De Florez Professor of Humanities and director of the comparative Media Studies program at MIT. He is the author or editor of eleven books on various aspects of media and popular culture, including *Textual Poachers: Television Fans and Participatory Culture, From Barbie to Mortal Kombat: Gender and Computer Games, Hop on Pop: The Politics and Pleasures of Popular Culture, The Wow Climax: The Immediacy of Popular Culture,* and *Convergence Culture: Where Old and New Media Intersect.*

LAURA KIPNIS is a professor of radio-TV-film at Northwestern University. Her most recent books are *Against Love: A Polemic* (2003) and *Bound and Gagged: Pornography and the Politics of Fantasy in America* (1996).

MARTY KLEIN is a sex therapist in Palo Alto, California. The author of five books about sexuality and relationships, he has trained tens of thousands of physicians, marriage counselors, psychologists, and social workers in human sexuality. He publishes the monthly electronic newsletter *Sexual Intelligence* (www.SexualIntelligence.org) and the popular website www.SexEd.org.

CHUCK KLEINHANS is the co-editor of *Jump Cut: A Review of Contemporary Media* (www.ejumpcut.org) and teaches in the radio/television/film department, Northwestern University. He has recently published articles on Court TV network, virtual child pornography, and Hong Kong cinema in relation to Hollywood.

PETER LEHMAN is a professor of English and director of Film and Media Studies and director of the Center for Film and Media Research at Arizona State University. He is the author of *Roy Orbison: The Invention of an Alternative Rock Masculinity* and *Running Scared: Masculinity and the Representation of the Male Body* and the editor of *Masculinity: Bodies, Movies, Culture.*

NINA K. MARTIN is an assistant professor of film studies at Emory University, where she teaches courses primarily on feminist film theory and criticism, experimental film, and animation. Her primary research areas are on intersections of gender and genre, especially in horror, action, and pornographic films. She is especially interested in the relationship between postfeminist discourses and contemporary U.S. female heterosexuality. Her book *Sexy Thrills: Undressing the Erotic Thriller* is forthcoming from the University of Illinois Press.

CONSTANCE PENLEY is a professor of Film and Media Studies and the co-director of the Center for Film, Television and New Media at the University of California, Santa Barbara. She has written and lectured widely on feminist media theory, popular culture, and science and technology studies. Her most recent book is *NASA/TREK: Popular Science and Sex in America*. Recent large collaborative art projects include Biospheria: An Environmental Opera and Primetime Contemporary Art by the GALA Committee as Seen on Melrose Place.

PAUL WILLEMEN was a member of *Screen*'s editorial group in the 1970s and edited *Framework* in the 1980s. He currently works as professor of film studies at the Ulster University in Northern Ireland. He is the author of *Looks and Frictions* (1994), co-author of the *Encyclopaedia of Indian Cinema* (1996), and co-editor of *Questions of Third Cinema* (1989).

LINDA WILLIAMS is former director of the film studies program at University of California–Berkeley. Her co-edited books include a volume of feminist film criticism (*Re-Vision*, 1984), an edited volume on film spectatorship, *Viewing Positions* (Rutgers University Press, 1993), *Reinventing Film Studies* (with Christine Geldhill, Arnold, 2000), and *Porn Studies* (Duke University Press, 2004). In 1989 she published a controversial study of film pornography, *Hard Core: Power, Pleasure and the "Frenzy of the Visible"* (2nd ed., 1999). Williams's latest book is *Playing the Race Card: Melodramas of Black and White, from Uncle Tom to O. J. Simpson* (Princeton University Press, 2001). She is currently writing a book about screening sex in American culture since the 1960s.

Index